RECOMMENDED BY THE
NATIONAL BIBLE ASSOCIATION

"DON'T KNOW MUCH ABOUT and will appeal to both longtime and novice students of the Bible. Like most really thoughtful books, it will inspire conversation and introspection and offers much fodder for study groups."
—*Chattanooga Free Press*

"Mr. Davis' book is an entertaining, informative must."
—*Dallas Morning News*

DO YOU KNOW:

- *Who wrote the Old Testament?*
- *Were there really apples in Eden?*
- *Who really killed Goliath?*
- *Was Solomon really so smart?*
- *Who is Gog and where is Magog?*
- *Did Jesus have brothers and sisters?*
- *Were there really "Three Kings," and where did they come from?*
- *What was the Last Supper?*

"Brimming with fascinating facts and fresh interpretations... wry and witty...A guaranteed bestseller sure to be in constant demand."
—*Booklist*

(Turn the page for more praise...)

DON'T KNOW MUCH ABOUT®

THE

BIBLE

Everything You Need to Know about the Good Book but Never Learned

KENNETH C. DAVIS

AVON BOOKS  NEW YORK

AVON BOOKS, INC.
1350 Avenue of the Americas
New York, New York 10019

The Eagle Brook edition contains the following Library of Congress Cataloging in Publication Data:
Davis, Kenneth C.
   Don't know much about® the Bible : everything you need to know about the Good Book but never learned / by Kenneth C. Davis.
      p.   cm.
   Includes bibliographical references and index.
1. Bible—Introductions. I. Title.
BS445.D35   1998   98-16744
220.6'1—dc21   CIP

First Avon Books Trade Paperback Printing: September 1999

To Joann—

A capable wife who can find?
She is far more precious than jewels.
The heart of her husband trusts in her,
and he will have no lack of gain.
(Proverbs 31:10–11)

Many women have done excellently,
but you surpass them all.
(Proverbs 31:29)

CONTENTS

There are more things in heaven and earth,
Horatio,
Than are dreamt of in your philosophy.
—WILLIAM SHAKESPEARE,
HAMLET

It ain't necessarily so—
The things that you're liable
to read in the Bible—
It ain't necessarily so,
—IRA GERSHWIN,
"IT AIN'T NECESSARILY SO," 1935

One of the reasons why religion seems irrelevant today is that many of us
no longer have the sense that we are surrounded by the unseen.
—KAREN ARMSTRONG,
A HISTORY OF GOD

INTRODUCTION

When I was in the sixth grade, a building was going up across the street from my school. Like most ten- or eleven-year-old boys, I preferred watching bulldozers in action and concrete being poured to whatever was being written on the blackboard. I spent a lot of sixth grade gazing out the window. I don't think I learned anything that year.

The redbrick structure I watched rising with such absorbed fascination was a church. Unlike the soaring Gothic cathedrals of Europe or the formidable fortress-like stone church my family attended, this was not a typical church. It was being built in the shape of a mighty boat. Presumably, it was Noah's ark. Most of us have a mental picture of Noah's ark and we all think it looks like a cute tugboat with a little house on top.

Except that Noah's ark didn't look anything like that. You can look it up yourself. Right there in Genesis, you'll find God's Little Instruction Book, a set of divine plans for building an ark. Unfortunately, like most directions that come with bicycles or appliances, these are a little sketchy, providing little more than the rough dimensions of 300 by 50 by 30 cubits (or roughly 450 feet long, 75 feet wide, and 45 feet high). God told Noah to add a roof and put in three decks. Beyond that, God's instructions came without a diagram, unless Noah threw away the blueprints when he finished. So we should count Noah putting this thing together in time to beat the rains as one of the first miracles.

Many years after I gazed out that classroom window, I discovered that the original Hebrew word for "ark" literally meant "box" or "chest" in English. In other words, Noah's ark actually looked like a big wooden crate, longer and wider than an American football field, and taller than a three-story building. So the architect who designed that church to look like the *Titanic* may have understood buttresses and load-bearing walls. But he didn't know his Bible.

He wasn't alone. Millions of people around the world own a Bible, profess to read it and follow its dictates. Many say they study it daily. But most of us have never looked at a Bible, despite insisting that it is important. According to one recent survey, nine out of ten Americans own a Bible, but fewer than half ever read it. Why? For most folks, the Bible is hard to understand. It's confusing. It's contradictory. It's boring. In other words, the Bible perfectly fits Mark Twain's definition of a classic: "a book which people praise and don't read."

Not only do we praise the Bible, but we quote it daily in public and private. It permeates our language and laws. It is in our courts for administering oaths. Despite the First Amendment to the U.S. Constitution, it is on the Capitol steps when America inaugurates a president. It is cited by politicians and preachers, playwrights and poets, peace lovers and provocateurs.

As its phenomenal sales prove, the Bible holds a special place in nearly every country in the world. The worldwide sales of the Bible are literally uncountable. It is even tough to keep track of all the translations of the Bible that exist around the world. There are complete Bibles in more than 40 European languages, 125 Asian and Pacific Island languages, and Bible translations into more than 100 African languages, with another 500 African-language versions of some portion of the Bible. At least fifteen complete Native-American Bibles have been produced. The first Native-American translation, completed in 1663, was made into the language of the Massachusetts tribe, which the Puritan colonists then promptly wiped out.

In English, there are more than 3,000 versions of the entire Bible or portions of the Bible. The King James Version, first produced in 1611, and the Revised Standard Version remain the most popular translations, but publishers thrive on introducing new versions and "specialty" Bibles every year. The *Living Bible*, one contemporary, paraphrased version, has sold more than 40 million copies since 1971. Around the world, active Bible study classes attract millions of students. So, whether we worship in some formal setting or not, it is clear that people of nearly every nation remain fascinated by the Bible and its rich treasury of stories and lessons.

To many of them, it is still the "Greatest Story Ever Told." For millions of Christians, the Old and New Testaments make up the "Good Book." For Jews, there are no "Old" and "New" Testaments, only the collection of Hebrew scriptures that are equivalent to the Christian Old Testament. In spite of these differences, the common chord for Christians and Jews is strong: these books have been the source of inspiration, healing, spiritual guidance, and ethical rules for thousands of years.

The Bible is clearly many things to many people. The problem is, most of us don't know much about the Bible. Raised in a secular, media-saturated world in which references to God and religion leave us in embarrassed silence, we have wide-ranging reasons for this ignorance. For some, it was simply being bored by the drone of Sunday school or Hebrew class. Others received their Bible basics from the great but factually flawed Hollywood epics like *The Ten Commandments*, *The Greatest Story Ever Told*, and *The Robe*.

But most people simply never learned anything at all about a book that has influenced the course of human history more than any other. Public schools don't dare go near the subject of religion—perhaps we should be grateful for that, given their track record on the other three R's. The media generally limits its coverage of religion to the twice-yearly Christmas-Easter stories, unless there is a scandal or a lunatic-fringe disaster, like those of the Heaven's Gate or Branch Davidian cults. We've stopped sending our children to Sunday school or synagogue, and stopped going ourselves. The ignorance doesn't stop at the churchyard gates. In a 1997 survey, the London *Sunday Times* found that only 34 percent of 220 Anglican priests could recite all of the Ten Commandments without help! All of them remembered the parts about not "killing" and not committing adultery. But things got a little fuzzy after that. In fact, 19 percent of these priests thought that the eighth commandment is "Life is a journey. Enjoy the ride."

At least they didn't think it was "Just do it."

Even those who *think* they know the Bible are surprised when they learn that their "facts" are often half-truths, misinformation, or dimly remembered stories cleaned up for synagogue and Sunday school. For centuries, Jews and Christians have heard sanitized versions of Scripture that left out the awkward, uncomfortable, and racier Bible stories. Sure, most people have some recollection of Noah, Abraham, and Jesus. But they are less likely to know about the tales of rape, impaling, and "ethnic cleansing" routinely found in the Bible. These are timeless stories with timeless themes: justice and morality; vengeance and murder; sin and redemption. *Pulp Fiction* and *NYPD Blue* have nothing on the Bible!

There was Cain knocking off Abel. Noah's son cursed for seeing his drunken father naked. Abraham willing to sacrifice the son he desired all his life. The population of Sodom and Gomorrah destroyed for its wanton ways. Lot sleeping with his daughters. A tent peg driven through a man's head in Judges. King Saul asking young David to bring him a hundred Philistine foreskins as a bride price to marry his daughter. King David sending a soldier into the front lines so he could sleep with the man's wife. Then there is that ever-popular tale of wise Solomon threatening to cut a baby in half. But did you know that the two women who brought King Solomon that baby were prostitutes?

Raised in a traditional, Protestant church with a full menu of Christmas pageants and confirmation classes, I thought I possessed a fairly solid biblical education. In the annual Christmas pageant, I rose from angel to shepherd to Joseph—a nonspeaking role; Jesus' earthly father stood mutely behind Mary with nothing to say. I never made it to the plum role—one of the "Three Kings" who call on the infant Jesus. They had the coolest costumes. Three very tall brothers in my church always got those parts. I didn't know until much later that they weren't three "Kings" at all but magicians from Iran.

While attending a Lutheran college and later, Jesuit Fordham University, I continued to study the history and literature of the Bible. But then, in writing an earlier book called *Don't Know Much About Geography*, I posed a few simple questions related to the Bible:

"Where was the Garden of Eden?"

"What is the world's oldest city?"

"Did Moses really cross the Red Sea?"

That's when I got some surprises. In researching the world's oldest city, for instance, I learned that Joshua's Jericho is one of the oldest of human settlements. It also lies on a major earthquake zone. Could that simple fact of geology have had anything to do with those famous walls tumbling down? Then I discovered that Moses and the tribes of Israel never crossed the Red Sea but escaped from Pharaoh and his chariots across the *Sea of Reeds*, an uncertain designation which might be one of several Egyptian lakes or a marshy section of the Nile Delta. This mistranslation crept into the Greek Septuagint version and was uncovered by modern scholars with access to old Hebrew manuscripts. While it would not have been as cinematically dazzling for C. B. DeMille to have Charlton Heston herd all those movie extras across a soggy bog, this linguistic correction made the escape from Egypt far more plausible.

To me, the fact that the Exodus, one of the key stories in the Bible, was garbled by a mistranslation was a striking revelation. And it set me to thinking. How many other glitches are there in the Bible? How many other "little" mistakes in translation have blurred our understanding of the real story? After all, the Bible has been through an awful lot of translations during the past two thousand years, including, only in fairly recent times, into English and other modern languages. Moses and Jesus never said "thee" and "thou." In fact, even the name Jesus is a muddled translation of the Hebrew name Joshua. In the words of one politician, "Mistakes were made." They were compounded over time. What if one of those medieval monks had slipped a bit with his quill when he was illuminating a manuscript? Or perhaps one of King James's scribes had too much sacramental wine the day he worked on Deuteronomy.

My questions about the Bible took a more troubling turn when I wrote *Don't Know Much About the Civil War*. I discovered that Christian abolitionists and defenders of slavery both turned to the Bible to support their positions. Slaveholders pointed to the existence of slavery in biblical times, as well as laws and biblical commands requiring slaves to be obedient, to justify America's "Peculiar Institution." Abolitionists cited Jewish laws for emancipating slaves and sheltering runaway slaves, New Testament verses that suggested freeing slaves, and Jesus' commandment to "do unto others as you would have them do unto you." How could the Bible be right for both of them? The moral quandary pitting slavery against abolition marked a turning point in American history: for the first time, doubt was cast on the Bible's authority.

The fact that the Bible was used to support an evil like slavery raises another uncomfortable fact. To many people, the Bible has been a weapon. For centuries, Jews have feared the anti-Semitic message drawn by some Christians from the New Testament and its emphasis that the Jews killed Jesus—a devout Jew himself. The Crusades, the Inquisition, and Catholics fighting Protestants are all part of the Bible's blood-soaked past. The nightly news is still filled with stories of Jews fighting Arabs over "biblical" lands. And in America, "biblical" issues permeate political debates. Abortion. Capital punishment. Homosexuality. Prayer in schools. On all of these burning social issues, people point to the Bible in justifying their positions.

Few biblical or religious questions have divided people more deeply in recent times than the role of women in the Scriptures. The Bible has been used as a cudgel against women for centuries. Biblical stories granting men supremacy over women—from the Garden of Eden through the early Christian church—seemingly conferred "divine authority" on women's second-class status. Second-class status in synagogues and churches cemented second-class status at home. The biblical role laid out for women seemed clear: make babies and make dinner.

The fact is, while we all know of the Bible's "macho men," such as Moses, David, and Samson, the Scriptures are also filled with stories of strong, brave women. Preachers and Hollywood have always focused on the Bible's "bad girls," like Delilah or Jezebel, but they've overlooked some compelling heroines. In my view, the daring Eve is far more interesting than gutless Adam; Ruth was a model of loyalty and faith; Esther a brave beauty queen who saved the Jews from history's first anti-Semitic pogrom; and Deborah was the Bible's answer to "Xena, the Warrior Princess."

My own curiosity about these troubling questions of biblical authority and accuracy come at a time when new discoveries and scholarship are challenging many accepted notions about the Bible. For instance, there have been startling discoveries drawn from the Dead Sea Scrolls, the ancient Hebrew Bible texts unearthed fifty years ago in some caves in the desert near the Dead Sea. These scrolls, the oldest known versions of the Hebrew scriptures that make up the Old Testament, have added immensely to an understanding of Bible texts and life at the time Jesus lived. Even more dramatic and controversial are questions raised in *The Gnostic Gospels*, a book that explores a cache of fifteen-hundred-year-old Christian documents very much at odds with the traditional New

Testament stories of Jesus. Discoveries such as these are prompting serious scholars to reexamine very fundamental questions: Who wrote the Bible? Did Jesus say everything we were taught he said? Did he say more?

Questions like these resonate deeply with many people, whether well schooled in the Bible or embarrassed by their lack of biblical knowledge. *Don't Know Much About the Bible* is aimed at answering these questions for an audience that still considers the Bible sacred and important but just doesn't know what it says. For instance, most people are astonished to learn that Genesis contains not one but two Creation stories, significantly different in details and meaning. In the first of these Creations, men and women are created simultaneously in "God's image." This is followed by a second Garden of Eden surprise: there was no apple. A few of the other widely held Bible misconceptions are equally remarkable. The commandment does not say "Thou shalt not kill." David didn't slay Goliath. Jonah wasn't in the belly of a whale. David didn't write the Psalms of David. Solomon didn't write Song of Solomon. Isaiah didn't write Isaiah. And King David and Jesus were both descended from prostitutes.

To clear away the cobwebs of misconception surrounding the Bible, this book traces the history of the Bible itself and how it came to be. Many of the events described in the Bible, such as the fifty-year captivity of the Jewish people in Babylon or New Testament events occurring during the heights of the Roman empire, can be matched to recorded history. While the ancient Israelites existed as a fairly small group of nomadic herders, the Egyptians built one of the most extraordinary civilizations in human history. (Do you find it curious that the Bible never mentions the pyramids?) Jesus lived and preached in a small outpost of the mighty Roman empire, whose language and laws continue to influence our lives.

By examining the Bible historically, one aim of this book is to show which Biblical teachings may have been just fine for an ancient, seminomadic world, and which may still apply to life at the dawn of the twenty-first century. There are many biblical laws that modern Jews and Christians no longer accept. For instance, even the most hard-core fundamentalists would probably agree that it is no longer necessary for a father to prove his daughter's virginity by displaying a bloody sheet in the town square. It is safe to say that most of us no longer believe that a mother must make a burnt offering after bearing a child or that a woman is "unclean" while menstruating. All these are drawn from the Laws of Moses.

Have you let your animals breed with a different kind? Sown your fields with two kinds of seed? Have you put on a garment made of two different materials? Well then, you've broken some of God's statutes as laid out by Moses in Leviticus.

How many still think that adultery should be punished by stoning, as Jewish Law provides? (Probably quite a few in the "First Wives Club"!) Anyone who wants a sense of biblical justice in the modern world might look at Afghanistan under the control of the Taliban, Islamic fundamentalists whose ideas of appropriate behavior and punishment are not too different from those of the ancient Israelites.

The questions I raise in *Don't Know Much About the Bible*, whether profound or irreverent, are aimed at dusting off some timeworn misimpressions and refreshing rusty recollections. Often these questions address "household" names and events from the Bible, such as what the Exodus was or who the "Good Samaritan" was, or what the Sermon on the Mount says. We know they're important, but we can't put our finger on exactly what they are and why we should know about them. But going beyond those, I pry open some bigger cans of worms. Why are there two Creation stories in Genesis? Why can't Moses enter the "Promised Land"? Was Jesus really born on Christmas? Was Mary Magdalene naughty or nice?

Of course, these sorts of questions challenge "traditional" notions about what the Bible says, and I suspect my approach will roil people who are possessive about the Bible. On balance, however, this is a book in which historical accuracy, cultural context, and removing confusion about archaic words and mistranslations are all given a place in understanding these ancient texts. I try not to "interpret" the Bible so much as explain what is actually in it.

As a historian, I know that "tampering" with the Bible is a risky business. In one attempt to make the Bible accessible to common folk who didn't understand Hebrew, Latin, or Greek, John Wycliffe, a renegade English priest, produced one of the first English Bible translations before his death in 1384. The authorities were not amused. Denounced as a heretic after his death, Wycliffe couldn't be executed. Church officials did the next best thing: they exhumed his corpse and burned it.

Another English priest, William Tyndale, didn't fare much better. Upset by the corruption he witnessed among his fellow clergymen, Tyndale (c. 1494–1536) believed the Bible should be read by everyone, not just the few who understood Latin, the language of the church. He set out to translate the Bible into English. Accused of perverting the Scriptures, Tyndale was forced to leave England, and his New Testament was ordered burned as "untrue translations." Arrested and imprisoned as a heretic, Tyndale was executed in Antwerp by strangling. His body was then burned at the stake in October 1536 for good measure.

In other words, you go into a job like this with your eyes open. There are plenty of people who feel that the Bible is just fine the way it is, thank you. Whenever a Tyndale comes along with different ideas, the Powers-That-Be usually lash out. Sometimes the Powers-That-Be realize they were wrong. It just takes a while. In the case of Galileo (1564–1642), the Italian physicist and astronomer who said the earth revolves around the sun, it took the Vatican three and a half centuries to admit that he was right. In 1992— 350 years after Galileo died—the Roman Catholic church reversed its condemnation of Galileo. William Tyndale is now honored as the "Father of the English Bible." Small compensation, perhaps, for having one's neck wrung and being barbecued.

While I don't expect that anyone will call for my execution or excommunication, I'm sure that some people will not be happy with this book because it challenges "conventional wisdom" by asking questions. Many people have been taught not to question the Bible. They fear that if you pull one loose thread, the whole thing will unravel like a cheap suit. Ultimately, the Bible is a book of faith, not history, biology, biography, science, or even philosophy. The questions I pose may be an affront to people who still believe that the Bible is the *unquestionable* "Word of God." But for centuries, scholars and thinkers, many of them devout believers, have been raising legitimate doubts about the Bible. People of faith shouldn't fear these inquiries. How strong is a faith that can't stand up to a few honest questions?

After all, some of the boldest inquiries ever made by men are explored in Job, a book that has the audacity to challenge a God who has made a bet with Satan. "Why?" a beleaguered Job asks God again and again. "Why have you made me your target?" One of history's most cynical fellows was called "the Preacher" in the book of Ecclesiastes. In the midst of all the Bible books praising God's wonders, "the Preacher" stops us short by asking, "What's the point if you live and work hard and then just die?"

If my questions upset you, blame Adam and Eve! After all, that Forbidden Fruit was plucked from the Tree of Knowledge. And knowledge is what this is all about. Underlying the *Don't Know Much About* series is the notion that "school" doesn't end when we leave the classroom. I believe it is crucial for people to question the easy assumptions they grow up with—about religion, history, or a Ford versus a Chevy. The world is a school; life about learning. In the words of poet William Butler Yeats, "Education is not the filling of a pail, but the lighting of a fire."

Beyond "lighting a fire," *Don't Know Much About the Bible* has more ambitious goals. We live in fascinating but confounding times. Rarely has the world seemed so "corrupt," yet rarely has there been such worldwide interest in religion and spirituality. Whether it is millennial curiosity or the weary rejection of modern life, many people are pondering their lives and searching for "something." Call it family values. Morality. Virtue. Perhaps even faith. For these searchers, *Don't Know Much About the Bible* sets out to offer some help in "attaining wisdom and discipline; for understanding words of insight; for acquiring a disciplined and prudent life, doing what is right and just and fair" (Proverbs).

An ambitious goal? Absolutely. In other words, for the modern spiritual journeyer, this book sets out to provide a readable road map through a Bible that remains morally instructive, vividly alive, and spiritually challenging. Can I bring you "faith"? Can I make you "believe"? I'm not even going to try.

If that is what you find, amen. If you don't find faith in these pages, however, I hope you will at least find wisdom.

Author's Note: When people heard I was writing this book, the most frequently asked question was "Which translation are you using?" It's a reasonable curiosity that points to one of the basic problems in discussing and understanding the Bible—there are so many Bibles. I have relied upon several translations, all of which are listed in the Bibliography. As a researcher, my preference is for *The New Oxford Annotated Bible*, a New Revised Standard Version (NRSV). The result of research by a broad range of scholars from diverse religions and denominations, it is a translation that reflects the latest discoveries in biblical scholarship and presents valuable notes regarding controversial, disputed, or conflicting versions. Bible verses cited in this book are generally from the Oxford NRSV unless otherwise noted. The most frequently cited alternatives include the King James Version (KJV), the Jewish Publication Society (JPS) edition of the Tanakh, and *The New Jerusalem Bible* (NJB).

Historical dates have traditionally been written as BC, for "before Christ," and AD, for "anno Domini" ("in the year of the Lord"). Both terms reflect a Christ-centered viewpoint. Many scholars now prefer a dating system that uses BCE ("before the Common Era") and CE ("Common Era"). I have adopted that dating system in this book.

DON'T KNOW MUCH ABOUT® THE BIBLE

part one

---❋---

WHOSE BIBLE IS IT ANYWAY?

The Devil can cite scripture for his own purpose.

—WILLIAM SHAKESPEARE,
THE MERCHANT OF VENICE

The Bible has noble poetry in it; and some clever fables; and some blood-drenched history; and a wealth of obscenity; and upwards of a thousand lies.

—MARK TWAIN,
LETTERS FROM THE EARTH

...what is it to me if Moses wrote it or if another prophet wrote it, since the words of all of them are truth and through prophecy.

—FIFTEENTH-CENTURY SCHOLAR JOSEPH BEN ELIEZER BONFILS

❋ What is the Bible?

❋ What's a "testament"?

❋ Are the Dead Sea Scrolls the "original" Bible?

❋ Who wrote the Hebrew Bible or Old Testament?

❋ Didn't Moses write the Torah?

❋ If not Moses, then who?

❋ Who were the Children of Israel?

❋ If they wrote it in Hebrew, where did all the Greek words come from?

My Bible or yours? Whose version shall we read? The King James? The Jerusalem Bible? The *Living Bible*?

Take a look at this brief passage from one Bible story as told in a version called *The Five Books of Moses:*

> The human knew Havva his wife,
> she became pregnant and bore Kayin.
> She said:
> *Kaniti*/I-have-gotten
> a man, as has YHWH!
> She continued bearing—his brother, Hevel.
> Now Hevel became a shepherd of flocks, and Kayin be-
> came a worker of the soil.

Havva? Kayin? Hevel?

"Who are these strangers?" you might ask.

Perhaps you know them better as Eve and her boys, Cain and Abel, whose births are recounted in Genesis. In Everett Fox's *The Five Books of Moses* you will also encounter Yaakov, Yosef, and Moshe. Again, you might recognize them more easily as Jacob, Joseph, and Moses. In this recently published translation of the Bible's first five books, Dr. Fox attempts to recapture the sound and rhythms of ancient Hebrew poetry, to re-create the feeling of this ancient saga as it was sung around desert campfires by nomadic herders some three thousand years ago. In doing so, Fox makes the comfortably familiar seem foreign. All of those art-museum paintings depicting a nubile, blond, blue-eyed European Eve holding an apple simply don't jibe with the image Fox conjures—of a primitive earth mother from a starkly different time and place. His unexpected presentation underscores a startling fact about the book we all claim to respect and honor: there is no one Bible. There are many Bibles. A stroll through any bookstore demonstrates that reality. You'll see Jewish Bibles, Catholic Bibles, African-American Bibles, "nonsexist" Bibles, "Husband's Bibles," and "Recovery Bibles" designed for those in twelve-step programs. Then there's the *Living Bible*—as opposed to the Dead Bible?—and *The Good News Bible,* both written in contemporary language. So far there is no "Valley Girl" or "Baywatch" Bible. Give it time.

So how to choose? The King James Version is still the most popular translation of all. But God, Moses, and Jesus didn't really speak the King's English, and all of those "thees" and "thous" and verbs ending in "eth" are confusing and tough on anyone with a lisp. The New Revised Standard Version is clear and readable, but it lacks poetic sweep. Then there are dozens of other versions, each proclaiming its superiority, some claiming to be more faithful to the "original" version. It brings to mind the words of the world-weary philosopher in the biblical book of Ecclesiastes: "Of making many books there is no end."

What would old "Ecclesiastes" say if he walked into a bookstore? Do too many translations spoil the biblical stew? This question lies at the heart of so much popular confusion about the Bible. We can't agree on a version. So how can we can agree on what it says?

Where did this Flood of Bibles come from? How did such an important document come to be so many different things to so many different people? Or as the English poet William Blake put it nearly two hundred years ago:

> Both read the Bible day and night,
> But thou read'st black where I read white.

All of these queries lead back to one very simple first question:

What is the Bible?

Most people think of the Bible as a book, like a long and complicated novel with too many oddly named characters and not enough plot. Pick up a Bible. Hold it in your hand. No question about it.

It is a "book." But it is vastly more. The word "Bible" comes from the medieval Latin *biblia*, a singular word derived from the Greek *biblia*, meaning "books." To add to this little word history: the city of Byblos was an ancient Phoenician coastal city in what is now Lebanon. The Phoenicians invented the alphabet we still use and taught the Greeks how to write. From Byblos, the Phoenicians exported the papyrus "paper" on which early "books" were written. (Papyrus is actually a reedlike plant; strips of the plant were soaked and woven together. When dried, they formed a writing "paper.") While *byblos* originally meant "papyrus" in Greek, it eventually came to mean "book," and books are therefore named after this city.

So, in the most literal sense, the Bible is not a single book but an anthology, a collection of many small books. In an even broader sense, it is not just an anthology of shorter works but an entire library. You might think of a library as a physical place, but it can also mean a collection of books. And the Bible is an extraordinary gathering of many books of law, wisdom, poetry, philosophy, and history, some of them four thousand years old. How many books this portable library contains depends on which Bible you are clutching. The Bible of a Jew is different from the Bible of a Roman Catholic, which is different from the Bible of a Protestant.

Written over the course of a thousand years, primarily in ancient Hebrew, the Jewish Bible is the equivalent of Christianity's Old Testament. For Jews, there is no New Testament. They recognize only those Scriptures that Christians call the Old Testament. Both the Jewish Bible and Christian Old Testament contain the same books, although arranged and numbered in a slightly different order. Unless you hold the Jerusalem Bible, popular among Roman Catholics; it contains about a dozen books that Jews and Protestants don't consider "Holy Scripture." But that's another story, one that comes a little later in the Bible's history. In Jewish traditions, their Bible is also called the Tanakh, an acronym of the Hebrew words *Torah* (for "law" or "teaching"), *Nevi'im* ("the Prophets") and *Kethuvim* ("the Writings"). These are the

three broad divisions into which the thirty-nine books of Hebrew
scripture are organized.

BOOKS OF THE HEBREW BIBLE OR OLD TESTAMENT

TANAKH   The order of the books of Hebrew scriptures

TORAH
Genesis
Exodus
Leviticus
Numbers
Deuteronomy

PROPHETS
Joshua
Judges
First Samuel
Second Samuel
First Kings
Second Kings
Isaiah
Jeremiah
Ezekiel
Hosea
Joel
Amos
Obadiah
Jonah
Micah
Nahum
Habakkuk
Zephaniah
Haggai

Zechariah
Malachi

WRITINGS
Psalms
Proverbs
Job
The Song of Songs (Song of Solomon)
Ruth
Lamentations
Ecclesiastes
Esther
Daniel
Ezra
Nehemiah
First Chronicles
Second Chronicles

KING JAMES VERSION   The standard order of the Old Testament books in most Christian Bibles

Genesis
Exodus
Leviticus
Numbers
Deuteronomy
Joshua
Judges
Ruth
1 Samuel
2 Samuel
1 Kings
2 Kings
1 Chronicles

2 Chronicles
Ezra
Nehemiah
Esther
Job
Psalms
Proverbs
Ecclesiastes
Song of Solomon
Isaiah
Jeremiah
Lamentations
Ezekiel
Daniel
Hosea
Joel
Amos
Obadiah
Jonah
Micah
Nahum
Habakkuk
Zephaniah
Haggai
Zechariah
Malachi

These thirty-nine books lay out the law, traditions, and history of the Jewish people and their unique relationship with their God. Starting "In the beginning," with the very Creation of "the heavens and earth," these thirty-nine books follow the lives of the ancient founders of the Jewish faith—the Patriarchs and the Matriarchs—and recount the story of the people of ancient Israel in good times and bad. While many of us recall childhood stories of such Israelite heroes as Abraham, Moses, Joshua, and David, the true centerpiece of these books is the code of divine laws primarily laid out in the first five books, or Torah, that both Jews and Christians believe was given by God to the prophet Moses more than three thousand years ago. Far more than just the familiar Ten Commandments—at least, they should be familiar—these laws regulated every aspect of Jewish religious and daily life, and provide the core of that "Judeo-Christian ethic" everybody's always talking about.

For Christians, who worship the same One God of Judaism, this Old Testament is a significant part of their religion and traditions, but it it is only part of the story. Because their Bible also includes a "second act" or sequel, the New Testament, which tells the story of Jesus, a man Christians believe was the son of God. Its twenty-seven additional books recount how Jesus' followers, most of them devout Jewish men and women, established the Christian church just about two thousand years ago.

But this quick, literal answer to the basic question of what the Bible is dodges the main issue. Some people would confidently reply that the Bible is the divinely inspired word of God, given to humankind through God's prophets. In other words, God dictated these Bible books word for word to men in his divine "stenography pool."

Centuries of research into the Bible presents a far more complicated picture: the Bible is the culmination of an extended process—covered with centuries of inky human fingerprints—of storytelling, writing, cutting and pasting, translating, and interpreting. That process began about four thousand years ago, and involved many writers working at different times—a fact that may still come as a distinct surprise to a good many readers.

What's a "testament"?

If the Bible really starts out as Jewish document, and they don't call it a "testament," where does that word come from? And what does it mean?

The word "testament" has come to mean several things. Most people prefer to put off thinking about the word when it comes to that unpleasantness, your "last will and testament." In this strictly legal sense, it means a document providing for the disposal of your earthly goods after you die.

Another common use for "testament" is as evidence of something—for instance, "The Holocaust is testament to Hitler's evil."

But the old way in which the word was used to describe these holy writings meant something quite different. "Testament" was another word for "covenant"—meaning an agreement, contract, or pact. For Christians, the Old Testament represented the ancient deal or "covenant" struck between God and his people. In the New Testament, however, Christians think they got a "New Deal" through the life, death, and resurrection of Jesus.

Many Christians think that this means they can simply throw out the old books and stick with the new, or skip over all that long, boring "old stuff." But the New Testament does not replace the Old. To Christians, it supplements, expands, and completes that "old contract." In the sports world, they call it a contract extension; the old agreement is renewed with more profitable terms.

Jesus himself was familiar with the "old contract." He was a good Jewish boy who studied the Torah, Prophets, and Writings. He could cite them by heart when he was twelve. Of course, Jesus wouldn't have possessed a Bible to study his lessons. When he was a boy, there was no "Bible." Books didn't exist. More likely he would have learned by rote from scrolls kept by local religious teachers, or "rabbis." The ancient books of Hebrew later collected as the Bible were written on papyrus or leather, stitched together, and rolled into long scrolls. Until recently, the oldest known copies of Hebrew scrolls came from medieval times, around the year 1000. Then fifty years ago a Bedouin boy scrounging around some caves in the desert wastelands near the Dead Sea made an intriguing and startling discovery.

Are the Dead Sea Scrolls the "original" Bible?

In the spring of 1947, while the British still controlled Palestine, Muhammed ed Dib was tending goats in the arid, rocky hills near the northern Dead Sea shore. The "Dead Sea" is actually a salty lake in the middle of a desert, the lowest point on the face of the earth, and one of the hottest and least inviting landscapes in the world. The fresh water flowing into it evaporates rapidly in the heat, leaving behind a thick mineral broth. Fish can't live in these waters—hence a "Dead Sea." In the hills that surround the Dead Sea, the young goatherd dropped a stone into a cave and heard it hit something. Investigating further, he came across ancient clay pots filled with scrolls and scraps of old leather covered in mysterious writing. His accidental find was the beginning of one of the most momentous, and controversial, discoveries in history: that of the "Dead Sea Scrolls."

Muhammed's find launched a wider search of the surrounding area, generally called Qumran, approximately ten miles south of Jericho, on a plateau overlooking the Dead Sea. After the initial discovery sent amateurs crawling all over these rocky hills, scurrying to find more scrolls, an orderly archaeological search of Qumran was eventually organized. Over the years, many more scrolls and remnants of scrolls were uncovered. Fifty years after that first find, researchers are still trying to piece together all of the tiny bits and pieces of leather fragments preserved by the dry desert air.

The painstaking work of sorting through these fragile old

leather scraps, a massive ancient jigsaw puzzle with no picture to work from, has stirred controversy. Set against the politics and intrigue of recent Middle East wars and history, the work proceeded in secret and very slowly. Too slowly for some critics, who saw a giant conspiracy to keep the world from learning some extraordinary truth. But even from the earliest days of the discovery of the Dead Sea Scrolls, as news of their contents trickled out, it was clear that these ancient scrolls included some of the oldest known texts of the Hebrew Bible ever found.

Written in both Hebrew and Aramaic—a Syrian language closely related to Hebrew, and the language spoken by Jesus— more than two hundred biblical documents have been found; some are almost complete, others are in fragments. The scrolls contain at least a portion of every book of the Hebrew Bible, except the book of Esther. Among the scrolls is a complete "book" of Isaiah, composed of seventeen separate pieces of leather stitched together to form a roll nearly twenty-five feet long. Sophisticated dating techniques have proven that some of these scrolls were written nearly three hundred years before Jesus was born. Others came from Jesus' own lifetime, a turbulent period in ancient Palestine when Rome controlled a contentious, rebellious Jewish people.

Besides these bits and pieces of the Bible, the scrolls also contained other ancient books that are not in our Bibles. There was also a great deal of information about the people who had copied and hidden these scrolls away in these Qumran caves. Known as the "Essenes," they were part of a Jewish sect, some of whom rejected mainstream Jewish life in Jerusalem for a monklike, celibate existence. A communal group, the Qumran Essenes adhered to strict regulations as they prepared for Judgment Day, like the Jedi Knights of *Star Wars*, awaiting a final battle between good and evil, the forces of light and dark.

The Dead Sea Scrolls make two facts clear. By the time Jesus was born, an official list, or "canon," of Hebrew books in the Bible had not yet been set. And while these old books are very similar to the Hebrew scriptures as they are known today, there were slightly different versions of some of these ancient Hebrew texts. While the scrolls from Qumran offer fascinating information about the Hebrew text of the Bible and life in first-century Palestine, they leave another big, tantalizing question unresolved.

Who wrote the Hebrew Bible or Old Testament?

A few years ago in the New York City subway system, there was a poster for a stenography school that read: "If U cn rd ths, u cn get a gd jb."

This subway advertisement achieved instant legend status in New York. Good for late-night comedians' laughs, it was also obscenely parodied on numerous T-shirts.

But now try this word puzzle—

"Mgn rdng ths bk wtht vwls. Sn't tht dffclt t cmprhd? Myb ftr whl y cld fll n sm f th blnks nd fgr t mst f t. Ftr ll, ts smpl nglsh. Bt nw, mgn ts prt f n ncnt lngg tht hs flln nt dss vr svrl cntrs. Tht s hw th Bbl nc pprd."

Would you like to "buy a vowel" as they say on the popular *Wheel of Fortune* game show? You might get this:

"Imagine reading this book without vowels. Isn't that difficult to comprehend? Maybe after a while you could fill in some of the blanks and figure out most of it. After all, it's simple English. But now, imagine it's part of an ancient language that has fallen into disuse over several centuries. That is how the Bible once appeared."

When commencing a new year of classes in Hebrew, a famous university professor was said to tell his students, "Gentlemen, this is the language which God spoke." The Hebrew alphabet comprises twenty-two letters, all of them consonants, a concept we find difficult to grasp. In fact, Semitic languages like Hebrew, Aramaic, and Arabic are still generally written without any vowels, although a system of dots and dashes above and below the line of writing has been added in recent times. In other words, readers of classical Hebrew, versed in its oral traditions, had to provide the vowel sounds from memory. The Greeks, who borrowed the basic twenty-two-letter alphabet used in Hebrew and Phoenician, added five new letters at the end of their alphabet—so the Greeks get credit for inventing the vowel system.

Now back to the fill-in-the-blanks puzzle. Imagine that the ancient scrolls and parchments on which this mysterious passage was found are falling apart. They are written from right to left, the opposite of what most Europeans and Americans are accustomed to reading. Complicating the fact that the vowels have been left out, these scrolls are filled with the names of obscure people about whom there are no other references in history. Anyone reading these scrolls knows the text had been hand-copied after centuries of being orally transmitted from one generation to the next, just as *The Iliad* and *The Odyssey* were. And they also know that, over the centuries, older versions of the scrolls have been lost or destroyed. All in all, it is a very confusing puzzle.

With all these difficulties to consider, is it any wonder that people are confused by what the Bible says? Or that a good many people dismiss the Bible as little more than a very elaborate set of myths, like those of the ancient Greeks or King Arthur's Round Table? Now you have some sense of what we're up against when we talk about understanding who wrote the Bible. As Winston Churchill said about Russia in 1939: "It is a riddle wrapped in a mystery inside an enigma."

Many readers of the Bible still possess the "Divine Light Bulb" notion of the Bible's composition. In this scenario, a man was sitting in his tent in the Sinai desert, when suddenly, in a glorious flash, the entire text of the Scriptures started flowing onto parchment or papyrus. Or perhaps it was whispered into his ear by an unseen spirit—Cosmic Dictation. Or the words were whirled out of some heavenly flames and carved into stone the way it was done for Charlton Heston in *The Ten Commandments*. As the Gershwins put it so succinctly, "It ain't necessarily so."

The history of the Holy Scriptures that modern Jews and Christians study is a fantastic story in itself, a tale out of an Indiana Jones movie. It is still unfolding with each new archaeological dig and discovery of an ancient scroll. Once armed with little more than pith helmets, pick and shovel, and a magnifying glass, modern researchers are now aided by satellite photographs, spectroscopes, and infrared readers that can date and analyze old parchments. Astonishing discoveries during the past few decades of great libraries of ancient writing have added immensely to our knowledge of biblical times and languages. And with the help of linguistic computers and instant communications links to vast worldwide libraries, scholars continue to unravel the secrets of the Bible.

Yet, while the depth of our knowledge grows, the answer to a basic and extraordinary question largely remains a mystery: Who wrote the Bible?

In spite of tremendous strides in scholarship and research dedicated to this question, the fact remains: no one really knows. And we will probably never know, short of some archaeological find of earthshaking significance. But it is safe to say that the King James Version familiar to most English-speaking Christians and all the other versions loading down the bookstore shelves are only recent links near the end of a long chain of troubled, sometimes badly garbled, and often conflicting translations.

This is the first blow to the plausibility of *The Bible Code*, the publishing sensation that claims that the Bible contains a systematic code that, when unscrambled, has predicted world events of the past, present, and future. The authors of that book claimed to use a version of biblical text that is "the original version of the Old Testament, the Bible as it was first written," and that there is "a universally accepted original Hebrew text." No such text exists. The Old Testament or Hebrew Bible exists in a variety of forms, all reflecting different translations over the past few centuries.

Questionable Bible codes aside, these various translations over the centuries have shaped perceptions of the Bible and what people believe it says. It still comes as a surprise to some English speakers that the Bible was not written in English—or to German speakers that it was not written in German. But research into ancient manuscripts, such as the Dead Sea Scrolls, and the discovery of other ancient libraries have provided many more clues about the people who did write the Bible.

First, researchers have learned that some of what appears in the most ancient sections of the Bible, including some of the stories in Genesis, was probably "borrowed" from other more ancient civilizations, particularly those of Egypt and Babylon. Various aspects of the Laws that God gives to Moses in Exodus are similar to Babylonian laws known as the Code of Hammurabi, which is a few centuries older than the Bible. The story of the infant Moses set afloat in a basket is similar to the Mesopotamian legend of an ancient king named Sargon. Some of the wisdom found in the biblical Proverbs sounds remarkably like the sayings of an Egyptian sage named Amen-em-ope who lived around the time of Solomon, the ostensible author of Proverbs. In other words, the authors of the Bible, like writers before and since, were not above liberal borrowing, or what modern writers call "fair use."

The beginning of the actual process of writing down what Jews call the Tanakh and what Christians call the Old Testament dates back more than three thousand years to approximately 1000 BCE. The actual process of writing down the Scriptures followed an oral tradition that goes back at least another thousand years.

The oldest of the Hebrew scriptures are the first five books of the Bible: Genesis, Exodus, Leviticus, Numbers, and Deuteronomy. In Jewish tradition, these five are called the "Torah" ("Law" or "Teaching"). They are also known as both the "Five Books of Moses" and, in Greek, the "Pentateuch" ("five scrolls"). For a very, very long time, it was assumed that Moses himself had written the five books of the Torah. While many devout Jews and Christians still hold to that belief, a majority of scholars and theologians accept that the Five Books of Moses were transmitted orally for centuries before being set down on scrolls beginning some time after 1000 BCE—approximately the time that King David and Solomon are traditionally thought to have ruled Israel. This writing process was not completed until about 400 BCE.

Didn't Moses write the Torah?

For centuries Moses was accepted as the author of the five books of Torah that are traditionally called the Books of Moses. The Torah stated that Moses wrote down what he was told, so this was not simply a scholar's opinion but an unquestioned matter of faith for both Jews and Christians. Some editions of the Bible still assert that Moses was the author of Genesis, and there are earnest believers who hold that as an article of faith.

In the past, daring to question that "fact" took guts—and more than a little "chutzpah." When an eleventh-century scholar pointed out that a list of kings mentioned in the Torah lived long after Moses died, he was called "Isaac the Blunderer" and his books were burned. Better his books burned than himself, Isaac undoubtedly mused. Four hundred years later, in the fifteenth century, new critics were raising awkward questions. Like: How could Moses write about his own death? Wasn't it odd that he called himself the "humblest man on earth"? A truly humble man wouldn't say such a thing. Besides recording his own death, Moses couldn't know of other later events that are mentioned in the Torah, like the long list of kings from nearby Edom who lived after Moses died. Traditional scholars tried to argue that Moses was a prophet, so he knew who those future kings would be. Others said that Joshua, Moses' successor, had merely tacked on a few lines after Moses died or that a later prophet updated the writings of Moses. But their arguments didn't stop the questions.

By the seventeenth century, as Europe entered the era of the Enlightenment, when rational thought and scientific observations were elevated over blind faith, other scholars began to question the authorship of Moses. A French priest who raised questions about Moses was arrested and forced to recant his views. In the grand tradition of the Roman Catholic church, his writing was banned and burned. The English translator of a book that claimed that the Torah was not the work of Moses also had to recant— which he did in 1688, "shortly before his release from the Tower," as Richard Elliott Friedman wryly notes in *Who Wrote the Bible?*, a comprehensive study of Torah authorship. The official church resisted these questions about Moses for the same reason it always does: to ask questions raises doubts. But their power rested on unquestioning belief. Let some troublemakers start asking about Moses, and before you know it they'll be asking why women can't be priests!

What these generations of scholars all noted was that the Books of Moses, in which the Laws of God had been laid out, contained contradictions in time, place, and numbers of things, and names that couldn't possibly belong in the time of Moses. Why were there duplicate versions of so many Bible stories, versions that did not always agree? Why, for instance, does Genesis open with two different versions of the Creation? Even more troubling, there were different names for God. If God had dictated these scriptures to Moses, why hadn't God used the same name all the time? Why did Moses—who had spoken to God—use so many different names for God? And finally, how could Moses write, at the end of Deuteronomy: "Then Moses, the servant of the Lord, died there in the land of Moab, at the Lord's command"? (Deut. 34:5)

These and other troubling questions raised by the mystery of Moses just wouldn't go away. And as the Enlightenment and Protestant Reformation chipped away at the pervasive power of the Church of Rome, the questions were asked by more and more people. No longer could church leaders explain away the numerous differences in style or the contradictions and anachronisms contained in the Torah as the "Word of God," take it or leave it. As generations of scholars pursued this mystery, it became clearer that Moses was *not* the book's author. They might be the Books *of* Moses, but they were not the Books *by* Moses. Equally important was the mounting evidence that the books attributed to Moses were composed at very different historical times. To many serious scholars, it seemed apparent that more than one author was at work. On many of these points, honest people still disagree. The difference is no one is being burned for heresy any longer.

If not Moses, then who?

Imagine taking apart an intricately woven tapestry and trying to figure out where each strand of thread came from, who had woven the cloth, and what they were thinking when they wove it. This is the seemingly impossible task that lay in front of biblical scholars trying to establish authorship of the Bible. As these scholars unraveled the threads of the Hebrew scriptures, they could see that very different strands had been woven together to tell the story. Often, these strands made references to events that happened much later than the events being described. Like the clock in Shakespeare's *Julius Caesar*, there were obvious anachronisms. Empires that didn't exist when Moses was alive were mentioned. A king of the Philistines was said to be around hundreds of years before the Philistines moved into the neighborhood. Camels were described in use before they were actually domesticated. In other words, it seemed obvious that some writers composed this material long after the events they described and added "details" that would be meaningful to the people they were addressing.

There are still many literalists who faithfully assert that the Bible is the "Word of God," dictated verbatim to "divinely chosen" individuals. However, most scholars now agree that there were at least four or five main authors, or groups of authors, of the Hebrew scriptures. They believe that they were composed over a long time, stretching from sometime around 1000 to 400 BCE. The idea that the Torah evolved from a combination of various sources is formally known as the "Documentary Hypothesis." This thinking gained such weight that, by 1943, even the Vatican under Pope Pius XII acknowledged it was time to solve these questions.

Today, the idea is widely accepted and taught by leading religious schools, including the divinity schools at Harvard and Yale, the Union Theological Seminary, and both the Jewish Theological Seminary and the Hebrew Union College. The precise identity of who wrote these books is an unsolved—and most likely an unsolvable—mystery, barring an archaeological find of the most revolutionary sort. But the principal "authors" have been given "names" and are identified by five letters of the alphabet: J, E, D, P, and R.

• **J** The oldest—and perhaps most celebrated—of these presumed authors is known as "J" from the German word *Jahwe*, the source of the word "Jehovah," another mistranslation now written in English as "Yahweh." The biblical writer code-named J consistently calls the Israelite God "Yahweh."

In a controversial but bestselling book of biblical scholarship, *The Book of J*, author Harold Bloom argued that the Bible's J was actually a woman. Many other scholars dismiss Bloom's theory, and it remains a question that may never be resolved. Male or female, J probably lived sometime between 950 and 750 BCE, in Judah (another reason "he" is called J), the southern half of a divided Hebrew kingdom. J is the Hebrew Bible's best storyteller, more interesting, more humorous, and more human than the others. J's Yahweh interacts with man easily and directly. J told the more famous and most folkloric version of the two Creation accounts, which begins in Genesis 2. It is J's Yahweh, for instance, who is walking in the Garden of Eden in the "cool of the day" (Gen. 3: 8), a lovely poetic image, and discovers Adam and Eve hiding themselves, ashamed of their nakedness. J is also responsible for the "Song of Deborah," an epic poem in the book of Judges about a Jewish "woman warrior."

• **E** Close on J's heels is E, the *Elohist*, so called because this author preferred to use the word *Elohim* for God. Although some scholars have placed E before or even contemporary with J, most think E came later, perhaps between 850 and 800 BCE. Most also agree that E is a much less colorful writer than J, and that E's contribution begins with the story of Abraham in Genesis 12. In the book of Judges, E tells a version of the Israelite heroine Deborah's story in prose (J's was a poetic version), and some of the details of the two accounts differ slightly.

• **D** The third Old Testament "author" is known as the "Deuteronomist," who most likely worked between 700 and 600 BCE and was responsible for large portions of the book of Deuteronomy. D is also thought to have shaped the later books of Joshua, Judges, Ruth, Samuel, and Kings—the major "historical" works of Hebrew scripture that describe the Conquest of Canaan and the establishment of the kingdom of Israel. In Deuteronomy, D depicts Moses giving a series of speeches that urge Israel to follow the Torah, but the law Moses offers in this section represents a revision of the earlier law books. Richard Elliot Friedman makes a case that D is the prophet Jeremiah, who lived in Jerusalem around 627 BCE and died in Egypt sometime after 587 BCE.

• **P** The texts credited to P, known as the Priestly author, include some of the most familiar words in western civilization— "In the beginning," the Creation account found in Genesis 1, and the first version of the Ten Commandments (Exodus 20:1–17). P's contribution was probably written sometime between 550 and 500 BCE. Highly concerned with the elaborate observances and duties of the ancient Jewish priesthood, P is responsible for nearly all of Leviticus. Dry and detail-obsessed, P was especially interested in codifying and justifying all of the ritual laws developed by the early Jewish priesthood, including the carefully worded descriptions of the Passover ritual, ordination ceremonies, the vestments of the high priest, and the sacred chest that held the Ten Commandments. P might as well have have been called "L," because he is so concerned with the Law, but he is also often as long-winded and tedious as a lawyer.

• **R** In addition to these four "writers," or groups of writers, there was probably another individual or group responsible for creating the Pentateuch and some of the other early books of Is-raelite history as they now stand. In some respects, this was the most extraordinary feat. R was the *Redactor*, or editor, who took the four existing strands, and spliced them together, probably around 400 BCE. Like the others, R's identity is a mystery. No one even knows whether there was more than one Redactor. The work of the Redactor is fascinating because of the way so many different and even contradictory strands of scripture were woven together. But it also raises a beguiling question. Were there any parts that R edited out of the picture? That is a mystery that remains in the realm of speculation.

This a vastly simplified overview of a question that scholars have puzzled over for more than a hundred years. Of course not everyone agrees with this multiple-author theory. Many "true be-lievers" reject it entirely. And some who accept the theory dispute those who say that the "Documentary Hypothesis" suggests that the Bible is just a collection of fables stitched together to suit each man who did the stitching. Historian Paul Johnson strikes this note in *A History of the Jews:*

> The Pentateuch is not therefore, a homogeneous work. But neither is it, as some scholars in the German critical tradition have argued, a deliberate falsification by priests, seeking to foist their self-interested religious beliefs on the people by attributing them to Moses and his age. . . . All the internal evidence shows that those who set down and conflated these writing, and the scribes who copied them . . . believed abso-lutely in the divine inspiration of the ancient texts and tran-scribed them with veneration and the highest possible standards of accuracy. (p. 89)

In other words, though, by about 400 BCE, the Pentateuch or Torah had arrived in something like the form we know it today. Some of these writers, compilers, or editors, particularly the three later writers—D, P, and R—were also involved in composing other parts of the Hebrew scriptures. As for the other thirty-four books of the Hebrew Bible—the Prophets and the Writings—evidence of authorship is either shaky or a complete mystery. Many of the books show the handiwork of writers working at different times and in different historical circumstances. But it is safe to say that David didn't write all, or even most, of the Psalms of David. Solomon didn't write Proverbs or the Song of Solomon, and Isaiah didn't write Isaiah. These "books," again transmitted orally for generations, were not finally set down in something like their present form until about 400 BCE, long after Moses and David. Some were not considered "Holy Scripture" for many more years. It was only around 90 CE that the Jewish rabbis closed the book on what they considered the "official" list of their Bible.

Who were the Children of Israel?

Why is there no evidence outside the Bible that such crucial personalities as Abraham or Moses existed? Why didn't the Israelites think to make sure that they kept track of which precise mountain was Mount Sinai of the Ten Commandments? Why does the Bible fail to mention the pyramids of Egypt, surely the most extraordinary structures then in existence?

These are bothersome questions for any thinking reader of the Bible. But they point to another underlying issue: most of us have no sense of the historical background of the Israelites and little idea as to who the people of the Hebrew Bible actually were. This brings us to a basic fact: it is nearly impossible to understand the writing and meaning of the Bible without understanding the history of the people who wrote it, the ancient Israelites. Of course, there are plenty of Hollywood images, which are practically useless. Most likely Samson didn't look like Victor Mature.

Who were these people, the first Jews? We use the words "Hebrew," "Jew," and "Israelite" almost interchangeably, but even these words came into use much later in history. So what was Israel like in the fifteen hundred years between the Patriarchs and the Prophets, roughly from 2000 to 500 BCE?

Located on the eastern coast of the Mediterranean, the world of the Bible is a tiny area—but it was a natural bridge between three continents, Africa, Asia, and Europe, as well as a natural beachhead for seafaring traders from the Mediterranean. And it was this geography that made the area such a collecting point for so many different groups who have had so much impact on history.

Though small in area, this land the Bible called Canaan features an extraordinary diversity of climate and features. A gentle coastline slopes up to mountains and the vast deserts beyond. The Jordan River flows from the steep, snow-topped mountains of Jordan, into a beautiful freshwater lake, the Sea of Galilee or Lake Tiberias, before plunging down to the lowest point on the surface of the earth, the Dead (or Salt) Sea. A lake thick with mineral salts, the Dead Sea is surrounded by an extremely hot, rocky wilderness. Into this land of such striking contrasts came waves of people, some as wanderers, some as traders, but many as invaders and conquerors. This was a blood-soaked piece of real estate, just as it continues to be today.

But long, long before the peoples of the Bible, long before the civilizations of Egypt or Mesopotamia, there were people here. They included some of the earliest known human settlers, a Stone Age people called Natufian. They were named for the Wadi en-Natuf, in the Judean hills, where a cave was discovered with evidence of some of the earliest known human settlements. The Natufians, dating to around 10,000 to 8000 BCE, were among the first people to live in permanent villages. Primarily hunter-gatherers, they also left evidence of grinding flour, and digs near the Sea of Galilee have yielded bone fishhooks and harpoons. These people practiced burial, and studies of their graves show that the dead were buried with jewelry and animals carved from stone and bone, evidence that from a very early time humans were interested, if not obsessed, with the "afterlife."

Over hundreds of centuries, a wide variety of people eventually settled these lands, evolving from primitive hunter-gatherers to nomadic herders, then settled farmers and finally city dwellers. One of the oldest of human settlements is Jericho, famed in the Bible as the city destroyed by trumpets. First excavated in the 1950s by British archaeologist Kathleen Kenyon, Jericho is nearly ten thousand years old, and has been almost continuously inhabited. By about 3000 BCE, about the time the first pyramid was built, Jericho had a strong defensive system, evidence of a high degree of social organization.

The names of the various groups who settled this land include the Canaanites, Edomites, Moabites, Amorites, Jebusites, and Hittites—all now lost tribes. Later arrivals included the Philistines, who apparently migrated from the Mediterranean islands of Crete or Cyprus and settled on the coastline sometime after 1200 BCE. To the north on the Mediterranean coast, in what is modern Lebanon, were the Phoenicians, the extraordinary sailors and dyers of cloth who also get credit for devising an alphabet that influenced our own.

Bracketing the land of Canaan were the two great superpowers of the ancient world. To the north and east was the land of Mesopotamia (from Greek for "between two rivers"), the "Cradle of Civilization" that sprang up in the fertile plains between the Tigris and Euphrates rivers and produced the Akkadians, Sumerians, Assyrians, and other "Babylonians." At the extreme other end of the land was Egypt, home of a civilization that lasted for thousands of years. Wedged into a tiny strip of land between sea and desert, Canaan served as bridge, buffer, and battleground between these two great ancient lands whose emperors vied for control of the area for centuries.

The land called Canaan in the Bible gradually grew to include both rural and urban people. A true melting pot, it was a land of herders, farmers, and traders. It was also a land of many gods and religions, although one group of Canaanite gods was most widely worshiped. The supreme god, the creator, was called El, a word that figures prominently in Genesis, as evidenced in such names as Israel and Bethel. El's son was the storm god Baal, another name that appears prominently throughout ancient Israel's violent history. And among Baal's consorts were Astarte and Asherah, mythical female goddesses who must have been very alluring to the Children of Israel. The followers of Moses and their descendants kept getting into trouble with their Yahweh God because they continued to worship these fertility goddesses instead of Yahweh. Since worshiping Baal and his goddesses probably meant having sex, or watching priests have sex, it was presumably more appealing to the masses than a religion that involved killing small animals and didn't allow women in the temple.

This "oversexed" Canaan was the little piece of land that the Israelites said they had been promised by their God. There is little historical or archaeological evidence to tell much about the people who came to be called "Hebrews"—a word possibly derived from an Egyptian word, *habiru,* a derogatory term for "outsiders"—or "Jews," derived from the later Roman name for the country, Judea. No one really knows when the "Children of Israel" arrived in Canaan. No one really knows precisely where they came from, although the evidence points to beginnings in the Tigris-Euphrates area. At some point, they moved into Canaan, and sometime after 2000 BCE some of them crossed into Egypt and remained there in the Nile Delta for a few hundred years. This group left Egypt, where they said they had been enslaved by an unnamed Pharaoh, and moved into the wastelands of either the Sinai or Arabian desert for forty years under the direction of a charismatic leader named Moses who said he spoke to God. Through Moses, the ancient promises that these people would one day possess Canaan were reconfirmed.

By around 1200 BCE, through conquest or gradual migration— the Bible has it both ways—they eventually took control of the land from the Canaanites, whose religious and sexual practices were so abhorrent to them. It's difficult to say precisely what these Canaanites did that was so abominable, but it can be assumed they had sex in their temples, and possibly didn't flinch at homosexuality, incest, bestiality, or human sacrifice.

The first piece of historical evidence of the existence of the Children of Israel is a stone plaque, or *stela*, from Egypt dated c. 1235 BCE. This stela from the reign of Pharaoh Merneptah mentions the complete destruction of the people of Israel. Merneptah's claim of a lopsided military victory, obviously inflated, is the first recorded reference to the people of Israel outside the Bible. Once the Israelites got their toehold in the interior hill country, they came to blows with another powerful group of recent arrivals, the Philistines, who had come from the Mediterranean and settled in cities along the coastline around 1200 BCE.

By around 1000 BCE, under the leadership of a dashing soldier-poet named David, who finally did in the Philistines, and his brilliant son Solomon, the Israelites finally controlled the land that they had been promised. But their empire was short-lived. After Solomon's death in 922 BCE, the kingdom was split in two in a civil war that left both halves of the divided nation vulnerable. The northern part was called Israel and the southern part Judah. The two nations vied for control over the land as well as authority in religious matters, each professing to be the true heirs of Abraham, Moses, and the promises from God.

The good times didn't last long. In 722 BCE, the Assyrians under Sargon II conquered Israel—the northern kingdom—and deported thirty thousand upper-class Israelites to the Euphrates River area in one of history's first recorded episodes of "ethnic cleansing." These ten northern tribes were dispersed throughout modern-day Iraq and Syria and became the so-called "Lost Tribes" of Israel. About one hundred years later, the southern kingdom, Judah, was conquered too, this time by the new superpower in the area, the Chaldeans (or Neo-Babylonians), led by Nebuchadnezzar. In 587 BCE, his troops captured and looted Jerusalem, destroyed the Great Temple built by Solomon, and set the city on fire. Thousands of the elite of Judean society were taken to Babylon in what is commonly known as the Exile. It is possible that they carried with them the "Ark of the Covenant," the sacred chest holding the stone tablets with the Ten Commandments, although this most holy object in Israel may have been destroyed with the temple. Somehow, in that fifty-year exile, the Ark of the Covenant disappeared without a trace or a mention. Of course, if you like Hollywood history, Steven Spielberg would have you think that the chest was found by Indiana Jones and is now locked up in some dusty U.S. government warehouse.

The final composition and editing of the Torah, along with the rest of the Tanakh, or Old Testament, largely took place over the stormy five hundred years between 900 and 400 BCE. And it was against that background of historical events—kings rising and falling, bitter disputes over religious authority, nations divided, conquests, and Exile—that the Hebrew scriptures were finally set down.

If they wrote it in Hebrew, where did all the Greek words come from?

Approximately two thousand years of history pass within the Bible's pages. Great empires came and went around the ancient Near East: Sumer, Akkadia, Babylon, Egypt, Assyria, Persia, and Greece. Along with those rising and falling empires and cultures, Hebrew and Aramaic fell into disuse, eventually replaced by Greek. And sometime around 250 BCE, when many Jews realized that they no longer understood the Hebrew of their ancient religion, someone decided to preserve those writings in a complete Greek translation of Hebrew scripture. An old tradition held that this Greek translation of the Hebrew holy scrolls was commissioned by Ptolemy II (282–246 BCE), one of the heirs to Alexander the Great who ruled Egypt after Alexander's death. Based on manuscripts sent from Jerusalem to the famed Library at Alexandria, this Greek translation was later called the Septuagint, meaning "seventy." According to the legend, seventy-two elders, six from each of the twelve tribes of Israel, did the translating. Each of these elders produced exactly the same translation in exactly seventy-two days. The number was rounded off to seventy. Of course, this sounds like the old notion that enough monkeys working at typewriters with enough time could produce the works of Shakespeare.

Modern scholars dismiss the connection with Ptolemy, as well as the seventy-two identical translations, as legend. In fact, the work was begun because the large Jewish community in Egypt and elsewhere in the Hellenized—or Greek-speaking—world needed a translation from Hebrew, which had fallen out of use during the Diaspora, or "dispersion" of Jews throughout the Mediterranean world.

The Greek Septuagint became the most popular form of the Hebrew Bible. It was the unofficial Scripture of the early Christians who read the Hebrew Laws and prophets in Greek. Roman Catholic Bibles, such as the Jerusalem Bible, still show this influence. Some of the books in the Septuagint were not considered "holy" by the Jewish rabbis who established the official "canon" of their Bible. When the Christian church split during the Protestant Reformation, the Protestants accepted the Jewish canon. That's why the Protestant Old Testament is the same as the Hebrew Bible, except for the order and numbering of some books. However, Roman Catholics considered the Septuagint holy, and Roman Catholic Bibles include eleven books that are not in the Hebrew or Protestant Old Testament. These books, called the deuterocanonical books, are represented in modern Bibles in the Apocrypha. (*Apocrypha*, not to be confused with *Apocalypse*, is from Greek by way of Latin and means "hidden.") To further confuse this issue, other Christian sects, such as the Eastern Orthodox churches, recognize even more books as sacred. In other words, for nearly two thousand years, humans have been deciding what should and shouldn't be read as the divine word of God. All of them claim to be inspired by God in making those judgments, but all don't agree.

The next major step in the process that led to the Bible as it is known today came when Latin, the language of the Roman empire, replaced Greek as the Western world's common language. By the time Christianity moved from outlaw religion to accepted faith after Emperor Constantine began to tolerate Christians in 313 CE, Greek was a dying language. Although Latin translations of parts of the Scriptures began to appear, there was no formal, official Latin version of the Bible. Beginning in 382 CE, a priest named Jerome began the process of bringing both Hebrew scriptures and the New Testament into Latin.

Working for twenty years in Bethlehem, the traditional birthplace of Jesus, Jerome went back to the original Hebrew and Aramaic texts, instead of simply translating the Septuagint Greek into Latin. Jerome supervised the translation of a Latin Bible that was completed by 405 CE. His work resulted in the *versio vulgata*, or "common translation," better known as the Vulgate Bible. To Jerome, *vulgata* meant "vulgar" in the sense of "commonly used," rather than the widespread modern meaning of vulgar as "dirty." But this is a perfect example of how words change meaning, a significant factor in understanding the Bible. Many words simply do not mean in the modern world what they meant in the Jerome's Latin fifteen hundred years ago, or King James's English of the 1600s. Among Jerome's decisions was to retain the use of the name "Jesus," which was how the first-century Greek writers of the New Testament had translated the Hebrew name Joshua.

At about the same time that Christians were transforming Greek into the Latin Vulgate, another crucial set of old Jewish scriptures was being maintained in its "official" Hebrew form by the Masoretes, a school of medieval Jewish scholars who worked between 500 CE and 1000 CE. They produced the original "Masoretic" text. The Masoretes made a crucial addition to the ancient Hebrew consonants-only writings—they included vowel signs, accent markings, and marginal notes, a kind of "Cliffs Notes" for the Hebrew Bible. These marginal notes provide a much clearer understanding of the ancient Hebrew texts, and the Masoretic texts have since become the standard used in studying ancient Hebrew scriptures. Yet even the oldest complete Masoretic texts—the Leningrad Codex and the Aleppo Codex—date only to about the year 1000 CE, practically a blink of the eye in the scheme of the Bible's composition. ("Codex," by the way, is a word for the earliest collections of bound pages; in other words, the first books were actually an innovation of the early Christians.)

When the Roman Catholic church became the predominant force in western Europe during the medieval era, the Latin Vulgate remained the standard by which European Christians knew the Bible. Of course, only priests and a few wealthy educated individuals could read the "Word of God." During this era, the Scriptures were still copied by hand in the famed illuminated manuscripts of the so-called "Dark Ages." Of course, few people could afford to own such a book and few ever saw one. Fewer still could read it. The Latin Mass, formalized and made into an elaborate ritual under Pope Damasus I (366–384), became the predominant form of worship in Europe. But most people had no idea what was being said in church. The advent of Gutenberg's printing press in 1450 meant the Bible could be mechanically produced, but even then, only about two hundred copies of the Gutenberg Bible were produced. And it was still in Latin.

But in the early years of the movement that came to be called the Protestant Reformation, begun in Germany in 1517 by Martin Luther, a few daring souls attempted to translate Holy Scripture from the Hebrew, Greek, and Latin into commonly used German and English. Like the mythical Prometheus, punished for bringing fire to mankind, some of these rebels would pay for their "crimes." Some died for their belief that the Bible was for all the people to read.

In England, another renegade priest, William Tyndale, also wanted to make the Scriptures available to all people. But he had to leave England to do so. Working in Germany, where Martin Luther had published his German New Testament in 1520, Tyndale also completed a New Testament first. Although some printers were prevented from publishing it, Tyndale's English New Testament appeared in 1526. His Old Testament began to appear in pieces in 1530. Again, the authorities were not amused. Tyndale was lured out of hiding and finally captured, arrested, and tried for heresy. In 1536, Tyndale was strangled. Just to make sure the message was clear, his remains were then burned. Tyndale died because he believed "that the boye that dryveth the plough shall know more of the scripture." It is a small measure of justice that Tyndale's work became the basis for the 1611 King James Version, the most influential and lasting of English translations. Now at last, "In the beginning" could be understood by all.

That is a brief glimpse at the long and sometimes painful trail of the Bible as it is known in the twentieth century. And that is why you have such a hard time when you go out to buy a Bible.

MILESTONES IN THE HEBREW SCRIPTURES

This timeline shows a simplified overview of the probable dates of the composition and later translation of the Hebrew scriptures, or Old Testament. Many of these dates are speculative and unconfirmed by archaeological or other historical sources and there is disagreement over some of them. The most questionable dates are marked with a ?.

Dates Before the Common Era (BCE)

2000–1700	Age of the Patriarchs (Abraham, Isaac, and Jacob) ?
1700–1500	Joseph in Egypt ?
1295–1230	The Exodus from Egypt ?
1240–1190	Israelite Conquest of Canaan ?
1020–1005	Reign of Saul
1005–967	Reign of David
967–931	Reign of Solomon
922	Division of Solomon's Kingdom

950–900	J (Jahwist) at work ?
850–800	E (Elohist) at work ?
722	Conquest of the Northern Kingdom; deportation of the Ten Tribes to Assyria—the "Lost Tribes of Israel"
650–600	D (Deuteronomist) at work ?
622	A "Book of the Law," similar to Deuteronomy, discovered in the First Temple
587/6	Fall of Judah; destruction of the First Temple; Babylonian Exile begins
550–500	P (Priestly source) at work ?
538	Return to Jerusalem from Exile
520–515	Construction of Second Temple
400	R (Redactor) at work ?
250–100	Septuagint: Translation from Hebrew to Greek
100	Earliest surviving Hebrew texts (Dead Sea Scrolls)

Dates in the Common Era (CE)

70	Destruction of the Second Temple by the Romans
90	Final canonization of the Hebrew Bible
405	Vulgate: Latin translation by Saint Jerome
500–1000	Masorah: Standardized Hebrew texts
1520	Luther's German New Testament
1526	Tyndale's English Pentateuch
1560	Geneva Bible (Shakespeare's Bible, also used by the Mayflower Pilgrims)
1611	King James Version

Map on next page: THE WORLD OF THE ANCIENT NEAR EAST
This map depicts many of the key locations referred to in discussing events in Hebrew scripture, the Old Testament. This map is meant to convey a general overview of the area, since the time period in question covers many thousands of years. Not all of the locations shown on this map existed at the same time. For example, while Babylon was a very ancient city, Alexandria in Egypt was not founded until the end of Old Testament times.

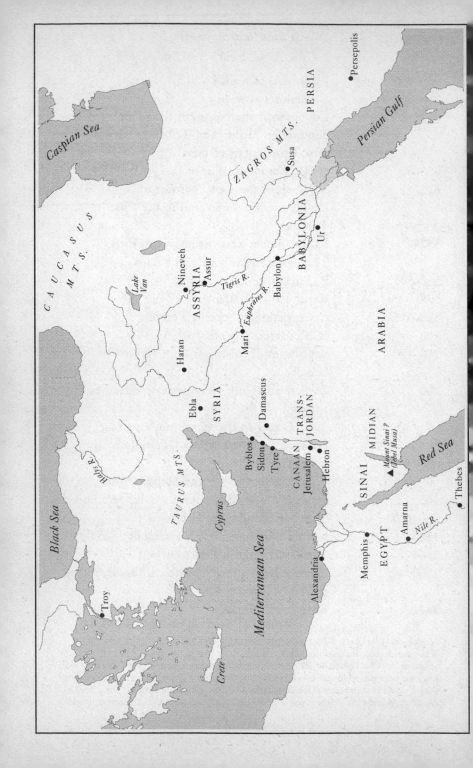

part two

———— ❊ ————

THE HEBREW
SCRIPTURES
OR
OLD TESTAMENT

Canst thou by searching out find God? (Job 11:7 KJV)

*I believe that our Heavenly Father invented man because he
was disappointed in the monkey.*

—MARK TWAIN, 1906

God is no saint, strange to say.

—JACK MILES
GOD, A BIOGRAPHY

Two Creations . . . No Apple

Genesis

*In the beginning God created the heaven and the earth.
And the earth was without form, and void; and darkness
was upon the face of the deep. And the Spirit of God moved
upon the face of the waters.
And God said, Let there be light: and there was light.
(Gen. 1:1–3 KJV)*

*But of the tree of the knowledge of good and evil, thou shalt
not eat of it: for in the day that thou eatest thereof thou shalt
surely die. (Gen. 2:17 KJV)*

✳ Why are there two Creations in Genesis?

✳ Who was right, Genesis or Darwin?

✳ Were there really apples in Eden?

✳ Was Eve really Adam's first woman?

✳ Where did Cain's wife come from?

✳ Do the "sons of God" sleep around in the Bible?

✳ Didn't Noah get some blueprints for the ark?

✳ Was Noah the first drunk?

✳ Do they "babble" in Babylon?

✳ Where did Abram come from?

✳ Why did Lot's wife turn into a pillar of salt?

✳ Would Abraham really have done it?

✳ What is Jacob's Ladder?

✳ How did Jacob become "Israel"?

❋ Was there a "coat of many colors"?

❋ What was the sin of Onan?

❋ Who was Joseph's Pharaoh, and could a slave become Egypt's prime minister?

Every stand-up comedian, speaker, or preacher knows that the best way to get an audience's attention is to tell a good story. If the story is funny, that's even better. A little sin and sex? Better still. That is why writers from Homer, Aesop, and the other Greeks right through Shakespeare and up to modern Hollywood have always dressed up their "messages" with great stories.

A good story makes us perk up our ears and pay closer attention. As the great American newspaperman Joseph Pulitzer is supposed to have said, "First fill the pews. Then preach."

That is one reason why the Bible is still around. It is full of great stories. And not just the simplistic "Virtue" tales many of us remember from Sunday school. The Hebrew prophets often cloaked their messages in stories. And Jesus certainly relied upon parables and short stories to teach.

But nowhere is the truth of the Bible being a great story more evident than in its opening book. Here is an entire account of the beginning of human civilization and God's unique relationship with humanity reduced to a series of fascinating narratives. This "miniseries" is filled with all the cliff-hanging action and humor that we expect from television or the movies. The stories are poignant, funny, compelling—and not a little troubling. On one hand, there is faith, goodness in the face of evil, and obedience to God. But on the other hand, there is betrayal, trickery, thieving, incest, and murder. These aren't the simplistic moralizing Sunday school tales of a bunch of "goody-goodies" who are well behaved and did exactly what God told them to do. And what God told them to do wasn't always so nice in the first place. That's one reason to believe that these characters were all real: if you were going to make up stories about your ancestors, you would not have them behave the way this bunch in Genesis does.

The English title Genesis is derived from the Greek words *Genesis kosmou* ("origin of the cosmos"). The Jews, who know each of the five books composing their Torah by the opening words or first significant word in the book, call it *Bereshith*—"In the beginning." Readers who return to Genesis after an absence may be surprised to discover that it is a much different story from the one they may dimly recall from childhood.

Genesis covers time, from the the beginning of the world through early human history and the rise of civilization to the establishment of God's special relationship with the Patriarchs, Matriarchs, and people of Israel—told through the compelling stories of Abraham and Sarah; Isaac, Rebekah, and their twin sons, Esau and Jacob, and Jacob's wives and family, the chief member of which was Joseph. It ends with the death of Joseph and the Israelite sojourn in Egypt, setting the stage for Exodus.

BIBLICAL VOICES

And God said, "Let us make man in our image, after our likeness: and let them have dominion over the fish of the sea, and over the fowl of the air, and over the cattle, and over all the earth, and over every creeping thing that creepeth upon the earth." (Gen. 1:26 KJV)

Why are there two Creations in Genesis?

One of the most sudden and shocking surprises to readers who might be vaguely familiar with the biblical Creation story but have never read the Bible is that there are actually two Creations in Genesis. Separate and unequal. They differ in style, order, facts, details—in fact, about the only thing they share is that God appears in both of them.

Version One begins comfortably with the well-known "In the beginning." Out of nothingness, and simply by speaking, God creates an orderly world and humanity. In this first Creation, which begins in the first chapter of Genesis, it takes God six days to create the heavens and earth, then come the animals, and finally, man and woman are created simultaneously, as apparent equals in "God's image." After a hard week at the office, God decides to put "his" feet up and take a day off—instituting the first sabbath. There is no mention of Eden, Adam, or Eve.

The second version of Creation—beginning in Genesis 2:4—is set in the Garden of Eden. It makes no mention of the number of days God took to accomplish this heavy lifting, and the order of creation is different from the first account. In the first, God had created "heaven and earth." This time, he creates "the earth and the heavens." More significant, in the second version, man is created before the trees and other animals. The other big difference in this second Creation is that man is created first and then woman is created out of man.

THE TWO CREATIONS

For centuries, people have taken the Chinese menu approach to the story of the Creation in Genesis. Choosing some from Version A and some from Version B, they have heaped together two different and conflicting stories to make a colorful but mismatched platter. The first account of the Creation is found in Genesis 1:1–2:3; the second Creation account is in Genesis 2:4–25. Side by side, they are are clearly two different stories featuring substantially different details.

VERSION A

"In the Beginning when God created the *heavens and the earth* . . . "

Over the course of "six days" God creates:

1. Light, then Day and Night
2. The Sky, separating the "waters from the waters"
3. The dry land is separated from the waters—Earth and Seas—and vegetation and trees
4. Sun, moon, stars, and seasons
5. Living creatures of the sky and sea: birds, sea monsters, fish
6. Living things of the earth: cattle, creeping things, wild animals. And lastly, mankind. Male and female are created together, both in God's image.

And on the seventh day, God finished and rested, blessing the seventh day. He also blesses the male and female, telling them to "be fruitful, multiply," and recommends a vegetarian diet. God concludes: "It was very good."

VERSION B
"In *the day* that the Lord God made the *earth and the heavens ...*"
God creates man from the dust of the ground.
He plants a Garden in Eden and puts the man there.
In the Garden is a Tree of Life and a Tree of the Knowledge of Good and Evil.
Man cannot eat of the Tree of the Knowledge of Good and Evil or else he will die.
God creates every animal and bird to be man's helper. The man names them all. But the man doesn't find a suitable partner from among the animals. God steps in and puts the man to sleep, takes out one of his ribs, and makes woman from the rib of man. Naked together, "they become one flesh," but "they felt no shame." God doesn't mention if that was very good; neither do Adam or Eve.

This is the where the "J versus P" version of biblical events discussed in Part One of this book first comes into focus.

The first of the Creation stories, found in Genesis 1, is attributed to P, the Priestly writer. God creates the heavens and the earth out of nothingness—a "void." On six successive days, P describes the Creator neatly making the universe, setting up shop on earth, and finally getting around to making people. In the words of the King James Version:

So God created man in his own image, in the image of God created he him; *male and female created he them*. (Gen. 1:27; emphasis added)

Most recent translations of the Bible, such as the New Revised Standard Version, make the point that the "man" in this verse was meant to encompass all humanity, rather than a single individual:

> So God created humankind in his image,
> in the image of God he created them;
> male and female he created them. (Gen. 1:27)

Clearly, in the first Creation account, there is no differentiating between male and female. There is no Eden. No forbidden tree. No women out of a man's rib. No submission of women. God creates both sexes at the same time, both "in his image."

Of course, this first Creation account raises all sorts of troubling questions on its own—even without a competing version in the next chapter. Who is this "us" that God mentions when he says, "Let us make man in our image"? So far, the Creation hasn't included anyone else. Is it the regal "us"? Or is it the three-part God (Father, Son, and Holy Ghost) of Christianity? Or is God speaking to the Heavenly hosts, all those angels, cherubim, and seraphim who work with God but get no credit line? And if mankind is created in God's image, does that mean we look like God? And would that image be black or white? European, Chinese, or Eskimo? If man and woman are created together, both can't literally be made in God's "image," can they? And if God says this Creation is good, why does it go so bad? Of course, questions like these have puzzled philosophers and religious thinkers for centuries, filling libraries with discourses on the nature of God and Creation.

Certainly, those problems are vexing enough. But Genesis 2 complicates matters as the Creation story is retold with significant changes. In this version, attributed to J, God creates earth and the heavens and then makes Adam "from the dust of the ground." He sets Adam down in Eden, where there are trees that are pleasing to the sight and good for food, as well as the Tree of Life and the Tree of the Knowledge of Good and Evil. After that, God makes the animals and birds to keep man company. Seeing that Adam is still lonely, God makes woman out of one of Adam's ribs. In this account, there is no mention of how many days this took and when—or if—God rested.

First of all, a brief Hebrew lesson. The word "Adam" is derived from the Hebrew word for "man" in the collective sense, as in humanity or mankind. It is also related to the Hebrew word *adamah*, which means "ground" or "earth." In other words, the author of this part of Genesis was engaging in wordplay. *Adam*, man, came from *adamah*, the ground. Puns, acrostics, and cryptics are all used widely throughout the Hebrew Bible. In later books, for instance, the name of a rival god, Baal, is changed to Baalzebub, which meant "lord of the dung." And many personal names in Hebrew scriptures, such as Abraham ("father of multitudes"), had some significance. Such wordplay was a highly valued poetic device in Hebrew writing.

Another significant aspect of these stories is that they were not entirely original. Both the first Creation account, in which God speaks and the world is made, and the second Creation account, starring Adam and Eve, share similarities to other creation myths of the ancient Near East. The very idea that God could "create" simply by speaking was not exclusive to the ancient Israelites. The myths of Mesopotamia and Egypt, the two great civilizations that bracketed the land of the Israelites, also celebrated the concept of a "divine word." In other words, the ancient Israelites drew upon commonly held beliefs about the Creation, ancient folklore that came from the lands and people that had the most impact on the ancient Near East. That basic fact will be repeated often throughout Genesis. The difference was that in Genesis it was shaped into an account of a special relationship between the Israelite God and humanity that had no precedent. The ancient nature gods, whose behavior was more human than divine, were transformed by the Israelites into a personal God with a very clear and rigid moral code. This God was going to make these people his favorites—but they had to toe a very sharp line of good behavior. Or else. Much of the Hebrew scriptures will tell the story of what happens when the Children of Israel don't keep up their end of the Promise.

Who was right, Genesis or Darwin?

The first letter published in the reader's mail section of the May/June 1997 issue of *Biblical Archaeology Review* is an interesting one. In it, the letter writer comments on the magazine's description of a "prehistory" archaeological dig. The writer asserts that this word is incorrect and concludes:

> This year [1997] marks approximately 6,000 years since the world's history began, when God created the heaven and the earth (Genesis 1:1). The terms "prehistory" and "Paleolithic" and "Neolithic" are a mockery of God's word, the Bible.

Set that letter against two recent news stories. In August 1997, scientists reported the discovery of fossilized footprints of anatomically modern humans that date back about 117,000 years. A few weeks earlier, in July, there was a report announcing the discovery of the most distant object ever seen in the universe. Combining observations from Hawaii's Keck telescope and the Hubble Space Telescope, two teams of astronomers reported sighting an infant galaxy *13 billion* light-years from the earth. In other words, this galaxy, "far, far away," came into being thirteen billion years ago. Smaller but brighter than our own Milky Way, it is so distant from the earth that we are just now receiving the news.

And you thought your mail was slow.

Here is the great raging war of the last few centuries reduced to a nutshell. How do you balance a belief that the world was created by divine pronouncement, a mere 6,000 years ago, with the scientific observation that modern humans walked 117,000 years ago and a galaxy was born 13 billion years ago? This is the war between science and faith. It's not simply some drawing-room argument or a nice academic debate over sherry in an ivory tower. The question of science versus faith has spilled into classrooms and courtrooms over such major controversies as cloning, Christian Science, Kevorkian, and Creationism.

Until Charles Darwin rolled into town in 1859 with his notion of "natural selection," most people accepted that God made the world in six days and then "he" rested. For nearly four thousand years, many people accepted Genesis as a perfectly viable account of the world's beginnings. Relying on biblical sources such as the chronologies and genealogies in Genesis, numerous people have attempted to pinpoint a time and date for the precise moment of the Creation. Ancient Hebrew scholars placed the moment as 3761 BCE. Perhaps the most famous Creation date was the one produced by Irish bishop James Ussher (1581–1656). Using Genesis, Ussher dated the moment of Creation to the early morning of the twenty-third of October in 4004 BCE (Ussher actually used the Julian calendar year of 710). Although it might seem silly to modern readers, Ussher's calculation was widely accepted by European Christians for centuries and was included in the margins of many editions of the King James Bible, giving it nearly divine "authority." There are still biblical literalists, such as the letter writer mentioned above, who accept Ussher's date as an article of faith.

Then science turned into the skunk at the garden party. When Leonardo da Vinci (1452–1519), the genius of the Italian Renaissance, found sea fossils in the Alps and asked how they got there, the conventional wisdom simply said it was proof that a Flood once covered the earth. When Copernicus, Kepler, and Galileo suggested that the earth revolved around the sun, they were mocked or worse. In 1616, Galileo was accused of heresy, placed under house arrest, and prohibited from further scientific inquiry. Then Darwin's *Origin of Species* (1859) proposed that man had evolved slowly, sharing common ancestry with the apes. Most of the religious world did not take kindly to this suggestion. It was one thing to discover that Galileo had been right about the solar system. It was another to accept that humankind was kissing cousin to the monkey.

Before Darwin, much of the world happily accepted the biblical version of Creation. After Darwin, many of the faithful continued that belief. Literalists past and present were never troubled by the fact that Genesis contains two Creations. Today, most biblical scholars accept the story of Adam and Eve for what it appears to be: a Hebrew story of human origins having much in common with the myths of other ancient peoples and also a good deal that is distinctive.

Where does that leave Darwin and his *Origin of Species*? The forces of science are still constantly pitted against the forces of religion. Aided by a media that loves to reduce complex issues to the simplicity of a Super Bowl, there is an ongoing contest between scientific knowledge and faith. Science is generally depicted in the media as dispassionate, rational, and nonbelieving. Religious people are generally represented in the media as conservative, backwards, trailer-park dwellers. Fundamentalists and "creationists" are usually featured only when attempting to get public schools to teach the Genesis version of the Creation alongside biology and evolutionary theory or eliminate Halloween celebrations from schools as a form of Satanic worship. Often these people are caught in the media spotlight when they refuse a child medical treatment out of their belief in the healing power of prayer and a faith in "God's will" being done. In "good faith," these people still hold tightly to their purely literal view of the Bible and history. The contest between these two sides is usually presented as one with no middle ground—that wouldn't make good headlines.

Yet a majority of scientists recently surveyed holds some religious beliefs, including a belief in God, as a *New York Times* article reported in 1997. The proportion of "believing" scientists hasn't changed much since a similar survey of scientists was conducted in the 1920s. And at another extreme, Pope John Paul II has recognized the validity of teaching Darwin's theory of evolution. So the challenge remains, more than a century after Darwin first proposed the ideas that formed the basis for modern evolutionary theory: can science and religion coexist? Nowhere is that battle more clearly defined than in the question over the Divine Creation. As many creationists like to point out, evolution is "just a theory." And that's true. In a purely scientific sense, all theories can only be disproven. But theories can also be supported by evidence. And the past hundred years have provided ample evidence to support and expand the scientific view, not only of human origins but of the origin of the universe. Putting Genesis in a biology or genetics class, however, makes about as much sense as teaching the changing of water into wine, Jesus' first miracle, in a chemistry class. Or calling a bat a "bird" because the book of Leviticus lists bats among flying creatures that may not be eaten.

But that does not mean that scientific and religious theory cannot somehow be brought together. As biblical scholar J. R. Porter writes: "The extended descriptions of creation . . . are not to be viewed as providing a scientific account of the origin of the universe. They are religious statements, designed to show God's glory and greatness, the result of theological reflection by which the older mythology was radically transformed to express Israel's distinctive faith." Genesis should be in our classrooms. Perhaps it can be placed alongside all the other religious and legendary creation stories in a comparative literature class.

As science explores further and further past the "known" world, whether it means seeing 13 billion years into the universe's past, or using DNA strains to push humankind's origins back another million years, or discovering the basic ingredients for life in a chemical stew that spews out of volcanoes at the bottom of the ocean, science is ultimately left with more questions. The notion that the universe is all energy has forced scientists who deal in the astonishing world of quantum physics to look past their equations to a universal creative force. At the same time, to accept that the Bible is filled with poetry, allegory, teaching parables, and other "stories" doesn't alter the fundamental truth to be found in the

Genesis accounts. As Pope John Paul II said when he gave support to Darwinian evolution: "If the human body has its origin in living material which preexists it, the spiritual soul is immediately created by God."

Of course, science can't speak of the creation, or even existence, of the soul. . . . The soul can't be removed, weighed, and dissected, as human organs can.

Why not see the Creation in Genesis as a magnificent metaphor for the Big Bang, an event that science acknowledges but does not yet fully understand? Viewing the opening words of Genesis as a poetic account of this cosmic instant of creation, when matter essentially burst out of energy, doesn't alter the essential "truth" of Genesis for those who believe it. As Robert Wright wrote in *Time* magazine in 1996, "Genesis isn't just about the beginning of the human race. It is also about the beginning of evil— about how and why sin and suffering entered human experience and stayed there. And here the verdict of science is more ambiguous."

The universe was created by some force—call it the Big Bang or God or Allah or Vishnu or simply Energy—that set in motion the cataclysmic string of events that brought the earth into being 4.5 billion years ago. So began the long line of chemical chain reactions that created the spark of life on earth. That miraculous process resulted in the appearance, a brief moment in time ago, of a two-legged creature that walked upright. This creature held tools in hands that were no longer needed for moving through the trees. He built fires and eventually held a sharp, pointed stick that made intricate symbols in pieces of hardening mud. It was the beginning of writing, the beginning of the Word.

BIBLICAL VOICES
Then the snake said to the woman, "No! You will not die! God knows in fact that the day you eat it your eyes will be

opened and you will be like gods, knowing good from evil."
(Gen. 3:4–5 NJB)

PLOT SUMMARY: ADAM AND EVE

Having made man ("adam") out of the dust ("adamah") and brought him into existence with the "breath of life," God places man in Eden, warning him not to eat from the Tree of the Knowledge of Good and Evil, threatening death if he does. Then God creates the rest of the animals to keep him company. The man names these animals but still doesn't have a proper partner. God then causes the man to sleep and removes one of his ribs—humanity's first "takeout ribs"—and forms woman.

The man and woman are naked in the Garden, unashamedly enjoying sex ("they became one flesh"). Along comes the serpent ("more crafty than any other wild animal") and the woman is convinced to eat from the forbidden tree. The serpent promises her that she will be "like God," or "gods," depending on the translation. The woman agrees, then gives the fruit to the man and he eats.

Their eyes now open to their nakedness, they feel shame and sew fig leaves into loincloths and try to hide from God. Out for a stroll, God finds them hiding and asks who told them they were naked. The man quickly establishes the human tradition of finger-pointing by saying, "The woman whom you gave to be with me, she gave me fruit from the tree, and I ate."

God is not happy. It is the first of several biblical moments in which he will wonder if this "man thing" was such a good idea after all. But instead of starting from scratch, God gets mad. Then he gets even. The serpent is cursed to crawl on his belly, and there will be permanent hostility between snakes and people. The woman will suffer the pain of childbirth and be ruled by her husband. (We know a man wrote that!) Instead of invoking the death sentence promised earlier, God curses the man to a life of hard work. Then the First Couple gets kicked out of the Garden.

Were there really apples in Eden?

Apples are supposed to be good for you. "An apple a day keeps the doctor away." You're supposed to bring an apple to the teacher. And what's more wholesome in America than apple pie? So how come apples got such a bad name in Genesis? Truth is, there was no apple in Eden. Genesis doesn't even mention "forbidden fruit." The Eden account mentions only the "fruit of knowledge" and the fruit of "everlasting life." The Garden of Eden version of Creation—the second Creation account in Genesis—traces its literary roots to the Tigris-Euphrates River area. Genesis mentions both these rivers in locating Eden, a word whose derivation is unclear. It might come from the Sumerian word for "plain," or the Hebrew for "delight." The identity of the other two rivers mentioned in Genesis, the Pishon and Gihon, is another mystery. Perhaps they were offshoots or tributaries of the Tigris and Euphrates, ancient rivers that later dried up. Eden is also said to be "in the East," a phrase commonly used in the Bible to describe the Mesopotamian region. In the ancient city of Mari, located near the Euphrates River in modern Syria, French archaeologists uncovered a library of twenty thousand tablets filled with descriptions of everyday affairs in Mesopotamia dating back to nearly 2000 BCE. Reconstructed murals from a magnificent palace there depict mythical gardens that recall Eden. One even shows a garden with two types of trees in its center.

So what fruits grew on those trees? Some historians have suggested a number of likely suspects as the "forbidden fruit," including apricots, pomegranates, or figs—a prime candidate since the leaves of the fig tree became the first unisex leisure wear. Fig trees also figure prominently in other spiritual tales, particularly that of the Buddha, who achieved enlightenment while sitting beneath a fig tree known as the Tree of Wisdom! This suggests that the fig may be more than just filling for Fig Newtons.

In other words, the image of Eve polishing up a nice red apple, fodder for great artists and political cartoonists throughout history, has no biblical basis. The apple wasn't connected to the Eden story until the European Middle Ages, when artists began to depict Eve with an apple, presumably as a way to give common people a familiar fruit.

In stark contrast to Genesis 1 with its simultaneous appearances of male and female, the story in Genesis 2–3 has woman created to be a companion and partner—but not a subordinate—to the man. Because the two of them eat the forbidden fruit, the man is destined to toil as a farmer in the fields of thorns and thistles, and the woman is destined to suffer pain in childbearing and be ruled by her husband. It is only in the aftermath of these divine pronouncements that the man names the woman as he had earlier named the animals, thus indicating his dominion over her.

The linguistic derivation of Eve's name also remains uncertain. For a long time, "Eve" was interpreted as "the mother of all living," because the name sounds similar to the Hebrew word for "living being" and Eve is the female ancestor of the entire human race. Another recent suggestion is that there is a connection with the Aramaic word for "serpent," and that the figure of Eve was originally a fertility goddess associated with snakes. The connection between the serpent and the Devil wouldn't be made until much later in Christian times. When Genesis was written, serpents had a much better image. Snakes were recognized as fertility objects in several ancient cultures because of their obvious phallic symbolism along with their ability to shed their skins—symbolic of reincarnation. In the epic of *Gilgamesh*, the Babylonian heroic epic that predates the Bible, a serpent acquires immortality by eating a magical plant.

More troubling is the question of why Eve takes the fall for the Fall. The fact that Eve takes the rap for humanity's loss of paradise has obviously had enormous consequences on relations between the sexes. The question is which came first. Did Eve's action cause woman to be divinely relegated to second-place status? Or was the Eve story, which is so at odds with the first Creation, in which men and women shared equal status, written to give a male-dominated society a divine sanction?

Genesis 3 offers no hint as to why the serpent addressed the woman. The passage even indicates that the man and the woman were together when the serpent spoke. In some views, Adam was not merely an innocent bystander but a coconspirator whose silence in the face of the serpent implies his willingness to go along. When offered the choice by Eve, Adam doesn't put up much of a fight in favor of obeying God. In other words, the first man was a bit of a wimp, a moral weakling who was simply a passive accomplice to the decisive, daring Eve.

But in eating from the tree, Adam and Eve acquire the capacity for rational and ethical judgments, one of the key ingredients in setting human beings apart from the rest of the animal world. If the First Couple had obeyed God, it would have meant that humanity would have lived in a paradise without wants, worry, or presumably violence. But what a boring paradise that might have been. A vegetarian paradise with no wants is like a life of eternal infancy—a Paradise without science, art, and the sort of rational distinctions that have brought humanity to its present state.

The biblical tale of the Fall is similar to other legends that contrast humanity's sufferings with an earlier time of perfection, a lost paradise or golden age. The Greeks' Pandora, like Eve, is responsible for the misfortunes of mankind because she disobeyed the order not to open the box out of which all the troubles of the world flew. The Blackfoot Indians of North America told of Feather-woman, a maiden who unleashes great ills when she digs up the Great Turnip after being told not to do so. For this, she is cast out of Sky-Country. Like all such myths of a lost golden age, the biblical Fall is an attempt to account for the problems of evil and human suffering and a symbol of how humans have always yearned for a better, but possibly unattainable, world.

And Eve's sentencing to the pain of childbirth? Perhaps that is also part of the cost of wisdom. As scientist-archaeologist Charles

Pellegrino notes in his book *Return to Sodom and Gomorrah*, "Child-birth is more difficult for human beings than for any other known species, a price apparently paid to accommodate the brain's tripling in size during the past two million years. The head is the largest part of the body and the first to emerge." In a manner of speaking, science and Genesis agree: women paid for the knowledge gained from eating from that tree by having babies with big brains.

Was Eve really Adam's first woman?

In the summer of 1997, the most popular rock concert in America was a collection of women musicians who barnstormed the country as the "Lilith" tour. Readers of *The New York Times* might have been surprised by the newspaper's statement that Lilith was Adam's first wife.

Was Eve really first? Or was there "another woman" in Adam's life?

In strictly biblical terms, Eve was the first woman and Adam's only wife. But Hebrew legend has another story that's a lot more spicy. As recorded in the medieval *Alphabet of Ben Sira*, Lilith was Adam's first wife, who preceded Eve. In this version, Lilith is created from the earth, as Adam was. In the Talmud, the vast collection of rabbinical teachings and commentaries on Jewish Law and learning, Lilith was also made out of dust, but her crime was even more specific: she balked at the way Adam wished to make love, with the man on top. When Adam refused Lilith's demand that she be regarded as his equal, she walked out on him. Then she uttered the unspeakable name of God and was sent to live with the demons, becoming a demon herself.

Lilith doesn't appear in Genesis, and the only biblical refer-ence to this mystery woman is a single line in Isaiah that mentions her as a female demon. A Canaanite demon called Lilitu who tor-mented men may have inspired the Hebrew Lilith, and the figure has been traced back even further to Babylonian mythology. The

Lilith demon was later depicted as a slayer of infants and women in pregnancy and childbirth who came out at night and drank human blood. In essence, Lilith was the first vampire, predating Count Dracula by thousands of years.

Scholars who approach the Bible from a "feminist" viewpoint suggest that Lilith was actually created before Eve, but male authors then introduced Eve as her opposite. In their view, Eve was more acceptable as the docile and dependent woman, a kind of biblical Betty Crocker. These feminist readings celebrate Lilith as headstrong, self-reliant, even sexually aggressive—a biblical version of rock and roll's Madonna. That is totally at odds with how women were viewed in the male-dominated society of the ancient Near East. In any case, if you stick to Genesis, there was no Lilith and Adam never had to choose between Betty Crocker and Madonna.

BIBLICAL VOICES
"Am I my brother's keeper?" (Gen. 4:9)

PLOT SUMMARY: CAIN AND ABEL
Cain and Abel are Adam and Eve's sons. Cain, the firstborn, whose name possibly meant "smith," was a farmer. Abel ("emptiness") was the first shepherd. Both bring offerings to God, but God rejects Cain's offering of grain without explanation, preferring Abel's, which was the firstborn of his flock. Angry that God rejects his offering, Cain decides to take it out on Abel and kills his brother. God discovers this act when he asks Cain where Abel is, and the famous "brother's keeper" reply is given. God curses Cain by making him a wanderer, the Original Fugitive, and marks him with an unspecified sign. This so-called "Mark of Cain" is actually a protective sign from God that will prevent anyone from murdering Cain, who heads off to the Land of Nod, "East of Eden." It is not precisely clear why God gives the murderer this mark of divine protection. Perhaps God wants to reserve judgment on Cain

for himself. After Cain leaves, Adam and Eve give birth to a third son, Seth.

Where did Cain's wife come from?

So we have Adam, Eve, and their sons, Cain and Abel. The story of Cain and Abel introduces many of the themes that will recur throughout Genesis and the Hebrew scriptures. Of course, it marks the first murder. But there is also the first appearance of sibling rivalry, and the enmity between brothers will be replayed throughout Genesis. The two characters also symbolically represent the farmer (Cain) and the nomadic herder (Abel). Tension between these groups was common throughout ancient times, so the story stands as a mythical explanation for the conflict between these two ancient callings—the true "oldest professions."

The most interesting, and misinterpreted, aspects of Cain and Abel's tale come after God discovers the crime. First the Lord asks Cain what happened, and Cain plays dumb. But God poignantly tells him, "Your brother's blood is crying out to me from the ground." God then sentences Cain to wander the earth and tells him that the ground will no longer yield to him. But Cain begs for mercy and, in fear, thinks that someone will kill him. God marks him, perhaps with a birthmark or tattoo of some kind. Widely viewed and long misunderstood as a sign of guilt, the so-called "Mark of Cain" is actually a symbol of divine mercy. Opponents of the death penalty point to this first murder, and God's merciful sentence on the murderer, as a biblical rejection of capital punishment. For his crime, Cain basically receives a life sentence of hard labor.

But Cain's request for mercy raises another question: Who was he afraid of, since nobody else existed? Which raises a related question: Cain goes off to the land of Nod—which means "wandering"—and finds an unnamed wife. Where did she come from?

The Scriptures contain no explanation for Cain's wife or the people Cain fears might murder him. One simplistic rationale—unsupported by the text—is that God kept creating more people after Adam and Eve. Another is that Adam and Eve had more children and they all were able to intermarry, as incest was not yet deemed out-of-bounds. This inconsistency is only one of many blows to the "literal" interpretation of the Bible. This is the chief argument for viewing the Genesis account as a mythical folktale tracing the primeval beginnings of humanity, steeped in the ancient folklore of the Near East.

Once married, Cain begins a family and his firstborn son is named Enoch. Cain also builds a city called Enoch. This is a typical Genesis combination of place and personal names. The notion that Cain builds a city also contradicts the curse that Cain would always be a wanderer; he was actually the founder of the first city. Maybe God issued a parole. Genesis doesn't say.

At this point in the narrative, two separate genealogies trace the descendants of Cain and his younger brother Seth, born after Abel's death. The two lists include very similar names and both lists include an Enoch and a Lamech. The Seth list, the more important of the two in that it leads to Noah, also contains specific and fantastic ages for each ancestor.

The Descendants of Adam

Cain	Seth
Enoch	Enosh
Irad	Kenan
Mehujael	Mahalalel
Methushael	Jared
Lamech	Enoch
Jabal, Jubal, and Tubal-cain	Methuselah
	Lamech
	Noah (becomes a father at five hundred years: his sons are Shem, Ham, and Japheth)

Before the introduction of the lineage of Seth, which traces a direct path from Adam to Lamech and then Noah, the list of Cain's descendants also leads to a Lamech, the Bible's first known polygamist, who takes two wives and has three sons. In a brief passage, an ancient song tells of Lamech avenging a murder, and it is commonly interpreted as an indication that man is falling into violent and sinful ways. But each of Lamech's three sons is a skillful innovator: Jabal is the ancestor of the people who live in tents and raise livestock; Jubal is the ancestor of all musicians; and Tubal-cain is the ancestor of metalworkers.

The Seth genealogy, so similar to Cain's, suggests that both developed out of a more ancient common source. The descendants of the protagonist of the Babylonian *Gilgamesh* epic are identified in a genealogy of ten individuals, each of whom lived extraordinarily long lives. And, like the ancients of the Bible, these Babylonian generations led up to a great flood.

Do the "sons of God" sleep around in the Bible?

Squeezed in between the generations after Adam and the time of Noah is a curious story (Gen. 6:1–4) about the mysterious "Nephilim," a group most Sunday school teachers would be at a loss to describe. In a brief biblical episode that echoes the tales of Greek gods who mated with mortal women, the verses describe the "sons of God," whose identity is unclear, though they might be angels who took wives from the daughters of humans.

After watching these goings-on, God decides this isn't a good idea and puts a stop to it. God also decides to limit human life spans to 120 years. The biblical passage then calls the offspring of these angelic-human marriages, the Nephilim, the "heroes that were of old, warriors of renown." Mentioned only once again in Hebrew scriptures, the Nephilim, which literally translates as "the fallen ones," have a confusing or contradictory fate. Supposedly giants possessing superhuman powers—like the half-divine Hercules of Greek myth—the Nephilim should have been wiped out in the Flood that would soon inundate the earth. But they are still in Canaan during the time of Moses, according to book of Numbers.

Some early theologians saw these "sons of God" and their children, the Nephilim, as the fallen angels who were responsible for sin in the world. But the Nephilim are rather ambiguous. They are either "heroes of old" or the result of naughty intermingling between gods and men. Their mention here, along with God's decision to limit the life spans of humans, hints at the fact that God is growing impatient with his most annoying creation. And that impatience is about to overflow.

BIBLICAL VOICES

The Lord saw that the wickedness of humankind was great in the earth, and that every inclination of the thoughts of their hearts was only evil continually. And the Lord was sorry that he had made humankind on the earth, and it grieved him to his heart. So the Lord said, "I will blot out from the earth the human beings I have created—people together with animals and creeping things and birds of the air, for I am sorry that I have made them." But Noah found favor in the sight of the Lord. (Gen. 6:5–8)

PLOT SUMMARY: THE FLOOD

People have become very wicked so God decides to clean the slate. Only Noah and his family, direct descendants of Adam, are good enough to save, so God orders Noah to build a boat, or an "ark" (from the Hebrew word for "box" or "chest"). Noah is told only to take his wife, their three sons, and their wives aboard, along with pairs of all animals and birds. This is where the ark story gets a little confused and it is clear that someone mingled the separate J and P accounts of the Flood into a single narrative that is sometimes contradictory. One account calls for pairs of every animal on the earth; the other calls for seven pairs of clean and unclean animals and seven pairs of each species of birds.

The Flood comes not just from the rains but up from below the earth in a kind of reverse Creation. Water covers the earth, killing everyone and everything, the innocent with the guilty. It rains for 40 days and 40 nights, but the account also says the water covered the earth for 150 days. When the water recedes, the ark comes to rest on "the mountains of Ararat." Then Noah sends out a series of birds. The first, a raven, doesn't return. The second, a dove, returns, as there is nowhere to land. The dove is released again and this time returns with an olive branch indicating that the waters have begun to recede. The dove is sent out once more and does not return. Finally, God simply tells Noah to go out of the ark and to "be fruitful and multiply on the earth." Noah and the missus and the kids then set out to repopulate the world.

Noah takes time to make a burnt offering of the animals and birds he has just saved from destruction. Pleased by Noah's thought, God says, "I will never again curse the ground because of humankind, for the inclination of the human heart is evil from youth; nor will I ever again destroy every living creature as I have done." (Gen. 8:21)

As a sign of this covenant, or promise, God sets a "bow" in the sky, presumably a folkloric explanation for rainbows after a rain. As a part of this new covenant or agreement, God blesses Noah, gives him a new set of dietary laws—meat is now in; the vegetarianism specified earlier in Genesis is out—and institutes a new sanction against murder because man has been made in God's image.

Didn't Noah get some blueprints for the ark?

While walking in the Alps, the famous Renaissance artist and inventor Leonardo da Vinci was surprised to discover the fossilized remains of sea creatures. Curious about their existence so high above the oceans, Leonardo still failed to arrive at the explanation that modern science accepts. The Alps were once at or below sea level but were thrust higher when Africa slammed head-on into Europe in the process of catastrophic mountain building. In Leonardo's day, however, there was a simpler explanation that seemed perfectly plausible to most folks: these remains of sea creatures high in the mountains of Italy were indisputable proof of the great Flood that the Bible said once covered the earth.

Almost every ancient culture has some sort of flood, or deluge, myth that shares much with the biblical Flood. In most of them, the gods send a catastrophic flood to destroy the world, but one good man is told of the coming disaster and his family is saved to continue human existence. For instance, one Sumerian myth told of a flood with which the gods curbed human overpopulation. Another Sumerian tale related the story of King Ziusudra, who survives a flood, offers a sacrifice to the gods, repopulates the earth, and gains immortality. The Greeks had the story of Deucalion. The son of Prometheus, Deucalion was another boat builder. When Zeus flooded the earth in one more of his fits of pique, Deucalion and his wife, Pyrrha, take refuge in an ark that lands on the top of Mount Olympus. Deucalion repopulates the earth with stones that represent the "bones" of "Mother Earth." But of these myths, the one most like Noah's story is from the Babylonian *Gilgamesh* epic. In this story, the hero, Utnapishtim, also survives the flood by building a boat, which comes to rest on Mount Nisir, in the same region as Noah's "mountains of Ararat."

All of these similarities suggest that these Near Eastern stories shared some common tradition, perhaps a memory of a catastrophic flooding of the Tigris-Euphrates plain. It is easy to imagine that people whose "world" constituted the area in which they lived could imagine that a devastating flood that affected them had actually destroyed the whole world. In fact, the Hebrew word for "earth" in Gen. 6:17 also means "land" or "country," which would suggest a much more limited flood.

Generations of archaeologists have looked for evidence of this all-encompassing Flood. When the pioneering British archaeologist Leonard Wooley (1880–1960) was investigating Ur, one of the most important ancient ruined cities in the Tigris-Euphrates area, he found a layer of silt with remains of human civilization both above and below it. He was initially convinced this was physical evidence of Noah's Flood. But Wooley later realized that this Ur-flood was local news, rather than an international story. He later wrote, "It was a vast flood (or series of floods) in the valley of the Tigris and Euphrates which drowned the whole of the habitable land between the mountains and the desert; for the people who lived there that was indeed all the world." It was later dated to a time too recent in human history to have been the Bible's Big Flood. Researchers working in Wooley's footsteps have since found evidence of numerous floods at sites in modern Iraq, some of them showing evidence of extensive destruction. Despite extravagant claims made by many in the past century, no one has discovered evidence of a flood that could have covered the whole earth.

For centuries, people have also searched for the remnants of Noah's ark, just as they searched for the actual Garden of Eden, and numerous false claims still crop up, attracting tabloid newspaper attention. Unlike many other biblical places and objects whose location or exact appearance is a mystery, the ark came with God's Little Instruction Book, a very rough set of directions. For all those parents who have sat down with a thousand bicycle parts on a child's birthday, Noah's predicament is understandable.

God gave Noah some fairly basic dimensions: 300 cubits long; 50 cubits wide; 30 cubits high. A cubit is roughly 18 inches (45 centimeters), giving the ark approximate dimensions of 450 feet (140 meters) long × 75 feet (22 meters) wide × 45 feet (12 meters) high. In other words, it was a very large box, the equivalent of one and a half American football fields. God told Noah to make it of "gopher wood" (in the King James Version), a wood mentioned nowhere else in the Bible, and translated elsewhere as "cypress." The wood was to be covered with pitch, another similarity with the *Gilgamesh* epic's boat. The ark was to have three decks, a door, and a roof. Besides these dimensions and rough outlines, God's

Little Instruction book was rather imprecise. It doesn't specify the roof dimensions. Was it partial? Or complete? It doesn't mention windows, although there was at least one.

In spite of the fact that this would have been a rather large object that Noah left behind, the search for the ark has turned up empty. Nobody ever found Eden and, so far, no one has unearthed the remains of the ark. Perhaps Noah chopped the ark into firewood because there was no dry wood around. For a long time, the search for the ark centered on Mount Ararat, even though Genesis specifically mentions that Noah's ark settled on "the mountains of Ararat." And where exactly are these mountains? The "mountains of Ararat" lie in a region surrounding Lake Van in modern Turkey, located midway between the Black and Caspian Seas.

Apart from its historical possibilities, the Noah story serves as a symbolic second creation tale. God realizes his flaws and starts over. It is not exactly a comforting picture of God. This God of the Flood seems rather impatient, unforgiving, and testy. Apart from Noah, who is described as "righteous," and his family, there is apparently no one else in all of Creation worth saving. The innocent, including the animals of the world, are caught up with the guilty.

Many of the images and the language of the Flood story recall the first biblical Creation. The deluge even suggests a reversal of the first Creation, in which the earth was created out of the formless deep. Then, once the flood recedes—we don't know what happened to all those drowned carcasses, but it must not have been a pretty sight—Noah is told to "be fruitful and multiply," just as his ancestor Adam was.

Was Noah the first drunk?

Things are not perfect in the new creation after Noah and the kids settle down, especially when "the fruit of the vine" makes its first biblical appearance. Noah becomes the first man to plant a vineyard, invents wine, and then discovers getting drunk. While Noah is lying in his tent, naked and drunk, his son Ham accidentally walks in and sees Dad in this state. He tells his brothers, Shem and Japheth, what he saw and they discreetly cover their father without looking at him. When Noah discovers that Ham has seen him in his birthday suit, he isn't too happy. Without explaining why this is such a bad thing, Noah curses his son. But there is some confusion here, because Noah places the curse on Canaan, Ham's son, rather than on the actual culprit, Ham:

> "Cursed be Canaan;
> lowest of slaves shall he be to his brothers."

He also said,

> "Blessed by the Lord my God be Shem;
> and let Canaan be his slave." (Gen. 9:25–26)

This confusion had long-lasting and ghastly implications. The point of this story would have been quite clear for the ancient Israelites. They were meant to rule over Canaan's descendants, the people who lived in the Promised Land. The Canaanites had a reputation for fairly lascivious sexual practices that were highly offensive in the eyes of the Israelites. Seeing one's father naked— and in some interpretations a homosexual act by Ham has been suggested—was associated with the lewd Canaanite sexual practices. In Leviticus, the phrase "to uncover nakedness" is a euphemism for sexual relations.

But the real historical impact of this passage was the later interpretation widely given to this story in seventeenth- and eighteenth-century America. Looking for moral justification for slavery, American slaveholders pointed to these biblical verses as divine sanction for the "Peculiar Institution." They argued—incorrectly—that Ham was the ancestor of Egypt, Cush, and Put as well as Canaan. These were the so-called "southern" tribes that included Africa. As the "Children of Ham," Africans were therefore meant to be slaves, a point of view that can only be charitably called way off base. Still, it was a widely accepted interpretation in England and America until well into the 1800s, when some Christian groups began to condemn slavery as a grave sin. Numerous other biblical verses were also cited in defense of slavery, although overlooked were some of the other Israelite laws regarding slavery, including invocations to free runaway slaves.

In America, this was a crucial moment. For the first time, the Bible provided arguments for two sides of a question. The dispute, ultimately settled by the American Civil War, led to deep, painful splits within several American churches, including the Baptists. (In 1994, the Southern Baptist Convention, the largest Protestant denomination in America, issued a formal apology for the "sin of slavery.")

The other two sons of Noah received great blessings, and the line beginning with Noah's son Shem eventually leads to the patriarch Abraham. The name Shem is the source of the word "Semite," which applies to all the groups who were descended from Shem, Jew and Arab alike.

BIBLICAL VOICES

And they said to one another, "Come, let us make brick, and burn them thoroughly." And they had brick for stone, and bitumen for mortar. Then they said, "Come, let us build ourselves a city, and a tower with its top in the heavens, and let us make a name for ourselves; otherwise we shall be scattered abroad upon the face of the earth." (Gen. 11:3–4)

PLOT SUMMARY: THE TOWER OF BABEL

Men migrate "from the east" and settle in the plain in the land of "Shinar." They all speak the same language and decide to build a tower that glorifies themselves. God comes down to take a look and doesn't like the scene of men making their way heavenward. Threatened by these men, God confuses their speech so the tower-builders cannot understand one another. For good measure, God scatters people over the face of the earth and they quit construction of the tower—or city—which is then named Babel.

Do they "babble" in Babylon?

There are several points of interest in this very brief but famous story of man trying to overreach his earthly bounds. First of all, it provides an ancient mythological explanation for the many languages spoken by humankind. Second, it offers an explanation for the existence of the large towers found throughout the ancient Near East. Called ziggurats, from an ancient Akkadian word for "high," these stepped towers built of sun-baked bricks were found throughout Mesopotamia. First the historical background. The "plains of Shinar" mentioned throughout Genesis is the plain beyond the Tigris and Euphrates rivers, or ancient Mesopotamia (Greek for "between two rivers"). Today the region is identified as southern Iraq.

This was part of the "Fertile Crescent" of your schoolbook history, the arc of land that stretched from Egypt, along the Mediterranean coastline of modern Israel and Lebanon, and then into modern Syria and Iraq. Watered by the key river systems—the Nile in Egypt and the Tigris-Euphrates in Mesopotamia—the area was the birthplace of much of what the Western world calls "civilization" and "history." The first wheel is supposed to have been used in ancient Mesopotamia, home to the Sumerians, in about 6500 BCE. By about 5000 BCE, the earliest cities were rising, and cattle were domesticated. Villagers began to cooperate on irrigation projects at about the time people were doing the same thing on the banks of the Nile. Over the next fifteen hundred years, the Sumerians gradually harnessed animals to plows, drained marshlands, and irrigated the desert to extend areas of cultivation. The increase in agricultural efficiency eventually led to the first "leisure class," allowing the development of priests, artisans, scholars, and merchants. By 3500 BCE, the Sumerians had developed bronze metalworking, sexagesimal counting—based on the number sixty, the reason we still have sixty minutes in an hour—and a written alphabet. Their myths and history had an unmistakable influence on the early sections of Genesis, and the "Sumerian King List" bears a striking resemblance to the biblical genealogies of Cain and Seth.

Part of a temple complex in these early cities, the towers—very similar to the stepped pyramids of Mexico and Central America—were topped by a chapel. The earliest of these ziggurats dates to around 2100 BCE, and they may have been influenced by the Egyptian pyramids, which were older by a few hundred years. The grandest of these ziggurats was the temple complex in the city of Babylon, a seven-staged pyramid that may have been built around 1900 BCE.

The Babel story had great significance for the early Israelites, because it provided an explanation for the name of the city of Babylon, which in the native Sumerian language meant "gate of the gods" but in Hebrew was related to the word for "to confuse." In other words, the composer of Genesis was using a bilingual pun to disparage the people who later captured the people of Israel and held them captive in the city of Babylon.

In another context, the story once again shows men trying to be "like gods" and how unfavorably God views that idea. It was an idea opposed not only by the God of the Israelites but by the gods of many mythologies. In other words, it just may be part of human nature to strive for the heavens, whether that means building towers in the desert, skyscrapers in the city, or sending rockets to the moon.

BIBLICAL VOICES

Now the Lord had said unto Abram, "Get thee out of thy country, and from thy kindred and from thy father's house, unto a land that I will shew thee. And I will make of thee a great nation, and I will bless thee, and make thy name great; and thou shalt be a blessing: And I will bless them that bless thee, and curse him that curseth thee: and in thee shall all families of the earth be blessed." (Gen. 12:1–3 KJV)

PLOT SUMMARY: THE CALL OF ABRAM AND HIS TRAVELS

Born the son of Terah in Ur, in a direct line from Noah, Abram was also directly descended from Adam. The founding patriarch of Jews and Arabs alike, Abram—whose name will later be changed by God to Abraham—had a brother named Haran, which was also the name of a city in northwestern Mesopotamia, in what is now modern Syria. Haran died, but had a son named Lot, who was Abram's nephew. Abram's wife was Sarai, who was also his half sister. Terah took his son Abram, Sarai, and Lot to Haran—a little confusion here because the place name is the same as the name of Abram's dead brother.

While in Haran, Abram is instructed by God to go to nearby Canaan, a land that God promises to Abram and his descendants. In Canaan, Abram sets up two altars and "invokes the name of the Lord." When a famine strikes, Abram goes to Egypt, where he is afraid that the Pharaoh will kill him in order to take his wife, Sarai, because she is so beautiful.

To save his own life, Abram tells Sarai to pretend she is his sister. Sarai is taken into the Pharaoh's household as a concubine and Abram prospers. But God sends a plague on the Pharaoh's house, and when the Pharaoh discovers Abram's deceit, he orders Abram to leave Egypt. Once back in Canaan, Abram and Lot decide to split up. Abram offers Lot the first choice of land, and Abram's nephew picks out a plain near the city of Sodom. Abram goes to the hill country of Canaan, where he is once more told by God, "I will make your offspring like the dust of the earth; so that if one can count the dust of the earth, your offspring also can be counted."

When four kings wage war on Sodom and Lot is taken hostage,

Abram leads a small army to rescue his nephew. Abram—identified for the first time as "the Hebrew"—defeats the four kings and gives a 10 percent share of the booty to King Melchizedek, who is also the high priest of the Canaanite cult El Elyon—the God Most High—in Salem, the place that will later be called Jerusalem.

Where did Abram come from?

If a man gives his wife to another man to save his own neck, we consider him a coward. If he sleeps with his wife's maid so he can have a son, we call him a pig. If he then kicks his son and that maid out of the house, we call him a deadbeat dad. And if that man were to threaten to kill his child and said, "God told me to do it," most people would agree that he should be locked up, even if he stopped short of committing the unthinkable. But the biblical patriarch Abram does all these things, and he is considered one of the heroes of the faith for his actions.

Revered as the "father of all nations" by Jews, Christians, and Muslims alike, Abram is a great example of the fact that the biblical heroes weren't always heroic—or even nice guys. Quite a few of them, in fact, were pretty pathetic characters. But in each case, they were singled out by God for special treatment and often extreme moral testing.

Abram is also the earliest biblical character who can be connected, rather remotely and speculatively, to recorded world history. This is not to say that we know that a man named Abram ever existed. There is no specific proof of this individual outside of the Bible. But with his arrival on the Genesis scene, there are the first clues that the biblical world he supposedly lived in was the world as history knows it.

Abram's birthplace is questionable. From the Bible account, he was from Ur, then a major city in southern Mesopotamia. But Genesis also says he was from Haran, another key city connected by ancient trade routes to Ur. One possible explanation: Abram was born in Haran, then traveled to Ur. Another notion put forth by eminent biblical scholar Cyrus Gordon is that Abram actually came from Urfa in northern Mesopotamia rather than Ur. The date of Abram's travels is also a matter of speculation and scholarly disagreement. Gordon has speculatively placed Abram around 1385 BCE; traditionally Abram was thought to have lived between 2000 and 1700 BCE. His travels correspond to known migratory and commercial routes before Ur was conquered and abandoned in 1740 BCE. Another problem is the mention of camels being given to Abram. Camels were not domesticated until the fourteenth century BCE. Another confusion: the Genesis account calls it "Ur of the Chaldeans." The Chaldeans were not on the scene in Mesopotamia until a much later date, and conquered Jerusalem in 612 BCE, sending the people of Jerusalem into the Exile in Babylon. A minority of scholars argue for this very late date for Abram's life, but most likely a scribe copying the Scriptures used "Ur of the Chaldeans" as a descriptive phrase that would have had great meaning for a Jewish audience that had lived through the Exile under their Chaldean conquerors.

Most widely accepted notions of Abram contend that he lived sometime in the second millennium BCE. Stone tablets from the period show that "Ibrahim" was a common name, which would make him roughly contemporary with Hammurabi, one of the most famous kings of Babylon. Of course, drawing that conclusion would be like finding a "John Smith" in a modern Manhattan telephone book and assuming he was the same "John Smith" who was a founder of Jamestown in colonial America.

While Abram exists only in faith—or legend—Hammurabi is a bit easier to nail down. An Ammorite (meaning "westerner") whose family swept into Sumer after 2000 BCE, Hammurabi conquered several Sumerian cities and developed a small empire, making him the first king to elevate Babylon from relatively small town to major power. Some scholars have conjectured that Hammurabi—generally dated as king of Babylon from 1792–1750 BCE;

some place him about 1706–1662—might be the mysterious King Amraphel, king of Shinar, mentioned in Genesis 14. There is no clear evidence to make that leap.

Hammurabi is best remembered for a code of law, set down toward the end of his reign on clay tablets and on stelae, or stone pillars, showing the sun god Shamash handing a code of laws to Hammurabi. These laws, derived from even older Sumerian law codes, are severe by modern standards, calling for the death penalty for a variety of offenses, including kidnapping and certain types of theft. These codes also covered traffic regulations on the Euphrates River and the rights of veterans. Written codes like these represented a major leap forward for human civilization, showing a move from primitive, arbitrary violence and vengeance to forms of justice, including protection for the weakest members of society—women, children, the poor, and slaves. There are clear parallels—and equally clear differences—between Hammurabi's code and the law Moses receives from God on Mount Sinai (see Exodus). The notion of an "eye for an eye" is in Hammurabi's Code and appears in Exodus, and there are other parallels regarding damages done by a farmer's animals.

But there is one key difference between these two sets of laws. Unlike the Ark of the Covenant containing the tablets with the Ten Commandments, you can actually see Hammurabi's laws as they were inscribed. A copy of the code, carved on a block of stone, was uncovered by French archaeologists in the ancient city of Susa, modern Shush, in Iran near the border with Iraq, early in this century. It remains on display in the Louvre in Paris.

PLOT SUMMARY: ABRAM, SARAI, AND HAGAR

Promised repeatedly that he will found "a great nation," Abram is getting worried—and not any younger. When he considers making one of his household slaves his heir, his wife, Sarai, suggests he take her Egyptian slave, Hagar, as a concubine. Any child she bore would still be considered Sarai's. Clay tablets found in the Near East confirm that this would have been a completely acceptable idea in that time.

But the story takes on a wonderful human quality when the barren Sarai becomes jealous of the pregnant Hagar and mistreats her. Hagar runs away into the wilderness, where God promises that her unborn child will also have many offspring, and she returns to Abram to bear his first son, Ishmael ("God hears"). Arabs trace their origin to the "Ishmaelites," the Bedouin tribes of the southern wilderness. This is the ancient connection between Arab and Jew through Abraham.

But God promises yet another son to the incredulous Abram, now ninety-nine years old, and Sarai, who is ninety. God tells Abram ("exalted ancestor") that he will now be called Abraham ("ancestor of a multitude"), promises him all the land of Canaan, and asks him to keep the deal by circumcising every male in his tribe. Abraham agrees and all the adult males, including thirteen-year-old Ishmael, are circumcised. The ritualistic removal of the male foreskin is not peculiar to the descendants of Abraham. It was practiced by many African, South American, and Middle Eastern people, including the Egyptians.

Sarai laughs at the seemingly ridiculous notion that she will bear a son at her age. God also changes her name to Sarah (both names are forms of "princess"). Later, Sarah gives birth to Isaac ("he laughs"), who will become Abraham's heir. Hagar is once more forced to flee because of Sarah's jealousy, and again the promise is made that Ishmael will found a nation. Left in the wilderness without water, Hagar begs not to see her son die. An "angel," an English word derived from the Greek word for "messenger," appears to Hagar and a well miraculously begins to flow.

BIBLICAL VOICES

Then Abraham came near and said, "Will you indeed sweep away the righteous with the wicked? Suppose there are fifty righteous within the city; will you then sweep away the place and not forgive it for the fifty righteous who are in it? Far be it from you to do such a thing, to slay the righteous with the wicked, so that the righteous fare as the wicked! Far be that from you! Shall not the Judge of all the earth do what is just?" (Gen. 18:23–25)

PLOT SUMMARY: SODOM AND GOMORRAH

Once again, people have turned very bad, especially in that biblical hot spot, Sodom, where Abraham's nephew Lot has chosen to settle. God looks down and once again doesn't like the scene. Evil is everywhere, especially in the form of unspecified sexual depravity, which is why certain sexual crimes are still gathered together under the catch-all term "sodomy." Once again, God decides to do away with at least some of his most troublesome creations. (Remember, God promised Noah that he would never again destroy everyone.)

But before God wipes anybody out, Abraham strikes a bargain with the Lord, persuasively arguing that God should not destroy the innocent with the guilty. Abraham haggles with God, negotiating down from fifty righteous men to forty-five, then forty, then thirty, then twenty. God finally agrees that for the sake of ten righteous men the town won't be destroyed.

Apparently ten aren't to be found. Two angels in human form, sent to warn Abraham's nephew Lot of Sodom's impending doom, are welcomed into Lot's home, fed, and offered beds for the night in the best tradition of ancient hospitality. But a lusty and unruly crowd of Sodom's men—"all the people to the last man"—demands that Lot turn over these "strangers" so that they might "know" them. Clearly the crowd is not the Welcome Wagon and has more in mind than a simple "We'd like to get to know you" visit. Faced with turning his guests over to a certain homosexual gang rape, Lot refuses, even going so far as to offer his two virgin daughters to the frenzied mob. He views his obligation as host as greater than his role as father. The crowd angrily presses in on him and Lot is pulled back into his house.

The angels tell Lot to take his family away. Sodom is about to be leveled. Lot's future sons-in-law don't believe them and refuse to leave. Even Lot is slow to take the hint, so the angels lead him, his wife, and their two daughters out of the city. Sodom and nearby Gomorrah—whose specific evils are curiously never spelled out—are destroyed. On the way out of town, Lot's wife ignores the warning not to look back. As fire and brimstone rain down on the wicked Twin Cities, she is turned into a pillar of salt.

The part of Lot's story that was left out in Sunday school is that Lot's motherless daughters have another worry: with all the available men in Sodom gone up in smoke and ashes, what will they do for husbands? They get their father drunk and each of them "lies with" him. Both become pregnant and each bears a son.

Why *did Lot's wife turn into a pillar of salt?*

The Sodom and Gomorrah story has always been useful as a simple moral tale of God destroying evil. But there is a subtext to the story that has been even more influential. It is all about the sin to which the name Sodom is attached, and this story has always been cited as one of the basic biblical justifications against homosexuality.

When God's messenger angels go to Lot's house, they are threatened with mass homosexual rape by the men of Sodom, who are all destroyed. This episode was long viewed as a fairly direct condemnation of homosexuality—sexual behavior condemned elsewhere in both Hebrew and Christian scriptures. Although many contemporary biblical scholars have argued that the specific act of homosexuality is not the real issue in Sodom, it is difficult not to accept that ancient Israelites viewed homosexuality as an "abomination," even though it was acceptable in other nearby cultures. One explanation is the sacredness of having children in the ancient Israelite view. Sex that did not produce offspring was therefore considered sinful.

As for Lot's incestuous daughters; each bears a son. The first is named Moab and becomes the ancestor of the Moabites, a neighboring tribe of Israel. The other is Ben-Ammi, ancestor of the Ammonites, another neighboring tribe. For the Israelites, this story, adapted from an old Canaanite folktale, mockingly explains the origin of two neighboring tribes. It also establishes that these tribes were not descended from Abraham and had no divine claim to the Promised Land.

The remains of the Twin Cities of Sin have never been found. Myth has it that they lie buried beneath the Dead (Salt) Sea. Apart from its moral implications, the story provides an explanation of two local phenomena. The Dead Sea area is rich in bitumen, or tar, supposedly left in the wake of the destructive "fire and brimstone" raining down from heaven. Bitumen was used in the Egyptian mummification process, and the Egyptian word for "bitumen" is *momiya,* from which "mummy" is derived. Bitumen was also used for "tarring" houses and was one of the key trade items in this area.

But Dr. Charles Pellegrino offers an unorthodox but fascinating speculation in *Return to Sodom and Gomorrah.* Pellegrino, a sort of "bad boy" of science, who has designed rockets, probed the wreckage of the *Titanic* with Dr. Robert Ballard, and once wrote an article about cloning dinosaurs that helped inspire *Jurassic Park,* likes to tweak conventional scientific wisdom. In his book, Pellegrino suggests that the Sodom story, like so many other early Israelite tales in Genesis, was adapted from Babylonian sources. He points to the fact that original names translated in Greek as "Sodom" and "Gomorrah" were Siddim (or Sedom) and "Amora"—Mesopotamian names—and that the warring kings who attacked Sodom and were defeated by Abraham were from Shinar, in the Tigris-Euphrates area. Pellegrino concludes, "Sodom, if it existed at all, existed in or near Iraq." (p. 180)

The account of Lot's wife is another version of a common mythic theme: someone is punished for looking back against divine or heavenly instructions. In the Greek myths, for instance,

Orpheus goes to the underworld to recover his beloved wife, Eurydice. As they leave the underworld, he ignores the instruction not to look back and Eurydice is lost to him forever. In the case of Lot's wife, the ancient tale has been cited to explain the peculiar salt formations that surround the Dead Sea.

PLOT SUMMARY: THE SACRIFICE OF ISAAC

Having waited until he was one hundred years old for the son and heir who would fulfill God's promise, Abraham is told by God to take the boy and offer him as a burnt sacrifice. Abraham never questions this directive in the Scriptures. He simply does as he is told, offering blind obedience to a God who would make him kill his beloved child. Even when the boy asks his father where the sacrificial lamb is, Abraham answers only, "God himself will provide the lamb."

Only as Abraham binds the boy, lays him on the altar, and holds the knife over him, does an angel stop him. Abraham is told that he has passed the test—he "fears" God. A ram is substituted for the young boy on the altar.

Would Abraham really have done it?

The story of Abraham sacrificing Isaac is a central moment in the Bible. But it raises a number of disturbing questions. Is that kind of devotion or obedience to a divine call acceptable? Would Abraham actually have gone through with it? And what kind of God would ask a parent to do this, even as a test? To many people, it has always seemed an unnecessarily cruel test of faith.

There is nothing that Abraham does in the story to suggest that he had any second thoughts about this divine request. He doesn't make the same kinds of arguments for his own son that he made for the citizens of Sodom—complete strangers. Sarah is also silent in this episode. Did she try to stop her husband? Did she know what he was up to? Would a mother have done what

Abraham did? Nor do we ever get Isaac's inner thoughts about lying there with a knife poised over his body. All interesting questions, but they lie in the realm of speculation.

Of course, whether this event actually happened is also purely speculation, just like the very existence of Abraham as a real person, rather than a mythic character. Maybe this episode was another legend designed to demonstrate what unshakable faith means and that God had done well in selecting Abraham to be the founder of the "Chosen People."

But there is another angle to this story, not usually discussed in Sunday school. In some cults and religions of the ancient Near East, human sacrifice was still practiced at that time. In fact, Hebrew Law even states that the firstborn offspring of humans and animals were to be offered to God. The aborted sacrifice of Isaac has been interpreted as a symbolic moment in which human sacrifice was rejected by God. Unfortunately, the practice didn't stop with Abraham. As the later history of ancient Israel shows, human sacrifice continued in Jerusalem for centuries.

Another question is raised by the episode. When God stays Abraham's hand, the passage says that Abraham "fears" God. What is the "fear of God," an expression still commonly used today, as it was meant in the Bible? The Hebrew verb for "fear" can be understood two ways. Occasionally it meant fear as we commonly think of it—the distressing psychological sense of being afraid. But very often the biblical "fear" meant awe or reverence for someone of exalted position. In other words, Abraham was not necessarily "afraid" of God, as he was holding him in profound respect.

BIBLICAL VOICES

Now Abraham was old, well advanced in years; and the Lord had blessed Abraham in all things. Abraham said to his servant, the oldest of his house, who had charge of all that he had, "Put your hand under my thigh and I will make you swear by the Lord, the God of heaven and earth, that you will not get a wife for my son from the daughters of the

Canaanites, among whom I live, but will go to my country, and to my kindred and get a wife for my son Isaac." (Gen. 24:1–5)

PLOT SUMMARY: ISAAC AND REBEKAH

After Sarah dies at age 127, Abraham buries her in a cave in Hebron. Significantly, he purchases the burial land from the local people, the Hittites, and the verses elaborately explain the great measures Abraham took to stake a legal claim to this land. This is a crucial passage, one of the oldest recorded real estate deals, which is viewed as a legal confirmation of possession of land that had already been divinely promised. In other words, God's word is one thing but a deed is better in court.

Abraham also realizes that his son Isaac should have a wife but does not want a woman of Canaan—one more dig at the Canaanites by the Genesis author. In one of the longest narratives in Genesis, Abraham sends a servant back to his homeland. At Nahor, near Haran, the servant encounters a beautiful girl at a well. Again there is a confusion of place and personal names. Nahor is the name of a town but it is also the name of another of Abraham's brothers. The girl draws water for him and Abraham's servant treats this as a sign from God that this is the girl for Isaac. She is Rebekah, the daughter of Abraham's nephew Bethuel. Abraham's servant is welcomed into the house by Rebekah's older brother Laban, and in an elaborate negotiation, the two strike a deal for Rebekah to become Isaac's wife.

After Sarah's death, old Abraham decides he's not done sowing oats yet either. He takes another wife, Keturah, who has six more of Abraham's children. These are the ancestors of other Arabic tribes, including the Midianites, who later figure in the story of Moses. When Abraham finally dies at age 175, he is buried alongside Sarah in the cave on the site he had purchased at Hebron. Another genealogy follows Abraham's death and traces the children of Ishmael, who also had twelve sons who were later organized into twelve tribes.

Like Abraham, Isaac is promised the land and many descendants. He is like Abraham in another respect too. Once again there is a famine and God tells Isaac to go to the land of King Abimelech, with whom Abraham had an earlier dispute. In a tale that mirrors Abraham's lie about his wife, Sarah, to the Pharaoh, Isaac tells the local people that Rebekah is his sister, because he too fears he might be killed because Rebekah is so desirable. When King Abimelech sees Isaac fondling Rebekah in a field, he says, "So she is your wife! Why then did you say, 'She is my sister'?" Abimelech orders no one to bother Isaac, who goes on to prosper. King Abimelech is identified here, and in an earlier episode, as the "King of the Philistines," the tribe that will play such a prominent part in the early history of Israel. This is another example of an apparent error in the chronology on the writer's part. The Philistines were part of the invasion of so-called Sea Peoples and did not enter this area in large numbers until after 1200 BCE, long after these events would have taken place.

PLOT SUMMARY: JACOB AND ESAU

Like Isaac's mother, the beautiful Rebekah is also barren but she conceives and bears twin sons after Isaac prays to God. The firstborn is Esau ("red"); the second son, born gripping his older brother's heel, is Jacob ("he takes by the heel" or "he supplants"). The common mythic theme of hostile twins is played out here as accounting for the two related tribes, the Israelites and the Edomites. Jacob, the younger, is a trickster, a classic mythic character, like Odysseus of Greek mythology. He becomes a shepherd and was favored by his mother. Esau is the hunter, slow-witted and easily deceived, but he is Isaac's favorite. Jacob first gets Esau to sell his birthright as the firstborn son for a pot of stew, also red, emphasizing the origin of the name Edom, which, like Esau, means "red."

In a more serious deceit, Jacob is prompted by his mother to trick his father, Isaac, who is losing his sight. Rebekah cooks

Isaac's favorite meal, then covers Jacob with a kid skin so that he will seem to be as hairy as Esau. Jacob tricks his father into giving him the deathbed blessing usually bestowed on the first-born son. When Esau finds out what Jacob has done, he poignantly asks his father for another blessing. Isaac tells Esau that he will live away from the fat of the land and shall live by the sword. His father also says Esau will serve his brother but that one day he will break free. (In the time of King David, when the text was probably written, Edom was ruled by Israel, but it later revolted.) After receiving this mixed blessing, Esau still threatens to kill Jacob.

What is Jacob's Ladder?

Unhappy that Esau has brought home two girls from the "wrong side of the tracks"—Canaanite women—and fearful that Esau may still try to kill Jacob, Rebekah schemes to have her younger son sent somewhere out of harm's way. In a story that mirrors the search for Isaac's bride, Jacob also sets off for Haran to find a wife. The narrative follows Jacob on a long journey, like that of the Odyssey, although not quite as perilous. It is still another ancient poetic tradition: the hero's wandering search, filled with mystical happenings and extraordinary events, and his eventual return home.

On the first night of his journey, Jacob uses a stone for a pillow and dreams of a ladder, reaching up to heaven. On it, angels are going up and down. God then speaks to Jacob, renewing the promise of land and descendants made to Abraham and Isaac. When Jacob wakes, he takes the stone he had used for a pillow and pours oil on it to sanctify this place that he calls Bethel ("House of God") and promises that the Lord who spoke to him shall be his God. He also promises God, as Abraham had done, to tithe, or give one tenth of all he receives.

While artists of the Christian era usually depicted "Jacob's

Ladder," immortalized in a widely sung hymn, as an actual ladder, the original word for "ladder" can also be translated as "ramp" or "stairway." Long before Led Zeppelin, in another words, the Bible was doing "Stairway to Heaven." In terms of archaeology, though, Jacob's dreamlike image related more precisely to the stepped towers, like the ziggurat of Babel, in Mesopotamia. And when Jacob names the place Bethel, he confirms the connection to a "gate of god" (Babylon).

PLOT SUMMARY: JACOB AND RACHEL

Jacob wants a girl just like the girl that dear old Dad got. So he too goes to Laban, Rebekah's brother, as Abraham's servant did. And he also meets a beautiful girl at the well. Unlike Abraham's servant, who carried a lavish treasure as a bride-price, Jacob is broke. He promises to work for Uncle Laban for seven years to pay for Rachel.

The plot thickens through a series of tricks played by each of the actors in this drama, which must have been popular as it was told around the campfires over the ages. On the morning of the wedding, Laban has his older daughter, Leah, dressed as the bride, veiled to conceal her identity, and she marries Jacob. After discovering this ruse, Jacob insists that he still wants Rachel, and promises to serve Laban for another seven years if he can have her too. Laban agrees and Jacob now has two wives and another seven-year hitch to serve. But he manages to keep busy in that time, siring a flock of children, even though his beloved Rachel is barren. First, Leah produces four sons. The envious Rachel gives her slave, Bilhah, to Jacob and Bilhah has two sons. Leah, who had stopped at four, wants more sons, so she gives Jacob her maid, Zilpah. She too produces two sons. Leah isn't finished after all and has another two sons and a daughter. Finally, Rachel's infertility is cured and she has two sons, although she dies in childbirth with her second son. Before very long, Jacob has a baker's dozen of children.

Jacob's Children

Leah
Reuben
Simeon
Levi
Judah
Issachar (after she thought she was barren)
Zebulun
Dinah, a daughter

Bilhah
Dan
Naphtali

Zilpah
Gad
Asher

Rachel
Joseph
Benjamin (Rachel dies after giving birth to Benjamin)

How did Jacob become "Israel"?

Jacob, the trickster, gets his own revenge on Uncle Laban when they make a business deal regarding the herds that Jacob has been tending so successfully. Jacob and Laban agree that Jacob can keep all the spotted and speckled sheep and goats and all the black goats in the flocks. But in the night, the crafty Laban tells his sons to remove all the striped male goats, the speckled female goats, and the black lambs from the herds. Jacob has a few tricks of his own though, and, in a story that combines magic with some early genetic engineering, Jacob places striped sticks in front of the healthiest and strongest animals of the flock in breeding time.

When the newborns arrive, the magical sticks have produced many striped, spotted, and speckled young. Jacob continues this process until he has successfully bred a strong herd of livestock that will be his, getting the better of his deceitful uncle.

Laban and his sons aren't happy about Jacob's ruse, and God sends an angel to Jacob, warning him to leave Laban's house. After twenty years of service to his uncle, Jacob sets off with his wives, children, and flocks, without telling Laban. Before leaving, Rachel steals her father's "household gods," the small, wooden or stone carved idols people kept around the house for good luck. Laban catches up to Jacob and his caravan and begins to search for anything Jacob might have stolen. Rachel sits on her father's gods, and when they come to search her she tells them she is menstruating and can't get up.

These "household gods" were idols, typical of the cults worshiped in Canaan and elsewhere in Mesopotamia. Small carved statues or fertility symbols, they were typically placed throughout a home, just as people still hang pictures of saints or crosses. The episode in which the menstruating Rachel hides these idols would have been told by the Israelites with derisive mockery as Rachel sat on the idols in her time of "uncleanness."

Jacob and Laban are reconciled and the father sends off his daughters. As Jacob journeys homeward, he must pass through his brother Esau's territory. Uncertain as to how his brother will receive him, Jacob splits his camp in two and sends messengers ahead with gifts for Esau. He will either win Esau over or lose only part of his camp. But before meeting Esau, Jacob has a strange encounter in the night. Left alone, Jacob wrestles with an unnamed man. Like all great heroes, Jacob possesses nearly superhuman strength and fends off this mysterious stranger until the man strikes his hip, dislocating it. Jacob still refuses to let go until the man blesses him. The "man" asks his name, and when Jacob tells him, he replies, "You shall no longer be called Jacob but Israel, for you have striven with God and with humans, and have prevailed." The name "Israel" is translated as "the one who strives with God" or "God rules," and the name would later be applied to the tribal confederacy formed from the twelve tribes, linking these groups not only by religious faith but by ancient blood ties.

One of the starkest revisions in the modern historical view of this "twelve tribes" picture is that local tribal groups in Canaan—later Israel—existed before they were given these names. According to recent archaeological and historical evidence, the "twelve tribe" explanation of these peoples' origin came much later to strengthen the unity of the confederation of local tribes—who may have had no connection to Jacob—that became the kingdom of Israel around 1000 BCE. According to J. R. Porter, "The tribal names were originally geographical names of parts of Palestine, but in Genesis they become the names of persons. The names of the tribal ancestors are all given popular etymologies, which in no way correspond to historical reality." (*The Illustrated Guide to the Bible*, p. 47) For instance, the tribe of "Dan," according to Cyrus Gordon's *The Bible and the Ancient Near East*, originated from another of the "Sea Peoples," the group known as the Danuna. (p. 96) There is plenty of evidence, even within the Bible, that many of the "Children of Israel" were already well established in the "Promised Land" before the Exodus from Egypt under Moses (see Exodus).

After wrestling with God, Jacob meets Esau, coming toward him with four hundred men. But instead of trouble, Jacob finds only welcome and forgiveness from his older twin. Esau embraces his brother, they kiss and weep together. The brother who was cheated, Esau, is usually remembered for his gullibility, but deserves a better image. He was duped, not once but twice—fooled by a manipulative, scheming mother and a willingly deceitful brother. Yet in the end he should be acknowledged for what he is: a true hero and model who, though cheated, offers his brother an emotional embrace and unconditional forgiveness.

PLOT SUMMARY: THE RAPE OF DINAH

While the legendary twelve sons got most of the attention, Jacob also had a daughter, Dinah. Her story was another of those uncomfortable ones that Sunday school conveniently skips over. But it is a reminder that these stories were set in a primitive culture of blood feuds and personal vengeance. After the peaceful settlement with Laban and Esau, Jacob and his family get into a nastier bit of trouble when they return to Canaan. They camp outside the city of Shechem and purchase a piece of land on which they can tend their flocks. But one of the local men, also identified as Shechem, takes Jacob's daughter by force. The young man's father expresses his regret and offers to have his son marry Dinah. He even proposes that the men of the city will be circumcised, implicitly recognizing Jacob's God, and the two groups can be joined through intermarriages. Jacob sees the wisdom in this and accepts the agreement; his sons sign on to the agreement but for different motives. Dinah, of course, has no say in the matter. As a woman of the time, she is her father's to do with as he wants. What *she* wants can only be guessed. Dinah remains with Shechem during the "negotiation." Is she a hostage, as the traditional view holds? Or has she fallen for the Canaanite Shechem? A few hundred years after this battle over a woman taken by a young man, there would be another similar war over a stolen woman. Was Dinah a violated hostage or, like Helen of Troy, a willing woman in love? The Bible doesn't tell us which.

As the men of Shechem lay in pain after being circumcised, Dinah's two full brothers, Simeon and Levi, kill Shechem and escape with Dinah. Jacob's other sons then plunder the city in reprisal for their sister's rape, going so far as to steal the wives and children of the men of Shechem. Jacob is furious at this turn of events, fearing reprisal from neighboring Canaanites. But the sons answer their father, "Should our sister be treated like a whore?"

Following this violent episode, Jacob travels on and makes altars to God. At the same time, he buries all of the foreign gods, household idols, earrings, and magical amulets carried by his family—a symbolic purging of the other local Canaanite deities.

Plot Summary: Joseph and His Brothers

After his long, eventful sojourn, Jacob returns to Canaan with his family and flocks. At age seventeen, Joseph has emerged as his father Jacob's favorite, the first son of the beloved Rachel. Joseph's brothers seem to find him a nuisance, especially when he rats on some of the brothers for something they had done wrong. Exactly what they did isn't spelled out, but Joseph "brought a bad report of them to their father." As Joseph's favored status grows, his brothers grow jealous of him. Jacob even gives him a special robe with long sleeves. Joseph makes things worse for himself when he tells his brothers about two dreams in which he is shown ruling over them and they bow down to him. The brothers first consider killing him, but Judah convinces the others to sell him instead, and Joseph is taken by a caravan of Midianite traders for twenty pieces of silver. The brothers then soak Joseph's robe with goat's blood, take it back to their father, and tell Jacob that Joseph was killed by an animal. The Midianites take Joseph to Egypt, where he is sold to Potiphar, captain of the Pharaoh's guard.

Was there a "coat of many colors"?

Sorry. Once again, bad translation by King James's men. The correct translation of Joseph's famous "coat of many colors" is a "long robe with sleeves." You can see why "coat of many colors" caught on—it has a much better ring than something that sounds like a fancy bathrobe. Such a robe is mentioned again later in the Bible and is said to be the dress of a princess. Either Jacob was conferring semi-royal status on Joseph or he wanted him to be a cross-dresser.

But it is clear that Joseph was favored and his brothers didn't like it. Once more the themes of Genesis are crystalized here. The sibling rivalry, the elevation of the younger over the older brothers, and, with Joseph's adventures in Egypt, the idea of exile and return—certainly one of the central themes in scripture for Jews and Christians alike. Finally, it is a story of forgiveness.

What was the sin of Onan?

In an interlude to the Joseph narrative is a pair of stories about Judah, the fourth of Leah's sons, and his family. Judah marries a Canaanite woman and has three sons, Er, Onan, and Shelah. Er marries a woman named Tamar, then commits some unspecified crime and the Lord strikes him dead. Judah then orders Onan to sleep with his dead brother's widow and raise up children for him, the duty of a brother-in-law at the time. Onan doesn't want to raise offspring who are his brother's heirs, so he "spills his seed" on the ground whenever he "went in to his brother's wife." God isn't pleased by his disobedience and also strikes Onan dead.

This brief passage has been the bane of adolescent boys ever since. The so-called "sin of Onan," later called "onanism," was mistakenly viewed for centuries as a biblical injunction against masturbation. Onan's "spilled seed" was the result of coitus interruptus, rather than "self-abuse," as they used to call masturbation. But failing to fulfill the law, a fraternal duty that required a brother to give his dead brother heirs, cost Onan his life. Pretty rough justice.

But Genesis isn't quite finished with Tamar, the widow who has seen two lovers die. Judah tells her to wait until his third son, Shelah, grows up. But when Shelah gets older, Judah reneges on the promise that Shelah will take care of Tamar. With her prospects for husband and children dimming, Tamar takes matters into her own hands. She trades in her widow's clothes for the veil of a prostitute and waits for Judah to pass by. He stops and, presumably failing to recognize his daughter-in-law, enjoys her services with a quickie by the side of the road. Short on shekels, Judah tells the "prostitute" that he will pay her with a kid from his flock some other time. But Tamar shrewdly asks for his signet—a ring used to stamp a signature—and cord and his staff, the ancient equivalent of taking his credit card.

When she becomes pregnant, Tamar is brought to Judah to be executed as a prostitute deserving death. That's when Tamar shows her trump cards—the signet, cord, and staff belonging to Judah.

This might all seem like a curious but insignificant subplot to the main story of Joseph. But one key footnote to this story is the identity of the offspring of Judah and Tamar. Another set of biblical twins, one sticks a hand out of the womb and is technically the firstborn, so the midwife ties a red string around the hand. Then the second twin is actually delivered first. His name is Perez. The brother with the red cord is named Zerah. Perez is an ancestor of David—and by further extension Jesus.

Who was Joseph's Pharaoh, and could a slave become Egypt's prime minister?

So what happened to Joseph? This is part of the brilliance of the Hebrew storytellers who composed the Bible. You can imagine everyone sitting around a desert campfire, listening to the story of Joseph. Just as the storyteller gets to Joseph's fate, he shifts attention away with the accounts of Judah and Tamar. The audience is left dangling. It is a technique that worked for Charles Dickens, Saturday afternoon serials, and television soap operas. It keeps the audience waiting expectantly.

When we left our hero, Joseph, he was not dangling off a cliff. But he had been sold by his brothers into slavery and taken to Egypt, where he was serving in the house of Potiphar, who is first identified as an Egyptian soldier. But God is with Joseph and he prospers, rising to become overseer in Potiphar's household. The Bible also says Joseph was "handsome and good looking." With her husband away, Potiphar's wife takes a heavy-breathing interest in the hunky Joseph, who resists her advances.

A scorned woman, Potiphar's wife cries "rape" and Joseph is thrown into prison, even though execution of a slave so accused would have been a reasonable outcome. Joseph's encounter with Potiphar's wife is apparently a revision of an Egyptian folk story known as "The Tale of Two Brothers," in which one brother is falsely accused by his brother's wife. In the Egyptian tale, the two brothers are reconciled. While in prison, Joseph rediscovers his skills as an interpreter of dreams—the very thing that got him into trouble with his brothers. His ability to explain dreams is so great that Joseph is brought to the Pharaoh, who tells Joseph his dreams. With God's help, Joseph explains that Egypt will experience seven years of good crops followed by seven years of famine. He advises the Pharaoh to store up grain during the good years to have it available during the bad years. Pharaoh is so impressed, he sets Joseph up as the prime minister of Egypt with authority to administer the food program.

Again Joseph prospers and marries the daughter of an Egyptian high priest who bears two sons, Manasseh and Ephraim. When the predicted famine comes, Joseph's brothers are sent by Jacob to Egypt, hoping to buy food. More than twenty years have passed since they sold Joseph as a slave, and the brothers do not recognize their brother, now an Egyptian official, when they come before him.

Joseph has no difficulty realizing these are his brothers. Instead of vengeance, Joseph secretly plans to reunite his family but first lays out an elaborate trick in order to teach his brothers a lesson. He has a gold cup placed in the brothers' baggage, and when it is discovered, Joseph demands that Benjamin, the youngest, be left behind as punishment. Troubled by his conscience over what he had done to his brother Joseph twenty years earlier, Judah offers himself in Benjamin's place.

Having seen that Judah had indeed learned his lesson, Joseph finally reveals his identity to his brothers and even tells them that his being sold into slavery was part of God's plan. At Joseph's insistence, his father, Jacob (Israel), and all his descendants make the trip to Egypt. They are given a prime piece of Egyptian real estate in Goshen, a fertile area on the Nile Delta. In a long poem, each of the twelve sons is given a blessing by their father, Jacob. This is an accounting of sorts for the twelve sons, and it is not good news for everybody. It actually reflects events as they occur a few centuries later, in King David's time.

Who was Joseph's Pharaoh, and could a Semite slave become the Egyptian prime minister? We know a lot about the Egyptians and how they lived, including how the pyramids were built by skilled wage laborers, not slaves. Elaborate court records survive of many of the Pharaohs before and after the presumed time of Joseph. But none of them mentions a Semite slave becoming a high official who had translated the Pharaoh's dreams and helped save Egypt in a time of extraordinary famine. Periodic drought and famine were not unusual in ancient times, and several periods of severe shortages are recorded, although none exactly matches the biblical scenario. So we don't know who Joseph's Pharaoh was. Many elements in the biblical story are consonant with what is known of Egypt at the time. Although considerable scholarship has been devoted to the question, the one widely accepted guess is that Joseph was in Egypt during the period of the Hyksos, a Semitic group that invaded and conquered parts of Egypt, holding onto the Nile Delta section for about a century.

Apart from the historical impact of the Joseph story and its consequences for the future of the Israelites, there is also a more significant spiritual meaning. Throughout Genesis, there has been a succession of stories about brothers mistreating and betraying one another. The first brothers, Cain and Abel, produced the first murder. Later brothers supplanted or tricked each other. And finally, Joseph's brothers actually contemplated killing him. In each case there is forgiveness. God is merciful toward Cain. Ishmael and Isaac reunite to bury their father, Abraham. Jacob and Esau are reconciled. And finally, in the Joseph story, the ultimate act of a brother's forgiveness is demonstrated. Forgiveness is ultimately the great theme that permeates the Bible. Men sin. God forgives.

BIBLICAL VOICES

Then Joseph said to his brothers, "I am about to die; but God will surely come to you, and bring you up out of this land to the land that he swore to Abraham, to Isaac, and to Jacob." So Joseph made the Israelites swear, saying, "When God comes to you, you shall carry up my bones from here." And Joseph died, being one hundred ten years old; he was embalmed and placed in a coffin in Egypt. (Gen. 50:24–26)

MILESTONES IN BIBLICAL TIMES I

All dates BCE ("before the Common Era"). Many of these dates are speculative and approximate.

4.5 billion years ago Earth is created, according to geological evidence.

3 million years ago An upright-walking australopithecine ape-man appears on earth.

1 million years ago Homo erectus develops; the toolmaker and fire-building ancestor of modern humans.

150,000 to 75,000 years ago Neanderthal man hunts, speaks, cares for sick, practices cannibalism, buries the dead.

125,000 years ago Earliest evidence of anatomically modern humans found in Africa.

100,000 years ago The Ancient Near East is inhabited by small bands of hunter-gatherers.

11,000 Vast fields of wild grain appear in parts of the Near East as the glaciers begin to retreat following the last Ice Age.

10,000–8000 "Natufian" culture in modern-day Israel, some of the first known human settlements.

8000 Agriculture begins in the Near East; digging sticks are used to plant seeds of wild grasses.

6500 The wheel is invented sometime in the next two centuries by Sumerians in the Tigris-Euphrates basin.

5508 The Year of the Creation, as adopted in seventh-century CE Constantinople and used by the Eastern Orthodox church until the eighteenth century CE.

5490 The Year of the Creation as reckoned by early Syrian Christians.

5000 The earliest cities are born as people begin to cluster in villages in the Fertile Crescent.

• Lands bordering Nile River begin to dry out; the first dikes and canals for irrigation are built, marking the beginning of civilization in North Africa.

4004 (October 23); *Date of Creation of Heavens and Earth* as calculated by Irish theologian James Ussher in 1650 CE.

3760 The Year of the Creation as calculated by Hebrew calendar that is used from the fifteenth century CE.

3641 (February 10) *The Date of the Creation* as calculated by the Mayans.

3500 Sumerian society develops in the Tigris-Euphrates valleys, where annual floods deposit fresh layers of fertile silt. The Sumerians gradually harness domestic animals to plows, drain marshlands, irrigate desert lands, and extend areas of permanent cultivation. The increase in agricultural efficiency creates the first "leisure class," permitting classes of priests, artisans, scholars, and merchants and a priestly administrative system evolves. Among the Sumerians' other accomplishments: animal-drawn wheeled vehicles and oar-powered ships; the making with bronze of objects that couldn't be made with softer copper; a written cuneiform alphabet.

3100 Egypt's 1st Dynasty unites northern and southern kingdoms under Menes, who founds a city called Memphis.

2680 Egypt's 3d Dynasty founded by Zoser, who rules for thirty years with aid of counselor Imhotep. Imhotep makes the first known efforts to find medical as well as religious methods for treating disease. Imhotep erects the pyramid of Zoser (Step Pyramid at Sakkara), the first large stone structure in the world.

2613 Egypt's 4th Dynasty founded by Snefru. His son Cheops (Khufu), who reigns for twenty-three years, constructs the Great Pyramid of Cheops at Giza.

2560 Egypt's Khafra (or Khafre) rules as the third king of the 4th Dynasty. The Great Sphinx at Giza, a 189-foot-long monument, is carved from rock under Khafra's reign.

2500 A third Egyptian pyramid is erected at Giza by Menkure of Egypt's 4th Dynasty.

2500 Sumerian cuneiform script simplified from earlier language of thousands of ideograms.

2350 The Akkadian empire, founded by Sargon I, rules Mesopotamia for the next two centuries.

c. 2000–1700 Abraham leaves Ur in Chaldea.

2000 Babylonians introduce decimal notation; Babylon has replaced Sumer as the dominant power in the Middle East.

1970 Founder of Egypt's 12th (Theban) Dynasty, Amenhet I dies after a thirty-year reign.

1792 208 years of Egypt's Theban Dynasty ends with death of Amenemhet IV.

1792–1750? Hammurabi rules Babylon and enacts a famous law code.

1700 Babylonians employ windmills to pump water for irrigation.

1660–1550 Semitic Hyksos tribesmen invade Egypt from Palestine, Syria, and farther north. Excellent archers, they wear sandals and use horses and chariots to dominate the Nile Delta for the next century.

c. 1650? The "cult of Yahweh," the earliest form of Judaism, begun by Abraham and carried on by his son Isaac is continued by his grandson Jacob, also named Israel.

LET MY PEOPLE GO

EXODUS

And he was there with the Lord forty days and forty nights; he did neither eat bread, nor drink water. And he wrote upon the tables the words of the covenant, the ten commandments.
(Ex. 34:28 KJV)

❋ Why did God try to kill Moses?

❋ Did the Hebrews build the pyramids?

❋ Which sea did the Israelites cross?

❋ When you sell your daughter as a slave, do you have to give a warranty?

How do we know Moses was a real man? Lost in the desert for forty years, he wouldn't stop and ask for directions.

At least when we get to Exodus, we have a perfect picture of biblical life and what people from the Bible actually looked like: Moses looked like Charlton Heston and the Pharaoh looked like Yul Brynner.

Cecil B. DeMille's religious epic, *The Ten Commandments* (1956), has probably shaped more common (mis)conceptions of the Bible and what it says than the last forty years' worth of scholarly dissertations, Sabbath homilies, and Sunday school classes put together. While those glorious cinematic visions—the Nile running with blood, the sea separating, those divine laws whirling out of the flames—were all visually exciting, there are some problems with the images. First of all, the "Red Sea" is now viewed as a mistranslation. Next, there is the problem of the missing Mount Sinai, sometimes called Mount Horeb. Nobody knows precisely which mountain is featured in Exodus, although the author of a controversial recent book, *The Gold of Exodus*, claims a pair of amateur archaeologists have discovered the site in the Arabian desert, a claim not verified by authoritative studies at this writing.

Another missing item is the single most important object in the history of ancient Israel, the Ark of the Covenant, the elaborate box God told Moses to build to hold the stone tablets inscribed with the Ten Commandments. It simply disappeared from the Bible without mention. After Jerusalem is destroyed in 586 BCE, the fate of the Ark is never discussed.

Then there is another troubling question: How can a million or two men, women, and children wander around for so long without leaving any trace of having been there? No signs of semipermanent dwellings or debris. Not a broken piece of pottery. No burial places. In other words, when it comes to the sojourn in the wilderness, researchers have (so far) found none of the remains typically left in the wake of ancient settlements. Always keep in mind Rule One of archaeology: Absence of evidence is not evidence of absence.

Yet there is Moses—or Moshe in Hebrew—the central (human) figure in the Hebrew Bible, the great law bringer, and for Christians, the symbolic model for Jesus. Moses is saved after a king orders the Jewish babies killed; Jesus is saved after a king orders the Jewish babies killed. Moses parts the waters; Jesus calms and walks on the waters. Moses spends forty days in the wilderness; Jesus spends forty days in the wilderness. Moses goes to a mountain and gives a sermon; Jesus gives a sermon on the mount. Moses delivers the covenant; Jesus delivers the new covenant.

Some Jews and Christians alike may be surprised to learn that Moses also gets high marks in Islam, which knows him as *Musa*. According to *Who's Who of Religions*, the Koran refers to him 502 times, more than any other prophet. In Islamic tradition, Moses urges Muhammad to negotiate with God (Allah) until the required number of daily prayers is reduced from fifty to five.

In spite of his exalted stature in three major religions, Moses is a mystery man. There is no evidence of his existence outside the Bible and the Koran. No existing copy of his writings. No references in Egyptian court records to a Moses raised in a Pharaoh's house. Nor do Egyptian sources mention the "Children of Israel" working as slaves and then escaping en masse. Modern scholars have no problem with that. It would have amounted to an embarrassing incident that Egyptian court historians covered up. That's right: governments past and present don't like to admit their embarrassments, mistakes, and failures.

While some scholars—but few believers—doubt the fact that Moses lived, the case for a "historical Moses" is secondary to what Exodus and the three following books of the Torah (Leviticus, Numbers, Deuteronomy) are about. Exodus (from the Greek *exodos*, "departure") recounts the events surrounding the deliverance of the Israelites from slavery in Egypt and the years of wandering that followed. Called *Shemot* ("Names") in Hebrew, Exodus falls into two major sections. First, it describes the rise of Moses and Israel's escape from Egyptian captivity. Then it relates Israel's sojourn in the Sinai desert, where the laws governing life and worship—not just the Ten Commandments—were given to Moses by God, binding Israel to its God in a unique covenant.

BIBLICAL VOICES

Then Pharaoh commanded all his people,"Every boy that is born to the Hebrews you shall throw into the Nile, but you shall let every girl live." (Ex. 1:22)

PLOT SUMMARY: MOSES

The opening chapter of Exodus seemingly skips over a few centuries of Israelite history—although even that idea is disputed—and finds the descendants of Abraham and Joseph in a changed set of circumstances. Favored by one anonymous Pharaoh in Joseph's time, the growing multitude of Hebrews is viewed as a threat by another anonymous Pharaoh, who has put them to work building cities and fortifications. This Pharaoh is so worried about them that he orders the murder of Hebrew boys. Still the Hebrews keep working.

Faced with the Pharaoh's genocidal death sentence, a Hebrew woman places her infant son in a basket woven of reeds and sets him down in the Nile—source of all life in Egypt. He is found by the Pharaoh's daughter, who decides to keep the Hebrew infant—obviously knowing that this was contrary to her father's decree. She names him Moses, an Egyptian name meaning "son of." The name is related to the Hebrew word for "draw out"; he is "drawn out" of the Nile, and will also draw his people out of Egypt. The infant's sister, sent to watch him float down the river, asks the Egyptian princess if she wants a Hebrew nurse to care for the child and brings the baby's true mother to the palace. One problem here is that Moses' brother, Aaron, is later said to be three years older than Moses. Why wasn't Aaron, the firstborn, thrown into the Nile? Was the Pharaoh's order retroactive or did it apply only to newborn children? Just another of those bothersome details the Bible doesn't flesh out.

Raised as a prince of Egypt, Moses witnesses an Egyptian overseer beating a Hebrew worker. In an attempt to save the Hebrew man, Moses kills the Egyptian and secretly buries him in the sand. When he later sees two Hebrews arguing, Moses again intervenes, but one of the men says to him, "Are you going to kill me like that Egyptian you buried?"

Fearing that the Pharaoh will hear of his crime, Moses flees to the land of the Midian, a tribe with ancient blood ties to Abraham, who live in the Sinai desert. There he finds a wife, Zipporah, one of seven sisters, at a well. There is another biblical name confusion here: Zipporah's father is identified first as Reuel and then later as Jethro and then Hobab. Moses marries Zipporah, becomes a shepherd, and the couple has two children.

One day, Moses is drawn to a strange sight on the "mountain of God," identified as Horeb and later Sinai. "An angel of the Lord" appears to him in a flaming bush. The bush burns but is not consumed. Then God calls to Moses out of the bush. The "God of your father" tells him that he must go back to Egypt and lead his people out of slavery.

Moses puts up a series of protests, finally complaining that he stutters and would not make a good spokesman, so God tells Moses that his brother, Aaron, can do the talking.

BIBLICAL VOICES
And God said to Moses, "I AM THAT I AM." (Ex. 3:14)

Why did God try to kill Moses?

One of the most fascinating and overlooked vignettes in the life of Moses is a brief section telling of his return to Egypt with his family. Apparently C. B. DeMille didn't want to go near this story because it has baffled scholars for centuries. The story is a paltry three lines in Exodus. As Moses and his family set out for Egypt, they camp for the night. The account reads, "On the way, at a place where they spent the night, the Lord met him and tried to kill him. But Zipporah took a flint and cut off her son's foreskin, and touched his feet with it, and said, 'Truly you are a bridegroom of blood to me!' So he let him alone. It was then she said, 'A bridegroom of blood by circumcision.'"

Whom does God try to kill and why? Moses or one of his two sons?

Whose feet (a frequent biblical euphemism for male genitals) get smeared with a bloody foreskin and why?

And what is a "bridegroom of blood"?

While centuries of scholars have plumbed this mystery, producing bizarre theories about the apparent assault on Moses, one explanation is that this was an ancient story reflecting the belief that circumcision could ward off demonic attack. Circumcision was originally a premarital or puberty rite before it was performed on infants. Since Moses was presumably not circumcised, the smearing of the blood on him may have protected him as well. The other point of the story is that without Zipporah and her handy flint knife, there might be no Moses. But most of us have never even heard of Zipporah, another of the overlooked biblical heroines.

Having survived this strange nocturnal attack, Moses returns to Egypt and asks Pharaoh—his stuttering is no longer a problem it seems—to release the Hebrews. His initial request is for a three-day leave to go into the wilderness for a religious celebration. Pharaoh isn't interested, and orders the Hebrew workload increased. As a show of power, Moses has Aaron cast down his staff, which turns into a snake. Interesting that the villain of Genesis is put to such good use by Moses. Pharaoh isn't impressed with this trick— his sorcerers can do the same trick. But Aaron's snake swallows those of the Egyptian court magicians, and Moses warns Pharaoh that worse is to come. A succession of divine calamities, known as the Ten Plagues, is then brought down on Egypt.

THE TEN PLAGUES

(Psalm 105 reviews the Exodus and does not mention all ten plagues; some scholars see in this further evidence of a combination of the two "J" and "P" accounts as one in Exodus.)

1. The water of the Nile and all its tributaries turns to blood.

   (The Nile occasionally reddens owing to volcanic deposits and algae.)

2. Frogs crawl out of the river and cover Egypt.

   (A result of the transformation of the river's waters.)

3. Gnats (also translated as "mosquitoes" or "lice") infest the people and animals of Egypt.

4. Flies (or swarms of insects) infest the land, but not Goshen, where the Hebrews live.

   (All of these severe insect infestations are typical natural occurrences in Egypt, especially after the annual river floods leave pools of water in which insects breed.)

5. Livestock pestilence on the Egyptians' horses, donkeys, camels, cattle herds, and flocks.

   (An outbreak of anthrax, perhaps spread by the preceding infestations of insects. An interesting modern note. The American military announced in 1997 that it would begin to vaccinate all military personnel against anthrax, a much feared biological weapon.)

6. Boils.

   (Aaron and Moses throw soot into the air, which turns to a dust that produces festering boils on the skin of the Egyptians and their animals—which were presumably killed by the fifth plague.)

7. The heaviest hail ever seen falls on Egypt but again doesn't touch Goshen.

8. Locusts.

   (A common pestilence in the ancient Near East.)

9. Darkness blots out the sun for three days.

   (The *khamsin*, a hot wind from the Sahara, produces thick dust clouds that block the sun, usually in March through May.)
10. The death of Egypt's firstborn, both human and animal.

God tells Moses to have the Hebrews daub their doorposts with lamb or goat's blood. In this way they will be protected when the angel of death "passes over" the land and kills the firstborn of Egypt. The final plague is commemorated in the Jewish festival of Passover. Most scholars believe that the Passover was actually a combination of two ancient festivals—an agricultural festival celebrating the barley harvest and a pastoral ritual in which an animal was sacrificed to ward off evil—later reinterpreted as a memorial of the deliverance from Egypt. Exodus reads, "This day shall be unto you for a memorial; and ye shall keep it a feast to the Lord throughout your generations." (Ex. 12:14)

In commenting on the plagues in *The Bible and the Ancient Near East*, Cyrus H. Gordon and Gary Rendsburg note that each of the plagues is aimed at specific gods in the Egyptian pantheon, ending with the sun god Ra, who is overpowered by darkness. Yahweh was not only demonstrating his power over men and nature but proved that this God is greater than any other gods.

With the death of the firstborn of Egypt—from wealthiest to poorest, human and animals—Pharaoh relents and tells Moses to "rise up and go away from my people."

Did the Hebrews build the pyramids?

There are no pyramids in the Bible. Despite the fact that these structures would have certainly been the talk of the ancient world, the authors of the Bible didn't consider them worthy of note. (There are no cats in the Bible either, an interesting curiosity only because the cat was one of the most significant animal figures in

Egyptian religion.) The missing pyramids are a strange oversight, but understandable; they played no part in the unfolding of the biblical narrative. However, the Bible also fails to record the names of the Pharaohs of Egypt, who held such great importance to the people of Israel, while it is filled with the names of many other ancient kings, some of them quite obscure from a modern perspective.

The first pyramids began to rise around 2900 BCE. The pinnacle of pyramid construction, the Great Pyramid of Khufu, and the extraordinary Great Sphinx built by his son Khafre, date from c. 2550 to 2500 BCE. Accepting a possible early date for Joseph in Egypt at around 1700 BCE, the pyramids would have existed well over a thousand years before any Hebrews arrived in Egypt. Maybe that meant they weren't such big news anymore. Maybe the Hebrews up in the Nile Delta never got to see the pyramids, like tourists who come to New York but never see the Liberty Bell in Philadelphia or the Lincoln Memorial in Washington, D.C. Or maybe the writers of the Bible didn't want to point out any of the accomplishments of their chief oppressor.

Contrary to the long-held notion, begun by the Greek Herodotus, "Father of History," that hundreds of thousands of slaves built the pyramids, recent research has shown that the pyramids were probably constructed by smaller work crews who were not slaves but conscripts or volunteers from farm villages. They were supported by thousands of bakers, brewers, cooks, and other "service people." The product of a highly developed and motivated society, the pyramids show an extraordinary degree of social organization. The laborers were paid in food and clothing, and as these enormous building projects demanded increasingly skilled artisans and workers, a trained working class gradually developed in Egypt.

The circumstances may have been very different for the Hebrews of Moses' time. There are numerous guesses and scenarios as to the timeline going from Joseph to Moses, a chronology complicated by very basic scholarly disagreements over Egyptian historical dates. Three of these scenarios are worth noting:

• The first, and perhaps most widely held theory, asserts that Joseph lived in Egypt in the time of the Hyksos, an Asiatic or Semitic group that invaded Egypt and held on to the Nile Delta area for a century, starting from around 1665 BCE. The Hyksos, who pioneered chariot warfare, gradually assimilated Egyptian practices and would have been open to another Semitic person, such as Joseph, rising to prominence. The Hyksos were driven out of the Nile Delta around 1570–1565 BCE by Ahmose (Amosis) I, first of the 18th Dynasty rulers of Egypt. This famous line of Egyptian rulers later included Thutmosis I and II, the female Pharaoh Hatshepsut, the "boy king" Tutankhamen, and the general-turned-Pharaoh Horemheb. During this period, any Asiatics, including the Hebrews, would have been viewed as a threat, and the Pharaoh's grim order to kill the Hebrew boys would have made strategic and historical sense.

In this time scheme, as Exodus suggests, the Hebrews remained in Egypt for several hundred years, and were enslaved by the Pharaohs of the 19th Dynasty, the first of whom was Ramses I, who came to power around 1309 BCE. Although Ramses I died after a one-year reign, to be succeeded by Seti (Sethos) I (1308–1291 BCE), the name Ramses is specifically mentioned in Exodus, although this might have been a later editor's addition. The cities that the Hebrews were forced to build fit in with the building program of Ramses II and his heirs. During this time, Egypt consolidated its power over the Nile Delta and moved aggressively into Canaan and an eventual confrontation with the Hittites, a powerful group moving south from their base in what is now Turkey.

In this scenario, the most likely culprit for the Pharaoh at the time of Moses is Seti's son Ramses II (1291–1224 BCE), and the Israelite Exodus occurs around 1290 BCE. Another possibility in this chronology is Seti's son Merneptah, who actually recorded a military victory over Israel around 1235 BCE, by which time the Israelites are thought to have been established in Canaan.

• Cyrus Gordon, one of the most esteemed historians of the

Bible and ancient Near East, and his coauthor Gary A. Rendsburg, make a case for a much later arrival of Joseph in Egypt. Using Egyptian and Mesopotamian sources, along with biblical genealogies, they select Seti I as Joseph's Pharaoh but maintain that Seti's son Ramses II was Pharaoh when Moses was born. Gordon and Rendsburg argue that the long stretch of time between Joseph and Moses mentioned at the beginning of Exodus is unlikely. They conclude that the biblical Exodus did not occur until around 1175 BCE, when Egypt was at war with the so-called Sea Peoples, a collection of Mediterranean groups who included the Philistines. The Exodus account supports this theory, as it says that the Israelites detoured away from the "way of the land of the Philistines" to avoid getting caught in the crossfire.

• A far more radical view comes from Charles Pellegrino in *Return to Sodom and Gomorrah*. Using a starkly different dating system, and geological evidence resulting from a tremendous volcanic eruption on the Mediterranean island of Thera in 1628 BCE, Pellegrino shows how each of the plagues—the red Nile, the darkened skies, etc.—could have been related to the aftermath of this explosion. The Thera eruption, Pellegrino argues, was fifty to one hundred times more powerful than the devastating 1883 CE explosion of Krakatoa. Pellegrino presses this notion further to suggest that the aftereffects of that eruption would have also affected the Mediterranean, spawning powerful tsunamis—or tidal waves—that might explain the parting of the seas and the drowning of the Egyptian army. In Pellegrino's view, this would push the dating of Moses in Egypt and the Exodus back much earlier than is commonly accepted. His choice for the Exodus Pharaoh is Thutmosis III.

Pellegrino writes:

> The biblical path taken by the people who left Egypt—
> south into Sinai—makes perfect sense if, indeed, one of
> the migrations took place during the time of Thera and
> Thutmosis III. . . . Anyone leaving Egypt, and not in the
> pharaoh's good graces, would have wanted to avoid both

Canaan and the shore road leading to it. The only safe route was south, into the Sinai Peninsula (whose coasts, incidentally, provided some of the best fishing in the world and could have easily sustained a population of migrants). Because Thutmosis III had placed military outposts along the north shore of Sinai and along the coast of Canaan, some of his soldiers would inevitably have come to harm from Theran tsunamis.... It then became but a small step from interpreting the tsunami and the ash fall as divine punishment on Egypt.... (pp. 240–241)

Does it really matter, a few hundred years here or there, one Pharaoh or another? Spiritually speaking, it doesn't really make a difference, if you accept the biblical version. But historians like things to be a little neater. Imagine in some distant future, a historical discussion in which the English "sea dog" Sir Francis Drake is said to have led a fleet of sailing ships against Hitler's navy. Drake's 1588 victory over the Spanish Armada is only 350 years removed from World War II, a blink of the eye when set against Egyptian history.

POSSIBLE EXODUS PHARAOHS
(Dates from *Chronicle of the Pharaohs* by Peter Clayton)

Ramses I	1292–1290 BCE
Sethos (Seti) I	1290–1279 BCE
	Cyrus Gordon's choice for Joseph's Pharaoh
Ramses II	1279–1212 BCE
	Consensus favorite for the Exodus Pharaoh
Merneptah	1212–1202 BCE
	He led Egypt in a battle against the Israelites, indicating that they were already in Canaan.
Amenmesses	1202–1199 BCE
Sethos II	1199–1193 BCE
Siptah	1193–1187 BCE

Teosret	1187–1185 BCE
Setnakthe	1185–1182 BCE
Ramses III	1182–1151 BCE
	Cyrus Gordon's choice for the Exodus Pharaoh

Whoever the cruel Pharaoh of Exodus was, there is another noteworthy footnote to the history of Jewish forced labor. King Solomon, one of the greatest Jewish kings, also put his own Israelite subjects to work constructing his massive public works projects a few hundred years later. His fellow Hebrews were no happier doing it for Solomon than they had been for the Pharaoh.

Which sea did the Israelites cross?

Crushed by the final, terrible plague, Pharaoh relents and Moses gathers the tribes to make a hasty getaway. Bread is prepared without leavening—hence the tradition of Passover matzoh bread, a reminder that eating a flat loaf as free people is better than a whole loaf as slaves. The account in Exodus claims that six hundred thousand men left Egypt. Adding women and children, more than a million Hebrews had to gather up their things on short notice and leave. Setting out for the Promised Land, the liberated Israelites are led by God in the form of a "pillar of cloud" by day and a "pillar of fire" by night. Then Pharaoh has a change of heart—actually God tells Moses he will "harden" the Pharaoh's heart, provoking him to follow Moses and the Hebrews. Pharaoh sends out six hundred chariots—three men to a chariot, or eighteen hundred soldiers—in hot pursuit of these million-odd people. Pressed up against the waters of the "Red Sea," with six hundred chariots bearing down on them, the Hebrews have second thoughts and wonder if they weren't better off as slaves. But Moses asks God for help and he is told to stretch his staff across the water. This is where DeMille and Charlton Heston fudged the biblical version. As the pillar of flame holds off the Egyptians, a strong wind blows all night; the parting is not instantaneous. The next day the waters divide, allowing the Israelites to pass through. When the Egyptians follow, the wheels of the chariots get stuck in the mud and the waters return, drowning the entire army in the waters of the "Red Sea."

Most scholars recognize that even if "Red Sea" had been correct, the Israelites would have crossed the Gulf of Suez, the northern arm of the Red Sea that reaches into Egypt, separating the Sinai Peninsula from Egypt. However, "Red Sea" is now recognized as a mistranslation. The commonly accepted correction is "Sea of Reeds," a mysterious body of water that has not yet been identified with certainty. One possible alternative is Lake Timsah, a shallow lake north of the Gulf of Suez. Another is the marshland on the Nile Delta where papyrus reeds commonly grow. An alternative suggestion is that the correct translation is "Sea at the End of the World," suggesting that the Israelites were leaving the known world of "Egypt" for a mysterious wilderness. The route to the Sinai is also a subject for speculation. The most commonly accepted Exodus route is south out of Egypt into the Sinai desert following the eastern shore of the Gulf of Suez to a temporary camp near the biblical Mount Sinai. This theory places Mount Sinai in the far south of the Sinai Peninsula, and is now traditionally associated with Jebel Musa ("Mount of Moses") in the southern Sinai Peninsula. That identification was made, however, by Christians around the fourth century CE. Others argue for a more northern route to "Shur," another obscure reference in Exodus, which places Mount Sinai/Horeb at Jebel Halal, much farther north on the peninsula, closer to modern Israel. The most recent theory to make headlines is that laid out in *The Gold of Exodus,* which places Mount Sinai in the Arabian desert. In Howard Blum's book, two amateur archaeologists claim that they found Sinai in a secret excavation performed without the permission of the Saudi authorities. Their claim has not yet been authenticated by anyone else.

Short of new discoveries, all of these theories of the Exodus remain just that. What is far more widely accepted is that the number of Hebrews who left Egypt had to have been far smaller than the hundreds of thousands mentioned in the Bible. There are several possible explanations for this incredible number. One is that the number in Exodus reflects a census made much later, in Israel. Others suggest a mistranslation of "thousand." If the word "thousand" is read instead as "troop," or a "contingent" of six to nine men each, it is far more plausible. A third suggestion is that in biblical numerology this figure represented a "perfect" number.

Besides "downsizing" the number of Israelites who depart from Egypt, most historians now accept the idea that other tribes who would later call themselves Israelites were already settled in Canaan when the wilderness contingent eventually arrives, as the Bible version itself later shows in Judges. This "revision" makes the Exodus an event that happened to a smaller number of Israelites who left Egypt and gradually relocated to Canaan in a natural wave of emigration rather than the "Conquest." But over time, that story was gradually expanded and embellished into the national epic that only emerged after centuries of retelling.

BIBLICAL VOICES

> Sing to the Lord, for he has
>   triumphed gloriously,
> horse and rider he has thrown into
>   the sea. (Exodus 15:21)

"The Song of Miriam," a victory chant led by the sister of Moses after the Israelites crossed the Sea of Reeds, is thought to be one of the oldest poetic verses in Hebrew scriptures; some scholars suggest that it may have been composed by an eyewitness to the event.

PLOT SUMMARY: THE TEN COMMANDMENTS

Having safely arrived in the Sinai desert, the Israelites find themselves dry but hungry. Like kids in the backseat on a long car trip, they start to complain, a problem that will become persistent for Moses. They are thirsty. They are hungry. These are not happy campers. Things were much better back in Egypt. It is not a flattering portrait of a group recently released from slavery and saved by God's miraculous intervention.

God again provides food in the form of "manna," an English translation derived from the Hebrew words *Man hu* for "What is it?" In *The Five Books of Moses*, Everett Fox suggests that an appropriate playful translation of *manna* is "whaddayacallit" (p. 348). Exodus mentions that quails came each evening and the manna was there in the morning, leading some to surmise it was bird droppings. Others suggest that there is a dewlike substance found on the tamarisk tree that is actually excreted by an insect. Whichever it was, it sounds unappealing, and any attempts at a natural explanation for "manna," as Everett Fox notes, miss the point of the story: divine providence kept the Children of Israel alive. Alive, but still complaining. They all remembered that Egyptian food was a lot better.

As the grumbling continues, God directs Moses to bring the people to the mountain; he will speak to them. God tells Moses to have the people wash their clothes, not to touch the holy mountain (Sinai here), and to refrain from sex for three days. In a cloud, accompanied by thunder and lightning and trumpets blowing, God descends from heaven to the top of Mount Sinai. God warns Moses not to let the people get too close and look at the divine presence. Moses reminds God that he already said the people can't touch Sinai, so God says, "Then go get Aaron." Then, in the first delivery of the Ten Commandments, God speaks. Afraid of the smoke and noise, the people think it would be a good idea for Moses just to go and talk to God alone.

THE TEN COMMANDMENTS (EXODUS 20: 1–17 KJV)

And God spake all these words, saying,

(1st) I am the Lord thy God, which have brought thee out of the land of Egypt, out of the house of bondage. *(In the Jewish tradition, this is the first "commandment," or more precisely, "statement.")*

Thou shalt have no other gods before me. *(Jewish tradition combines this with the following verse to make the second commandment/statement.)*

(2d) Thou shalt not make unto thee any graven image, or any likeness of anything that is in heaven above, or that is in the earth beneath, or that is in the water under the earth:

Thou shalt not bow down thyself to them, nor serve them: for I the Lord thy God am a jealous God, visiting the iniquity of the fathers upon the children unto the third and fourth generation of them that hate me.

And shewing mercy unto thousands of them that love me, and keep my commandments.

(3d) Thou shalt not take the name of the Lord thy God in vain; for the Lord will not hold him guiltless that taketh his name in vain.

(4th) Remember the sabbath day, to keep it holy.

Six days shalt thou labor and do all thy work:

But the seventh day is the sabbath of the Lord thy God: in it thou shalt not do any work, thou, nor thy son, nor thy daughter, thy manservant, nor thy maidservant, nor thy cattle, nor thy stranger that is within thy gates:

For in six days the Lord made heaven and earth, the sea, and all that in them is, and rested the seventh day: wherefore the Lord blessed the sabbath day, and hallowed it.

(5th) Honor thy father and thy mother: that thy days may be long upon the land which the Lord thy God giveth thee.

(6th) Thou shalt not kill.

(7th) Thou shalt not commit adultery.

(8th) Thou shalt not steal.

(9th) Thou shalt not bear false witness against thy neighbor.

(10th) Thou shalt not covet thy neighbor's house, thou shalt not covet thy neighbor's wife, nor his manservant, nor his maidservant, nor his ox, nor his ass, nor any thing that is thy neighbor's.

The first round of commandments is given orally—no mention of tablets is made yet. Moses must go back onto the mountain for forty days and is given a long set of specifications for how to build the Ark (chest) of the Covenant that will hold the tablets, and descriptions of how priests should dress. Only at the end of those forty days does Moses come back with the "two tablets of the covenant, tablets of stone, written with the finger of God." (Ex. 31:18)

The Ten Commandments: A Modern Take on Some Ancient Laws

A cartoon by the madcap artist Gahan Wilson once appeared in *Playboy* magazine. In it, a group of people in elaborate vestments bowed and worshiped before an enormous letter "N." The caption read, "Nothing is sacred."

If anything is still widely considered sacred today, presumably it is the Ten Commandments. Two cases that attracted wide media attention in America recently gave proof of that perception. First, the state legislature in Tennessee attempted to pass a law requiring that the Ten Commandments be posted on the walls of all public buildings, including courts and schoolrooms. Then in Alabama a judge was told to remove a plaque featuring the Ten Commandments from his courtroom wall. When he refused, the judge became a hero to thousands of people. The state's governor, throwing his support behind the judge, threatened to call out the militia to defend the judge's right to post the commandments. While the sacredness of the Ten Commandments has always been held up as central to American law and virtue, people through the centuries have done a pretty poor job when it comes to obeying them. Even Israel's greatest national hero, King David, didn't fare too well when it came to following the commandments. He broke the Sabbath rule at least once—as Jesus also later does—and he murdered, committed adultery, and coveted. God struck many people dead—Onan and the people of Sodom come to mind—for much less grievous sins.

With that in mind, take a closer look at the Ten Commandments and see just how well modern society does in observing this basic, presumably immutable, set of rules.

First of all, most people would be hard-pressed to name all ten. In his book *Sources of Strength*, Jimmy Carter cites the man who thinks the seventh commandment is "Thou shalt not *admit* adultery." The fact is that most of the adulation given to the Ten Commandments is little more than lip service. The version shown above is the King James Version, the most commonly known Christian translation. Besides changing the order of the Hebrew commandments, the "Authorized Version" mangled some of the ancient Hebrew words, and more faithful translations show some interesting and very significant differences, especially regarding the sixth commandment, against "killing," and the substitution of "impassioned God" for "jealous God" in the second commandment.

1. *"I am the Lord thy God, which have brought thee out of the land of Egypt, out of the house of bondage.*
   Thou shalt have no other gods before me."
Interesting. God didn't say, "I am the only God," but rather that he is Number One. God doesn't even say don't worship any other god, only not to put another god before him. This is a reflection of the times and circumstances. The tribes of Israel were wanderers in lands of many gods—Canaanite, Egyptian, Mesopotamian. Moving into the "Promised Land," they confronted the fertility cult gods of Canaan, including the creator god El, whose name was adapted by the Hebrews, the notorious storm god Baal, and his numerous consorts, including Asherah and Astarte. We have come to take for granted the idea that Judaism invented the notion of "One God" right from the start. But the original conception of Israel's Yahweh was the greatest among many, and only over time did Yahweh evolve into the "One God," meaning the *only* God.

Most modern believers have no trouble with the first commandment, taking it in the most literal sense. Although it does give pause to wonder if the God of an Orthodox Jew is the God of Pat Robertson or Jesse Jackson or the God (Allah) of an Iranian ayatollah.

The notion of a single God as the "True God" opens up the gates of intolerance. If people are really expected to hold the Ten Commandments, with its Judeo-Christian God, as an ideal for behavior, what does society do about all the other gods worshiped in a modern, pluralistic world? And then what happens to all those who choose to deny God's existence? Granting this commandment the authority of "law of the land" clearly places such people in jeopardy of being second-class citizens, or even worse, dispensable.

But there is another way to look at the first commandment. What do people really worship? There are many "other gods" worshiped in the modern world. They just have different names. Money. Alcohol. Success. Sex. Shopping. All of these are, in varying degrees, objects of worship. Lesser gods, perhaps, but still pursued with the kind of devotion that old Yahweh wanted to reserve for himself. Maybe the admonition to have no "other gods" is still a wise one.

2. *"Thou shalt not make unto thee any graven image, or any likeness of anything that is in heaven above, or that is in the earth beneath, or that is in the water under the earth...."*

This was clearly another rule reflecting the time and place in which Moses delivered the commandments. Idol worship, household gods, and magic amulets were all in widespread use at the presumed time of the Exodus and for centuries after, especially in Canaan.

In a modern context, few people worship "idols" in the sense given in Exodus. In his insightful book, *Biblical Literacy*, Rabbi Joseph Telushkin offers a useful insight on this commandment:

> From Judaism's perspective, idolatry occurs when one holds any value (for instance, nationalism) higher than

God. Thus, a person who, on the basis of "my country
right or wrong," performs acts that God designates as
wrong is an idolater; his behavior makes it clear that he regards his country's demand to do evil as more binding than
God's demand to do good. Such a person's claim to worship God—an assertion that was actually made by S.S. officers who worked in concentration camps—is plainly false;
the person is an idolater, not a follower of God. (p. 425)

That still leaves open the problem posed by Michelangelo or
the University of Notre Dame's "Touchdown Jesus." Michelangelo's ceiling of the Sistine Chapel, with its God reaching out to
give Adam life, and the *Pietà*, a statue of Mary and the dead Jesus,
are clearly "images" of God. There can be little question that
Notre Dame's famed statue of Jesus, hands upraised like a football
referee, is a "sculptured image." Taking the commandment literally, what do we make of highly venerated Christian statues honoring saints or the Mother of Jesus or even a medallion of the
crucified Jesus?

The commandment is quite clear—"You shall not make for
yourself a sculptured image, or any likeness of what is in the heavens." (Ex. 20:4 JPS) The best case to be made for all the great
religious artworks of the past few centuries is that they might
break the letter of the law but not the spirit. Michelangelo surely
expected the Pope who commissioned him to appreciate his artwork without worshiping it. On the other hand, many devout believers fervently kneel before statues in hopeful prayer. Are they
"worshiping" graven images?

Some Christians, particularly those Protestant denominations
that emerged during the Reformation, rejected elaborate church
buildings and certain religious practices in favor of a "purer" religion devoid of symbols and statuary—that's how the "Puritans"
got their name. To them, the religious statues and the magnificent
cathedrals built to display these artistic works contradicted the
commandment and the spirit of Jesus' teachings. One of the clear-

est themes in the ministry of Jesus is his contempt for outward expressions of empty piety in favor of the importance of inner, spiritual "wealth." He also railed against material riches on a number of occasions, telling one would-be disciple to sell all his belongings if he wanted to follow him. It is difficult to imagine that the Jesus who counseled that the rich would have a hard time getting into the kingdom of heaven would be pleased with the earthly treasures piled up by churches in his name during the past two thousand years.

3. *"Thou shalt not take the name of the Lord thy God in vain."*

Taught to most of us when we were children as an injunction against shouting "G————t" when you bang your finger with a hammer, this commandment is another that has slipped a few notches in terms of universal acceptance.

In Jewish tradition, the commandment came to be viewed as a prohibition against saying or writing the name of God at all. However, the original intent was more specific. The law related to the misuse of God's name in attempting to cast a magic spell or perform any sort of incantation of divination. In another sense, it related very clearly to giving sworn testimony, a sense better conveyed by the Jewish Publication Society translation: "You shall not swear falsely by the name of the Lord your God; for the Lord will not clear one who swears falsely by His name." In modern terms, the commandment might say, "Don't perjure yourself."

The society that developed in ancient Israel is notable for its very highly defined sense of legality. Just as other ancient Near East cultures were beginning to develop law codes to order society, the Israelites held to a highly rigid code, given to them by God, that regulated religious, personal, social, and commercial conduct. These cultures were all trying to move from primitive justice codes to a well-ordered society in which the law, not simply the king's will, was obeyed. With that in mind, the belief that testimony given in a "court" was sacred was an enormous step forward for establishing the supremacy of "law and order."

Another interpretation is that the verse relates not just to words but also to actions taken in God's name, reflected in certain translations of the Hebrew that read "You shall not carry the name of the Lord." This commandment, as Rabbi Joseph Telushkin comments, is also aimed at those who commit sins in "the name of God." Telushkin writes: "If they 'carry' God's name in promotion of a cause that is evil (e.g., the medieval crusaders who murdered innocent people in the name of God, or members of racist organizations such as the Ku Klux Klan that claim what they do is God's will), then they violate the Third Commandment." (*Biblical Literacy*, pp. 426–427)

4. "Remember the Sabbath day, to keep it holy."

First of all, note it does not say the Lord "hallowed it for NFL football." Does watching six to eight hours of sports on Sunday count as keeping the Sabbath holy? "Sabbath" is derived from an ancient Hebrew word that meant "coming or bringing to an end" that evolved into the word *shabat*, "rested." The idea of Sabbath has changed immensely in the modern world. Anyone who likes shopping in the mall on Sunday may have forgotten the days when many businesses were not permitted to open on Sunday. There was a time not so long ago in America when local "blue laws" kept stores shuttered on Sunday in an attempt to legislate compliance with the God-ordained Sabbath—the Christian Sabbath, that is. The Jewish Sabbath, commencing on Friday at sunset through Saturday, was never the Sabbath honored in Christian-dominated America.

For the most part, these old laws legislating Sabbath morality have gone the way of many other social dinosaurs, but there are still vestiges of Sabbath blue laws in America. In New York City—long famed as "Sin City"—you still cannot buy a bottle of wine or vodka from a liquor store on Sunday, even though you can buy beer in a grocery store after noon and order a drink in a restaurant. Go figure.

Of course, Christians have no monopoly on circumventing Sabbath holiness rules. Many observant Jews have long found ways to get around the spirit, if not the letter, of the law. Before the days of modern electrical timers that could turn televisions and other appliances on or off, Jews commonly employed Christians—"sabbath goys"—to perform certain predetermined services, such as turning on their lights. This might seem a rather lighthearted issue. But in Israel, there is a serious contemporary conflict over doing business on the Jewish Sabbath. Politically powerful Orthodox Jews respect the Sabbath Commandment, and the Israeli government respects that view. This is not a new argument. When the Maccabees of Israel rebelled against their Syrian rulers in 166–164 BCE, some of the most faithful Jews refused to fight on the Sabbath, preferring death to desecrating the holy day. While not as ultimate a sacrifice, sports fans and moviegoers may recall the Olympian who refused to race on the Sabbath, the story told in *Chariots of Fire*. And baseball fans of a certain age may remember Sandy Koufax, one of the greatest pitchers of all time, who wouldn't pitch on Jewish holy days.

This is one commandment that Jesus openly disobeyed. He and his disciples were accused by the priests and rabbis of Jerusalem of violating the commandment by "laboring" on the Sabbath. Jesus responded to his Sabbath-day critics in two ways. First, he said the things he was doing on the Sabbath, such as healing the sick, were too important to put off. And Jesus also professed a belief that internal holiness, an inner sense of spirituality, was more important than the "show-off" piety, typified by the Sabbath templegoers who outwardly kept God's commandments but then behaved badly the rest of the week.

While it is clear that the Sabbath "ain't what it used to be," it might be worth reexamining its value. In a society that has increasingly placed work above all else—either in the form of multiple jobs to make ends meet or bringing home the laptop to crunch some numbers—it might be a good thing for people to respect the significance of creating "holy" time. Whether people use it to go back to traditional religious observations, or to quietly meditate, or simply to spend more time together as families, most of us would do well to "consecrate" some time not just for "resting" but for reflection, contemplation, and good works.

5. *"Honor thy father and thy mother: that thy days may be long upon the land that the Lord thy God giveth thee."*

This is the commandment every parent loves. They use it to tell their kids what to do all the time. American politicians adhere to it as well. Old people vote more than young people, so they have become a potent political force and their wishes are "honored."

Again, it is a commandment that demands an examination of its historical context. In a semi-nomadic desert culture, the elderly were often more of a burden than a blessing. This commandment was aimed at protecting the elderly and sick from being abandoned to the elements once they were no longer productive members of the tribe. It was easy to drop Grandpa off by the side of the camel path instead of dragging him around every time you packed up the tents.

Christians need to double-check this one against Jesus' words because, on several occasions, he said and did things that seemed to flout the fifth commandment. He spoke of his own mother and other family members in what seem to be disparaging terms. "No one can come to me without hating his own father, mother, sister, brother." (Luke 14:26). Hardly sounds like "honor," though Jesus was clearly saying that membership in his spiritual "family" was stronger than ties of blood.

Many people doubt that such a commandment demands unqualified acceptance. Does the physically or emotionally abused child have to "honor" an abusive parent? Sadly, an observer of the modern world might conclude that, in an era of increasingly commonplace physical and sexual abuse of children, perhaps a better commandment would be "Honor thy children."

6. *"Thou shalt not kill."*

Oops. This is another critical King James Version mistranslation of the original Hebrew. The correct reading is "You shall not murder" (NRSV, JPS, and others). As the rest of the Hebrew scriptures clearly indicate, God had no problem with certain forms of killing: the death penalty was invoked for a wide variety of offenses, including house burglary, striking one's parents, adultery, bestiality, and homosexuality. God also gave very unambiguous directions that Israel's enemies were to be killed in the conquest of Canaan and in the later battles with the Philistines. God not only sanctioned killing Israel's enemies but often acted as an accomplice.

So killing for some moral purpose—killing a killer to prevent a death, or killing a Hitler—is viewed as acceptable. Of course, that opens up a nasty can of worms: Who decides what is "moral" killing? Before the the American Civil War, abolitionist John Brown felt that killing was justified to free slaves. In the fall of 1997, during the Iraq weapons inspection crisis, *New York Times* columnist Thomas Friedman suggested assassinating Saddam Hussein. Some extreme anti-abortionists believe killing doctors who perform abortions is "moral." A significant number of Americans believe that Dr. Kevorkian's "assisted suicides" should be legal. Which ambiguous forms of killing, such as abortion, suicide, euthanasia, and capital punishment, fall under the constraints of the sixth commandment? It all falls on your definition of "murder."

7. *"Thou shalt not commit adultery."*

Not even in the White House. Adultery ain't what it used to be. In an era when the private lives of public people are displayed on the evening news and at the supermarket checkout, it is definitely time to rethink adultery. In 1997, a young woman pilot was kicked out of the U.S. Air Force for having an affair and then lying about it. That's actually two broken commandments: adultery and false witness. Pretty soon, the Pentagon was issuing more Scarlet

Letters than Purple Hearts. A couple of generals got into trouble over their old affairs and a potential candidate for the highest-ranking post in the American military was forced to withdraw from consideration because of an affair he had thirteen years earlier. These stories were all a prelude to the "Clinton Follies," a series of scandals that left the American people shrugging their shoulders at the thought of their president being unfaithful to his wife.

Viewed against this upheaval in social attitudes, this is a commandment that first must be viewed through ancient eyes. Adultery in ancient Israel was not exactly the crime we think of today. Ancient Israel was a polygamous society, so this commandment was primarily directed at women. Although it applied to a man who committed adultery with a married woman, adultery was viewed as a crime against the husband and it demanded the death penalty.

Jesus complicated things for Christians with this one because he said that just looking at a woman the wrong way was the moral equivalent of adultery. In his Sermon on the Mount, Jesus says everyone who looks at a woman with lust in his heart has already committed adultery.

When President Jimmy Carter once told an interviewer from *Playboy* magazine, of all places, that he'd committed adultery many times "in his heart," Carter had Jesus' admonition in mind and was expressing the highly moralistic view that conceiving the sin is as bad as doing it. While the modern take on adultery is considerably more forgiving, it is still somewhat schizophrenic. We think it's wrong but don't stone adulterers in the town square any longer. Most Americans—and even more Europeans—seem to shrug off adultery. Poor Hester Prynne, Nathaniel Hawthorne's nineteenth-century heroine. She was just ahead of her time. Adultery certainly isn't *The Scarlet Letter* any longer.

8. *"Thou shalt not steal."*

This one is pretty straightforward, although Jewish commentators note that the eighth commandment referred to kidnapping as well as the simple theft of goods—and kidnapping was a death-penalty offense. Rabbi Telushkin also points out that the law code specified penalties for crimes such as stealing, and compensation to the victim was mandated. A thief was required to repay double the value of what was stolen; servitude was required if the thief could not pay the fine.

Again with this commandment there are some moral imperatives to weigh: Would you steal food to feed a starving child? Would it be wrong to steal military secrets relating to the creation of destructive weapons from an enemy to defend your nation?

9. *"Thou shalt not bear false witness against thy neighbor."*

Although it is now thought of as an injunction against lying in general, this commandment originally referred to telling the truth in a legal dispute, reinforcing the sacredness of testimony in court already noted in the third commandment.

Even if taken in the widest sense of "lying," the false-witness commandment still has some gray areas. Certainly the people who concealed Anne Frank and her family in their attic to protect them from the Nazis "lied" to the Gestapo. But most would agree that in breaking the commandment, they had done nothing wrong. On the contrary, to have told the truth would have been the real crime against God.

Another broader interpretation of the commandment likens "false witness against neighbors" to gossip, the malicious, destructive whispering that can destroy reputations. Imagine if breaking this commandment brought down a bolt of heavenly lightning. No more talk-show television or supermarket tabloids!

10. *"Thou shalt not covet thy neighbor's house, thou shalt not covet thy neighbor's wife . . . nor any thing that is thy neighbor's."*

The American Heritage Dictionary says that to covet is "to feel blameworthy desire for that which is another's" or "to wish for longingly." This commandment is somewhat unique in that it sees sin in thought as opposed to a specific action.

The problem with the tenth commandment is that most modern consumer economies and the entire advertising industry are built on "coveting." The whole purpose of TV and magazine commercials or billboards is to get us to "wish for longingly"—to covet that Mercedes or that cigarette. So does that make us all sinners? Rabbi Telushkin offers this wisdom: "It is not wrong to want more than you have. What is wrong is to want it at your neighbor's expense. There's no evil in desiring a Jaguar, only in wanting the one belonging to the person next door."

BIBLICAL VOICES

And you are not to ascend my slaughter-site by ascending steps, that your nakedness not be laid-bare upon it. (Ex. 20:23 *Five Books of Moses*)

When you sell your daughter as a slave, do you have to give a warranty?

When they told you about the Ten Commandments, they didn't mention that God didn't want you looking under the priest's skirt either? Moses got a great many laws from God. And more than a few of them need some explaining.

Witnessing God's amazing sound and light show on top of Sinai—seeing the lightning and smoke, and hearing the thunder—the Israelites decided it would be better if Moses went up and talked to God one-on-one while they stood "at a distance." So Moses drew near to the "thick darkness" where God was. Then God proceeded to give Moses a much longer list of laws. The Ten Commandments were only the beginning of the Law, the tip of a *Titanic*-sized iceberg at that. The commandments might be called the "Big Ten," but the next few chapters in Exodus, referred to as the "Book of the Covenant," along with the rest of the Torah, were devoted to an extensive set of laws that governed everything from basic morality and religious behavior to a wide array of social guidelines for almost every aspect of an Israelite's life.

The simple notion that Moses went up once, got the tablets, and came down has no relation to the far more complex story of the giving of the laws, as laid out in in Exodus. Moses goes up and down Sinai like a yo-yo, making eight trips that take several months to complete. In some places it says God wrote the laws, and in others, Moses wrote the laws. This is one more major section of the Bible where scholars have shown convincingly that at least three separate versions of the events at Mount Sinai—back to good old J, P, and E, those authors introduced back in the first section of this book—were woven together to get the somewhat jumbled version told in Exodus.

This is also a place where the Bible gets tricky for those who still want to take the Bible and biblical law literally. Jewish tradition identifies 613 Laws in the Torah. Many of them governed sacrificial rites no longer performed by Jews or Christians. In other words, most of us no longer believe that "worship" and the forgiveness of sins require cutting up small animals.

What follows is a small sampling of some of the many laws that Moses gave to the people of Israel in Exodus. They should remind modern readers that the Bible was composed a long time ago for a very different group of people. This is where people have to determine what is law appropriate to desert nomads four thousand years ago, and which are universal laws that transcend time and setting:

• "When you buy a male Hebrew slave, he shall serve six years, but in the seventh he shall go out a free person, without debt. . . . But if the slave declares, 'I love my master, my wife and my children; I will not go out a free person,' then his master shall bring him before God. He shall be brought to the door or the doorpost; and his master shall pierce his ear with an awl." (Ex. 21:2–6)

Here is a good example of the altered ethical and moral standards from biblical times to the present day. Many passages in the

Bible condone slavery, one reason it was justified by American Christian slaveholders. We can only consider slavery an inhumane and immoral institution, a very clear case of something that was acceptable in the time of Moses but is now considered reprehensible.

• "When a man sells his daughter as a slave, she shall not go out as the male slaves do. If she does not please her master, who designated her for himself, then he shall let her be redeemed; he shall have no right to sell her to a foreign people.... If he designates her for his son, he shall deal with her as with a daughter. If he takes another wife to himself, he shall not diminish the food, clothing or marital rights of the first wife." (Ex. 21:7–10)

The connotation of this passage, confirmed elsewhere many times over, is that a woman in ancient Israel was approximately the equivalent of a slave. While there are people who still believe that this is the way things were meant to be between the sexes, that is no longer the majority view.

• "Whoever curses father or mother shall be put to death." (Ex. 21:17)

The Hammurabi code, usually much more stern and containing many more death-penalty offenses, actually saw this law differently. For the same offense, Hammurabi said the person should lose a hand, not his life.

• "When people who are fighting injure a pregnant woman so that there is a miscarriage, and yet no further harm follows, the one responsible shall be fined what the woman's husband demands. ... If any harm follows, then you shall give life for life, eye for eye, tooth for tooth, hand for hand, foot for foot, burn for burn, wound for wound, stripe for stripe." (Ex. 21:22–24)

This often misquoted passage meant that punishment and justice must be evenhanded and compensation should be equal to the crime. It was meant to limit people from exacting vengeance out of proportion to the wrong that had been done to them.

• "When an ox gores a man or a woman to death, the ox shall be stoned, and its flesh shall not be eaten; but the owner of the ox shall not be liable. If the ox has been accustomed to gore in the past, and its owner has been warned but has not restrained it, and it kills a man or a woman, the ox shall be stoned, and its owner shall be put to death. . . . If the ox gores a male or female slave, the owner shall pay to the slave owner thirty shekels of silver, and the ox shall be stoned." (Ex. 21:28–33)

• "If someone leaves a pit open, or digs a pit and does not cover it, and an ox or a donkey falls into it, the owner of the pit shall make restitution, giving money to its owner, but keeping the dead animal." (Ex. 21:33–34)

• "If a thief is found breaking in, and is beaten to death, no blood guilt is incurred; but it if happens after sunrise, blood guilt is incurred." (Ex. 22:2–3)

To incur "blood guilt" meant to be considered a murderer. In other words, you could legally kill a thief in your home in the night; but in the light of day, one would presumably have other means of stopping a thief besides killing.

• "Nor put a curse upon a chieftain among your people." (Ex. 22:27)

This law prohibits cursing the leader of one's nation. Remember that when your taxes are due.

Following a section of "case law" dealing with making restitution for lost, damaged, or stolen sheep and other livestock, Exodus adds:

• "When a man seduces a virgin who is not engaged to be

married, and lies with her, he shall give the bride-price for her and make her his wife. But if her father refuses to give her to him, he shall pay an amount equal to the bride-price for virgins." (Ex. 22: 16–17)

- "You shall not permit a female sorcerer to live." (Ex. 22:18)
- "Whoever lies with an animal shall be put to death." (Ex. 22:19)
- "You shall not wrong or oppress a resident alien, for you were aliens in the land of Egypt." (Ex. 22:21)

These last four laws, rather incongruously grouped together, point up the vagaries of "obeying" the Bible. Obviously, modern folks have very different ideas about virginity, marriage, and bride-prices than Moses did. The women who offer advice on "Psychic Hot Lines" are annoying, but do you want to strap them into the electric chair? Bestiality is indeed icky to most of us. But a capital crime?

Plot Summary: The Golden Calf

Moses has been up and down the mountain once, and then goes back again, this time for forty days and nights. He is going to be given a very specific set of directions on how to build the sacred dwelling place for God, the Tabernacle designed to be portable so the Israelites can carry it with them, and the special Ark of the Covenant in which the tablets with the Ten Commandments are to be stored. But while Moses and God are sorting out the design plans and the laws, the people get impatient. They tell Aaron, the brother of Moses, to make them a new god. Aaron doesn't put up much of an argument and takes all the gold earrings and rings in the camp, melts them down, and casts them into a golden calf that the people dance around.

God is not happy about this and sends Moses down. He smashes the tablet containing the law and grinds the calf into dust. Then he spreads the dust on the water and makes the people drink it. God follows this with a plague on the camp. Moses asks for the loyal to stand by him, and all the Levites rally to his side. They take out their swords and kill three thousand people.

For his role in this mischief, Aaron gets away scot-free, and his alibi is amusing: he tells Moses he threw the gold into the fire and the calf emerged! Moses apparently accepts his brother's explanation.

After this purge, Moses gets two more pieces of stone for new tablets. This gets a little tricky because God says he will write them. Then a few verses later God tells Moses to write the laws, which he does, bringing back the fresh set of commandments.

BIBLICAL VOICES

The Lord said to Moses, "Go, leave this place, you and the people whom you have brought up out of the land of Egypt, and go to the land which I swore to Abraham, Isaac and Jacob, saying, 'To your descendants I will give it.' I will send an angel before you, and I will drive out the Canaanites, the Amorites, the Hittites, the Perizzites, the Hivites, and the Jebusites. Go up to a land flowing with milk and honey; but I will not go up among you, or I would consume you on the way, for you are a stiff-necked people." (Ex. 33:1–3)

Forty Years on the Road

Leviticus, Numbers, Deuteronomy

Thou shalt love thy neighbor as thyself. (Lev. 19:18 KJV)

And your children shall wander in the wilderness forty years. (Num. 14:33)

Thou shalt love the Lord thy God with all thine heart, and with all thy soul, and with all thy might. (Deut. 6:5 KJV)

✳

❋ What is "kosher"?

❋ Why can't Moses enter the Promised Land?

❋ What did the speaking donkey have to say?

❋ What is the "Great Commandment"?

❋ How does God feel about cross-dressing?

As good storytelling goes, the next three books of Moses—Leviticus, Numbers, and Deuteronomy—pale against the epic nature of the first two. All three books largely focus on restating, adding to, or even reinterpreting the elaborate ritual and religious law codes of Israel. That's one reason why you find another slightly different version of the Ten Commandments in Deuteronomy 5. It essentially says the same thing as the first, but has some alternative wording. You might think it was just fine the way it was the first time. And if Moses had written it down, why couldn't he keep it straight and read it the same way? But these sorts of repetitions and occasional contradictions in these books all serve to strengthen the multiple-author theory of Bible composition, where the hand of more than one writer is clearly at work.

While Genesis and Exodus were primarily "story books," Leviticus, Numbers, and Deuteronomy read more like the "fine print" in a contract that most folks try to avoid reading.

Leviticus

Leviticus (in Hebrew, *Vayikra*, "and he called") is primarily concerned with the laws given by God on a range of ritual and other religious matters. The English title, derived from the Greek and Latin versions of the Hebrew Bible, refers to the tribe of the Levites who were set apart as a priestly order. With little of the great narrative drive of the earlier books, Leviticus also lacks their memorable poetry and dramatic sweep. However, it is the book in which the biblical version of the "Golden Rule" first appears.

The elaborate laws outlined in Leviticus cover sacrifices and burnt offerings; the consecration of priests; the distinction between what is clean and unclean, including elaborate discussions of dietary laws; skin diseases such as leprosy; how to get rid of mold on your tents; rules regarding purification rites after childbirth and menstruation; the ceremony for the the annual Day of Atonement, or Yom Kippur, which was not celebrated before the sixth century BCE; and laws governing Israel's life as a holy people and the holy calendar.

It is now widely believed that Leviticus was compiled by priests of the Jerusalem Temple in the fifth century BCE. Composed as a training manual for the priesthood, the book painstakingly details how to sacrifice animals and the appropriate ceremonies for ordaining priests. The ancient Jewish practice of animal sacrifice, described in precise and elaborate detail in these books, was the centerpiece of Jewish worship for centuries. That practice ended with the destruction of the rebuilt Jerusalem Temple, the only place such sacrifices could be made, in 70 CE by the Romans. Then the discussion moves into the realm of the clean and unclean, focusing on which animals may or may not be eaten.

What is "kosher"?

Once every year, many supermarkets, particularly in metropolitan areas, clear off shelves to make room for foods that are "Kosher for Passover." Many non-Jews believe that "kosher" poultry and meat are cleaner, safer, and even better-tasting than nonkosher. And many people, Jew and Gentile alike, commonly ask if something is "kosher," loosely using the term to mean is it permissible or "okay." *Kosher* is a Yiddish word for "proper" that derives from the Hebrew word *kashrut*. Although the modern sense commonly associates "kosher" only with dietary laws, the notion of what is "proper" covers a broad range of items that must be done accordance with the law. The dietary laws, found in Leviticus and the following Torah books, not only specify which animals are proper to eat but also describe the precise methods by which the animals must be slaughtered and prepared. While many people think that kosher laws somehow relate to health issues—such as the notion that the pig was forbidden because it was responsible for diseases—most of the distinctions regarding "proper" foods relate to a more elusive and even subjective notion of "holiness" and "purity."

Okay to Eat:
- "any animal that has divided hoofs and is cleft-footed and chews the cud" except the camel, the rock badger, the hare, the pig
- "all that are in the waters" if they have fins and scales
- poultry, except for those below

Not Okay:
- eagle, vulture, osprey, buzzard, kite, raven, ostrich, nighthawk, seagull, hawk, little owl, cormorant, great owl, water hen, desert owl, the carrion vulture, the stork, the heron, the hoopoe, and the bat (not a bird of course, but this is the Bible, not a zoology text)
- shellfish
- all winged insects, unless they have "four legs and walk on the ground"
- all that walk on their "paws": the weasel, the mouse, the great lizard, the gecko, the land crocodile, the lizard, the sand lizard, and the chameleon
- all creatures that "swarm upon the earth," "whatever moves on its belly," and "whatever has many feet"

  There are also several specific warnings about "boiling a kid in its mother's milk," a somewhat mysterious rule that lives on in the kosher rule against mixing meat and dairy.

Moving from food to matters of birth, there are elaborate laws for purification after menstruation and childbirth. These are followed by long series of rules for coping with leprosy and other skin diseases and with mold in houses, before arriving at the question of the uncleanness of a man who has a "discharge from his member." Leviticus doesn't say there's anything wrong with this, only that you have to clean up afterward. "If a man has an emission of semen, he shall bathe his whole body in water, and be unclean until the evening." (Lev. 15:16)

BIBLICAL VOICES

The Lord spoke to Moses, saying,

"Speak to all the congregation of the people of Israel and say to them: You shall be holy, for I the Lord your God am holy. You shall each revere your mother and father, and you shall keep my sabbaths: I am the Lord your God. Do not turn to idols or make cast images for yourselves: I am the Lord your God. . . .

"You shall not steal; you shall not deal falsely; and you shall not lie to one another. And you shall not swear falsely by my name, profaning the name of your God: I am the Lord.

"You shall not defraud your neighbor; you shall not steal; and you shall not keep for yourself wages of a laborer until morning. You shall not revile the deaf or put a stumbling block before the blind; you shall fear your God: I am the Lord.

"You shall not render an unjust judgment; you shall not be partial to the poor or defer to the great: with justice you shall judge your neighbor. You shall not go around as a slanderer among your people, and you shall not profit by the blood of your neighbor: I am the Lord.

"You shall not hate in your heart anyone of your kin; you shall reprove your neighbor, or you will incur guilt yourself. You shall not take vengeance or bear a grudge against any of your people, but you shall love your neighbor as yourself."
(Lev. 19:1–18)

These verses, which lay out a plan for a "life of holiness," recap the commandments and expand them. While they remain valuable and valid rules of conduct, this "holiness code" is immediately followed, somewhat incongruously, by rules of a very different sort:

"You shall not let your animals breed with a different kind; you shall not sow your field with two kinds of seed; nor shall you put on a garment made of two different materials."

We don't know how God felt about mixing plaids and stripes.

Numbers

The English title refers to the census of the twelve tribes that opens the book. The Hebrew title, *Ba-Midbar* ("In the Wilderness"), is more accurately descriptive because the book begins with the decision to leave Sinai and cross the desert toward the Promised Land. The Israelites finally reach the oasis of Kadesh-barnea, where they spend most of the forty years in the wilderness. While much of the book is still concerned with laws, it also contains several highly charged dramatic episodes, including two separate rebellions against Moses and God, and the death of Aaron.

BIBLICAL VOICES

> The Lord bless you and keep you;
> the Lord make his face to shine
>   upon you, and be gracious
>   to you;
> the Lord lift up his countenance
>   upon you, and give you
>   peace. (Num. 6:24–26)

This is the "Aaronic benediction," given by God to Aaron. It is considered an extremely ancient blessing and is still widely used in temples and churches alike.

PLOT SUMMARY: DEPARTURE FROM SINAI

Finally, God gives Moses marching orders. After nearly a year spent at Sinai, the tribes move out. Once again, there is whining as the "rabble" voice their craving for meat. They are tired of manna. God is annoyed and sends so many birds over the camp the Israelites are nearly knee-deep in poultry, which they eat. But just to remind them who is in charge, God sends a plague on the complainers.

Aaron and Miriam get in the complaint line too. Miriam, Moses' sister, who had saved his life as a child and then helped Moses lead the people out of Egypt, and Aaron carp about their baby brother. Why is Moses so special? They consider themselves to be prophets and leaders of the people too. Why does Moses get all the attention from God? It's sibling rivalry gone cosmic. On top of that, they don't like Moses' wife, who is a "Cushite." This complaint is a little confusing and has led to some speculation— did Moses have a second wife? Zipporah was Midian, not a Cushite. Also, "Cushite" has been interpreted as "African," although Cush might be another word for Midian. Was Zipporah black? Was there a second wife? The Bible doesn't really say.

Annoyed at Aaron and Miriam's quibbles, God lashes out at the two renegade siblings. Miriam is afflicted with a skin disorder like leprosy and becomes "white as snow." Moses asks God to forgive her, and Big Sister is sent out of the camp for seven days until she is healed and "purified," or made ritually clean. Aaron, on the other hand, seems to get off easily, just as he did after making the golden calf. Most likely, the priestly writers saw themselves as, or actually were, descendants of Aaron and gave him good press. In other words, it's a little like reading a Republican party biography of Richard M. Nixon that glosses over Watergate and his resigning in disgrace.

BIBLICAL VOICES

> The Lord said to Moses, "Because you did not trust in me, to show my holiness before the eyes of the Israelites, therefore you shall not bring this assembly into the land that I have given them." (Num. 20:12)

Why can't Moses enter the Promised Land?

When God gets annoyed, look out. Even Moses gets in trouble. The reason for God's anger at Moses is not entirely laid out, although most interpreters believe that Moses and Aaron either took too much of the credit for a miracle when Moses struck a rock and water flowed out, or they didn't do it the way God told them to do it.

Aaron, whose death on Mount Hor, near Kadesh, is recorded in Numbers, and Moses both die without entering the Promised Land.

But God doesn't let up with just the two of them. Fed up with the constant grumbling and grousing of the Israelites, God later tells Moses, "Not one of these—not one of this evil generation— shall see the good land that I swore to give to your ancestors." (Deut. 1:35)

With the exception of Joshua and Caleb, none of those who left Egypt in the Exodus will enter the Promised Land.

What did the speaking donkey have to say?

"A horse is a horse of course of course/Unless, of course, he's a talking horse." So goes the theme song to one of American television's landmark comedies, *Mister Ed*.

A talking donkey is a different matter. Especially when it talks in the Bible. The biblical version of *Mister Ed* appears in a curious story of a magician named Balaam, who is asked to put a curse on the tribes of Israel. Having left Kadesh, the Israelites must pass through the territory of several tribes, including Edom—the descendants of Esau—and Moab, where the descendants of one of Lot's daughters live. Threatened by the Israelites, the king of Moab asks a powerful magician to come to Moab and curse the Israelites. Balaam, this Mesopotamian wizard, saddles up his donkey and goes off to help King Balak.

The account gets a little confused as it proceeds because God is angry that Balaam seems to be doing exactly what he was told to do by God. Then Balaam's donkey takes center stage. As Balaam is riding down the road, the donkey sees an angel of the Lord in the way and refuses to move. Unable to see the angel, Balaam strikes the donkey three different times in an attempt to get the animal moving. Finally, the donkey turns around and asks the magician, "What have I done to you that you have struck me these three times?"

God finally opens Balaam's eyes and he sees the angel blocking the road. The heavenly messenger tells the magician to go to the king of Moab and say whatever he is divinely told to say. When the king tells Balaam to curse Israel, the magician blesses Israel instead. Although his donkey was always more famous than Balaam himself, according to *The Oxford Illustrated Guide to the Bible*, Balaam may have actually existed. "Fragmentary Aramaic texts of the ninth century BCE from Deir Alla refer to a Balaam who, as in the Hebrew scriptures, was the son of Beor. He is said to have a vision of a disaster that befalls his city, at which he weeps." (p. 67)

Deuteronomy

At the end of Numbers, the people of Israel are camped out in the plains of Moab, preparing to assault Canaan from the east. Moses gives them his valedictory speeches. To many people, "Deuteronomy" may be a very old cat in Andrew Lloyd Weber's musical. But the biblical title comes from the Greek words *deuteros* ("second") and *nomos* ("law"); the book does not present new laws so much as reiterates earlier rules.

Modern biblical scholars view most of the contents of this book as material that was passed down orally until it was recorded in the seventh century BCE, lost, then rediscovered, as reported later in the book Kings. A "Book of the Law" was discovered in the First Temple in 621 BCE during the reign of the Judean king Josiah (see Kings). With the discovery of this book, Josiah realizes that his people have not been following the laws properly. He sets the country on a rigorous period of religious reform in which strict Mosaic Law is again enforced. Deuteronomy is essentially Moses' farewell address—actually three addresses—in which he rehashes the acts of God. Solemnly warning of the temptations of the ways of Canaan—especially cautioning against the naughty Canaanite women—Moses pleads for loyalty to and love of God as the main condition for life in the Promised Land. A distinctive teaching of Deuteronomy is that the worship of God is to be centralized in one place, so that the paganism of local shrines may be eliminated. When Deuteronomy was composed, the Jerusalem Temple was regarded as the central sanctuary.

What is the "Great Commandment"?

"Hear, O Israel! The Lord is our God, the Lord alone [or, "the Lord our God is one"]. You shall love the Lord your God with all your heart and with all your soul and with all your might." (Deut. 6:4–5 JPS)

This is the *Shema*, the most commonly spoken prayer in Judaism, and also traditionally called the "Great Commandment." Many Christians may know it in the form that Jesus uses (Mark 12:29) when he is asked which commandment is the first. They may not realize that Jesus is quoting Hebrew scripture. Jesus adds, "You shall love your neighbor as thyself" (Mark 12:31) as the second commandment, and none are greater.

The "Golden Rule," as has often been pointed out, is a widely expressed idea. Besides its biblical appearances in Leviticus and in Jesus' words, other significant versions include:

Confucius—"What you do not want done to yourself, do not do to others."

Aristotle—"We should behave to our friends as we would wish our friends to behave to us."

Hillel—"What is hateful to you do not do to your neighbor. That is the whole Torah. The rest is commentary." (A famous first-century CE rabbi, Hillel lived in Jerusalem. Though many people speculate that Jesus knew his teachings and may have even been his student, there is no evidence of that.)

The Earl of Chesterfield—"Do as you would be done by, is the surest method I know of pleasing." (Philip Dormer Stanhope, the Earl of Chesterfield, lived from 1694 to 1773. His many aphorisms, reminiscent of Benjamin Franklin's pithy advice, were culled from letters to his son.)

He subjected you to the hardship of hunger and then gave you manna to eat, which neither you nor your fathers had ever known, in order to teach you that *man does not live by bread alone*, but that man may live on anything that the Lord decrees. The clothes upon your back did not wear out, nor did your feet swell these forty years. Bear in mind that the Lord your God disciplines you just as a man disciplines his son. (Deut. 8:3–5 JPS; emphasis added)

Once again, Christian readers may be more familiar with this verse from the time of Jesus' temptation by the devil during his forty days in the wilderness. When Jesus says, "One does not live by bread alone but by every word that comes from the mouth of God" (Matt. 4:4) he is quoting Deuteronomy.

How does God feel about cross-dressing?

Milton Berle, Lucille Ball, New York mayor Rudolph Giuliani, the singer k.d. lang, and the notorious basketball player Dennis Rodman may all be in trouble. According to Deuteronomy 22: "A woman shall not wear a man's apparel, nor shall a man put on a woman's garment; for whoever does such things is abhorrent to the Lord your God."

That makes it pretty clear—God doesn't go for cross-dressers.

This is one more example of a specific prohibition against a practice that was common in other ancient Near Eastern societies. Many of the Torah's prohibitions were aimed at a variety of acts, including idol worship, cultic prostitution, incest, homosexuality, even bestiality and infant sacrifice, that were acceptable in other neighboring cultures, including the Canaanites and the Egyptians.

The cross-dressing prohibition was apparently aimed at keeping Israelites from taking part in Canaanite practices where worshipers simulated a sex change, perhaps as a fertility rite.

Canaanite religion centered on worship of Baal, a fertility god responsible for rain, obviously a significant figure in an agricultural community that bordered the desert. The rains came, according to Canaanite belief, when Baal had sex, with his semen falling in the form of life-giving rain. Instead of a simple "rain dance," Canaanite priests imitated Baal by having sex, apparently coupling with men, women, and beasts. Many of the Mosaic Laws were specifically aimed at sexually charged Canaanite worship that must have held enormous appeal for many of the Children of Israel.

Apart from its disdain for the commingling of sex and God, the law code in Deuteronomy, like the laws elsewhere in the Torah, dealt very specifically with sexual relations, including marriage customs:

> "Suppose a man marries a woman, but after going in to
> her, he dislikes her and makes up charges against her, slan-
> dering her by saying, 'I married this woman but when I lay
> with her, I did not find evidence of her virginity.' The fa-
> ther of the young woman shall then submit the evidence
> of the young woman's virginity to the elders of the city at
> the gate. . . . Then they shall spread out the cloth before
> the elders of the town. The elders of the town shall take
> the man and punish him. . . . She shall remain his wife; he
> shall not be permitted to divorce her as long as she lives.
>
> "If, however, this charge is true . . . then they shall
> bring the young woman out of the entrance of her father's
> house and the men of her town shall stone her to death."
> (Deut. 22:13–21)

BIBLICAL VOICES

Then Moses went up from the plains of Moab to Mount Nebo, to the top of Pisgah, which is opposite Jericho, and the Lord showed him the whole land: ... The Lord said to him, "This is the land of which I swore to Abraham, to Isaac, and to Jacob, saying, 'I will give it to your descendants'; I have let you see it with your eyes, but you shall not cross over there." Then Moses, the servant of the Lord, died there in the land of Moab, at a valley in the land of Moab ... but no one knows his burial place to this day. (Deut. 34:1–6)

OVER THE RIVER

JOSHUA

Joshua "fit" the battle of Jericho, Jericho, Jericho.
Joshua "fit" the battle of Jericho,
And the walls came tumblin' down.
—African-American spiritual

And it came to pass, when the people heard the sound of the
trumpet, and the people shouted with a great shout, that the
wall fell down flat, so that the people went up into the city.
(Joshua 6:20 KJV)

❉

❋ How did a prostitute help destroy Jericho?

❋ How did King David and Jesus descend from a pair of biblical prostitutes?

❋ If God sanctions "ethnic cleansing," does that make it okay?

B ack in the wicked days of disco, throngs of "beautiful people"
stood on a line outside Studio 54, hoping, praying, and plead-
ing to be let into New York's notorious nightclub. Many of them
were devastated when the all-powerful doorman didn't beckon
them forward. They simply weren't among the select, the "chosen
people."

With that in mind, imagine the disappointment if you've been
waiting for forty years to get into a place and then at the last
minute you're told, "Sorry. You're not good enough to come in."
That's basically what happened to the Hebrews who left Egypt
with Moses. When Moses died at the age of 120, he was buried
in a place known only to God. He and Aaron weren't able to enter
the Promised Land and neither were any of the people who came
out of Egypt, because of their sin and griping in the wilderness.
Permission came at last for the Israelites to "conquer" the Promised Land after forty years of waiting, and the book of Joshua tells
the story of that "Conquest," an account that has undergone considerable revision. Evidence in the following book of Judges, as
well as archaeological discoveries during the twentieth century,
have shown that the Israelite conquest of Canaan was not the
grand holy war it was cracked up to be in Joshua.

The military leader chosen by Moses as his successor, Joshua
was, according to tradition, the book's author. Most modern scholars believe, however, that Joshua's material was drawn from different sources. The only widely accepted fact is that the oldest
passages of the book, which may date from around 950 BCE, were
completely rewritten in the seventh century BCE. Later on, probably after 500 BCE, someone else revised and rewrote much of the
book's second half, which is largely devoted to issues concerning
the priesthood.

The God of Joshua is a War God, a purely nationalistic deity
who seems far removed from the Lord who had ordered Israel,
only a few chapters earlier in Leviticus, to love its neighbors. The
central theme of Joshua is that God will lead the people to great

victories if they observe the law but will turn from them if they deny the Lord.

PLOT SUMMARY: THE CONQUEST OF CANAAN

Like many war stories, Joshua is not a pretty picture. The story opens with the miraculous passage of the Israelites over the Jordan River, which temporarily stops running, and the bloody sack of Jericho. It goes on to recount how the Hebrew armies moved from the Jordan Valley up into the highlands to capture the city of Ai, and records a great battle with the chieftains of five other Canaanite cities. The Israelites could prove to be quite ruthless in war, as violently illustrated in the complete devastation of the cities of Jericho and Ai. A final battle in the north results in the complete destruction of Canaanite power in Palestine. Following a brief summary of Joshua's triumphs, the book describes the division of the land among the tribes.

How did a prostitute help destroy Jericho?

Before leading the Israelites into Canaan, Joshua sent two spies to check out the land, and the city of Jericho in particular. In Jericho, the spies go directly to the house of Rahab, a prostitute, who shelters these Israelite spies from Jericho's king. The spies promise this "holy hooker" that when the Israelites conquer Jericho, Rahab and her family will be spared if she will tie a crimson cord to her house to identify it and gather her family inside the house.

The spies safely return to Joshua and the Israelite camp. After waiting on the banks of the Jordan River for three days the tribes finally cross the river. When the priests carrying the Ark of the Covenant touch the water of the Jordan River, the water stands still. The priests stand in the dry riverbed while the entire Israelite nation crosses into Canaan, a symbolic reminder of the escape from Egypt when the Sea of Reeds was parted. The chapter records that forty thousand armed men—there's that mystical number forty again—lead the Israelite tribes. The priests come out of the riverbed and the water begins to run again, overflowing its banks.

To commemorate this crossing of the Jordan, twelve river stones are set in a pile at Gilgal. The first Passover in the Promised Land is celebrated here and a mass circumcision is performed with flint knives—Ouch!—because all the men born in the wilderness had not been circumcised. That is why Gilgal means "Hill of the Foreskins." Lovely mailing address!

While standing near Jericho, Joshua sees a man and asks if he is a friend or foe. The man replies that he is "commander of the army of the Lord." Joshua knows he will have help in the battles to come.

When the Bible comes to the legendary attack on Jericho, history begins to stick its awkward nose into the picture. Unlike the Garden of Eden, Mount Sinai, the Sea of Reeds, and many other biblical locales whose geographical identity or precise location is unknown and debatable, Jericho is a very real place. During the past century, it has been one of the most carefully excavated sites in the Holy Land.

Located approximately eight miles north of the Dead Sea, at 840 feet (258 meters) below sea level, Jericho is the lowest city on earth. Situated twenty-three miles east of Jerusalem, Jericho—which probably meant "moon city," reflecting the worship of a local deity—is also one of the oldest human settlements in the world. Archaeologists have now dated Jericho's beginnings quite thoroughly. The extensive digs in and around Jericho and nearby Tell es-Sultan suggest that hunters were drawn to the area in the ninth millennium BCE by a spring. By about 8000 BCE, a permanent settlement of some two thousand people had been established. With an irrigation system, a large tower, and a defensive wall, Jericho is justifiably called the world's oldest city. Around 6800 BCE, the original settlers were displaced by a new group. A third group took over the site around 4500 BCE and it was then occupied continuously until the middle of the Late Bronze Age.

In your Sunday school version, Jericho was destroyed when

the tribes marched silently around Jericho, once a day for six days, led by seven priests blowing seven ram's horns. On the seventh day, they march around the city seven times and, on the last lap, the priests blow their horns and the people let out a great shout. The walls fall down flat and the city is captured. They probably didn't mention what happens to the people of Jericho whose homes are now rubble. Joshua minces no words. All of Jericho's inhabitants are put to the sword, except for the prostitute Rahab and her family.

How did King David and Jesus descend from a pair of biblical prostitutes?

The story of Rahab, the prostitute who was censored out of most of the "clean" Sunday school versions, deserves a longer look. There are two rather compelling points to consider. Remember Tamar, the woman who pretended to be a prostitute with Judah back in Genesis? When her twins were born, a red cord was tied around the hand of one, Zerah. That cord provides a symbolic connection to the red cord Rahab dangles out her window. According to other Jewish accounts, Rahab was the ancestor of several prophets. But New Testament genealogy in Matthew says Rahab was the mother of Boaz, who marries Ruth (see Ruth) and is another ancestor of David. That means the great king of Israel—as well as Jesus, whose lineage is traced to David—is descended from a pair of prostitutes whose exploits are generally overlooked.

But what sort of prostitutes? There were actually two kinds in the Hebrew scriptures. The run-of-the-mill "streetwalker" variety, obviously tolerated in this otherwise sexually restrictive culture, and the "cultic prostitute" of Canaanite religion. Traditionally, Canaanite religion was thought to have employed temple prostitutes who had sex with worshipers and priests in fertility rites. That view has undergone some revision. The word traditionally translated as "temple prostitute" is more accurately a "consecrated" person. While sex with the Canaanite priests was probably part of the job description, some scholars now suggest that these women served in other roles, perhaps as midwives, or women who sang holy songs or otherwise served in the Canaanite temples. (An fascinating overview of prostitution in the Hebrew scriptures can be found in Jonathan Kirsch's *The Harlot by the Side of the Road: Forbidden Tales of the Bible.*) Tamar of Genesis was described as both common harlot and temple prostitute. Rahab, the prostitute in Jericho, was a *zonah*, in Hebrew a common prostitute.

Recent archaeology has tempered the biblical account of the Conquest. In the thirteenth century BCE, the likely date of the entry of the Israelites into Canaan, Jericho was an unfortified village. In other words, the familiar account was most likely embroidered upon in later tellings. The Jordan River valley in which Jericho lies sits on a major rift, or geological fault zone. One explanation for the river stopping and the walls tumbling is that both events were earthquake-induced. However, there is no archaeological evidence of those tumbled walls at Jericho.

For evidence of how old war stories get embellished and overlaid with notions of "divine intervention," one needn't look too far in the ancient Mediterranean neighborhood. At about the same general historical time period that Joshua may have been leading the loose confederation of Israelite tribes into Canaan, there was a long-running battle between a loose confederation of Greek tribes and the inhabitants of another fortified town on the coast of what is now Turkey. This extended but otherwise historically insignificant battle fought over "Ilium" around 1193 BCE was transformed into a much bigger story. Transmitted orally, like the Bible stories, it was finally written down more than three hundred years later in 850 BCE by a poet we call "Homer" and is titled *The Iliad* (its sequel is *The Odyssey*).

Following Jericho's capture, the town was destroyed, pillaged, and cursed, but there was some unpleasant fallout from the destruction of Jericho. One of the Israelites illicitly kept some of the booty of Jericho that had been promised to God. For this crime, God punished all of Israel with a military defeat when Joshua and his armies moved on to Ai (which means "ruin"). After the guilty party was discovered, he and his family were stoned to death, and Joshua captured Ai, which is near Bethel, through a clever military ruse, instead of divine intervention.

The casualty reports after the battle for Ai are grim: "When Israel had finished slaughtering all the inhabitants of Ai in the open wilderness where they had pursued them, and when all of them to the very last had fallen by the edge of the sword, all Israel returned to Ai, and attacked it with the edge of the sword. The total of those who fell that day, both men and women, was twelve thousand—all the people of Ai. . . . So Joshua burned Ai, and made of it forever a heap of ruins, as it is to this day." (Josh. 8:24–28)

If God sanctions "ethnic cleansing," does that make it okay?

Bosnia. Lebanon. Nanking. The "removal" of Native Americans. The "Peculiar Institution." You don't have to look very hard to find evidence of people justifying the rape, enslavement, murder, and genocide of "godless heathens." These are just a few examples from fairly recent history, and there are plenty more. Of course, in history's worst episode of "ethnic cleansing," the descendants of Joshua were nearly wiped out in the Nazi Holocaust.

The vivid biblical description of the cruel treatment of the Canaanites in Ai and other cities comes wrapped in the cloak of divine approval, pointing up one of the great ethical contradictions of the Bible. When a supposedly "evil" people is eradicated at God's direction, does that justify it? Remember, God's own commandment said not to "murder," leaving some "wiggle room" for cases of killing that could be justified.

Ironically, recent research into this period seems to be chipping away at the biblical version of the Conquest, so the worst of the killing done by the Israelites seems to have been embellished with retelling. More likely, in current scholarly opinions, the Israelites gradually took over Canaan in a much longer process of "Settlement," combining emigration and negotiations, while scattered conflicts between localized groups went on for a much longer time. But saying "It didn't really happen that way" is the easy way out of this moral bind.

The traditional response is that the Canaanites were so bad they had it coming to them. Throughout the Torah, stories of Canaanites frequently demonized these people, just as the Philistines would be demonized when they later became Israel's chief adversary. It is much easier to destroy others—or put them in chains—if you convince yourself that they are godless, pagan, heathen, or morally bankrupt. Most European "discoverers" or settlers of the Americas, from Christopher Columbus and the Spanish conquistadors to the English in Virginia and Massachusetts, were convinced that the Native Americans they encountered were godless heathens. Slaveholders were convinced that Africans were pagan savages. The Germans were convinced that the Jews were the source of all their troubles. It is a very short leap from condemning another race or culture as "immoral" to justifying their enslavement or worse.

BIBLICAL VOICES
"And now I am about to go the way of all the earth, and you know in your hearts and souls, all of you, that not one thing has failed of all the good things that the Lord your God promised concerning you; all have come to pass for you. . . ." (Josh. 23:14)

Having fulfilled his role of bringing the tribes into Israel and dividing the Promised Land among them, Joshua died at the age of 110.

MILESTONES IN BIBLICAL TIMES II
1568 BCE TO 1000 BCE

Prehistoric dating is often speculative and subject to substantial scholarly debate and revision. The following dates are generally used by a broad range of historians in a variety of books and publications. However, there are alternative dates suggested for some of these events. Among the most controversial is the radically different chronology suggested by Charles Pellegrino in his recent book *Return to Sodom and Gomorrah*. By pushing the date of the eruption of the volcano at Thera back to 1628 BCE (see 1470 below), Pellegrino creates a chronology that differs by a few hundred years from the traditional view of ancient Near East history. Accepting Pellegrino's view has a significant impact on the dating of the dynasties of Egypt, the Exodus, the fall of Jericho, and a number of other biblical events discussed in this book.

1568/5 Ahmose I (Amosis, Amasis) expels the Hyksos from Egypt and begins the 18th Dynasty, or New Kingdom.

1545 Amosis I dies after twenty-year reign; his son succeeds as Amenhotep I.

1525 Amenhotep I dies after twenty-year reign; his successor will be known as Thutmose (Thutmosis) I.

• Thutmose I restores the Temple of Osiris at Abydos and builds the first tomb in the Valley of Kings.

1512 Thutmose I is deposed; his bastard son will reign as Thutmose (Thutmosis) II with his wife (and half-sister) Hatshepsut.

1504 Thutmose II dies; Hatshepsut rules as queen and regent for her infant nephew Thutmose (Thutmosis) III.

c. 1480 Thutmose III comes of age and begins a thirty-three-year reign in which Egypt will reach the heights of its power. The title "Pharaoh," or "Great House," will come into use under him. He attempts to obscure all references to his aunt Hatshepsut by building walls around her obelisks at Karnak.

1470 Volcanic eruption at Thera destroys Minoan civilization based on Crete. Seismic waves 100 to 160 feet high temporarily drop water level on eastern shores of Mediterranean; Egyptian lands are inundated by seawater from seismic waves; famine ensues. Many surmise that this culture provided the basis for the myth of the Lost City of Atlantis.

1450 Thutmose III dies; his son Amenhotep II invades Judea and Mesopotamia.

1419 Amenhotep II dies after thirty-four-year reign; succeeded by son Thutmose (Thutmosis) IV.

1400 Iron Age begins in Asia Minor as methods for smelting are devised.

1386 Thutmose IV dies and is succeeded by son Amenhotep (Amenophis) III the last great ruler of the New Kingdom.

1349 Amenhotep III dies after a thirty-eight-year reign. He is succeeded by his son, Amenhotep IV (also called Akhenaten, Ikhnaton, Akhnaton). During this period Egypt weakens when Hittites build an empire extending south from Anatolia (modern Turkey) to the borders of Lebanon.

• Amenhotep IV introduces a form of monotheism to Egypt; the Pharaoh establishes a new cult worshiping the sun god; he opposes the priests of Amen, due to the influence of his first and most famous wife, Nefertiti.

1334 Amenhotep IV dies after sixteen-year reign; succeeded by his nine-year-old son, Tutankhamen.

1321 Egyptian soldier Harmahab (Horemheb) seizes throne; Tutankhamen is buried at Thebes with a vast treasure.

1300 Alphabetic script developed in Mesopotamia is a refinement of the simplified cuneiform alphabet of *2500 BCE*.

1293 Harmahab dies and is replaced by Ramses I, who dies two years later and is succeeded by son Seti (Sethos) I.

1278 Seti (Sethos) I dies after defeating Libyans west of the Nile and making peace with Hittites in Syria. Seti's son will reign as Ramses II.

c. 1275 Battle of Qadesh, a decisive Egyptian victory over the Hittites.

c. 1260? A forty-year Israelite migration begins after three centuries of Egyptian captivity and oppression.

1246 Egypt's Ramses II marries a Hittite princess, sealing a permanent peace treaty between these two powers. He devotes his reign to massive construction projects: completion of Seti's temple at Abydos; additions to the temples at Karnak and Luxor; construction of temples at Thebes with a colossal statue of himself; and construction of rock-cut temples at Abu-Simbel in Nubia.

1238/5? Merneptah's battle with "Israel."

1212 Ramses II dies after a sixty-seven-year reign in which he has used forced labor, presumed to include the Israelites, to build the treasure cities of Pithom and Ramses. His son Merneptah succeeds him.

1207 Egypt invaded by Libyans but they are defeated by Merneptah.

1202 Merneptah dies after a ten-year-reign and is succeeded by a series of lesser Pharaohs, ending the 19th Dynasty.

1200 Lower Egypt's remaining Jews are expelled in the confusion following the end of the 19th Dynasty.

   • The *Gilgamesh* epic, the first known written legend, is recorded in Sumerian cuneiform. It tells of a great flood in which man was saved by building an ark. Foods mentioned in the *Gilgamesh* epic include caper buds, wild cucumbers, ripe figs, grapes, several edible leaves and stems, honey, meat seasoned with herbs, and bread—a kind of pancake made of barley flour mixed with sesame-seed flour and onions.

1193 Destruction of Troy, by Greek forces under King Agamemnon after a ten-year siege.

1182 Egypt's 20th Dynasty begins under Ramses III. He will rally the Egyptians against a confederation of "Sea Peoples"—Mediterranean invaders including the Philistines, Sardinians, and Greeks.

1150 The Philistines establish five cities on the Mediterranean coast of Canaan. Israel begins to emerge as a network of settlements in the Galilean and central hill country.

1146 Nebuchadnezzar I begins a twenty-three-year reign as king of Babylon.

1141 Israelite armies lose more than thirty-four thousand men in battles against the Philistines.

• The Ark of the Covenant is captured by the Philistines and taken to their city Ashdod.

1116 Tiglath-pileser I begins a thirty-eight-year reign that will take the Middle Assyrian Empire to its zenith.

1100 Assyrian forces under Tiglath-pileser I reach the Mediterranean after having conquered the Hittites.

1020 The prophet Samuel anoints Saul, who will reign as king of Hebron until *1012*.

1005 Saul and his son Jonathan die in battle of Mount Gilboa against the Philistines. Jonathan's friend David succeeds to the throne.

WHY, WHY, WHY, DELILAH?

JUDGES, RUTH

Then Jael . . . took a nail of the tent, and took a hammer in her hand, and went softly unto him, and smote the nail into his temples, and fastened it to the ground, for he was fast asleep, and weary: so he died. (Judges 4:21)

With the jawbone of an ass . . . have I slain a thousand men. (Judges 15:16)

❇

❋ Who was Deborah?

❋ If a father kills his daughter, does God mind?

❋ Were the Philistines really all that bad?

❋ Did Delilah snip more than just hair?

Y ou say you hate sex and violence? Stomach not strong enough for *Pulp Fiction?* Then you might want to stay away from Judges, one book that definitely deserves an "R" rating. Nails driven into heads, rape and dismemberment, a daughter sacrificed—with God's approval—by her father, men and women incinerated. Judges has it all and more. "The oddest assortment of rogues, outlaws, and lowlifes in all of the Bible . . . seducers and harlots, assassins and mercenaries, rapists and torturers." That is how Jonathan Kirsch's *The Harlot by the Side of the Road* neatly sums up the characters introduced in Judges.

The book recounts the history of Israel from the death of Joshua to the time just before the birth of the Hebrew prophet Samuel, roughly a two-hundred-year span stretching from the end of the Israelite conquest of Canaan, the "Promised Land," to the beginning of the monarchy around 1000 BCE. This creates a slight chronological problem because the book of Judges seems to cover four hundred years of history. The book combines a series of tales of the exploits of various tribal leaders. Although called "judges," they didn't sit around in black robes and decide legal cases. These "judges" have been described as "warrior-rulers," but even that description doesn't quite fit them all. The most notorious "star" of Judges is Samson, among the most famous yet least understood of these Israelite "heroes," whose behavior makes the term very questionable.

Traditionally ascribed to the prophet Samuel, the book is now considered part of a large historical work that ran from Deuteronomy to the time of the Exile under the Babylonians (538 BCE). Although some sections of Judges, such as the "Song of Deborah," are believed to be among the oldest preserved Hebrew writings, other parts of the book are considered additions made after the Babylonian Captivity.

BIBLICAL VOICES

Then the Israelites did what was evil in the sight of the Lord and worshipped the Baals; and they abandoned the Lord, the

God of their ancestors, who had brought them out of the land of Egypt; they followed other gods, from among the gods of the peoples who were all around them, and bowed down to them; and they provoked the Lord to anger. They abandoned the Lord, and worshipped Baal and the Astartes. (Judges 2:11–13)

Who was Deborah?

One thing is clear right away in Judges. The Children of Israel weren't very good at following God's requests. Joshua's body wasn't cold before the Israelites "did what was evil in the sight of the Lord." The Children of Israel obviously found the Canaanite gods, Baal, Astarte, and Asherah, far more appealing than Yahweh. Asherah was associated with the sacred tree of life and she was often depicted with a tree springing from her pubic area. In *The Bible and the Ancient Near East*, Cyrus Gordon and Gary Rendsburg point out that the Torah laws relating to sexual practices were a response to Canaanite sexual practices. "In the Canaanite fertility cult, the relationship of Baal to the earth was compared to that of a human couple having intercourse. . . . In a type of ritual drama . . . temple prostitutes would perform the very act that Baal was to perform." (pp. 161–162)

Since the Israelites wrote very specific laws condemning incest, bestiality, transvestitism, and temple prostitution, it is safe to assume that these were all Canaanite practices. Is it any wonder that the Children of Israel had such a hard time sticking with Yahweh, who wasn't a party kind of god? Even more intriguing is the discovery, made in the 1980s, of an inscription that mentioned "Yahweh and his Asherah." Without more evidence, the inscription invites the question: Did God date? Perhaps some ancient Israelites combined their Yahweh with the Canaanite Asherah. This certainly would have counted as "evil in the sight of God."

Many more times, according to Judges, the Israelites "did what was evil in the sight of God," only to be punished. Each time, a tribal leader, or "judge," rose up to rescue Israel, and each time the people slid backward soon after. When the Israelites once again found themselves in trouble, Deborah, described as a prophetess and the only woman judge, emerged as savior. A woman warrior in a time in which few women held such roles, Deborah's rise to prominence is unexplained in the Bible. It is simply stated as a fact, but Deborah establishes herself as a forceful leader, massing an army against a Canaanite enemy, and then drawing up the plan of battle. Although she is as epic a character as Xena, the Warrior Princess of modern pop culture, Deborah is overlooked as a biblical character when compared with some of her more notorious male compatriots. Is that biblical sexism? How else to explain the general ignorance of this heroic warrior, the Jewish Joan of Arc?

There are two accounts of Deborah's leadership in Judges, one in prose, the second in poetry, again reflecting the combination of two separate accounts. In the first, Judges 4, Deborah leads the army and unites her people, but another woman, named Jael, also emerges a hero. When the defeated enemy general Sisera enters Jael's tent, she greets him. But as the general is sleeping, Jael takes a tent stake and, "drove the tent peg into his temple, until it went down into the ground."

This episode is followed by the "Song of Deborah" (Judges 5), a poetic rerun of the story, which is thought to be one of the oldest portions of the Hebrew Bible and is attributed to J, the oldest of the biblical authors described in Part I of this book. J is also the author whom some historians think might have been a woman, and they point to the story of Deborah, one of the Bible's great heroines, as evidence that J was fond of writing about strong, bold females. In J's poetic version of Deborah's victory, the details change. When Sisera's chariots attack, God sends a downpour that bogs down the chariots. This must have been a reassuringly familiar tale to the Israelites who remembered a story of how their God once sent six hundred Egyptian chariots to a watery grave. Escaping from the battle, Sisera went to Jael's tent, where she shattered his skull with a mallet. The "Song of Deborah" has been dated to about 1100 BCE and may have written shortly after the event that inspired it took place. The prose version of Deborah's conquest was probably written about 750 BCE.

If a father kills his daughter, does God mind?

The story of Deborah is followed by those of two more judges, Gideon and Jephthah. Gideon defeats the Midianite kings who had killed his brothers. He then refuses the offer of kingship.

After a time, the Israelites once more did what was evil—this time they not only bow to Canaanite gods but are said to worship the gods of Aram, Sidon, Moab, the Ammonites, and the Philistines. This time, a "mighty warrior" named Jephthah rises up. The illegitimate son of a prostitute, Jephthah was an outcast from his father's family and became an outlaw, an ancient Hebrew "Robin Hood." Hardly the image of a "judge." Jephthah asks God for help, but makes a terrible vow: he will sacrifice whoever greets him if he is victorious. Of course, he wins his battle against the Ammonites and is then greeted by his own daughter, who must be sacrificed. The pious, virtuous girl—who is unnamed—agreeably goes to her death. And you thought old Abraham had wiped out the practice of human sacrifice. So why doesn't God stay Jephthah's hand? The Bible doesn't tell us so. The only conclusion to be reached: Jephthah's daughter was not as precious as Abraham's son.

There is a brief follow-up to this story when Jephthah's men fight with the tribesmen of Ephraim, another Israelite tribe, who apparently did not join Jephthah to help in his battle. Afterward, whenever an Ephraimite came to the river, Jephthah's men would ask him to say "Shibboleth," a word that means either "ear of corn" or "flood torrent." But due to regional dialects, these men couldn't pronounce the "sh" sound, and said "sibboleth" instead. According to Judges, forty-two thousand men had this speech deficiency and died at the Jordan. In *The Harlot by the Side of the Road*,

Jonathan Kirsch recounts the story from World War II in which Dutch resistance fighters were able to cull out Nazi infiltrators who couldn't pronounce a particular Dutch name. "Shibboleth" has since come to mean a word or catchphrase that is distinctive to one group.

Were the Philistines really all that bad?

With the most famous character in Judges, the legendary Samson, and his naughty wife, Delilah, the villains have changed. The abominable Canaanites have been replaced by the barbarous Philistines.

History has not been kind to the Philistines, whose name was picked up by the Greeks and Romans and applied to the entire area as "Palestine." They are on the losing end of one of western civilization's "shortest sticks." For a long time, when someone was called a "Philistine," it was an insult—a derogatory term for a boorish, classless, ill-educated person with no appreciation of life's finer things. The French have a different word for such a person— "American."

Were the Philistines really all that bad? Or were they a kinder, gentler nation of barbarians? Recent archaeological discoveries have softened the harsh image of the Philistines, who were among the so-called "Sea Peoples" of the Mediterranean who entered the ancient Near East in the last years of the thirteenth century BCE, destroyed the Hittite empire, and then threatened Egypt until Ramses III defeated them around 1190 BCE. At about that time, the Philistines settled on the southern coast of Canaan, in what is now the area around Gaza, the name of one of five established Philistine cities. From this coastal base, the Philistines pressed inland, coming into collision with the Israelite tribes who were spreading themselves down from the hill country toward the coast. A well-organized military force, the Philistines were a major threat to the more loosely organized Israelite tribes. Presumably from either the island of Cyprus or Crete, the Philistines left pottery that shows the influence of the early Mycenean culture. And just as many of the Israelites were attracted to the Canaanite religion, the Philistines also assimilated the local divinities. The Philistine deities, Dagon, Ashtaroth, and the notorious Baal-zebub were all related to Canaanite gods.

Did Delilah snip more than just hair?

The most famous of the Judges characters was not a "judge" at all. He wasn't even a very good boy. Most people probably recall something about Delilah cutting off his hair—she didn't even do it, she brought in a barber—but the story of Samson is a lot more than just Delilah's deceitful hair-cutting skills. Samson was the product of another biblical miraculous birth. His barren mother is promised she will conceive, but the unborn Samson is pledged to God as a "nazirite," a term for a person who has made specific vows in dedicating his life to God (laid out in Numbers 6). Nazir-ites could not drink wine, have any contact with dead bodies, or allow a razor to cut their hair. While Samson is still in the womb, his greatness is predicted. The vow dedicating Samson to God, and not his hair alone, is the source of Samson's superhuman strength, first demonstrated when he kills a lion with his bare hands. This feat is one of several parallels between Samson and the Greek strongman Heracles—Hercules to the Romans—whose first act was also to kill a lion.

The story of Samson is basically a string of grudges and fights over women escalating into warfare—not unlike the story of Troy. Samson falls for a Philistine girl and marries her. At the wedding feast, Samson tells a riddle and bets that the wedding guests can't solve it. When his bride tricks Samson into revealing the secret of the riddle, the guests win the bet, and Samson has to kill thirty men to pay off the bet. Angrily, Samson abandons his wife, who is then given to Samson's best man! When he learns about that,

Samson sets the Philistine wheat fields, olive groves, and vineyards on fire by tying burning branches to the tails of three hundred foxes tied together in pairs and setting them loose. The Philistines retaliate by burning Samson's wife and father-in-law to death. Samson escalates this tribal grudge match by killing more Philistines. When the Philistines come for him, Samson is captured and turned over by fellow Israelites, who want to avoid trouble. But God breaks the ropes that bind him and Samson slaughters a thousand Philistine men with the "jawbone of a donkey."

After that, Samson returns to the Philistine city of Gaza to visit a prostitute. But when the Philistines attempt to capture him in the brothel, Samson rips down the city gate.

Finally, he falls for Delilah. Although widely assumed to be a Philistine woman because Samson had a taste for "foreign" girls, Delilah—whose name may be related to the Arabic word for "flirt"—is not identified in the biblical account as either Philistine or Israelite. The Philistine leaders bribe Delilah to uncover the secret of Samson's strength. After telling Delilah several false stories, Samson finally reveals the truth. Despite Hollywood images of Hedy Lamarr with her trimming shears, she doesn't do the cutting. Instead, she calls for a barber who cuts off Samson's sacred locks. His vow broken, Samson's strength is gone. While there is plenty of Freudian-style speculation that it wasn't Samson's hair that got trimmed but another aspect of his masculinity, there is no biblical evidence that the Israelite strongman was castrated.

Once Samson is captured, he is blinded and put to work turning a millstone. The none-too-bright Philistines forget to keep shaving his head and Samson's hair grows back. Brought out to entertain the crowds during a festival, Samson asks God for his strength once more and pulls down the temple, killing himself and thousands of Philistines all at once. Having received her promised payoff for discovering Samson's secret, Delilah disappears from the story. There is no word as to whether she is among those thousands who were killed when Samson brought down the house.

If the preceding stories in Judges haven't satisfied the baser appetites, the book closes with an even gorier tale. A traveling Levite (priest) and his concubine stop to spend the night in a town called Gibeah. As in the story of Lot in Sodom, a group of men from the tribe of Benjamin want to have sex with the Levite. And just as Lot did back in Sodom, the Levite's host offers his own daughter and the concubine to this lust-driven crowd, but the men aren't satisfied. To save his own skin, the Levite turns the concubine over to the crowd and she is raped until she dies. In order to incite the other tribes to take vengeance on the Benjaminites of Gibeah, the Levite cuts the dead concubine into twelve pieces and sends a piece to each tribe. The intertribal war that follows costs 22,000 Israelite lives. Then God intercedes in the battle and 25,100 Benjaminites were killed in one day. Another 18,000 Benjaminites die in the ensuing slaughter and their wives are put to the sword and whole towns are burned.

The story would have been bad enough if it had ended there, but the other tribes then realize that the tribe of Benjamin, part of the Israelite confederacy, will be totally destroyed if the surviving men of Benjamin have no wives. The leaders of the other tribes decide to kill the people of Jabesh-gilead, the one town that did not join in the attack on the tribe of Benjamin. Twelve thousand Israelite soldiers kill the people of Jabesh-gilead, "including the women and the little ones." Four hundred virgins are then turned over to keep the tribe of Benjamin from extinction. When even those four hundred prove insufficient for the men of Benjamin, they are allowed to kidnap some girls from the town of Shiloh who come out to dance.

As the last words of Judges bluntly put it: "In those days there was no king in Israel; all the people did what was right in their own eyes."

Ruth

In the Christian Old Testament, Ruth follows Judges. The Hebrew Bible places Ruth among its third section, called "Writings," or *Kethuvim*. It is placed here to maintain chronological continuity. The date of its composition is uncertain.

An ancient Hebrew short story probably based on an earlier folktale, Ruth is ostensibly set in the days of Judges, but it has little in common with that book's bloody tales of intertribal warfare. Ruth is from neighboring Moab, not Israel. The opening verses tell of Ruth's marriage to a Hebrew man and how she chose to return to Judah with her mother-in-law after her husband's death. Her loyalty and kindness are rewarded, and she becomes the great-grandmother of King David.

BIBLICAL VOICES

"Whither thou goest, I will go; and where thou lodgest, I will lodge; thy people shall be my people, and thy God my God." (Ruth 1:16 KJV)

PLOT SUMMARY: RUTH

During a famine in the time of the Judges, a woman named Naomi from the ancient town of Bethlehem takes refuge in the neighboring land of the Moabites, who occupied the land east of the Dead Sea. According to Israelite tradition, the Moabites were descended from one of Lot's daughters. While there, Naomi's sons both marry Moabite women. When her husband and two sons die, the bereaved Naomi decides to return to Bethlehem and she urges her two daughters-in-law to remain in Moab. One of them, Ruth, loyally insists on returning with Naomi, and they reach Bethlehem at the beginning of the barley harvest.

Back in Bethlehem, Naomi sees some marital possibilities for Ruth in Boaz, a distant relative, and she suggests Ruth go and lie next to Boaz and "uncover his feet," a biblical euphemism for the male sex organ. Ruth takes Naomi's advice, and when Boaz wakes up to discover Ruth cuddled up nearby, she tells him to spread his cloak over her, another euphemism suggesting more than just getting cozy under the blankets. Boaz is definitely interested, but under the law, another kinsman has the right of first refusal. When that man passes Ruth up, Boaz marries her. Despite the fact that Ruth is a foreigner, she becomes the great-grandmother of King

David. Besides its importance to Jewish tradition, this line of descent is doubly significant because Jesus was also born from this lineage, a fact noted in the genealogy given at the beginning of Matthew in the New Testament.

As a literary character, Ruth has been viewed in two compelling lights. First of all, despite aggressively climbing into the sack with Boaz and seducing him, she is otherwise the model of a virtuous, loyal woman who does what is right. Although the Bible's bad girls—Eve, Bathsheba, Delilah, Jezebel—have gotten most of the publicity, many of the "good girls" were far more significant in Israelite history. Ruth belongs to this group, who have taken a backseat to the more familiar male heroes. Ironically, women in ancient Israeli society were little more than slaves with few legal rights. But the roster of Hebrew heroines who took matters into their own hands is impressive: Deborah of Judges; Rachel, whose quick thinking when she sat on her father's idols in Genesis saves her husband, Isaac; Miriam, who rescues the infant Moses and then helps lead the Exodus; Rahab, the prostitute who helped capture Jericho; and Tamar, who played the resourceful prostitute to win her just due from Judah (see Genesis) and was, like Ruth, an ancestor of King David, Israel's greatest national hero—and by extension ancestors of Solomon and Jesus as well.

So far removed from the violence, sexual savagery, and warfare of Judges, the simple, folksy Ruth has been interpreted in various ways. Although it is set before the Exile, some scholars believe it was written after the Exile in Babylon and its message was aimed at the harsh decrees opposing Jewish intermarriage in the period after the Exile when Jewish men were urged to divorce their foreign wives (see Ezra). The emphasis on the fact that the virtuous Ruth is a foreigner, her acceptance by Boaz despite this fact, and her place in the genealogy of King David all seem to underscore the acceptability of foreign wives. But others see Ruth as a much simpler "virtue" tale that proves that God is open to those outside of Israel.

Uneasy Lies the Head That Wears a Crown... Part 1

1 & 2 Samuel

So David prevailed over the Philistine with a sling and with a stone. (I Sam. 17:50 KJV)

❋ Who really killed Goliath?

❋ Was David a traitor?

❋ Were David and Jonathan more than just friends?

❋ Did King David even exist?

After the mayhem in Judges, with its cast of lesser-known characters, getting back to more familiar biblical turf might come as a relief. In the two books of Samuel, readers will re-encounter some characters they may fondly recall from childhood: the "Sweet Psalmist" David and "Wise" Solomon. However, the level of sexual misdeeds and bloodbaths found in Judges drops off only marginally when the Bible comes to these "heroes." Some of their stories may not be the ones you remember. David and Solomon, in particular, are the biblical version of JFK: once-sainted leaders whose spotty histories and difficulties with women have tarnished their reputations.

Originally the two books of Samuel and the two books of Kings were each a single book in the Hebrew canon of the Bible, telling the history of the kingdom of Israel. Once they were translated into Greek in the Septuagint, they no longer fit on single scrolls and were expanded into four books. In Hebrew Bibles, the expansion of Samuel into two books did not appear until the middle of the fifteenth century CE. Samuel contains the history of the prophet Samuel—the last judge of Israel—and the stormy relationship of Israel's first two kings, Saul and David. Theirs is a conflict of characters worthy of Shakespeare in terms of the rich plot twists, political machinations, and psychological depth. *Macbeth* has nothing on the stories of Saul and David. Although a relatively short period in history, the time covered in Samuel is a significant one in which the monarchy was first established and the Israelite tribes united in one kingdom with its capital at Jerusalem.

Traditionally viewed as having been written by Samuel himself, Samuel is the work of several authors and author/editors working from a number of different sources, modern scholars generally agree. One of these, the "Early Source," probably dates from the reign of Solomon (c. 961–922 BCE). The second, or "Late Source," was probably composed between 750 and 650 BCE. Whatever their origin and authorship, the two books of Samuel have been long appreciated for their remarkable value as history and literature, and some authorities have called the author or authors of these books the first "historian," a title traditionally given to the Greek Herodotus (485–424 BCE).

BIBLICAL VOICES

The Lord said to Samuel, "Listen to the voice of the people in all that they say to you; for they have not rejected you, but they have rejected me from being king over them. Just as they have done to me, from the day I brought them up out of Egypt to this day, forsaking me and serving other gods, so also they are doing to you. Now then, listen to their voice; only—you shall solemnly warn them, and show them the ways of the king who shall reign over them." (1 Sam. 8:7–9)

PLOT SUMMARY: SAMUEL

Like the mother of Samson, Hannah is another previously barren woman who is divinely blessed after she makes a vow that her son will be consecrated as a "nazirite." He will not touch a razor to his head or drink any wine. She is blessed and gives birth to Samuel. As a young boy Samuel is placed with a priest named Eli for training, and his gift for prophecy soon makes him honored throughout Israel as a judge, priest, and prophet.

During Samuel's judgeship, a major crisis strikes when the Philistines attack, killing thirty thousand Israelite soldiers and capturing the Ark of the Covenant, which holds the tablets containing the Ten Commandments and is the dwelling place of Israel's God. Possessing the Ark is dangerous for unbelievers, as the Philistines learn. When the Philistines place the Ark in the temple of their god Dagon, the idol of Dagon falls down and the bubonic plague strikes the Philistines. Quickly realizing that they'd better return the Ark, the Philistines send the sacred chest back, but even some of the Israelites who retrieve the Ark are killed. Once the Ark is restored to the Israelites, Samuel tells the people that they can only defeat the Philistines if they stop worshiping false gods.

To combat the Philistine threat, the Israelites tell the aging Samuel they need a king to lead them. Taking the priestly position that they only need God's leadership, Samuel warns the people to be careful; they may get what they are asking for. In Samuel's eyes, a king will only mean trouble, taxes, and forced labor. Sounding a bit jilted when he learns that his people want an earthly king, God tells Samuel, "Listen to the voice of the people in all that they say; for they have not rejected you, but they have rejected me from being king over them." God then helps Samuel find Saul, the son of a wealthy Benjaminite.

BIBLICAL VOICES

And Samuel said to all the people, See ye him whom the Lord hath chosen, that there is none like him among all the people? And all the people shouted, and said, God save the King. (1 Sam. 10:24)

If God had chosen the king, his first draft choice wasn't so great. Saul's reign (c. 1020–1012 BCE) was tainted. He is what the ancient Greeks called a "tragic" figure, a noble character possessing fatal flaws. Although he won some early victories, Saul failed to thoroughly defeat the Philistines and never established a firm rule over the loose-knit Israelite tribal confederation. The biblical account traces all of Saul's flaws as a leader back to a split with Samuel, who clearly never liked Saul or the idea of a king in the first place.

The entire Samuel-Saul conflict is basically a "church versus state" argument and reflects the view of the priests who wrote the Hebrew scriptures: only God, through his priests, should rule Israel. The priesthood felt that kings, who were a threat to their authority, were not a good idea, and the composers of these histories ultimately blamed the monarchy for all the misfortunes that befell Israel. The trouble begins when Saul tries to make a sacrifice before a battle and he mucks things up. As in a union whose rules dictate who does which jobs, making sacrifices was the priest's job, and Samuel and the rest of the "priest union" are not happy when Saul infringes on their sacred turf. Before long, Sam-

uel is secretly looking for a new and improved king. The aging
prophet goes off to the little town of Bethlehem where the seven
sons of a man named Jesse are paraded past him, but none of them
passes muster. Samuel asks if there are any other sons and is told
the youngest is out tending sheep. A young boy enters, handsome
and eyes shining. He is the one, Samuel is told by God, and the
old priest secretly anoints this shepherd boy: "And the spirit of
the Lord came mightily upon David from that day forward."

BIBLICAL VOICES

> And there came out from the camp of the Philistines a cham-
> pion named Goliath of Gath, whose height was six cubits and
> a span. He had a helmet of bronze on his head, and he was
> armed with a coat of mail; . . . He stood and shouted to the
> ranks of Israel, "Why have you not come out to draw up for
> battle? Am I not a Philistine, and are you not servants of Saul?
> Choose a man for yourselves, and let him come down to me.
> If he is able to fight with me and kill me, then we will be
> your servants; but if I prevail against him and kill him, then
> you shall be our servants and serve us." (1 Sam. 17:4–9)

Who really killed Goliath?

This is how you probably remember it. After rejecting some armor
loaned by Saul because it is too large, little David accepts the
Philistine champion's challenge, picks up five smooth stones and
his shepherd's sling, and sets out to meet this giant. The ten-foot-
tall ("six cubits and a span") Goliath laughs at the sight of the
smallish shepherd. Then the first stone catches Goliath between
the eyes and he falls down, unconscious. David takes Goliath's
sword, kills him, and calmly lops off the Philistine giant's head.

Now a few "facts." At the end of the Goliath story, Saul
doesn't know who David is. But in an earlier passage, David is

seen playing the harp for Saul. Either Saul knows David or he doesn't. This is another compelling piece of evidence for the idea that various sources were woven together to create this narrative—and the weaving wasn't always done seamlessly. This problem crops up again because later in the story somebody else kills Goliath.

First of all, Goliath was only four cubits and a span, according to another version of the story found in the Dead Sea Scrolls, making him about six feet nine—a very healthy size, to be sure, and nice for professional basketball—but he was no ten-foot giant. Then there is Elhanan, a soldier who kills Goliath in 2 Samuel 21. So who really killed Goliath? Probably not David, who may have killed another Philistine who was later called Goliath. The King James translators of 1611 tried to cover up the discrepancy by inserting the words "brother of" before the second mention of Goliath, but older texts don't bear that version out. In other words, after David was famous, the authors of the Hebrew scriptures may have tried to dress up David's military exploits with a few embellishments. This is an old story that keeps being replayed, as recently demonstrated in the sad episode of an American admiral who had exaggerated his service record and then committed suicide when he was about to be exposed in the media. There was also a much-publicized case of an American diplomat who fabricated his World War II service and a war-related injury, a lie discovered after the man was buried in Arlington National Cemetery, America's most sacred military burial ground.

David knew how to win friends and influence people. From playing harp for Saul, he became best friends with Saul's son Jonathan, a friendship that has led to speculation (see below) about its intimacy, and was soon elevated to leadership in the army. Like many notable generals in history, including Napoleon, Washington, Eisenhower, and Schwarzkopf, David learned that military victories equal huge popularity with the hometown fans. Everyone was happy with David. Except Saul, who could hear the people chanting:

"Saul has killed his thousands,
and David his tens of thousands."

Inflamed by jealousy and obviously threatened by David's charismatic abilities, Saul began to plot David's death, even going so far as to use his daughters as bait. That plan backfired when Saul's daughter Michal fell in love with David, but Saul was willing to use even his daughter's love to get David. He asks David for a "marriage present," or bride-price, of a hundred Philistine foreskins, assuming David will die in the process. The idea of giving a young hero an impossible task is a common one in legends. In Greek myth, Jason must deliver the golden fleece and Perseus must bring the head of the Medusa. Like these other ancient Near East warrior-heroes, David surprises Saul by delivering the goods. In some versions of the Hebrew text, David actually goes Saul one better and delivers *two hundred* foreskins.

The details of how these foreskins are presented to Saul are vague in this account. But the ritual stripping of some body part of a dead enemy—a battle trophy that provided in modern military parlance a "body count"—was typical of ancient Near Eastern cultures. Heads or hands were the usual proof, so Saul's request for the delivery of enemy body parts was not unusual in the ancient world. But foreskins? Cyrus Gordon explains that Egyptians, who were circumcised like the Hebrews, usually took hands or heads of their defeated enemies. However, when it came to uncircumcised Libyans, "uncircumcised phalli were often amputated for counting." (*The Bible and the Ancient Near East*, p. 187)

Again bested by David, Saul is forced to keep his side of the bargain and David becomes Saul's son-in-law, as well as a thorn in his side. Driven to near madness, Saul openly discuses his plans to kill David with his oldest son, Jonathan. But even Saul's children like David better, and Jonathan immediately warns his friend of Saul's murderous intentions. After throwing a javelin at David, Saul sends assassins to kill David while he is sleeping, but Saul's daughter Michal saves David by making a dummy and putting it in the bed. When David escapes another of Saul's traps, the raging Saul orders the murder of eighty-five priests who had sheltered David. This certainly didn't help Saul's standing with the priests who later recorded this history.

Was David a traitor?

On two occasions, the biblical account reports how David spared Saul's life when he could have killed him. Reduced to bandit status, David rides with a few hundred loyal men who "take no prisoners." While in this "Jesse James" phase of his career, David takes time to acquire two new wives, and the account reports without comment that David's first wife, Michal, was given to another man by her father, Saul. This regal muscle-flexing is a move to diminish David's stature. While married to the king's daughter, David had a claim to the throne. David's new wives are the result of politically astute marriages, made in an attempt to shore up loyalty to him among some of the tribes. All of these wives being taken and given with little thought for the women paints a very clear picture of a woman's role at the time.

Convinced that Saul is still after his skin, David does the seemingly unthinkable; he joins the Philistines. The biblical account leaves no doubt: David is a mercenary in the Philistine employ. There is no word as to how God views this shift in loyalty.

At about the same time, in a scene rivaling the three witches of the heaths in Shakespeare's *Macbeth*, Saul visits a medium at En-dor, a practice forbidden by Mosaic Law. She summons up the spirit of the dead Samuel, who has bad news for Saul; he and his sons and the Israelites will fall to the Philistines in battle. In the meantime, some of the Philistines have second thoughts about David and his loyalties, although their leader thinks David is doing a fine job. So David and his men leave the Philistine camp, just as the Philistines march out to battle Saul at Mount Gilboa. It is a matter of some conjecture as to whether David actually left the

Philistines when they fought Saul or the later writers amended the history to keep David's involvement in Saul's defeat out of the biblical picture. In a total rout, Jonathan and two of Saul's other sons are killed and the first king of Israel commits suicide with the help of his armor-bearer—the equivalent of the Roman tradition of falling on one's sword to avoid disgrace. When found by the Philistines, Saul and his sons are stripped of their armor, decapitated, and their bodies hung on a wall.

In *The Bible and the Ancient Near East*, Cyrus Gordon and Gary Rendsburg have drawn fascinating parallels between the epics of Homer and the biblical accounts of the Philistine-Israelite wars. They write:

> David has more in common with the heroes of the *Iliad*
> than with Ezra and Nehemiah. His command of a band of
> rough men, his impetuousness, his winning of a princess
> by slaying Philistines . . . his amours—all of these and other
> features fit rather into the milieu of Homer's heroic age
> than the framework of synagogue and church. . . . The historic
> context leaves no doubt as to what happened: Saul
> was killed by the Philistines, who were of the same East
> Mediterranean origin as the Myceneans in the Trojan War.
> . . . The early histories of the Hebrews and Greeks were
> intricately interrelated, and neither can be understood in
> isolation from the other. (pp. 107–108)

BIBLICAL VOICES
How the mighty have fallen
   in the midst of the battle!
Jonathan lies slain upon your high places.
   I am distressed for you, my
      brother Jonathan;
   greatly beloved were you to me:
   your love to me was wonderful,
   passing the love of women. (2 Sam. 1:25–26)

Were David and Jonathan more than just friends?

This elegy and other verses concerning the friendship of Jonathan and David ("And Jonathan . . . loved him [David] as he loved his own soul" 1 Sam. 20:17) have led to more than raised eyebrows. Some modern commentators state outright that Jonathan and David were homosexual lovers. While the ancient Israelite writers condemned homosexuality, other nearby cultures accepted it. Even among warriors, homosexuality was condoned because of the bond it created between men. Traditionalists like Rabbi Joseph Telushkin call this idea "slanderous." They completely refute the idea that David was gay, or more accurately bisexual, since he had plenty of wives, arguing that the verses simply describe an extraordinary platonic friendship between two men who loved each other as brothers. Others have tried to read between the lines and say it was more than that. Given the unconditional condemnation of homosexuality throughout Hebrew scriptures, it is difficult to imagine that this particular "abomination" would have been overlooked had it been true. But David sure got away with a lot and came out looking squeaky clean. Did David's biblical "spin doctors" gloss over this particular "sin" and leave David's numerous heterosexual dalliances as proof of what a macho guy he really was? It's a question that goes unsettled.

Did King David even exist?

Until recently, asking this question was akin to asking if Odysseus or King Arthur was real. Heroic characters, celebrated in song and epics, they were undoubtedly based upon somebody, and the facts were embellished over time. Until 1993, there was no historical or archaeological evidence outside the Bible to substantiate the existence of an Israelite king named David. That changed with the discovery of a wall fragment found at Tell Dan on the headwaters of the river Jordan. The Phoenician script carved in stone appears to refer to "the king of Israel" and the "House of David." Although this single inscription in a piece of wall that was broken and reused has provoked considerable scholarly disagreement, it is still widely accepted as the first mention of a Davidic dynasty outside the Bible.

After Saul's death, David consolidates power within his own tribe of Judah and the intensity of the palace intrigues and tribal infighting increases. David goes to war with Saul's surviving son, Ishbaal. At the same time, Ishbaal (also called Ish-bosheth) is caught in a power struggle with one of his generals who has slept with one of Saul's concubines, an attempt to stake a claim to the throne. The general defects to David, who presses Ishbaal for the return of Michal, his first wife, who has been given to another man. Ishbaal is then assassinated. With this coup, David is accepted as king by the northern tribes of Israel. He further solidifies his power with victories over the Philistines and then selects Jerusalem as the site of his capital. A small and previously obscure Canaanite town, Jerusalem is an excellent strategic and political choice. Occupying high ground at a crossroads with highways running in four directions, Jerusalem is virtually impregnable from assault on three sides and contains a perennial water supply from the Gihon spring. The choice of Jerusalem is politically astute because it was not affiliated with any of the tribes. David then strengthens the significance of the "city of David" by moving the Ark of the Covenant there, making Jerusalem the center of worship of Yahweh.

David celebrates this triumphant moment with a frenzied, ecstatic dance. But his first wife, Michal, now back in his household but clearly no longer in love with David, does not approve of David's doing the "Full Monty." She complains that David had "uncovered himself today before the eyes of his servants' maids as any vulgar fellow might shamelessly uncover himself." In other words, he had been dancing naked. David, clearly disinterested in his first wife, tells her he will dance all he wants. A poignant loser in every way, Michal is left childless, either because she is barren or because David will no longer sleep with her.

BIBLICAL VOICES
"Set ye Uriah in the forefront of the hottest battle." (2 Sam. 11:15 KJV)

PLOT SUMMARY: DAVID AND BATHSHEBA
In his famous and often misquoted 1887 remark, Lord Acton said, "Power tends to corrupt and absolute power corrupts absolutely."

King David proves no exception. The "Sweet Psalmist" becomes an adulterous murderer whose power makes him believe that he is above the law and eventually is responsible for the death of one of his own sons.

The problems start when David sees a beautiful woman bathing nearby. The interested David is told that she is Bathsheba, the wife of Uriah the Hittite. As Mel Brooks once put it, "It's good to be the king." David has her brought over, they sleep together, and she gets pregnant. Uriah is called back to sleep with Bathsheba in an attempted cover-up, but Uriah refuses: soldiers are supposed to abstain from sex before battle to keep themselves "pure." Next, David orders Uriah into the front lines and has the rest of the army withdrawn, leaving Uriah vulnerable, and he is killed. After a suitable mourning period, Bathsheba marries David and bears him a son. But through the prophet Nathan, God lets David know he's done wrong and promises that there will be trouble in David's own house. As part of the punishment, David and Bathsheba's first son is struck by God and dies. "The sins of the father . . ."

David and Bathsheba have another child, who is named Solomon, but their dysfunctional family troubles have just begun.

PLOT SUMMARY: THE RAPE OF TAMAR

David has a son named Absalom and a daughter named Tamar by one marriage. He has another son, his firstborn and heir, Amnon, by still another wife. Amnon wants to sleep with his half sister, Tamar, but she refuses. Amnon doesn't take no for an answer and rapes her. Waiting two years before striking back at his half brother, Absalom avenges the rape of his sister Tamar by getting Amnon drunk and killing him. Not only is it an act of revenge, but Absalom has moved himself to the front of the line to succeed David by removing the first heir, Amnon.

But Absalom is impatient. Unwilling to wait for David to die, Absalom stages a nearly successful coup. With a small army, he forces his father to flee Jerusalem, leaving behind "ten concubines." Absalom sets up a tent on the roof of David's house and sleeps with each of his father's ten concubines in a symbolic demonstration that he has taken the throne and all that goes with it. With the aid of a group of mercenaries, David finally puts down the rebellion of his son and Absalom is captured. In a scene that must have been told for great comic effect, Absalom is captured when his head, or his hair—depending on the translation—gets caught in a tree and the mule he is riding keeps going. Some commentaries suggest that the "tree" in which Absalom's head is caught is a euphemism for pubic hair and Absalom is actually caught *in flagrante*. Against David's orders, his renegade son Absalom is killed.

A second coup by a "scoundrel named Sheba" is also ruthlessly put down. But the family intrigues of David are not over. David's reign was a passion play of fraternal conspiracies that equal anything that took place in the courts of Caligula or Nero of Roman infamy.

Uneasy Lies the Head . . . Part 2

1 & 2 Kings, 1 & 2 Chronicles, Lamentations

Let a young virgin be sought for my lord the king, and let her wait on the king, and be his attendant; let her lie in your bosom, so that my lord the king may be warm. (1 Kings 1:1–4)

Divide the living boy in two; then give half to the one and half to the other. (1 Kings 3:25 KJV)

Nebuzaradan the captain of the bodyguard, a servant of the king of Babylon, came to Jerusalem. He burned the house of the Lord, the king's house, and all the houses of Jerusalem; every great house he burned down. . . . Nebuzaradan the captain of the guard carried into exile the rest of the people who were left in the city and the deserters who had defected to the king of Babylon—all the rest of the population. (2 Kings 25:8–12)

❋ Was Solomon really so smart?

❋ What did Solomon's Temple look like?

❋ Where is Sheba?

❋ Was Jezebel really so bad?

❋ Who was Baal-zebub?

❋ Is mocking a bald man any reason to kill children?

❋ Who wrote the "Book of the Law"?

❋ Why are the stories in Chronicles different from those in other Bible books?

❋ Was the Exile all that bad?

I f the stories of David in the preceding chapter didn't disillusion you, buckle your seat belt. Solomon, generally presented as a paragon of wisdom and virtue, was not much better than his illustrious—and lusty—father.

In both Hebrew scriptures and Christian Old Testament, the two books of Kings immediately follow the two books of Samuel and form a continuing narrative account of the kingdoms of Israel and Judah from the death of David and the enthronement of Solomon to the Babylonian Exile, a period extending roughly from 1000 BCE to the destruction of Jerusalem in 587 BCE. Traditionally ascribed to the prophet Jeremiah, the books are are now thought to be the work of two or more anonymous authors or editors. These writers relied upon a number of earlier sources, now lost, several of which are actually mentioned in the biblical text. These missing sources include "The Book of the Acts of Solomon," "The Book of the Chronicles of the Kings of Israel," and "The Book of the Chronicles of the Kings of Judah," all of which probably belonged to the official court archives and historical records. The biblical books called Chronicles are different books compiled at a later time and are discussed at the end of this chapter.

The work of the first writer of Kings is thought to date from just before the death of the Judean king and religious reformer Josiah (609 BCE). The second writer probably worked from about 550 BCE, mainly because the last historical event recorded in the book took place in 561 BCE, and no mention is made of the conquest of Babylon by the Persians in 539 BCE.

BIBLICAL VOICES

King David was old and advanced in years; and although they covered him with clothes, he could not get warm. So his servants said to him, "Let a young virgin be sought for my lord the king, and let her wait on the king, and be his attendant; let her lie in your bosom, so that my lord the king may be warm." So they searched for a beautiful girl throughout all the territory of Israel, and found Abishag the Shunammite, and brought her to the king. The girl was very beautiful. She became the king's attendant, but the king did not know her sexually. (1 Kings 1:1–4)

Quite an image of the virile young shepherd boy who once danced naked in the streets!

Now a decrepit old man, unable to keep warm, David nears the end of his life a somewhat pathetic character. However, before reaching this age of dotage, when he needs a "bed warmer" to fight off chills, David further strengthened his control over Israel by executing seven descendants of Saul by impaling; only one other of Saul's descendants, the crippled son of Jonathan, is allowed to live. David and Bathsheba have agreed that their son Solomon will take the throne. In a compelling scene, David advises Solomon about which enemies to eliminate, a scene that author Jonathan Kirsch points out was "artfully copied" when Don Corleone similarly counsels his son and successor, Michael, in *The Godfather*.

BIBLICAL VOICES

As David's life drew to its close he laid this charge on his son Solomon, "I am going the way of all the earth. Be strong and show yourself a man. Observe the injunctions of Yahweh your God, following his ways and keeping his laws, his commandments, his ordinances and his decrees, as stand written in the Law of Moses, so that you may be successful in everything you do and undertake, and that Yahweh may fulfill the promise which he made me, 'If your sons are careful how they behave, and walk loyally before me with all their heart and soul, you will never want for a man on the throne of Israel.'

"You know too what Joab son of Zeruiah did to me, and what he did to the two commanders of the army of Israel, Abner son of Ner and Amasa son of Jether; how he murdered them, shedding the blood of war in time of peace and staining the belt round my waist and the sandals on my feet with the blood of war. You will be wise not to let his grey head go down to Sheol in peace. As regards the sons of Barzillai of Gilead, treat them with faithful love, let them be among those who eat at your table, for they were as kind to me when I was fleeing from your brother Absalom. You also have with you Shimei son of Gera, the Benjaminite from Bahurim. He called down a terrible curse on me the day I left for Mahanaim, but he came down to meet me at the Jordan and I swore to him by Yahweh that I would not put him to death. But you, you must not let him go unpunished; you are a wise man and will know how to deal with him, to bring his grey head down to Sheol in blood." (1 Kings 2:1–9 NJB)

After David's death, his eldest son, Adonijah, made a futile grab for the throne by asking Bathsheba if he might sleep with David's virgin concubine, Abishag. Bathsheba reports this request to Solomon, knowing that Solomon will understand the implications of Adonijah's design. Solomon has his half brother Adonijah assassinated. He will make short work of the few other possible threats to his rule, proving himself as ruthlessly cold-blooded as his father was. When God later commends him for not asking for the life of his enemies, Solomon must have snickered. He had already dispensed with all of them.

BIBLICAL VOICES

God said to him, "Because you have asked this, and have not asked for yourself long life or riches, *or for the life of your enemies,* but have asked for yourself understanding to discern what is right, I now do according to your word. Indeed I give you a wise and discerning mind; no one like you has been before you and no one like you shall arise after you. I give you also what you have not asked, both riches and honor all your life; no other king shall compare with you." (1 Kings 3: 11–13; emphasis added)

Was Solomon really so smart?

In the ancient joke, when the comedian is asked, "Who was that lady?," the famous reply goes, "That was no lady. That was my wife."

The punch line changes when it comes to Solomon: "Those were no ladies. They were prostitutes."

Think of Solomon and we think of wisdom, the ancient Israelite equivalent to the Judge Wapner on television's *People's Court*, coolly making wise judgments at a moment's notice. In a dream, the newly crowned King Solomon asked God for wisdom. Impressed by the request, God grants Solomon's wish but also gives him everything else he *didn't* ask for. While Kings asserts that Solomon "spake three thousand proverbs," the biblical evidence of his smarts rests largely upon a story told over and over again. But the story that most people remember is not the whole truth and nothing but the truth.

In this well-known folktale, two women bring a baby to King Solomon. One woman's child has died in the night. Both women live in the same house and both claim this live baby as their own. Solomon ponders the case for a moment and orders the baby to be cut in half, and a half given to each mother. One woman shrieks and says to give the child to the other. Solomon knows that she is the real mother. Such wisdom. All Israel is impressed.

What they didn't tell you in Sunday school was that those two women were prostitutes. So what were two prostitutes doing in King Solomon's palace? There are two choices here. One is that they were simply harlots of the sort readers of the "real" Bible should now be accustomed to encountering. The other possibility is that they were cultic prostitutes, also well known throughout the Hebrew scriptures. At the end of 1 Kings, mention is even made of male temple prostitutes who were finally cleaned out of Jerusalem by King Jehoshaphat during his reign in 873 BCE.

A grim archaeological dig, reported in *Biblical Archaeology Review* (July/August 1997), offers evidence that prostitution continued long afterward in this part of the world. Near the remains of a Roman-era building that may have been a brothel in the city of Ashkelon, two archaeologists found the remains of many infant children, leading them to speculate that the prostitutes of this later era did not share the same maternal concerns as the two prostitutes who presented themselves to Solomon.

Even though Solomon is conventionally viewed with reverence for building the first Temple in Jerusalem, he allowed other religions and cults to flourish in his kingdom, especially to keep his many wives and concubines happy. The number of Solomon's "strange women," according to the text, reached seven hundred princesses and three hundred concubines. They included the daughter of a Pharaoh, a marriage made to secure a peace treaty and defensive pact with Egypt. For many of these wives and mistresses, Solomon constructed shrines, or "high places," including one dedicated to the Canaanite god Molech (or Moloch), the "abomination of the Ammonites," the most reprehensible of foreign gods who demanded infant sacrifice, a practice that apparently continued in Judah despite the biblical condemnation. Built in Solomon's time, the Tophet, the actual temple where infants were burned, was in a nearby valley called Gehennah, a word that understandably came to be a synonym for Hell.

Solomon had grandiose plans for his empire. Besides building the first Temple in Jerusalem, he wanted palaces for himself and his wives along with their numerous shrines. Solomon's lavish plans required two things: labor and taxes. Ancient Israel was no different from most places. People don't like taxes and they don't like forced labor. A conscription program, essentially no different from the one used by the Pharaohs to build the pyramids, required Israel's men to work one month out of three for Solomon and was especially unpopular. In other words, while Solomon enjoyed himself at court in Jerusalem, antagonism was building throughout the country toward the Jerusalem regime with its wealth, excess, and blasphemous disregard for God's rules. He may have been "Wise" but Solomon wasn't very smart.

What did Solomon's Temple look like?

While it wasn't the largest building built during Solomon's reign, the Jerusalem Temple was probably the most important. Seven years in the making—Solomon's palace took thirteen to build—the Temple construction job was let out to an outside contractor, King Hiram of Phoenicia, who supplied materials and labor. That meant the great Temple, center of Judaism and dwelling place of Yahweh, was probably designed in the style of a Phoenician or Canaanite temple. A clear picture of King Solomon's Temple is somewhat difficult because some of the descriptions of it in the Bible are obscure. But its plan followed that of the portable Tabernacle described to Moses by God in the wilderness, and the Tabernacle had been with the Israelites ever since. David had brought it to Jerusalem, where Solomon planned to convert it into a permanent building.

The building was rectangular, with an open "porch" facing east and an inner sanctuary, the Holy of Holies, believed to be the actual dwelling place of Yahweh. The overall dimensions of the building were 60 by 20 cubits (roughly 100 by 33 feet, or 30 by 10 meters) and rose to a height of 30 cubits (about 50 feet, or 15 meters). The Temple was built of quarried stone, but the inner walls were lined with cedar and the entire structure was lined with gold. The Temple building had two sections. The large exterior room contained candelabra, two altars, and a golden table on which twelve new loaves of bread were placed each week. At the back of the Temple, a set of steps led to an inner room, the cube-shaped Holy of Holies whose sides were each 20 cubits. It was the resting place of the Ark of the Covenant, the chest holding the tablets of the Ten Commandments. This room was entered by the high priest only once each year on the Day of Atonement.

The Temple building was surrounded by two open-air court-yards. The inner one—the court of the priests—was enclosed by a wall constructed of three courses of stone and one of cedar beams. Inside this enclosed courtyard was the outdoor altar where animals were sacrificed and a large metal basin—10 cubits in diameter—called the "sea," supported by twelve bull statues, an animal that was typically associated with the Canaanite god Baal. A larger, outer great court probably also enclosed the royal buildings.

Daily temple worship included prayers and sacrifices made by the priests. Sacrifices were made for a variety of reasons, including gratitude, ritual purification, and the expiation of sins. In keeping with the requirements laid out in Leviticus, the Temple priests performed the sacrifices using only unblemished male animals. The priest slaughtered the animal with a sharp knife and its blood was sprinkled or smeared on the altar. The carcass was flayed and cut into pieces, which were then burned. Offerings of wine, cereals, and oils were also burned. Pigeons and doves were available as substitutes for the large—and presumably more costly—animals. These were dispatched by the priests, who slit their throats with a fingernail. The contents of the animal's stomach were discarded—in case it had eaten something impure—and the wings were pressed flat without breaking them before the carcass was burned. That daily processional of ritual sacrifices continued in Jerusalem from the time of Solomon until the Temple was destroyed in 586 BCE. Temple sacrifices were restored in 516 BCE, after the return from the Babylonian Exile, and continued until 70 CE, when the Temple was destroyed by the Romans.

Where is Sheba?

Besides the famed baby-slicing incident, a visit made to King Solomon by the "Queen of Sheba" stands as the other memorable episode in Solomon's life. This meeting of royals has fueled his-

torical speculation and several legends. What exactly went on between these monarchs when they met? And where did the Queen
of Sheba come from? Both questions are still matters of mythology.
Ethiopians who claimed that Meroe, the ancient capital of Ethiopia, was the biblical "Sheba" decided that their first emperor was
the offspring of a liaison—unmentioned in the Bible account—
between Solomon and the Queen of Sheba. This provided the link
allowing the last Ethiopian emperor, Haile Selassie, to call himself
the "Lion of Judah" and claim descent from Solomon. This story
gets more complicated because, according to Ethiopian legends,
the regal offspring of Solomon and the Queen of Sheba's alleged
dalliance, Menelik I, returned to Jerusalem and stole the Ark of
the Covenant from the Temple and took it back to Ethiopia,
where it remains to this day.

Good legend. Bad geography.

The biblical Sheba was actually a state in southern Arabia—in
the area of present-day Yemen, a region that produced those famed
biblical spices, frankincense and myrrh. The Queen of Sheba's
visit, if it actually happened, was most likely a diplomatic mission
made to iron out some differences regarding the spice trade, which
Solomon was attempting to get a piece of. The fact that the
territory had a queen was historically interesting because it demonstrated that women could hold such power in these male-
dominated times.

PLOT SUMMARY: THE DIVIDED KINGDOM

After Solomon's death between 930 and 925 BCE, political and
religious differences quickly shattered the kingdom built by David
and Solomon. When Solomon's son Rehoboam foolishly told the
northern tribes that he planned to be even tougher than his father
had been, the policy did not sit well with his already disgruntled
subjects. Led by the rebel Jeroboam, supported by the Egyptian
Pharaoh Sheshonk (called "King Shishak of Egypt" in the Bible),
the ten tribes in the north broke away from the southern tribes of
Judah and Benjamin. In the wake of this "secession," two weaker

kingdoms were left: Judah in the south and Israel in the north. To assert his religious and political independence from Jerusalem, Jeroboam set up two shrines with golden bulls, recalling the Exodus story, an act of idol-worship for which the northerners would eventually pay.

Jeroboam's twenty-year reign over Israel was followed by that of his son, who was soon deposed by a military coup. A series of rebellions followed until an army officer named Omri gained the throne and established a period of relative order, proving to be one of the ablest kings in Israelite history, a fact that the southerners who wrote this story conveniently overlooked. It would be like a Confederate historian writing about the American Civil War and saying that Lincoln was an American president—but nothing else. Omri set up a new capital in the town of Samaria, recovered previously lost territory—conquering neighboring Moab, a fact omitted from the Scriptures—and established an orderly succession with his son Ahab following him. In Assyrian court records, Israel was actually known as the "House of Omri."

RULERS OF THE DIVIDED KINGDOM

(Dates of reign in parentheses; these dates are imprecise but generally accepted. All dates are BCE.)

ISRAEL (NORTH)	JUDAH (SOUTH)
Jeroboam I (922–901)	Rehoboam (922–915)
	Abijam (915–913)
Nadab (901–900)	Asa (913–873)
Baasha (900–877)	
Elah (877–876)	Jehoshaphat (873–849)
Zimri (876)	
Omri (876–869)	
Ahab (869–850)	
Ahaziah (850–849)	Jehoram (849–842)
Jehoram (849–842)	Ahaziah (842)
	Athalia (842–837)
Jehu (842–815)	Jehoash (837–800)

Jehoahaz (815–801)   Amaziah (800–783)

Jehoash (801–786)

Jeroboam II (786–746)   Uzziah (783–742)

Zechariah (746–745)

Shallum (745)

Menahem (745–738)   Jotham (742–735)

Pekahiah (738–737)   Ahaz (735–715)

Pekah (737–732)

Hoshea (732–721)   J U D A H (A F T E R

           T H E F A L L O F

           I S R A E L)

           Hezekiah (715–687)

           Manasseh (687–642)

           Amon (642–640)

           Josiah (640–609)

           Jehoahaz (609)

           Jehoiakim (609–598)

           Jehoiachin (598–597)

           Zedekiah (597–586)

(Source: *New Oxford Annotated Bible*)

In the period of the divided kingdom, the focus of the Bible books moves away from the kings to the exploits of a series of "prophets" who try to counsel—usually with little success—the rulers and people of Israel and Judah. There had been prophets or "seers" earlier in Israelite history, including Samuel and Deborah, the prophetess and judge. But in the period of the divided kingdoms, the various prophets emerge as the crucial biblical characters, overshadowing the kings to whom these prophets often tried to preach. Hebrew "prophets" aren't easily defined; they were more than "fortune-tellers." In general, the prophets were men or women who received divine messages—generally through dreams or visions. These messages were then communicated to the entire nation or to individuals, such as kings. The first of this generation of prophets were Elijah, one of Judaism's great folk heroes, and his successor, Elisha.

BIBLICAL VOICES

The dogs shall eat Jezebel by the wall of Jezreel. (1 Kings 21:23 KJV)

Was Jezebel really so bad?

Few names in biblical lore conjure up as negative an image as that of Jezebel, now synonymous with an evil, scheming woman, with a smattering of sexual temptress thrown in as well. The biblical Jezebel was a Phoenician princess, wife of King Ahab, Omri's son. While he is viewed as one of the great scoundrels in the Bible, historical records show Ahab to have been an effective ruler who increased Israel's strength in the region during a reign of nearly twenty years. When a coalition of Canaanite nations united to fend off an Assyrian invasion in 853 BCE, Ahab supplied the largest contingent: two thousand chariots and ten thousand fighting men. He even improved ties with the southern kingdom of Judah by marrying his daughter to the southern king Jehoram. The biblical authors—from southern Judah—did not think too highly of this northern king and glossed over his accomplishments, focusing instead on his shortcomings, the greatest of which was his wife: "But there was none like unto Ahab, which did sell himself to work wickedness in the sight of the Lord, whom Jezebel his wife stirred up." (1 Kings 21:25 KJV)

To the authors of Kings, Ahab was merely a pawn of his scheming wife. He willingly allowed her to promote the worship of Baal, the chief Canaanite god, and Baal's consorts Astarte and Asherah. To counter the growth of Baal worship under Jezebel and Ahab, God sent a drought and famine on Israel, then dispatched the prophet Elijah to preach to the sinful rulers and people. Hav-

ing been miraculously fed in the wilderness by ravens and then at
a widow's home by food that never ran out, Elijah was a wonder-
worker whose powers were much greater than simple prophecy.
He also raised a child from the dead. But his essential mission was
to bring all of Israel back to Yahweh's fold.

To prove God's superiority, Elijah challenged four hundred and
fifty prophets of Baal and four hundred prophets of Asherah, "who
eat at Jezebel's table," to a contest. The Baal prophets danced in a
frenzy and hacked at themselves with swords, an accurate depiction
of Baal worship in which priests mutilated themselves in a ritual of
mourning for their dead god, who was then supposed to rise from
the dead. When nothing happened after these priests performed,
Elijah taunted the Baal worshipers, saying their god was either
sleeping or "has wandered away," a euphemism for defecating. Elijah then called down heavenly fire on the altars of Baal, and the
Israelites slaughtered the four hundred and fifty priests of Baal.

Unhappy with the decimation of her priests, Jezebel threatened to kill Elijah, who escaped back into the wilderness. Jezebel's capacity for evil was then illustrated in a story in which she
trumped up a false charge against a neighbor who owned a vineyard that Jezebel's husband, King Ahab, wanted. Using witnesses
she had bribed, Jezebel had the neighbor, Naboth, convicted of
blasphemy and he was stoned to death. Ahab took Naboth's vineyard for himself.

Ahab and Jezebel were cursed horribly by Elijah, who told the
king that dogs would eat Jezebel and anyone belonging to Ahab.
Sure enough, when Ahab died in battle, the biblical account of his
life ends with dogs licking the blood from his chariot and "prostitutes washing themselves in it."

Who was Baal-zebub?

When Ahab's son and successor, Ahaziah, fell from a balcony, he
asked a god named Baal-zebub if he would recover. *Baal-zebub*

(also translated as Beelzebub) is a pun on the Canaanite name meaning "Lord Baal," "Baal the Prince" or "lord of the divine abode." In Hebrew, it is mockingly translated as "lord of the flies," or in Aramaic, "lord of dung." In later times, Beelzebub (or Beelzebul) became identified with Satan, and in the New Testament Jesus is accused of casting out demons on the authority of Beelzebul, the ruler of demons.

When Elijah the prophet tells Ahaziah that he will die from his injuries, the king sends his guard to kill the prophet, but heavenly fire destroys the soldiers.

Soon after this episode, Elijah is taken up to heaven, only the second biblical figure besides Enoch in Genesis to be taken directly to heaven, and his mantle is taken up by his disciple Elisha:

> There appeared a chariot of fire, and horses of fire, and parted them both asunder; and Elijah went up by a whirlwind into heaven. (2 Kings 2:11 KJV)

Is mocking a bald man any reason to kill children?

After the death of the prophet Elijah, his mantle was passed—literally—to Elisha, who emerged as the next leader of a "company of prophets," a powerful force in court politics of the day. Unlike priests, these prophets were itinerants who roamed the countryside, sometimes in bands. While some achieved a high degree of power and influence with the rulers of the time, many of the prophets were viewed as troublemakers. Besides the similarities in the names of Elijah and Elisha, there are numerous parallels of miracles performed by these two prophets in the biblical account. It seems likely that stories of the two men may have been confused and merged by later writers.

Elisha's first miracle was to purify a spring at Jericho (still called Elisha's Fountain). But the account of Elisha's second "miracle" is more troubling. When some boys came out of the town to make fun of his bald head, Elisha cursed them in God's name. Two she-bears emerged from the woods and mauled forty-two of the boys.

They weren't the only children to die in this biblical episode. During a battle between the allied forces of Israel, Judah, and Edom against Moab, the king of Moab offered his son as a burnt sacrifice in the midst of the fighting. Impressed by this horrifying act, the forces of Israel withdrew, but would suffer for allowing this human sacrifice to sway them in battle against God's direct orders.

Unlike Elijah, and later prophets who were often viewed as gadflies and thorns in the royal side, Elisha and his followers, "the company of prophets," became power brokers in the courts of a succession of kings. They led the forces of Israel in wars and turned the tide of battle with their miraculous powers. Elisha's influence at court eventually led to his counseling Jehu of Israel (842–815 BCE), a general who engineers a coup and purges the surviving members of Ahab's dynasty.

BIBLICAL VOICES

When Jehu came to Jezreel, Jezebel heard of it; she painted her eyes, and adorned her head, and looked out of the window. . . . He looked up to the window and said . . . "Throw her down." So they threw her down; some of her blood spattered on the wall and on the horses, which trampled on her. (2 Kings 9:30–33)

After Ahab's death, Jezebel had remained the power behind the Israelite throne while her sons ruled. But in a coup led by Jehu, the general backed by Elisha, Ahab's sons were overthrown and Jezebel was killed, fulfilling Elijah's curse, and finally removing any vestiges of Baal worship from Israel. While Jehu emerges from the Bible with flying colors, in historical terms, he doesn't fare as well. Jehu foolishly broke Israel's alliances with neighboring

Phoenicia and Judah, seriously weakening the nation at a time when the Assyrian empire, based in the Tigris River area and led by Shalmaneser III (859–824 BCE) was expanding its power. Shalmaneser reduced Israel to a vassal state, forced to pay heavy tribute. Assyria also went into a period of decline after the death of Shalmaneser, and Israel and Judah were able to recover some lost territory and a measure of independence. King Jehu was first in a dynasty that lasted for about a century in Israel. Among his heirs was Jeroboam II, little noted in the Bible but an effective ruler whose forty-year reign was a period of relative stability and wealth for Israel. After Jeroboam II's death in 746 BCE, however, Israel once again fell into a period of chaotic instability.

BIBLICAL VOICES

Then the king of Assyria invaded all the land and came to Samaria; for three years he besieged it. In the ninth year of Hoshea the king of Assyria captured Samaria; he carried the Israelites away to Assyria. . . . This occurred because the people of Israel had sinned against the Lord their God, who had brought them up out of the land of Egypt from under the hand of Pharaoh king of Egypt. They had worshiped other gods and walked in the customs of other nations whom the Lord drove out before the people of Israel, and in the customs that the kings of Israel introduced. (2 Kings 17:5–8)

Under Tiglath-pileser III (745–727 BCE), the Assyrian identified as "Pul" in the Bible, an invigorated Assyrian empire rose again to dominate the Near East. The Assyrians extended their empire all the way to the Nile and their great capital city of Nineveh, with a magnificent temple honoring the city's patron goddess Ishtar, rose on the banks of the northern Tigris River. Once again, Israel was reduced to a client state forced to pay huge tributes to the Assyrians. One of the Assyrians' most effective methods of controlling conquered territories was to deport the elite of their defeated enemies back to Mesopotamia. When

Israel's last king, Hoshea, attempted to revolt against the Assyrian overlords with Egyptian assistance, Tiglath-pileser's son, Shalmaneser V, invaded Israel and the capital of Samaria fell. In 721 BCE, Sargon II made Israel a province of Assyria and he deported 27,290 inhabitants of Israel to territory in the northern Tigris-Euphrates area. This was the end of the kingdom of Israel. The members of the ten tribes deported from Israel became the "Lost Tribes of Israel."

Sargon II also introduced new settlers into the territory of former Israel, which was renamed Samaria, and its people became known as Samaritans. Curiously, Sargon sent an Israelite priest to instruct these people in the "law of the god of the land." While the Samaritans adopted some Hebrew laws and customs, they continued many of their own practices, which then included human sacrifice. This historical event explains the enmity that existed between Jews and Samaritans, carrying over to New Testament times as evidenced in Jesus' parable of the "Good Samaritan."

RULERS OF ASSYRIA
(All dates are approximate and BCE)

Ashur-dan II	934–912
Adad-nirari II	912–891
Tukulti-Ninurta II	891–884
Ashurnasirpal II	884–859
Shalmaneser III	859–824
Shamshi-Adad V	824–811
Adad-nirari III	811–783
Shalmaneser IV	783–773
Ashur-dan III	773–755
Ashur-nirari V	755–745
Tiglath-pileser III	745–727 (Identified as Pul in the Bible)
Shalmaneser V	727–722
Sargon II	722–705
Sennacherib	705–681

Esarhaddon	681–669
Ashurbanipal	669–627
Ashur-etel-ilani	627–624
Sin-shumu-lishir	624–623
Sin-shara-ishkun	623–612
Ashur-uballit II	612–609

(Source: *The Illustrated Guide to the Bible*)

Based on the plains of the Tigris River, the Assyrian empire dominated the ancient Near East for three hundred years (between 900 and 600 BCE). Its greatest period came under a succession of kings who appear in the Bible and often are made to be instruments of God in their oppression of Israel. The most famed city of the Assyrian empire was Nineveh, a splendid capital dedicated to the goddess Ishtar, and the city to which the noted prophet Jonah would be sent by God. While their art and libraries, which preserved older Sumerian cultures, were sophisticated, the Assyrians also had a reputation for ruthlessness. As Cyrus Gordon and Gary Rendsburg put it in their history of the period, "Brutality was justified from the Assyrian viewpoint on religious grounds. The god Assur had willed that his country and his king should achieve world domination; and all other gods, kings, and peoples had to be subservient to Assur's will. Any resistance meant rebellion against the great god and was put down with . . . severity." (*The Bible and the Ancient Near East*, p. 249)

Does that assessment have a familiar ring? Sounds a lot like another God we all know.

As cruel as they might seem, the Assyrian methods of mass deportations of conquered people are certainly not unique. The "removals" of Native Americans by the U.S. government in the early nineteenth century, as well as the "ethnic cleansing" of the twentieth century, are merely updated versions of an ancient practice. As another biblical writer would later put it in Ecclesiastes, "There is nothing new under the sun."

Who wrote the "Book of the Law"?

When the northern kingdom of Israel fell, the southern kingdom of Judah tried to maintain its independence but suffered from a combination of weak kings and the onslaught of the powerful Assyrian empire. Among these "bad" kings was Ahaz, who attempted to curry favor with the Assyrian overlords by placing an Assyrian altar in the Temple of Jerusalem. That was clearly not an idea that sat well with the Temple priests.

In stark contrast, Ahaz's son Hezekiah (715–687 BCE) was a king regarded favorably by the priestly authors of the Bible. He attempted to make religious reforms and destroyed some of the alien shrines that remained scattered throughout Judah. But what works for God doesn't always work in the realm of ancient Near Eastern power politics. In his attempt to fend off the Assyrian threat, Hezekiah made alliances with kings in Babylon and Egypt, but their combined strength could not stave off the Assyrian advance. The strategic city of Lachish fell in 702 BCE. Biblical accounts diverge from other historical material in describing the Assyrian threat to Jerusalem. According to the Bible, the city was saved by a divine miracle. Other sources suggest that Hezekiah paid off the Assyrians.

Hezekiah was followed by one of the most notorious kings of Judah, Hezekiah's son Manasseh (687–642 BCE). Hoping to preserve his throne, he tried to negotiate with the Assyrians and reintroduced Assyrian idol worship to Jerusalem. In the view of the authors of the Bible, his actions were so reprehensible to God that they ultimately caused the kingdom's downfall. Manasseh's tactics proved feeble anyway; he was carted off to Babylon in shackles. His son Amon ruled Judah for two years but was assassinated.

A crucial moment in biblical history occurred in 621 BCE, during the reign of King Josiah, Manasseh's grandson, who had taken the throne at age eight, and was presented in the biblical accounts as the ideal king who ruled for thirty-one years. A scroll, perhaps hidden in a money box or in some rubbish about to be removed from the Temple, was discovered by a priest. When he read the scroll, Josiah tore his clothes in anguish because he knew how far the people had fallen from God. He began a vigorous reform movement in which all objects of foreign worship, like altars and idols, were removed from Jerusalem.

This "Book of the Law" found in Josiah's time is generally thought to be an early version of Deuteronomy, a Torah book that places special emphasis on removing any trace of idolatry from the worship of God. For the first time since the time of the judges, before the rise of the monarchy in Israel, the Passover was properly celebrated. There is a discrepancy between the Kings account and a later account in Chronicles, which states that King Josiah began his reforms before the "Book of the Law" was found. This is typical of the contradictions between the versions of the "history" of Israel and Judah presented in Kings and Chronicles (see 1 and 2 Chronicles, page 207).

With Assyria's power in decline, Josiah hoped to reunite Judah with the remnant of Israel in the north, restoring the nation as one, as well as continue his major religious reforms. But Josiah's vision of a reunited Israel loyal to God's law died with him in 609 BCE when he was killed in battle at Megiddo against Egypt's Pharaoh Necho II, and Judah became an Egyptian territory.

By that time, a new regional power was emerging from a collection of tribal groups known as the Chaldeans (also called "Neo-Babylonians" to distinguish them from earlier Babylonians). They conquered Nineveh, the Assyrian capital, and defeated the Assyrians in 612 BCE and the Egyptians in 605 BCE. Their first great king was Nabopolassar, and it was this empire, based in a revived and rebuilt Babylon, that would finally bring about the fall of Jerusalem.

Rulers of the Chaldeans (Neo-Babylonians)
(All dates are approximate and BCE)

Nabopolassar	625–605
Nabu-kuduri-usur II	605–562 (Also called Nebuchadrezzar or Nebuchadnezzar)
Amel-Marduk	561–560 (Evil-Merodach)
Nergal-shar-usur	559–556 (Neriglissar)
Labashi-Marduk	556
Nabu-naid	555–539 (Nabonidus)
Bel-sharra-usur	552–542 (Belshazzar, Baltasar)

BIBLICAL VOICES

In the fifth month, on the seventh day of the month—which was the nineteenth year of King Nebuchadnezzar, king of Babylon—Nebuzaradan the captain of the bodyguard, a servant of the king of Babylon, came to Jerusalem. He burned the house of the Lord, the king's house, and all the houses of Jerusalem; every great house he burned down. . . . Nebuzaradan the captain of the guard carried into exile the rest of the people who were left in the city and the deserters who had defected to the king of Babylon—all the rest of the population. But the captain of the guard left some of the poorest people of the land to be vinedressers and tillers of the soil. (2 Kings 25:8–12)

The Chaldeans first attacked Jerusalem in 597 BCE, and King Jehoiachin and the Judaean nobility were taken captive to Babylon, the Chaldean capital. The actual numbers deported are unclear. Ten thousand captives were deported, according to one verse; 8,000 in another; and 3,023 in a third account in Jeremiah. Established as a puppet king in Jerusalem by the Chaldeans, Zedekiah bravely but unwisely rebelled, and in 587 "David's city" was destroyed. A number of Jewish leaders were executed and more captives—832 according to a later account—were taken to Babylon. Zedekiah was captured, forced to watch the execution of his sons, then was blinded and later died in captivity, the last king of Judah.

1 & 2 Chronicles

Our days on the earth are as a shadow. (1 Chron. 29:15 KJV)

Why are the stories in Chronicles different from those in other Bible books?

If the Bible includes some of the earliest written history, as many scholars profess, it also includes some of the earliest "revisionist history." The two books of Chronicles, in fact, practically define the notion of "revisionism" as changing historical facts to suit a specific purpose. These books, when read objectively, present some of the best evidence for the multiple—and very human— authorship of the Bible. These are awkward books, difficult to explain away in their numerous contradictions of other biblical materials. That is one reason they occupy different places in the Hebrew and Christian versions of the Bible. In the Hebrew scriptures, the books of Chronicles are placed at the end of the section called "Writings," making them the final books in the Tanakh. In the Christian Old Testament, the two books of Chronicles follow Kings, falsifying the original order of the Hebrew scriptures.

The two books of Chronicles and the books of Ezra and Nehemiah may have once formed one longer book, and some scholars regard all four books as the work of a single author. Ancient Jewish authorities attributed the books to Ezra himself, but there is no proof of that. Whether he also wrote the other books or not, the "Chronicler's" name and identity are a mystery. The manner in which the story is told and the way details have been altered in Chronicles suggest that the author was a Levite, or a member of the priestly clan. Recent scholarship suggests that the book was probably composed between 350 and 300 BCE.

Put simply, Chronicles is the ancient *Reader's Digest* version of everything that has already taken place in the Bible, from

Genesis on. It is abridged, condensed, simplified, and a lot of the nasty parts have been left out. That's why it is a perfect example of revisionism. Essentially someone set out to tell the story of Israel and Judah from the creation of Adam to the beginnings of the Persian empire, culminating with the decree of Persia's King Cyrus that the Jews exiled in Babylon could return to Jerusalem. But "he" wanted to tell a safer version with some considerable changes in details. These weren't small details. For instance, David's relationship with Bathsheba, a central event in the Samuel version, is ignored, and David's role in planning the Temple is greatly enhanced. Solomon's worst excesses are similarly glossed over, and Chronicles dwells on his more glorious achievements in constructing the Temple.

If tedium—or genealogy—is your cup of tea, the first nine chapters of 1 Chronicles may be for you. They contain long tables of "begats," showing the descendants of the Israelite tribes, from Adam down to the time of King David. The rest of 1 Chronicles and most of 2 Chronicles deal with the reigns of David and Solomon and the subsequent history of the kingdom of Judah until the time of the Babylonian Exile. The material in Chronicles was clearly based upon the accounts in Samuel and Kings, which are quoted verbatim though never mentioned by name, as well as Genesis, Exodus, Numbers, Joshua, and Ruth. In addition, some sixteen other sources are mentioned, such as "The Chronicles of Samuel the Seer," "The Chronicles of Nathan the Prophet," and "The Commentary on the Book of Kings," titles that may refer to parts of a single book, now lost.

The "Chronicler" freely altered the facts to bring his version of history in line with his priestly viewpoint. As a "southerner," he wrote as little as possible about the northern kingdom of Israel, since to him it did not represent the "true Israel." His account emphasized the descendants of Judah in the genealogies. He omitted almost all information about the prophet Samuel and King Saul, the political difficulties and personal misdeeds of David and

Solomon, and nearly all historical information about the northern kingdom. He also gives previously unrecounted details of the building and rituals of the First Temple and pays close attention to the roles of the Levites and priests and temple singers. The "Chronicler" was interested in advocating a strict religious life for his own day, and to indicate what a proper kingdom of his people under God would be like. His portrait of the reigns of David and Solomon is an idealized vision; the two kings are depicted not as they had been, but as they should have been.

In 2 Chronicles, the author takes up the story of the monarchy after Solomon's death, recounting the period of the divided kingdoms of Judah and Israel. This version emphasizes the priestly view that the calamities striking the nation were the outcome of the nation's sins. The past is viewed as a warning for his own time and for the future. Unlike Kings, which ends on the depressing news of Jerusalem's destruction, the "Chronicler" fast-forwards his account to a more hopeful moment, the return to Jerusalem.

BIBLICAL VOICES

In the first year of King Cyrus of Persia, in fulfillment of the word of the Lord spoken by Jeremiah, the Lord stirred up the spirit of King Cyrus of Persia so that he sent a herald throughout all his kingdom and also declared in a written edict: "Thus says King Cyrus of Persia: The Lord, the God of heaven, has given me all the kingdoms of the earth, and he has charged me to build him a house at Jerusalem, which is in Judah. Whoever is among you of all his people, may the Lord his God be with him! Let him go up." (2 Chron. 36: 22–23)

Since these books are placed last in the Hebrew canon, the Hebrew scriptures end on a liberating note, with echoes of the Exodus.

Lamentations

> How lonely sits the city
> that once was full of people!
> How like a widow she has become,
> she that was great among the
> nations!   (Lam. 1:1)

Lamentations is a brief book of sorrowful poems, some in the form of alphabetic acrostics, recalling the grim fate of Jerusalem following its destruction by the Babylonians in 587/6 BCE. In Christian Old Testaments, it appears after Jeremiah, but it is placed in the Writings, the third part of the Hebrew canon. Jews entitle the book Ekhah ("O How!"), the first word of the Hebrew text, or Kinoth ("Dirges" or "Laments"). The English title is derived from the Septuagint Greek Threnoi, for "Dirges," and the Vulgate's *Threni Id Est Lamentationes Jeromiae Prophetae*, Latin for "Dirges, That Is, Lamentations of the Prophet Jeremiah." While these songs were traditionally ascribed to the prophet Jeremiah, he is not the likely author. The anonymous author, or authors, certainly may have experienced the destruction of the city, and the poems are bitterly sad elegies for the "dead" city. Still, they express the hope that God will restore a humbled and repentant Israel.

BIBLICAL VOICES

> Our ancestors sinned; they are
>   no more,
>   and we bear their iniquities.
> Slaves rule over us;
>   there is no one to deliver us from their hand.
> We get our bread at the peril of our lives,
>   because of the sword in the wilderness,
> Our skin is as black as an oven
>   from the scorching heat
>   of famine.

Women are raped in Zion,
　　virgins in the towns of Judah.
Princes are strung up by
　　　their hands;
　　no respect is shown to the elders.
Young men are compelled to grind,
　　and boys stagger under loads
　　of wood.
The old men have left the city
　　　　gate,
　　　the young men their music.
　　The joy of our hearts has ceased;
　　　our dancing has been turned
　　　　to mourning.
The crown has fallen from
　　our head;
woe to us for we have sinned!
Because of this our hearts are sick,
　　because of these things our eyes
　　　have grown dim.
But you, O Lord, reign forever;
　　your throne endures to all
　　　generations.
Why have you forgotten us
　　completely?
Why have you forsaken us these
　　many days?
Restore us to yourself, O Lord,
　　　that we may be restored;
　　renew our days as of old—
unless you have utterly rejected
　　　us,
　　and are angry with us beyond
　　　measure. (Lam. 5:7–22)

Was the Exile all that bad?

The period of the Exile in Babylon, lasting approximately from 586 to 538 BCE, was momentous in terms of shaping Judaism and the Bible. Without the Temple in Jerusalem as the focal point of Yahweh worship, the exiles were forced to create a new form of communal ritual, with the earliest beginnings of the synagogue (a Greek word for "place of assembly") as a center of prayer, Torah study, and teaching. Unable to make legitimate sacrifices outside the now-destroyed Jerusalem Temple, and eager to distinguish themselves, Jews began to emphasize the Sabbath, circumcision, dietary laws, and other purity rituals that would set their community apart. The notion that their God was not one of many but the only God truly emerged in this era. Jews also accepted the idea that the destruction of Jerusalem did not mean that their God was powerless against or weaker than foreign gods but was punishing Israel for its sins. This focus on personal and national sin—as well as redemption—emerged as the predominant religious theme of the Exile, expressed in prophecy and song.

Among the exiles, the spirit of hope for an eventual return to Jerusalem and the restoration of the Temple took on new fervor. The bleak doom and gloom of the Hebrew Prophets before and during the Exile was usually tempered by hope. Jews began to look for a Messiah, a new leader or savior—an optimistic spirit that yearned for a better life in this world, rather than some afterlife or next life—that would be unique to Judaism.

The other great development of the Exile was the final stages of the composition of the Hebrew scriptures, and during these years in Babylon, the Hebrew Bible gained much of its present shape. The Pentateuch, or Torah, approached the form it now holds, and the history of Israel, from Joshua through Kings, and the earliest prophetic writings were all composed during the Exile.

Despite the images of being enslaved or held captive in Babylon, things couldn't have been all bad for the exiled Jews. When the Exile was officially ended under Persia's Cyrus the Great in 538 BCE, only a minority of the Jews in Babylon took advantage of the offer to return to Judah and rebuild Jerusalem (see Ezra, Nehemiah). Many of these people had been living in Babylon for two generations. Intermarriage had become commonplace; many Jews had profited from and were accustomed to life among the pleasures to be had in the splendid ancient city of Babylon—the "Great Whore," as it was later called. Babylon remained a vibrant, active center for Jewish life and scholarship, the place where the "Babylonian Talmud," an extensive collection of teachings about the scriptures, was later compiled. The period of the Exile and Return also marks the beginnings of the "Diaspora," the great dispersal of Jews throughout the Mediterranean world and eventually into Europe. Some Jews had entered official government service, as shown in the cases of Nehemiah, "a cupbearer" to one Persian king, and Mordecai, a Jew who also serves a Persian king (see Esther, page 261).

As Gordon and Rendsburg point out in *The Bible and the Ancient Near East*,

> The success of various Jews in government service is to be explained as follows: since Jews were not bound by close ties to their gentile neighbors, they were free to serve the king without conflicting loyalties. Thus men like Nehemiah or Mordecai were in a position to serve the king well, to attain positions of influence, and to secure royal protection for their coreligionists when necessary. This, of course, stirred up jealousy and hatred so that with the Diaspora appears anti Semitism. As long as the Hebrews were a nation on their own soil, they had normal feuds and friendships with their neighbors. But anti-Semitism is a product of the Diaspora, as exemplified by Haman, the villain in the Book of Esther (p. 303).

Gordon and Rendsburg's point is clear from history. Setting aside the Pharaoh's legendary order to kill the Hebrew babies, the history of the Jewish people before the Exile is essentially no different from that of peoples in other nearby lands. They lived and fought with their neighbors for all the usual reasons. Land, power, ancient feuds. But something changed after the Exile as Jews, compelled to integrate into the non-Jewish world, sought ways to set themselves apart. It is a view that in essence blames Jews for what others did to them, and doesn't account for other "separate" sects through history who have not been singled out. But many scholars have asserted this religious, ritual, and social "separateness" contained the roots of what is now called anti-Semitism.

"Anti-Semitism," as most people will readily acknowledge, does not mean hatred of Semites, who include Arabs and other Near Eastern groups. As historian Peter Schäfer explains in *Judeophobia*, "Its literal meaning, 'hostility against Semites,' reveals its absurdity, since it aims, in its original racist context, not precisely at all 'Semitic peoples,' but solely at the Jews." Greatly worsened in the Christian era by the widely preached sentiment—one of the great bloodstains on Christian history—that Jews were "Christ-killers," there was a powerful anti-Jewish feeling among both the Greeks and Romans. Scholars have long debated whether that sentiment is essentially religious, as opposed to social or political. But none of those explanations ultimately satisfies a question pointedly phrased by Rabbi Joseph Telushkin. "What is it about this small group of people that can unite the far left and the far right, rich and poor, religious and anti-religious in opposition to them?" (*Jewish Literacy*, p. 468)

While the hateful idea of "anti-Semitism" may be ancient, the expression is not. The phrase itself is only about a century old and was coined by a Jew-hating German agitator named Wilhelm Marr who wanted to purge Jewish influences from German culture. Marr formed the League of Anti-Semites, as a more socially acceptable way to say "Jew-haters," in 1879.

MILESTONES IN BIBLICAL TIMES III
1000 BCE–587 BCE

1005 David unites the tribes of Israel and breaks the power of the Philistines. The Ark of the Covenant is brought to Jerusalem, "David's City," capital of a united Israel.

c. 965–960 David dies and his son Solomon assumes the throne in Israel. He reigns until *928,* making treaties of alliance with Egypt and Phoenicia. Under his rule, ancient Israel reaches the height of its power and civilization.

• Solomon begins building the Great Temple of Jerusalem to house the sacred Ark of the Covenant; Solomon also builds a new palace and city walls using forced labor and introduces taxation to finance these projects.

945 Egypt's throne is usurped by the Libyan Sheshonk, beginning the 22nd Dynasty that rules Egypt for the next two hundred years.

928 Solomon dies and is succeeded by his son Rehoboam I; ten northern tribes balk at taxation and establish a kingdom (Israel) with Jeroboam I as king. The southern kingdom is known as Judah.

884 Assyria's King Ashurnasirpal II begins a twenty-four-year reign in which he will defeat Babylonia and revive the Assyrian empire.

853 Israel's King Ahab defeated by Assyria's Shalmaneser.

850 *The Iliad* and *The Odyssey* are composed by Homer.

841 King Jehu of Israel pays tribute to Shalmaneser III.

814 Carthage is founded in North Africa by Phoenicians ("Punians").

776 Greece's first recorded Olympic Games are held at Olympia.

760–690 The Hebrew prophets Amos and Hosea in Israel; Isaiah and Micah live and prophesy in Judah.

753 Rome is founded, according to legend, on a wooded hilltop overlooking the Tiber.

745 Assyria's Tiglath-pileser III begins a seven-year reign in which he will conquer Syria and Israel.

722 Fall of Samaria, capital of Israel, to Assyrian forces after a

three-year siege. The victory belongs to Sargon II, who succeeds
Shalmaneser V; thirty thousand Israelites are taken prisoner and
deported to central Asia; they will disappear from history (the
"Lost Tribes of Israel").

710 Ethiopian invaders conquer Egypt.

705 Assyria's Sennacherib begins a twenty-three-year reign during
which Nineveh becomes a great city.

701 Lachish, a stronghold in Judah, falls to Assyria's Sennacherib.

693 Babylon is destroyed by Assyria's Sennacherib.

670 Judah's King Manasseh pays tribute to Assyria's Esarhaddon.

626 Assyria's King Ashurbanipal dies after a forty-three-year reign
that had brought prosperity to the country; his empire will crumble
over the next twenty years.

621 Athenian lawgiver Draco issues a code of laws that make
nearly every offense punishable by death.

• A "Book of the Law," thought to be Deuteronomy, is found
in the Jerusalem Temple. Hebrew prophets Nahum, Zephaniah,
Habakkuk, and Jeremiah are active.

612 Fall of Assyrian capital of Nineveh to the Chaldeans ("Neo-
Babylonians"). The Assyrian empire disappears soon after.

609 Judah's King Josiah slain by Egyptian Pharaoh Necho II.

605 Egypt's Necho is defeated by the Chaldean who begins a
forty-three-year reign as Babylon's Nebuchadnezzar II.

• The Persian religious leader Zoroaster (Zarathustra) founds
a faith that will dominate Persian thought for centuries.

597 Nebuchadnezzar II conquers Jerusalem; Judah's King Jehoia-
chan is deported to Babylon, now a magnificent city of public
buildings faced with blue, yellow, and white enameled tiles, broad
avenues, canals, and winding streets. It is the site of the Hanging
Gardens, one of the seven wonders of the ancient world, exotic
shrubs and flowers irrigated by water pumped from the Euphrates.

587 Fall of Jerusalem; destruction of the Great Temple and beginning of fifty-year Exile in Babylon. During the Babylonian Captivity, many of the orally transmitted books of Hebrew scripture
are first written down.

EIGHT MEN OUT

THE PRE-EXILE PROPHETS

✳

❋ Why are the Children of Israel the "Chosen People"?

❋ What is the difference between a "virgin" and a "young woman"?

❋ Who is the "suffering servant"?

❋ What is a jeremiad?

I f you were drawing up a guest list for a party, you might want to leave the prophets off. While David and Solomon deserve the title of ancient Israel's "party animals," the prophets were the "party poopers." Represented by the fifteen individual books, the Hebrew prophets ringingly denounced evil, corruption, and immorality as they saw it. As noted earlier, the term "prophet" is a loose one. While the earliest sense of the word was "seer," these men (Deborah in Judges was a prophetess, but very few other women are given the title) were far more than simple fortune-tellers or diviners. Their role might more accurately be defined as human messengers of God; occasionally they were reluctant witnesses, as in the case of Jonah in particular.

Although primarily targeting the people of Israel and Judah, the prophets also took aim at neighboring societies, and their words can still ring uncomfortably true in discussing sin, corruption, and human fallibility. These books offer few biographical details about these men, and in many cases, portions of their books were composed long after the individual prophets lived. For the most part uncompromisingly harsh, and often vividly poetic, the body of literature left by the prophets is unique among the world's religions.

The prophetic books also mark a departure point for Hebrew and Christian scriptures. In the Hebrew scriptures, the three "major" and twelve "minor" prophets follow the "historical books" of Joshua through Kings, all under the heading of "Prophets" (*Nevi'im*). The Christian Old Testament continues a "historical" progression in which Kings is followed by Chronicles, Ezra, Nehemiah, and Esther, and the prophets are placed much later.

To maintain a narrative continuity tracing the history of ancient Israel, this survey of the prophets breaks them into two groups; the first group covers the eight prophets who preceded the fall of Jerusalem and the Exile. The prophets of the Exile and Post-Exile periods are covered in a later chapter.

The three longest prophetic books, Isaiah, Jeremiah and Ezekiel, have traditionally been labeled the "Major Prophets." The other twelve books are called the "Minor Prophets," but the characterization does not reflect their relative importance. The "minor" prophets are not less significant, but the books are much shorter in length. However, calling them the "Short Prophets" might have made them sound like a Hebrew version of the Seven Dwarfs.

THE PRE-EXILE PROPHETS

PROPHET	DATE (BCE)/Place
Amos	c. 760–750; Israel under Jeroboam II
Hosea	c. 745; Israel under Jeroboam II
Isaiah	742–701; Judah under Uzziah, Jotham, Ahaz, and Hezekiah
Micah	c. 750; Judah under Jotham, Ahaz, Hezekiah
Nahum	625–610: Judah under Josiah
Zephaniah	c. 621; Judah under Josiah
Habakkuk	615–598; Judah?
Jeremiah	627–587; Judah to the fall of Jerusalem

• **Amos**

> But let justice roll down like
> waters,
> and righteousness like an ever-flowing stream. (Amos 5:24)

Amos is attributed to a herdsman—Richard Elliot Friedman calls him a "cowboy" in *Who Wrote the Bible?*—from a Judean village who goes to Israel during the time of the northern King Jeroboam II (786–784 BCE), a prosperous time in Israel. But Amos sees these good times as a time of moral decay and ethical corruption in both Judah and Israel.

BIBLICAL VOICES

> Because they sell the righteous
> for silver,
> and the needy for a pair of
> sandals—

they who trample the head of the
poor into the dust of
the earth,
and push the afflicted out of
   the way;
father and son go in to the
   same girl,
so that my holy name is profaned. (Amos 2:6–8)

Preaching in a time of relative wealth and political stability, Amos attacked the oppression of the poor by the rich, empty piety, and immoral religious practices—the "father and son going in to the same girl" may have referred to the continuing popularity of temple prostitutes. According to Amos, God despises sacrifices, festivals, and songs if they are not accompanied by ethical behavior, and he stressed personal responsibility. If the people did not mend their corrupt ways, Amos said they would be destroyed. It wasn't a popular message, and Amos was banished from Israel by Jeroboam because his words were so harsh. Obviously Amos's message is not limited to its times.

In the book's closing verses, Amos predicted eventual redemption, peace, and prosperity for the people of Israel, but these verses may have been added by a later editor.

Why are the Children of Israel the "Chosen People"?

One of the most significant lines in Amos is the prophet's message to Israel from God: "You alone have I singled out of all the families of the earth—that is why I will call you to account for all your iniquities."

This is the essence of the Jews' designation as the "Chosen People." From the time of Abraham, the Israelites believed that they had been selected by God. But selected for what? The best seat at the table? Good tickets for the opera?

The idea of being "special" isn't unique to Judaism; almost every culture sees itself as somehow better than others—that is what is known as "ethnocentrism." Both Christians and Muslims have adopted the idea that they are "chosen." However, the concept of "chosenness," which is tied closely to the historical resentment of Jewish people and finds its ultimate expression in virulent anti-Semitism, has nothing to do with a view that Jews are somehow "favored" by God. For Amos, God's covenant with the people—being "chosen"—did not entitle them to special favors. In essence, their being "chosen" increased their responsibility to show exemplary obedience to God's law. While the reason for choosing Abraham and his descendants is never made clear in the Torah, the Israelites were chosen for a unique function: to spread the word of God and make his nature and laws known to the world. As Rabbi Joseph Telushkin writes in *Jewish Literacy*, "Does Judaism believe that chosenness endows Jews with special rights in the way racist ideologies endow those born into the 'right race'? Not at all. . . . Chosenness is so unconnected to any notion of race that Jews believe the Messiah himself will descend from Ruth, a non-Jewish woman who converted to Judaism." (p. 506)

Amos underscores this point when he adds this note to the Jewish people: " 'To Me, O Israelites, you are just like the Ethiopians,' declares the Lord." (Amos 9:7)

• **Hosea**

For I desired mercy, and not sacrifice; and the knowledge of God more than burnt offerings. (Hos. 6:6)

Hosea is attributed to a prophet who lived in the northern kingdom a little later than Amos. His story counts as one of the oddest among the prophets because in the opening verse God tells Hosea to marry a prostitute. He does as he is told, although his wife, Gomer, is later called an adulteress, rather than a prostitute. In modern terms, Hosea was the prophet of "unconditional love."

No matter what Gomer did, Hosea loved her and always took her back. Once, he was even forced to purchase her—although from whom is unclear—with a payment of silver, barley, and wine. (Some writers contend that Hosea actually purchased a second wife, and there has been considerable disagreement over this interpretation.)

An unfaithful wife provides Hosea with his prophetic metaphor. He compares the relationship of a man married to an adulteress to that between God and Israel. Hosea, the betrayed husband, is like God. His wife runs around with other men, just as the people of Israel sin with other gods. She will be punished severely, but each time she will be forgiven and even bought back because her husband's love will always turn away his anger.

Hosea's statement that God preferred "mercy," or righteous behavior, to empty shows of piety ("sacrifice") was a key theme in the teachings of Jesus as well.

BIBLICAL VOICES

I will heal their disloyalty;
    I will love them freely,
    for my anger has turned
        from them
I will be like the dew to Israel. (Hos. 14:4–5)

On the whole, Hosea is a curious book. The God who has inveighed so heavily against adultery, ordering adulterous wives to be stoned to death in the Mosaic Laws, now discusses forgiving the adulterous wife.

Talk about mixed messages.

• Isaiah

Be your sins like crimson,
    They can turn snow-white;
Be they red as dyed wool,
    They can become like fleece. (Isa. 1:18 JPS)

Every year at Christmas and Easter, concert halls, cathedrals, and churches overflow with the sound of people cranking out Handel's *Messiah*. Written in just eighteen days in 1742, Handel's masterpiece is filled with glorious music and words. Audiences still rise in honor of the "Hallelujah Chorus." But Handel had help. George Gershwin had Ira. Rogers had Hammerstein. And Elton John has Bernie Taupin. Handel and his librettist had Isaiah.

"For unto us a child is born." "Comfort ye, comfort ye my people." "Every valley shall be exalted." "The voice of him that crieth in the wilderness." "Surely he hath borne our griefs, and carried our sorrows." "All we like sheep have gone astray." All of these and more come from the book of Isaiah (through the King James Version).

The longest prophetic book in Hebrew scripture, Isaiah has had a remarkable impact on our language. Besides providing Handel with great lyrics, Isaiah gave us:

- "White as snow" (or "Snow-white" according to the Jewish Publication Society)
- "Swords into plowshares/spears into pruning hooks"
- "Neither shall they learn war any more"
- "The people that walked in darkness"
- "The wolf also shall dwell with the lamb, and the leopard shall lie down with the kid . . . and a little child shall lead them"
- "They shall mount up with wings as eagles"
- "Be of good courage"
- "They shall see eye to eye"
- "A lamb to the slaughter"

The use of so many of Isaiah's phrases in crafting Jesus' life into the *Messiah* isn't a surprise. Perhaps more than any other book of Hebrew prophecy, Isaiah has played a central role for Christians and has even been called "The Fifth Gospel" because so many of the book's prophecies seem to have been fulfilled in the life of Jesus. This points to an essential difference between Jews and

Christians when it comes to reading the Bible. For Jews, Isaiah spoke to his times, as well as a messianic future to come. For Christians, Isaiah's prophecies were fulfilled in Jesus.

PLOT SUMMARY: ISAIAH

What is known of Isaiah can basically only be drawn from the book itself, including the fact that Isaiah didn't write all of the book bearing his name. Born into an aristocratic family in Jerusalem, around 740 BCE, Isaiah was an adviser to four kings of Judah, the southern kingdom—Uzziah, Jotham, Ahaz, and Hezekiah. According to tradition, Isaiah was martyred between 701 and 690 BCE. His prophetic career was set against the political turmoil and foreign intrigues swirling around Judah in the time of the Assyrian empire. References to events long after he lived were certainly added by a later writer or writers who edited Isaiah. Most scholars now consider it a composite of at least three separate narratives that attained its present form as late as 180 BCE.

Like other prophets, Isaiah combines warnings of doom about Jerusalem's wicked ways with hopes for prosperous times. He announces a coming judgment and arrival of a messianic era when a king from David's line will rule in peace and righteousness.

BIBLICAL VOICES

Behold, a virgin shall conceive, and bear a son, and shall call him Immanuel. (Isa. 7:14 KJV)

Look, the young woman is with child and shall bear a son, and shall name him Immanuel. (Isa. 7:14)

What is the difference between a "virgin" and a "young woman"?

The two translations of a single verse above provide another clear case of "Whose Bible Is It?" Variations in languages and the failure to convey the precise meaning or sense of words in translation has caused trouble for centuries. Often these misunderstandings and mistranslations account for fundamental differences in the way Jews and Christians perceive the Scriptures. For Christians, much of what happens in their Old Testament is seen in relationship to prophecies of the coming of Jesus. Jewish readers obviously don't make those connections. A perfect example of the Jewish-versus-Christian understanding, or interpretation, of the Scriptures, is found in the prophecy Isaiah made to King Ahaz around 735 BCE. Like English, Hebrew usess different words for "virgin" and "young woman." A young woman *might* be a virgin but she doesn't have to be. Jewish commentators point out that Isaiah was specifically telling King Ahaz that his wife, the "young woman" of the verse, would soon bear another son. That son was Hezekiah, who was a devout and good king, loyal to traditions and obedient to the laws.

Christian readers and the author of Matthew's Gospel saw something else in Isaiah's words—not just a prophecy of a new prince for Israel but a future messianic deliverer they believed was Jesus. In the two accounts of his miraculous birth in the New Testament, Jesus was born to Mary, said to be a virgin. One of those accounts, in the Gospel of Matthew, repeated the errant Greek translation of "virgin" when Isaiah's prophecy was used to refer to Mary, mother of Jesus. In other words, whether or not Mary was a virgin, she did not have to be a virgin to fulfill Isaiah's prophecy, which spoke only of a young woman. While some modern Christian scholars have begun to debate the concept of the "virgin birth" more vigorously (see page 361), Isaiah's original words clearly refer to a "young woman" or "maiden" and not a virgin.

BIBLICAL VOICES

> Here is my servant, whom I uphold,
> my chosen, in whom my soul delights;
> I have put my spirit upon him;
> he will bring forth justice to the nations. (Isa. 42:1)

I gave my back to those who struck me,
and my cheeks to those who pulled out the beard;
I did not hide my face from insult and spitting. (Isa. 50:6)

See, my servant shall prosper;
he shall be exalted and lifted up
and shall be very high. (Isa. 52:13)

But he was wounded for our transgressions,
crushed for our iniquities;
upon him was the punishment that made us whole,
and by his bruises we are healed. (Isa. 53:5)

The righteous one, my
    servant, shall make many
    righteous,
        and he shall bear their iniquities. (Isa. 53. 11)

Who is the "suffering servant?"

As with the "virgin" birth Isaiah prophesied, Christians and Jews differ on another key portion of Isaiah's prophecies, found scattered throughout Isaiah chapters 42, 49, 50, 52, and 53 in songs that speak of a "suffering servant of God." When Isaiah speaks of a despised, rejected man of suffering who is led like a lamb to slaughter, Christians see another symbolic prophecy of Jesus. The verses describe specific sufferings that reflect the torture Jesus endures before his death on the cross. The "suffering servant" not only suffers for the sake of the people but actually bears their sins, a description of the central belief of Christianity in which Christ dies for the sins of man. Jewish readers prefer to view this as either a reference to Isaiah himself, the prophet who suffers because his words are unpopular, or to the people of Israel, who soon suffer for the nation's sins through a catastrophic defeat by a foreign invader.

• **Micah**

> He has told you, O mortal, what
> is good;
> and what does the Lord require
> of you
> but to do justice, and to love
> kindness,
> and to walk humbly with
> your God? (Mic. 6:9)

Micah began to prophesy before the fall of the northern capital of Samaria in 721 BCE and his prophecies tell of impending doom for both the northern and southern kingdoms. Most scholars now agree that it is a composite work, and only the first three chapters are believed to have come directly from Micah.

Like Amos and other prophets, Micah warns of God's coming punishment upon Israel and Judah because of the oppression of the poor by the rich, the corruption of the priests and prophets, and the irresponsibility and immorality of the political leaders. As a consequence of these evils, Micah predicts that Jerusalem and the Temple will both be destroyed, an event that came in 586 BCE.

Some of the later chapters of Micah, which were probably written after the Babylonian Exile, contain prophecies of a new age of universal peace when Israel will once again be ruled by a descendant of King David. This "shepherd king" will be born, as King David was, in Bethlehem, and Micah's prophecy has been interpreted by Christians as a prediction of the birth of Jesus.

Micah's "three requirements"—to love justice, do good deeds, and walk humbly with God—sum up the essence of a godly person.

• **Nahum**

Very little is known about Nahum, except that he is really more of a poet than a prophet. And a very good poet at that. The

first part of Nahum is an incomplete acrostic poem, each line of
the poem beginning with a different letter of the Hebrew alphabet. His literary effort constituted a prediction of the imminent
defeat of Nineveh, the Assyrian capital, which fell to Chaldean
invaders in 612 BCE. Comparing this evil city to a prostitute, Nahum spoke of the city's impending destruction in vivid imagery,
although his message can still be read as a much broader attack
on evil, corruption, and immorality.

BIBLICAL VOICES
Ah! City of bloodshed,
    utterly deceitful, full of booty—
    no end to plunder!
The crack of whip and rumble
      of wheel,
    galloping horse and bounding
      chariot!
Horsemen charging,
    flashing sword and glittering
      spear,
piles of dead,
    heaps of corpses,
dead bodies without end—
    they stumble over the bodies!
Because of the countless
      debaucheries of
      the prostitute,
gracefully alluring, mistress
      of sorcery,
who enslaves nations through her
      debaucheries,
and people through her
      sorcery,
I am against you,
    says the Lord of hosts,

and will lift up your skirts over
　　your face;
　　and I will let nations look on your nakedness
and kingdoms on your shame.
  I will throw filth at you
　　and treat you with contempt,
　　and make you a spectacle. (Nah. 3:1–6)

Nahum also provides an excellent example of the problems inherent in various translations of the Bible. Here are four versions of a single line from Nahum 2:11:

The faces of them all gather blackness. (KJV)
The faces of them all are as the blackness of a kettle. (Douay)
All faces grow pale. (NRSV)
All faces turn ashen. (JPS)

• **Zephaniah**

　　　　　I will bring distress on the people,
　　　　　And they shall walk like blind men,
　　　　Because they sinned against the LORD;
　　　　Their blood shall be spilled like dust,
　　　　　And their fat like dung.
　　　　Moreover, their silver and gold
　　　　Shall not avail to save them.
　　　　On the day of the LORD's wrath,
　　　　　In the fire of His passion,
　　　　The whole land shall be consumed;
　　　　For HE will make a terrible end
　　　Of all who dwell in the land. (1:17–18 JPS)

Traditionally attributed to a prophet who was said to be a descendant of the good King Hezekiah (the boy whose birth was predicted by Isaiah), Zephaniah prophesied during the reign of the reformer king Josiah, who instituted a sweeping set of religious reforms meant to restore pure worship in Judah. Zephaniah complains about all the usual sins: defiling the worship of God through foreign religious rites; adopting foreign customs; and violent and deceitful behavior.

An imminent day of judgment is predicted, and the people of Judah are urged to repent so that God's anger may be appeased. Jerusalem is specifically condemned to destruction for refusing to mend its corrupt ways.

In the end, Zephaniah sounds a hopeful note, promising the restoration of Jerusalem. He also predicts that all the Gentile, or non-Jewish nations, will be converted, and a faithful, righteous remnant of Judah will be saved. While "Gentile" has acquired a modern sense meaning "Christian," it traditionally had a broader sense. It comes from the Latin *gens* (literally, "nation"), a translation of the Hebrew *goy*. It referred to non-Jews or anyone outside the Jewish covenant. In many newer Bible translations, the word "Gentile" commonly used in the King James Version has been replaced by "nation" as a more accurate meaning of the original Hebrew.

Part of Zephaniah's oracle on the terrible "day of the Lord" inspired the well-known Latin hymn *Dies Irae*:

> The great day of the Lord is near,
>   near and hastening fast;
> the sound of the day of the Lord
>   is bitter,
> the warrior cries aloud there.
> That day will be a day of wrath,
>   a day of distress and anguish,
> a day of ruin and devastation,
>   a day of darkness and gloom,
> a day of clouds and thick
>   darkness,
>   a day of trumpet blast and
>   battle cry

    against the fortified cities
    and against the lofty
    battlements. (Zeph. 1:14–16)

• **Habakkuk**

    O Lord, how long shall I cry
                for help?
        and you will not listen?
    Or cry to you "Violence!"
    and you will not save? (Hab. 1:2)

Virtually nothing is known about the prophet Habakkuk, and
the dates given to him are fixed by references he made in his book
to the coming of the Chaldeans (Neo-Babylonians), an event that
took place around 597 BCE. Habakkuk is somewhat unusual among
the prophets in that he questions God about the suffering of the
righteous and the fact that the wicked go unpunished, a moral
question that is further explored in the book of Job.

In his response, God assures the prophet of the coming judgment, and the Chaldeans are specifically mentioned as the nation,
all-conquering and violent, that will carry out God's plan. Habakkuk concludes his revelation by asserting that "the righteous shall
live by their faith" (2:4) and with a great psalm, or hymn, extolling
God's wonders in nature.

• **Jeremiah**

    Can the Ethiopian change his skin, or the leopard his spots?
                (Jer. 13:23 KJV)

What is a jeremiad?

Born around 650 BCE, Jeremiah was the son of a powerful priest,
Hilkiah, and began his prophetic career in 627 BCE. He died sometime after the Babylonian conquest of Jerusalem in 586 BCE. Jeremiah is told by God not to marry or to have children because

they will only end up dead. Carrying that sort of knowledge around with him couldn't have made Jeremiah a very pleasant fellow to be with. He actually had few friends after he started to preach his prophecies of doom and gloom for Jerusalem.

Jeremiah probably took part in the reform movement of King Josiah and was protected by powerful friends at court until Josiah's death in 609 BCE. After that, Jeremiah fell from favor among both religious and political leaders. At different times, he was placed under house arrest, denied a public forum, and thrown into a dry cistern or well that served as a dungeon. He was also widely regarded as a traitor and defeatist because he counseled against fighting the Chaldeans. After the final defeat of Jerusalem, Jeremiah was carried off to Egypt against his will and, according to legend, was eventually murdered around 587 BCE.

God called Jeremiah to preach the destruction of Israel and Judah on account of the religious and moral impurity of its people, and that is how we come by the word "jeremiad"—a sad, angry, doom-laden tirade. To Jeremiah, even the priests were lax and corrupt, and he urged the Israelites to repent and turn once more to God. Foreign invasion was inevitable, he warned them, and the people of Jerusalem would suffer, their weak faith providing no security. He lambasted the people and graphically depicted the horrors of war and the coming deportation to Babylon. Human endeavors—wisdom, strength, wealth—are meaningless, God told Jeremiah, and he described in vivid terms how "human corpses shall fall like dung upon the open field."

BIBLICAL VOICES

But the army of the Chaldeans pursued them, and overtook Zedekiah in the plains of Jericho; and when they had taken him, they brought him up to King Nebuchadnezzar of Babylon, at Riblah, in the land of Hamath; and he passed sentence on him. The king of Babylon slaughtered the sons of Zedekiah at Riblah before his eyes; also the king of Babylon slaughtered all the nobles of Judah. He put out the eyes of

Zedekiah, and bound him in fetters to take him to Babylon. The Chaldeans burned the king's house and the houses of the people, and broke down the walls of Jerusalem. (Jer. 39:5–8)

(In the Christian Old Testament, the book of Jeremiah is followed by Lamentations [see page 210], a collection of sad songs commemorating the destruction of Jerusalem in 587 BCE. The Hebrew Bible places Lamentations among its third section, Writings. Most scholars agree that Jeremiah did not write Lamentations.)

YOU CAN GO HOME AGAIN

EZRA, NEHEMIAH

Then Ezra the priest stood up and said to them, "You have trespassed and married foreign women, and so increased the guilt of Israel. Now make confession to the Lord the God of your ancestors, and do his will; separate yourselves from the peoples of the land and from the foreign wives." Then all the assembly answered with a loud voice, "It is so; we must do as you have said." (Ezra, 10:10–12 KJV)

❋

❋ Mixed marriages: kosher or not?

The American novelist Thomas Wolfe may have been mistaken when he famously titled his work *You Can't Go Home Again*. For the exiled Jews in Babylon—or at least some of them—returning home was very possible. For others, Babylon had proven to be more than a nice place to visit—they wanted to stay.

The books of Ezra and Nehemiah deal with the history of Judah after the return from Exile in Babylon. The books not only describe the reconstruction of the Temple but the restoration of a "godly remnant" whose mission was to restore and uphold the true faith. Considered a single book until around 300 CE, when the material was divided into two parts, the books known as Ezra and Nehemiah were thought to have been written by the same person who wrote Chronicles. Although there are some discrepancies regarding the precise dates when Ezra and Nehemiah made their trips to Jerusalem, the time frame of the Return to Jerusalem, often called the "Post-Exile," is well within the bounds of documented "history," unlike many other earlier periods in the Bible. The biblical accounts have been supported by Persian and other Near Eastern archives.

Ezra opens with the decree of Cyrus, the king of Persia, following his capture of Babylon in 539 BCE, that those who want to may leave Babylon and return to Jerusalem to rebuild the Temple. Unlike other "foreign" kings and Pharaohs of the Bible who were usually viewed as scoundrels, sinners, and murderers, Cyrus gets pretty good reviews from the Bible's composers. Founder of an extensive empire that lasted more than two hundred years, Cyrus was an extraordinary leader. Under Cyrus and his successors, much of the ancient Near East, from India to Egypt and the borders of Greece, was brought under one ruler, a feat neither the Egyptians nor earlier Babylonian empire builders had accomplished. Even the later Greek writers, who had no great love for the Persians—classical Greece's archrival—considered Cyrus a model ruler. Unlike other ancient conquerors who attempted to enforce their own religions and practices on conquered peoples, Cyrus and his successors permitted the "captive nations" to preserve and restore their own institutions.

RULERS OF THE PERSIAN EMPIRE
(All dates are approximate and BCE)

Cyrus ("The Great")	550–529	(Captures Babylon in 539; allows Jews to return to Jerusalem in 538)
Cambyses II	529–522	(Captures Memphis, capital of Egypt)
Darius I	522–486	(Jerusalem Temple completed in 516; defeated by Greeks at Marathon in 490)
Xerxes I	486–465	
Artaxerxes I	465–425	(Sends Ezra to Jerusalem in 458; Nehemiah in 445? and again in 433?)
Xerxes II	425–424	
Darius II	424–404	
Artaxerxes II	404–359	
Artaxerxes III	359–338	
Arses	338–336	
Darius III	336–330	

In 330 BCE, the Persian empire fell to Alexander the Great, beginning the "Hellenistic Era" in which Greek civilization and language spread and predominated throughout the Near Eastern world.

PLOT SUMMARY: EZRA

Most scholars agree with the biblical record that the Return of exiled Jews to Jerusalem was not a mass, sudden movement but took place gradually, in waves. In the year after Cyrus captured Babylon, "without shooting a single arrow," as ancient Near Eastern authority Cyrus Gordon puts it, the initial group of Jews came back to

Jerusalem starting in 538 BCE. They were led by Sheshbazaar, a "prince of Judah" despite his Persian name, who served as territorial governor. Under his leadership, reconstruction of the Temple commenced almost immediately. But a conflict soon arose between those Judeans who had been left behind and the returning Jews. Over the nearly fifty years of Exile, the mostly poorer Judeans who had been allowed to remain behind had staked claims to some of the land left behind by the Exiles, who had been the elite of Judean society, mostly aristocrats or members of the priestly class. Animosity was natural between those who had stayed and the returnees who expected to return to their previous status. The conflict between the two groups brought work on the Temple to a halt.

About seventeen years later, a second wave of returnees were permitted to return during the reign of Darius I, a twenty-eight-year-old soldier and relative of Cyrus who took the Persian throne in 522 BCE following a series of intrigues and plots. Now led by Zerubbabel, the grandson of King Jehoiachin and a descendant of King David, and the high priest Jeshua, work recommenced on the temple in 520 BCE. Encouraged by the prophets Haggai and Zechariah (see Post-Exile Prophets), the returnees completed the second Temple in 516 BCE.

The Judah of the Return was a far cry from Solomon's empire, and the second Temple, completed in March/April of 516 BCE, was a modest affair, reflecting these changed circumstances. Judah was a fraction of the size of Solomon's Israel, and territory once controlled by the Jews was now in the hands of neighboring Edom and the Samaritans. Despite the fact that Cyrus provided funding for rebuilding the Temple, the new center of Jewish worship was not as grand as Solomon's in all its glory had been. There is very little description of the rebuilt Temple in the book of Ezra except that it was to be sixty cubits (approximately one hundred feet, or thirty meters) high and sixty cubits wide, with walls constructed of three courses of stone and one of timber. All of the gold and silver vessels that had been salvaged from the original Temple and taken to Babylon were also returned to Jerusalem. But unmentioned here or elsewhere in the Hebrew scriptures is the fate of the Ark of the Covenant, Judaism's most sacred object. Whether it was destroyed in 586 BCE when Jerusalem was sacked and the Temple burned by Nebuchadnezzar's army or salvaged and taken to Babylon by the captives remains a biblical mystery.

In 458 BCE, more than fifty years after the Temple was dedicated, a third wave of returning Exiles came back during the reign of Darius's successor, Artaxerxes. Ezra, a Jewish official of the Persian government, was sent to ensure that Jewish Law was being strictly observed. To his great dismay, Ezra discovered that many of the former exiles, as well as those who had remained in Judah, had been intermarrying with non-Jews.

BIBLICAL VOICES

After these things had been done, the officials approached me and said, "The people of Israel, the priests, and the Levites have not separated themselves from the people of the lands with their abominations, from the Canaanites, the Hittites, the Perizzites, the Jebusites, the Ammonites, the Moabites, the Egyptians, and the Amorites. For they have taken some of their daughters as wives for themselves and for their sons. Thus the holy seed has mixed itself with the peoples of the lands, and in this faithlessness the officials and leaders have led the way." When I heard this, I tore my garment and my mantle, and pulled hair from my head and beard, and sat appalled. Then all who trembled at the words of the God of Israel, because of the faithlessness of the returned exiles, gathered around me while I sat appalled until the evening sacrifice. (Ezra 9:1–4)

Mixed marriages: kosher or not?

In Jewish history, law, and theology, Ezra is a character of great significance. Some Hebrew scholars rank him second only to

Moses as a lawgiver and prophet. A Jewish official of the Persian government who was responsible for the administration of Jewish religious affairs, Ezra was sent to Jerusalem to stabilize the Jewish community there and reestablish the Law of Moses. He was accompanied by some seventeen hundred Babylonian Jews, including some Levites apparently not too eager to make the trip.

Upon returning to Jerusalem in 458 BCE, Ezra reestablished the Mosaic Laws and rituals. In *Who Wrote the Bible?*, Richard Elliot Friedman argues that Ezra was the biblical "R" author, or "Redactor," who cut and pasted together the earlier J, E, P, and D strands into the Torah in much the form it now takes. Considered by some as the second founder (after Moses) of the Jewish nation, Ezra was responsible for the extensive codification of the Laws, including those governing Temple worship and the scriptural canon. He also contributed to the eventual replacement of priests by rabbis, or learned teachers.

But one of Ezra's first decisions was none too popular and from a modern perspective, cruel. He decided that all Jewish men had to get rid of their foreign wives and their children. Over a period of a few months the men reluctantly agreed, and Ezra ends poignantly with the words, "All these had married foreign women, and they sent them away with their children."

The biblical account offers no clue as to what becomes of these banished families. There is some ambiguity that the men singled out in Ezra as having foreign wives comply with the law. While the NRSV Ezra concludes: "All these had married foreign women, and they sent them away with their children," the Jewish Publication Society version reads: "All these had married foreign women, among whom were some women who had borne children." But the implication is that these women and their children were abandoned. Ezra apparently didn't consider the possibility of conversion.

Seemingly overlooked are the many "foreign" women who were crucial heroines in Israelite history. Among these is Tamar (see Genesis), the Canaanite woman who tricked Judah but bears Perez, an ancestor of King David, and Rahab, the prostitute in

Jericho. Many scholars have suggested that Ruth (see page 169), a story of a model foreign wife who converts, was specifically written to counter Ezra's decree.

The issue of intermarriage is still a divisive and emotional question among contemporary Jews. One reason: the definition of who is a Jew. According to Jewish Law, a Jew is one who is born to a Jewish mother or is converted to Judaism. Although Reform Jews have regarded children of Jewish fathers as Jews since 1983, Orthodox and Conservative Jews do not share that view. Orthodox Jews also reject Reform and Conservative conversions to Judaism, the vast majority of such conversions. While this is an emotional issue that speaks to the very survival of Judaism in many places, it has an even greater impact in modern Israel, where the question of who is a Jew and who makes that decision has serious political implications as well.

- **Nehemiah**

BIBLICAL VOICES

Thou art a God ready to pardon, gracious and merciful, slow to anger, and of great kindness. (Neh. 9:17 KJV)

PLOT SUMMARY: NEHEMIAH

Approximately eighty years after the initial Return from Exile, things were still not going well in Jerusalem. Ezra may have been great at the law and a true genius if he is the man who crafted the Torah, but his divorce ruling hadn't made him popular among the locals. When Ezra also proved ineffective as a civil administrator, the Persian king Artaxerxes dispatched a Jewish "cupbearer"—an official presumably charged with testing the king's drinks for poison—named Nehemiah, living in Susa (Shush in modern Iran), to Jerusalem in 445 BCE. In the geopolitics of the period, Artaxerxes was interested in establishing a strong, loyal ally in Jerusalem to counter any potential threat from Egypt. The king commissioned Nehemiah to supervise repairs to the walls of Jerusalem, which had been breeched and damaged in the Babylonian invasion in

587 BCE and had crumbled from neglect during the intervening years. Nehemiah quickly began a repair program, endearing himself to the locals in the meantime by canceling all debts, since Jews were not supposed to charge fellow Jews interest. This move proved far more popular with the citizens of Jerusalem than Ezra's decision to make them give up their non-Jewish wives had been.

Much of Nehemiah is concerned with the reconstruction of Jerusalem's walls and watchtowers. When these public works were completed, Ezra was invited to rededicate the city by reading from the book of Moses. Nehemiah returned to Persia but, in his absence, laxity set in and he had to return to Jerusalem once more, possibly in 433, to lay down a new set of local laws. Gates were closed to merchants on the Sabbath and the issue of intermarriage was pushed to center stage once more.

In the historical sense, the Ezra-Nehemiah period also reflected a change in political realities for the Jewish people. Recognizing the power of Persia, Nehemiah made no attempt to reestablish the Davidic line of kings. Without a viable monarchy in the post-Exile period, authority over Jewish internal affairs rested with the Temple officials. The new Judah was a "theocracy" in which the priesthood held power over local religious and social life; all political and military power remained with the Persian kings.

Under Ezra and Nehemiah, the Second Temple became the focal point of Jewish religion, customs and power. The one God manifested himself in this place, the only place where sacrifices could be offered to God. The Temple's central role was made even stronger by obligating Jews to make a pilgrimage to Jerusalem for three major religious festivals.

BIBLICAL VOICES

All the people gathered together into the square before the Water Gate. They told the scribe Ezra to bring the book of the law of Moses, which the Lord had given to Israel. Accordingly, the priest Ezra brought the law before the assembly, both men and women and all who could hear with understanding. . . . He read from it facing the square before the Water Gate from early morning until midday, in the presence of men and the women who could understand; and the ears of all the people were attentive to the book of the law. . . . So they read from the book, from the law of God, with interpretation. They gave the sense, so that people understood the reading. (Neh. 8:1–8)

The last line of this verse refers to the fact that most Jews no longer understood Hebrew. By the time of the Return, Aramaic, a related Semitic language that originated in Aram (modern Syria) had replaced Hebrew as the common language of the ancient Near East, used for both trade and diplomacy, and the Law of Moses had to be translated for the Jews who gathered in Jerusalem to hear Ezra read. Later books of the Bible, including some late additions to Isaiah, parts of Ezra, and other books, were composed in Aramaic.

FROM DRY BONES TO FISH BELLIES

THE POST-EXILE PROPHETS

❈

✺ Who is Gog and where is Magog?

✺ What happened to Jonah's whale?

The events that fall between 586 and 516—the destruction of Jerusalem, the Exile, Return, and reconstruction of the Temple—all combine to mark a crucial point in the history of the Jews and the Bible, just as the Civil War does in American history. Everything that came before and after can only be viewed in light of these turning points. Since much of the Hebrew scriptures reached their present state after this period of turmoil and uncertainty, everything in these books has to be viewed against the backdrop of this turmoil.

For the Jews, the stark realization was that the Kingdom of God—an empire that would reign supreme on earth—was not the kingdom they were going to get. As time went by, and generations of Jews began to spread abroad in the great Diaspora, or dispersion, that reality became more pronounced. The sense that everything had changed forever was reflected in the voices and words of the prophets who lived and preached during and after the Exile in Babylon. These prophets increasingly spoke of a future day of the Lord, a day of judgment, a future messianic time, when God would ultimately rule the world. A few politically minded, militaristic Jewish firebrands took that to mean a warrior-king like David would rise up to make Israel great once more, and there were sporadic nationalistic movements over the next few centuries. Other Jews would come to believe the fulfillment of their prophecies had come through Jesus, and these Jews became the first Christians. Other faithful Jews still wait for the words of the prophets to be realized.

THE POST-EXILE PROPHETS

PROPHET	DATE (BCE)/Place
Ezekiel	597–563; Babylonian Exile
Haggai	520; Jerusalem in the post-Exilic period
Zechariah	520–518; Jerusalem in the post-Exilic period
Malachi	460–450; Jerusalem after the Temple is rebuilt
Obadiah	460–400

Joel   350
Jonah   Jonah lived c. 750; the book of Jonah is
                        written c. 350

• **Ezekiel**

   "O ye dry bones, hear the word of the Lord."
                        (Ezek. 37:4 KJV)

The prophet Ezekiel, whose wife had died during the last
siege of Jerusalem, was among the Jewish captives deported to
Babylon in 597 BCE, before the fall of Jerusalem and destruction
of the Temple, making him the first of the prophets to live outside
the Promised Land. His role as prophet and priest dates from
about 592, when he symbolically swallowed a scroll and received
his call to prophesy "among the exiles by the river Chebar"—
thought to be a canal near Babylon. Ezekiel's familiarity with
Temple rites and the unholy forms of worship that had been introduced into the Temple indicate that he may have been a priest
before the Exile. His prophecies fall into three general phases. He
is a harsh prophet of doom and destruction before the fall of Jerusalem; a comforter to the exiled community after the fall; and
lawmaker and designer of the form and structure of the restored
Temple and Jewish worship following the Return to Jerusalem.

In strictly literary terms, Ezekiel was one of the greatest individual writers in the Bible. He was a rich stylist, and the most
famous sections of his book are dreamlike, mystical visions of God,
filled with terrifying imagery, threats, and violence. His early
prophecies include stinging, graphic denunciations of the behavior
of the Israelites. He singles out for specific condemnation the practices permitted in the Temple, including the worship of other
gods, such as the Mesopotamian agricultural deity Tammuz, who
supposedly died each year and then returned, bringing new crops.
Ezekiel mentions the continuing practice of human sacrifice as
well. His description of life during the siege before Jerusalem's

capture suggests that the people in the city were probably forced to resort to cannibalism.

In one of his sharpest denunciations of the people of Israel, Ezekiel describes, in euphemistically sexual language, how God had treated Israel like a lover:

> "I passed by you again and looked on you; you were at the age for love. I spread the edge of my cloak over you, and covered your nakedness; I pledged myself to you and entered into a covenant with you. . . . Then I bathed you with water and washed the blood from you, and anointed you with oil." (Ezek. 16:8–9)

But in spite of this loving attention, the unfaithful wife becomes degenerate:

> "You trusted in your beauty, and played the whore because of your fame, and lavished your whorings on any passer-by. . . . You took your sons and your daughters, whom you had borne to me and these you sacrificed to them to be devoured. As if your whorings were not enough! You slaughtered my children and delivered them up as an offering to them. . . ." (Ezek. 16:15ff.)

> "Therefore, O whore, hear the word of the Lord: Thus says the Lord God, Because your lust was poured out and your nakedness uncovered in your whoring with your lovers, and because of all your abominable idols, and because of the blood of your children that you gave to them, therefore I will gather all your lovers, with whom you took pleasure, all those who loved you and all those you hated; I will gather them against you from all around, and will uncover your nakedness to them, so that they may see all your nakedness. I will judge you as women who commit adultery and shed blood are judged, and bring blood upon you in wrath and jealousy." (Ezek. 16:35–38)

This image of God as the angry, jilted lover who will turn his wife out naked to be raped and punished is very much at odds with the prophetic image in Hosea (see page 222) in which the adulterous wife is punished but then forgiven.

Of Ezekiel's prophetic visions, the most famous and memorable is his description of the Valley of the Dry Bones:

> The hand of the Lord came upon me, and he brought me out by the spirit of the Lord and set me down in the middle of a valley; it was full of bones. He led me all around them; there were very many lying in the valley, and they were very dry. He said to me, "Mortal, can these bones live?" I answered, "O Lord God, you know." Then he said to me, "Prophesy to these bones, and say to them: O dry bones, hear the word of the Lord. Thus says the Lord God to these bones: I will cause breath to enter you, and you shall live. I will lay sinews on you, and will cause flesh to come upon you, and cover you with skin, and put breath in you, and you shall live and know that I am the Lord."
>
> So I prophesied as I had been commanded; and as I prophesied, suddenly there was a noise, a rattling, and the bones came together, bone to its bone. (Ezek. 37:1–7)

Over the centuries, this prophetic vision has been interpreted in various ways. In his own time, Ezekiel was describing the revival of Judah after the Exile. More recently, Jews have seen it as a prophecy of the post-Holocaust creation of the modern state of Israel. And others see it more broadly as the promise of a resurrection after death, a concept central to Christian beliefs but which has figured less prominently in Jewish theology.

Summing up Ezekiel's message in *A History of the Jews*, historian Paul Johnson wrote,

> In essence this weird and passionate man had a firm and powerful message to deliver: the only salvation was

through religious purity. States and empires and thrones did not matter in the long run. They would perish through God's power. What mattered was the creature God had created in his image: man. . . . The Christians were later to interpret this fearsome scene [The Valley of the Dry Bones] as an image of the Resurrection of the dead, but to Ezekiel and his audience it was a sign of the resurrection of Israel, though of an Israel closer to and more dependent on God than ever before, each man and woman created by God, each individually responsible to him, each committed from birth to the lifelong obedience of his laws. . . . It was Ezekiel and his visions which gave the dynamic impulse to the formulation of Judaism. (pp. 81–82)

Ezekiel's book concludes with a vision of Jerusalem, restored to life by the divine breath or spirit—an act recalling the very Creation in Genesis—through which Israel is revived. Following the Return, Ezekiel describes how the new and perfect Temple is to be rebuilt, a place where the divine presence can return.

Who is Gog and where is Magog?

Another of Ezekiel's visions has led to a great deal of continuing speculation because of its prophecy warning of a great apocalyptic battle to come, a prophecy that the Christian author of the New Testament book of Revelation seized upon to refer to a coming Satanic invasion. In Ezekiel, the "chief prince" Gog is a foe who will come from "Magog," to the north, to attack Israel. After a cataclysmic battle, Gog will be defeated and God will be acknowledged by all nations. In historical context, the identity of Ezekiel's Gog and Magog is a mystery, although it seems likely that the prophet was referring to Babylon, traditionally identified as the greatest source of evil in the Hebrew world. Following the decline of Babylon as a political force, literalists throughout history have suggested a variety of alternative nations as the biblical "Magog." More recently, fundamentalist Christians, in particular, have pointed to the Soviet Union, now dismantled and presumably no longer a threat, Russia, or Iran as this evil empire that would come "from the north." Magog has been loosely identified as an area in the Caucasus Mountain region near the Caspian Sea.

• **Haggai**

> Go up to the hills and bring wood and build the house, so that I may take pleasure in it and be honored, says the Lord. You have looked for much, and, lo, it came to little; and when you brought it home, I blew it away. Why? says the Lord of hosts. Because my house lies in ruins, while all of you hurry off to your own houses. (Hag. 1:7–9)

Nothing is known about the life of the prophet Haggai, to whom the book is attributed, other than that he was in Jerusalem to help oversee reconstruction of the Temple in 520 BCE, a year of blight, drought, and general dissatisfaction for the exiles who had returned from Babylon. Haggai attributed all of these misfortunes to the failure to complete the new Temple. Haggai says that God is punishing the people for concentrating on the decoration of their own houses before completing the house of the Lord. Haggai urges Zerubbabel, the governor of Judah, and Joshua (Jeshua), the high priest, to rally the people to the crucial task of completing the Temple.

After work commences again, the people must be further encouraged, and Haggai rallies them a second time by prophesying that the spirit of God will remain with them, that God will bring silver and gold from all nations, and that the new Temple will one day be even greater than the first, a prophecy that did not literally come to pass. As previously noted, the Second Temple, whose precise dimensions are unknown, was far less grandiose than Solomon's Temple had been.

While Haggai lacks the great poetic visions or sweeping dramatic voice of many of the other prophets, the book is valuable because it documents the history of the period of the Return from Babylon. Besides Ezra and Nehemiah, only Haggai and the short Zechariah (see below) cast any light on this significant period.

- **Zechariah**

> Not by might, nor by power, but by my spirit, says the
> Lord of hosts. (Zech. 4:6)

Like Haggai, Zechariah, a priest and prophet, also spoke to the returning Jews, urging them to finish the restored Temple during the reign of Darius I (522–486 BCE). But only the first eight chapters of the book could have been written by Zechariah. The later chapters are occasionally obscure visions of a messianic era to come and they differ from the first eight chapters in style, language, theology, and historical background. These later chapters contain references to the Greeks, whose influence did not become great until after the era of Alexander. Scholars suggest that these sections may have been written more than two centuries after Zechariah lived, or between 300 and 200 BCE.

However, the first eight chapters reflect the period immediately after the Babylonian Captivity (538 BCE) and are concerned with the reconstruction of the Temple and Jerusalem in preparation for a coming messianic age. Jewish tradition held that the Messiah ("anointed one") would be a descendant of King David, who would reign once more in the land of Israel. The Messiah would gather all Jews and restore full observance of the Torah, ushering in an age of world peace. Many Jewish people expected a warrior-king like David to overthrow the string of empires— Persian, Greek, Syrian, Roman—that oppressed the people of Israel. Several rebel leaders over the course of the next few centuries attempted to claim that they were the Messiah. Christians hold that Jesus fulfilled the prophecy of a Messiah.

Zechariah preached repentance, obedience, inward spirituality, and a peaceful world in which Jew and Gentile would worship together. His prophecy included a series of eight night visions that Zechariah experienced in 519 BCE. He also thought Zerubbabel, a descendant of King David, might continue the kingly line, but Zerubbabel quietly disappears from this story and from biblical history without further mention. A good guess is that the Persian king Darius viewed Zerubbabel as a threat and deposed him. With any hopes for a nationalistic restoration dashed, Zechariah looked to a messianic future in which the coming leader would banish the "warrior's bow," bringing about a time of universal peace.

The remaining six chapters of Zechariah constitute some of the most obscure portions of Hebrew scripture. They include a series of oracles that prophesy the restoration of Israel after the defeat of Israel's enemies, the coming of the Messiah from David's line to lead Israel, and a great "day of the Lord," when the covenant will be reestablished and the God of Israel will be universally worshiped. Christians attach special significance to several passages in these last six chapters, regarding them as prophecies later fulfilled by Jesus. Among them:

> "Behold, thy king cometh unto thee . . . lowly, and riding upon an ass. (Zech. 9:9 KJV)

(Believed to pertain to Jesus' entry into Jerusalem)

> "So they weighed for my price thirty pieces of silver." (Zech. 11: 12 KJV)

(Seen as a prediction of Judas's betrayal of Jesus, for which he receives a payment of silver)

> "What are these wounds in thine hands?" . . . "Those with which I was wounded in the house of my friends." (Zech. 13:6)

(Viewed as a prophecy of the wounds suffered by Jesus during his crucifixion)

- **Malachi**

Have we not all one father? Has not one God created us? Why

then are we faithless to one another, profaning the covenant of our ancestors? (Mal. 2:10)

Nothing is known about "Malachi," a name that may be a pseudonym, as it means "my messenger." This book was once thought to have been written by Ezra, but biblical scholars now consider it unlikely that he was the author. Although Malachi stands as the last book of the Christian Old Testament, and the last of the twelve "minor" prophetic books in the Hebrew Bible, it was not the last composed. The historical evidence suggests it was written some fifty years after Haggai and Zechariah and the reconstructed Temple but prior to the reforms carried out by Nehemiah (see page 242).

A very brief book, Malachi is mostly concerned with the laxity of the priesthood in the new Temple who are using sick and blemished animals for sacrifices. Malachi predicts punishment for the priests if they persist in ignoring their obligations. He later condemns divorce and marital infidelity. But like many of the prophets, Malachi decries crimes and sins in terms that remain as timely today as they were twenty-five hundred years ago:

BIBLICAL VOICES
Then I will draw near to you for judgment; I will be swift to bear witness against the sorcerers, against the adulterers, against those who swear falsely, against those who oppress the hired workers in their wages, the widow and the orphan, against those who thrust aside the alien, and do not fear me, says the Lord of hosts. (Mal. 3:5)

The book ends with two appendixes that tell the people to remember the Law and prophesy that the prophet Elijah will return to herald the arrival of the messianic age, when "the sun of righteousness shall rise, with healing in its wings."

Malachi's prophecies of a "messenger" who will prepare the way are connected to the coming of the Messiah, who Christians believe is Jesus.

• **Obadiah**

> For the day of the Lord is near
> against all the nations.
> As you have done, it shall be done
> to you;
> your deeds shall return on your
> own head. (Obad. 1:15)

The shortest book of the Hebrew scriptures, Obadiah consists of only one chapter of twenty-one verses. While it is generally agreed that the book was written after the Exile, several verses specifically refer to the fall of Jerusalem in 586 BCE. But nothing else is known of this prophet whose name means "servant of the Lord."

The first part of Obadiah foretells the fall of Judah's traditional enemy, Edom, because the Edomites assisted the Babylonians in the destruction of Jerusalem. The remainder of the book forecasts a "day of the Lord," at which time Edom and other neighboring nations will be punished for their behavior toward Israel. Afterward, Israel will possess all of its former territory, a prophecy that modern Zionists point to in the establishment of the modern state of Israel.

• **Joel**

> Your old men shall dream dreams, your young men shall see
> visions. (Joel 2:28)

Other than the name of his otherwise obscure father (Pethuel), and that his own name means "Yahweh is God," nothing is known of Joel. That makes it difficult to precisely place him and his work, although most scholars agree that Joel belongs to the post-Exile period and was written around 350 BCE. Joel is first concerned with a terrible plague of locusts sweeping the land, and it is not known if this was a reference to an actual event or a prophetic metaphor for the troubles Israel had experienced. Joel summons the people to a solemn fast and they are urged to pray for deliverance. Interpreting the plague as an omen of the coming day of judgment, Joel warns the people that only heartfelt repentance can save them. If they repent, the Lord will restore the land to its former fruitfulness.

In the book's second part, Joel looks to an age of deliverance, in which God will gather all the nations for a final judgment. In a stark contradiction to the hopeful predictions of a coming day of peace voiced by some prophets, Joel foresees a coming holy war. In a reversal of the famous pacifist vision of Isaiah and Micah about weapons being converted into farming tools, Joel instead says:

> Prepare war,
>> stir up the warriors.
> Let all the soldiers draw near,
>> let them come up.
> Beat your plowshares into swords
>> and your pruning hooks into
>>> spears;
>> let the weakling say, "I am a
>>> warrior." (Joel 3:9–10)

Christian theologians have also found considerable significance in Joel. The apostle Peter believed that a passage in Joel about God's Spirit being poured out was a prophecy concerning the descent of the Holy Spirit, and he cited the following passage on the day of Pentecost.

BIBLICAL VOICES
> Then afterward
>> I will pour out my spirit on
>>> all flesh;
> your sons and daughters shall
>> prophesy,
>> your old men shall dream
>>> dreams,

and your young men shall
    see visions.
Even on the male and female
    slaves,
    in those days, I will pour out
      my spirit. (Joel 2:28–29)

- **Jonah**

  And Jonah was in the belly of the fish three days and three
  nights. (Jonah 1:17)

What happened to Jonah's whale?

First of all, there was no whale. Perhaps one of the most popularly
known stories of the Bible, the tale of Jonah is another familiar
legend that has been vastly oversimplified in retelling over the
centuries. Most people still don't know what Jonah was doing in
that fish's belly in the first place.

Although this book describes events in the time of Jeroboam
II (786–746 BCE), when the Assyrians based in Nineveh threatened
Israel, the book was written much later. Rather than a depiction
of events that happened to the actual Jonah, a prophet who lived
around 750 BCE, the book is regarderd by most scholars as a parable
that was written around 320–350 BCE. The style of the Hebrew
used by the writer and his familiarity with later biblical books are
evidence of this late date. Historical records from ancient Assyria
contain no reference to the events described in Jonah.

PLOT SUMMARY: JONAH

    The prophet Jonah is commanded by God to go to Nineveh,
the wicked capital city of the Assyrians, to preach repentance. Instead, Jonah attempts to run away, booking passage on a ship going
to Tarshish in southern Spain, the farthest known earthly point to
which a man could then travel. When a storm comes up, the fright-
ened sailors believe someone on board is responsible for making

the gods angry. They throw Jonah overboard at his own request. Swallowed by "a great fish," Jonah prays in its belly for three days and nights. Obviously sick of this praying man, the fish vomits Jonah out on dry land and he is again commanded by God to go to Nineveh and preach to the people there, calling them to give up their wicked ways. Jonah does as he is told and the Assyrian people, even though the are not Jews, repent and are spared by God.

Everybody is happy with this turn of events but Jonah. He was hoping for a little fire and brimstone to come raining down on Nineveh. In a lesser known conclusion to this tale, Jonah sits under a bush, or large gourd, to get some shade. God sends a worm to attack the bush. So Jonah is left sitting in the hot sun, angry about the loss of his shade. God tells him, "You're concerned about the bush, for which you did not labor. . . . Should I not be concerned about Nineveh, that great city, in which there are more than a hundred and twenty thousand persons who do not know their right hand from their left, and also much cattle?" (Jon. 4:10–11)

In other words, the God of Jonah is no longer presented as the God of vengeance on Israel's enemies but as a caring, loving Creator concerned for everything he has made in the world. The God of Jonah has come a long way from the days of Noah.

For Jews and Christians alike, the story of Jonah and the "great fish" who swallowed him illustrates God's universal mercy. Even the sinners of Nineveh, the most awful place on earth, are worthy of forgiveness and salvation if they repent. Other Jewish commentators saw the tale of the reluctant Jonah as a parable about the unwillingness of Jews to proclaim God's Word to Gentiles, so it has also been cited to underscore the significance of taking God's message to the entire world, even to the least likely listeners, a message that has since been applied to Christians as well. In Christian tradition, the three days in the fish's belly are also viewed as symbolic of the death and resurrection of Jesus Christ. Jesus himself compared his entombment with Jonah's confinement "in the belly of the sea monster" (see Matt. 12:39–41).

A GODLESS BOOK

ESTHER

Haman ... the enemy of all the Jews, had plotted against the Jews to destroy them, and had cast Pur—that is "the lot"—to crush and destroy them; but when Esther came before the king, he gave orders in writing that the plot he had devised against the Jews should come upon his own head, and that he and his sons should be hanged on the gallows. Therefore these days are called Purim, from the word Pur. (Esther 9:24–26)

K nown to Jewish readers as the source of the Purim festival—and unfamiliar to many Christians—the book of Esther has a distinction shared with only one other Bible book. It never mentions God. The Lord sits this one out.

Set in the time of the Persian empire, it is the story of a brave Jewish heroine, Esther (Hadassah in Hebrew), who saves her people from a genocidal plot. As scripture, Esther was a latecomer to the Hebrew canon. The rabbis who fixed the canon of official Hebrew scriptures debated well into the fourth century CE whether this story, essentially a Hebrew Grimms' fairy tale, belongs with the rest of the divine books. Not only is God a "no-show," but the book contains few elements typical of most other biblical books. There are no laws, miracles, prayers, or mention of Jerusalem. It's not even a very moral story, concluding with a bloodbath in which more than seventy-five thousand Persian enemies of the Jews are massacred.

Probably inspired by a Persian court tale, it is not a "historical" book and it has the feel of a Hebrew *Cinderella*. Apart from the name of the king in the story, "Ahasuerus," who is most likely the Persian ruler Xerxes I (486–465 BCE), there is no evidence linking the tale to authentic Persian history, and it was probably written sometime after 200 BCE by an anonymous author.

PLOT SUMMARY: ESTHER

The Persian king Ahasuerus gives a grand banquet at his capital, Susa. In his cups, Ahasuerus decides to display his beautiful queen, Vashti. But Vashti, apparently uninterested in being put on display like a prize heifer, refuses to attend. The king issues a decree that all women must obey their husbands (once again, we know a man wrote that!), and Vashti is deposed as queen. Deciding a new wife is in order, the king orders all the beautiful, young virgins of the kingdom—the Persian empire then spread from India to Egypt—collected for what is essentially a massive beauty contest.

Concealing her Jewish identity, the beautiful Esther, a young woman brought up by her cousin Mordecai, is selected to be the new queen of Persia. Esther and Mordecai then help foil a plot against the king's life. But Cousin Mordecai refuses to bow in deference to the king's chancellor, Haman. Infuriated at this show of disrespect, the enraged Haman determines to seek revenge on the Jewish Mordecai by eliminating all the Jews in the empire, the first anti-Semitic pogrom in history. He persuades the king to decree death to a "certain people" who keep their own laws.

Learning of Haman's plot to destroy the Persian Jews, Mordecai prompts Esther to invite Ahasuerus and Haman to a banquet. There she tells King Ahasuerus that she is under threat of death from the king's decree, and that it is Haman's doing. The horrified king rescinds his decree and orders Haman and his ten sons to be hanged on the very gallows that had been set up for the Jews. Mordecai is promoted to chancellor, and the Jews are given license to take revenge on their enemies in the empire. Esther's triumph is celebrated in the Jewish festival called Purim, a holiday with roots in an ancient agricultural festival celebrating the arrival of spring.

THE DEVIL MADE ME DO IT

JOB

Job feels the rod,
Yet blesses God.
—THE NEW ENGLAND PRIMER, 1688

Then Satan answered the Lord, "Does Job fear God for
nothing? Have you not put a fence around him and his house
and all that he has, on every side? You have blessed the work
of his hands, and his possessions have increased in the land.
But stretch out your hand now, and touch all that he has, and
he will curse you to your face." (Job 1:9–11)

❋ Why does God make bets with Satan?

One of eleven books in the third section of the Hebrew Bible collected as Writings, Job is a familiar yet widely misunderstood story that sets out to explain the mystery of why the righteous must suffer. Or in modern terms, why bad things happen to good people. Based on an ancient folktale set in the land of Uz in the desert regions to Israel's southeast, it is about a saintly man—never identified as a Jew—who suffers unthinkable pain and tragedy after Satan challenges God to a bet. While the precise date of its composition is unknown, Job supposedly dates from the time of the Exile in Babylon or soon after the Return to Jerusalem. As Karen Armstrong points out in *A History of God,* "After the exile, one of the survivors used this old legend to ask fundamental questions about the nature of God and his responsibility for the sufferings of humanity." (p. 65)

Written when Jewish society was seen as divided between the pious and the unfaithful, the book does not set out to explain the problem of evil and disease in the world, but specifically addresses why righteous believers must suffer if God is truly just. It is a question that appears elsewhere in Hebrew scriptures (several Psalms and certain prophets raise it, for instance) and has troubled not only Jewish thinkers but people in many cultures and times, before and since. A Babylonian poem called "A Dialogue About Human Misery" may have influenced the style and content of Job, and in recent times the troubling story has inspired modern writers such as Archibald MacLeish, whose play *J.B.* is based on Job, and political columnist William Safire, whose book about Job is called *The First Dissident.*

PLOT SUMMARY: JOB

God is boasting about how faithful a servant Job is when Satan (or in Hebrew, "the Accuser" or "Adversary") says, "Sure he's a good guy. He has everything. Take it all away and see how good he is."

Accepting Satan's dare, God allows Satan to do his worst. Job loses everything, including his ten children who die when their house collapses in a windstorm. Despite the terrible tragedy, Job stands strong. Challenged a second time, God allows Satan to further test Job by covering his body with painful sores. When Job's wife tells him, "Curse God, and die"—in other words, just put an end to your misery—Job faithfully answers that he must take both the good and the bad from God. That's how most people thought the story ended, with a dutiful, obedient Job refusing to question the Lord. But it is really just the beginning.

Three of Job's friends—Eliphaz, Bildad, and Zophar—arrive to offer "sympathy," or at least discuss the subject of divine justice. The consoling friends quickly assume that Job must have done something wrong to deserve the punishment he is receiving. Angrily protesting his innocence and railing against his fate, Job curses the day he was born, no longer appearing quite the faithful servant of God meekly accepting his fate. Another character, Elihu, appears and attempts to vindicate his own view of God's mysterious ways, but Job counters each of his arguments with continuing protests of innocence, pointing out how evil people seem to prosper.

Ultimately, God himself arrives to speak directly to Job from a whirlwind, telling him that for humans to discuss how God functions is presumptuous, since God is utterly beyond mortal understanding. At the same time, God's showing up for a face-to-face encounter with this mere mortal is supposed to demonstrate how much God cares for Job. This occasionally sarcastic God—"Surely you know, for you were born then, and the number of your days is great," God cuttingly says to Job—argues that Job doesn't even comprehend what a big task being God is. From ordering the heavens to letting "the wild ass go free," God has lots of balls to juggle. Chastened by God's unanswerable questions to him, Job is repentant. Instead of getting a clear answer to the questions he had posed to God, Job recognizes God's awesome power and realizes that he can never comprehend God's purpose. He repents for his weakness in questioning God.

With that, God reproaches Job's three friends and orders them to make a special sacrifice. God then restores Job and his fortunes, bringing him even greater happiness and prosperity than he had enjoyed before. Scholars debate whether the family given to Job at the end of the book is the same seven sons and three daughters he had at the beginning, or whether they are ten new children. However, the book closes with Job giving the three girls names: Jemimah ("Dove"), Keziah ("cassia" or "cinnamon"), and Keren-happuch ("horn of eye cosmetic"). If they were his own children, why would Job give them new names?

BIBLICAL VOICES

Then the Lord answered Job out of the whirlwind:
> "Who is this that darkens counsel
>> by words without
>> knowledge?
> Gird up your loins like a man,
>> I will question you, and you
>> shall declare to me.
> Where were you when I laid the
>> foundation of the earth?
>> Tell me, if you have
>> understanding.
> Who determined its
>> measurements—surely you
>> know!
>> Or who stretched the line
>> upon it?
> On what were its bases sunk,
>> or who laid the cornerstone
> when the morning stars sang
>> together
>> and all the heavenly beings
>> shouted for joy?" (Job 38:1–7)

Why does God make bets with Satan?

For about twenty-five hundred years, the meaning of Job has puzzled people. The traditional depiction of Job was an oversimplification, presenting a picture of a good man who is true to God, no matter what happens, whose complete obedience is rewarded with greater prosperity. A closer reading shows that Job is a far more complicated character who challenges God. Some have called Job the "first existentialist," because he questioned the seeming isolation of humanity in a hostile universe and then discovered that there were no answers. The more complicated, and not entirely satisfying, message of Job and his questioning of God is that humans, in the cosmic sense, "just don't get it." It is a message that seems more of a dodge than spiritually comforting. As Karen Armstrong wrote in discussing Job:

> Together with his three comforters, Job dares to question the divine decrees and engages in a fierce intellectual debate. For the first time in Jewish history, the religious imagination had turned to speculation of a more abstract nature. The prophets had claimed that God had allowed Israel to suffer because of its sins; the author of Job shows that some Israelites were no longer satisfied by the traditional answer. Job attacks this view and reveals its intellectual inadequacy, but God suddenly cuts into his furious speculation. He reveals himself to Job in a vision, pointing to the marvels of the world he has created: how could a puny little creature like Job dare to argue with the transcendent God? Job submits, but a modern reader who is looking for a more coherent and philosophical answer to the problem of suffering will not be satisfied with this solution. The author of Job is not denying the right to question, however, but suggesting that the intellect alone is not

equipped to deal with these imponderable matters. (*A History of God*, pp. 65–66)

The message for the Israelites of the time Job was composed may have been clearer: Yes, the righteous must sometimes suffer, but if they maintain their faith in God their fortunes will be restored, just as Israel was restored by God in 538 BCE. But Job, along with many other biblical accounts of God, seems to raise more troublesome questions than it fitfully answers. Most troubling of all is the none too flattering portrait the book paints of God, who is rather boastful in the first scene, like an overly proud parent crowing over a precocious child. Challenged by Satan, this God seems insecure, uncertain when pressed about his loyal servant Job. Is God so weak as to be pricked by an almost adolescent dare from Satan? Why does God have to prove anything to one of the "heavenly company"?

The Satan of Job, from the Hebrew *ha-Satan*, is more of a figure, say, a prosecuting attorney, than the figure of pure evil as Satan is now commonly conceived. Job's Satan, who disappears from the stage after the opening scenes, not to be heard from again, is presented as a member of the heavenly company. Only in later Jewish and Christian writings did Satan become the chief of a group of fallen angels. The connection between the Satan of Job and the serpent who tempts Eve in Genesis was not made until the author of Revelation, the last book of the Christian New Testament, identified the serpent with the Devil.

To Jack Miles, author of *God: A Biography*, the book of Job represents a climactic event in the Bible, a moment in which the Lord faces the fact that even God can do bad things, or as Miles puts it, has a "fiend-susceptible side." Noting that in the Hebrew scriptures Job marks the last time God speaks personally, rather than through some messenger, Miles writes:

The climax is a climax for God himself and not for Job or for the reader. After Job, God knows his own ambiguity as he has never known it before. He now knows that . . . he has a fiend-susceptible side and that mankind's conscience can be finer than his. With Job's assistance, his just, kind self has won out over his cruel, capricious self just as it did after the flood. But the victory has come at an enormous price. Job will father a new family, but the family he lost during the wager will not be brought back from the dead; neither will the servants whom the devil slew. And neither will God's innocence. The world still seems more just than unjust, and God still seems more good than bad; yet the pervasive mood, as this extraordinary work ends, is one not of redemption but of reprieve. (p. 328)

Just as the character Job himself learns that there are no easy answers, Job is not an easy book. It stands as testimony to the questioning nature of the human spirit, perhaps the leftovers from that "Forbidden Fruit" Adam and Eve enjoyed in Eden. The fact that the people who decided on what should be in the Bible included a book with so many unanswered questions is also a "testament" of their recognition of God's mysterious ways and the legitimacy of wondering about them. This is not a book that celebrates blind faith or Abraham's unconditional "fear of God." Job leaves readers with a tentative grasp of faith. Its message still seems subversive, leaving behind an uneasy sense that this somewhat capricious God of Job offers his "servant" the time-honored but frustrating response so many children get from their parents: "Because I said so."

Out of the Mouths
of Babes

Psalms

❋

God's Greatest Hits! A collection of 150 hymns or, more accurately, poems, Psalms is the first book in the Hebrew "Writings" but follows Job in Christian Bibles. The Hebrew title is *Tehillim*, "Praises" or "Songs of Praise," but that is not a completely accurate description. These are often intensely personal songs of despair, woe, and depression as well as songs celebrating the glories of God.

In ancient Jewish and Christian tradition, King David was considered the author of Psalms, but modern biblical scholars agree that the book was has multiple authors. The biblical text actually attributes seventy-four psalms to King David, twelve psalms to Solomon, and one to Moses; thirty-two psalms are identified with other individuals, and the rest are anonymous. The most widely accepted notion is that the psalms were composed over a long period, from the Exodus to the time of the Return to Jerusalem in 538 BCE. While historic setting is important to the Psalms, as C. S. Lewis noted in his *Reflections on the Psalms* (1958):

> The Psalms were written by many poets and at many different dates. Some, I believe are allowed to go back to the reign of David. I think certain scholars allow that Psalm 18 might be by David himself. But many are later than the "captivity," which we should call the deportation to Babylon. . . . What must be said, however, is that the Psalms are poems, and poems intended to be sung: not doctrinal treatises, nor even sermons. . . . Most emphatically the Psalms must be read as poems; as lyrics, with all the licenses and all the formalities, the hyperboles, the emotional rather than logical connections, which are proper to lyric poetry. (pp. 2–3)

The Bible has traditionally been thought of as God speaking to people. But in Psalms people speak to God, in some of the world's greatest poetic literature. David Rosenberg, a poet who strives to capture the human voices at work in the Hebrew scriptures in his book *A Poet's Bible,* makes this point in discussing the intimate, human quality of Psalms. "One day, translating a psalm that I thought was written in anger and is usually presented as such, I suddenly realized it was not anger at all but an intense depression, a self-conscious awareness of failure. The psalmist was facing depression and not allowing himself to respond with anger. Instead, even as his voice speaks bitterly, he overcomes despair with his song's ironic sense of never ending, echoing into eternity. And I felt the poet's utterly real presence." (p. 3)

While Jews and Christians share the entire Hebrew scriptures, or Old Testament, Psalms might be the most emotionally and intensely shared book of Hebrew scripture. Rabbi Joseph Telushkin calls Psalms the "backbone of the Hebrew prayerbook" and notes that because the psalms are so omnipresent in prayer services, Jews know many of the book's verses by heart. Jesus often quoted or referred to Psalms, notably during his temptation, in the Sermon on the Mount, and at his crucifixion. It is likely that early Christians used selections from the book in their services. Saint Augustine, the fifth-century church scholar, called the book the "language of devotion," and Martin Luther regarded psalms as "a Bible in miniature." The 150 "rosaries" later instituted by the Roman Catholic church are in honor of the 150 psalms.

Greatest Hits from the Psalms

While most people would agree that the most familiar psalm, the twenty-third, is the greatest of all, the following highlights come from some of the other most beautiful, memorable or frequently cited psalms. (See Appendix 2 for the full text of the twenty-third psalm in two translations.)

Psalm 1

Blessed is the man that walketh not in the counsel of the ungodly, nor standeth in the way of sinners, nor sitteth in the seat of the scornful.

But his delight is in the law of the Lord; and in his law doth he meditate day and night.

And he shall be like a tree planted by the rivers of water, that bringeth forth his fruit in his season; his leaf also shall not wither; and whatsoever he doeth shall prosper.

The ungodly are not so: but are like the chaff which the wind driveth away. (1:1–4 KJV)

Psalm 8
Out of the mouths of babes and
    infants
you have founded a bulwark
    because of your foes,
to silence the enemy and the avenger.
When I look at your heavens, the
    work of your fingers,
the moon and the stars that you
    have established;
what are human beings that you are mindful of them,
mortals that you care for them?
Yet you have made them a little lower than God [or angels].
(8:2–5 NRSV)

Psalm 13
How long, O lord? Will you forget me forever?
How long will you hide your face from me?
How long must I wrestle with my thoughts and every day have sorrow in my heart?
How long will my enemy triumph over me?
    Look on me and answer, O Lord my God.
Give light to my eyes, or I will sleep in death; my enemy will say, "I have overcome him" and my foes will rejoice when I fall.
But I trust in your unfailing love;
my heart rejoices in your salvation.
I will sing to the Lord,
because he has been good to me. (KJV)

Psalm 14
Fools say in their hearts, "There is
    no God." (14:1 NRSV)

Psalm 19
The heavens declare the glory of God,
    the sky proclaims His handiwork.
Day to day makes utterance,
    night to night speaks out
There is no utterance,
    there are no words,
    whose sound goes unheard
Their voice carries throughout the earth,
    their words to the end of the world. (19:1–4 JPS)

The precepts of the Lord are just,
    rejoicing the heart;
    the instruction of the Lord is lucid,
    making the eyes light up.
The fear of the Lord is pure,
    abiding forever,
    the judgments of the Lord are true,
    righteous altogether,
    more desirable than gold,
    than much fine honey
    than drippings of the comb. (19:9–10 JPS)

Psalm 22
        (The "crucifixion" psalm, quoted by Jesus on the cross)
My God, my God, why have you forsaken me?
    Why are you so far from
        helping me, from the
        words of my groaning?
O my God, I cry by day, but you
    do not answer;
and by night, but find no rest. (22:1–2 NRSV)

Psalm 24

Who shall ascend the hill of the Lord?
    And who shall stand in his holy place?
Those who have cleans hands and pure hearts,
who do not lift up their souls to what is false,
and do not swear deceitfully. (24:1–4 NRSV)

Psalm 27

The Lord is my light and my salvation;
    whom shall I fear?
    The Lord is the stronghold of my life;
    of whom shall I be afraid?
When evildoers assail me to devour my flesh—
my adversaries and foes—they shall stumble and fall.
Though an army encamp against me, my heart shall not fear;
though war rise up against me, yet I will be confident. (27:1–3)

Psalm 37

Refrain from anger, and forsake wrath.
    Do not fret—it leads only to evil.
    For the wicked shall be cut off,
    but those who wait for the Lord shall inherit the land.
Yet a little while, and the wicked will be no more;
though you look diligently for their place, they will not be there.
But the meek shall inherit the land,
    and delight themselves in abundant prosperity.
(37:8–11 NRSV)

Psalm 42

As the deer pants for streams of water,
so my soul pants for you, O God.
My soul thirsts for God, for the living God
When can I go and meet with God?
My tears have been my food day and night,
while men say to me all day long, "Where is your God?"
(42:1–3 KJV)

Why are you downcast, O my soul?
Why so disturbed within me?
Put your hope in God, for I will yet praise him, my Savior and my
God. (42:5–6 KJV)

Psalm 66

Make a joyful noise to God, all the earth;
    sing the glory of his name;
    give to him glorious praise.
Say to God, "How awesome are your deeds!
    Because of your great power, your enemies cringe before you.
All the earth worships you; they sing praises to you, sing praises
to your name." (66:1–4 NRSV)

Psalm 84

How lovely is Your dwelling place,
    O Lord of hosts,
I long, I yearn for the courts of the Lord;
    my body and soul shout for joy to the living God.
Even the sparrow has found a home,
    and the swallow a nest for herself
    in which to set her young,
    near your altar, O Lord of hosts,
my king and my God.
Happy are those who dwell in Your house. (84:1–5 JPS)

Better one day in Your courts than a thousand [anywhere
    else];
    I would rather stand at the threshold of God's house
    than dwell in the tents of the wicked. (84:11 JPS)

Psalm 100

Make a joyful noise to the Lord,
    all the earth.
    Worship the Lord with
      gladness;

come into his presence with
singing.
Know that the Lord is God.
It is he that made us, and we
are his;
we are his people, and the sheep
of his pasture.
Enter his gates with thanksgiving,
and his courts with praise. (100:1–4 NRSV)

Psalm 137
By the rivers of Babylon,
there we sat,
sat and wept,
as we thought of Zion.
There on the poplars
we hung up our lyres,
for our captors asked us there for songs,
our tormentors, for amusement,
"Sing us a song of Zion."
How can we sing a song of the Lord
on alien soil?
If I forget you, O Jerusalem,
let my right hand whither;
let my tongue stick to my palate
if I cease to think of you,
if I do not keep Jerusalem in memory
even at my happiest hour. (137:1–6 JPS)

Psalms Your Sunday School Left Out
That's the familiar part of Psalm 137, a picture of Israel held
captive in Babylon, awaiting deliverance. Fewer people may have
read this part of the psalm:

Fair Babylon, you predator,
a blessing on him who repays you in kind

   what you have inflicted on us;
   a blessing on him who seizes your babies
   and dashes them against the rocks. (137:8–9 JPS)

As this grim verse proves, not all of the psalms painted a rosy picture. Here are a few lines from some of the other psalms that Mother never taught you:

Psalm 68

But God will shatter the heads of
   his enemies,
 the hairy crown of those who
   walk in their guilty ways.
The Lord said,
  "I will bring them back from
   Bashan,
   I will bring them back from the
   depths of the sea,
 so that you may bathe your feet
   in blood,
 so that the tongues of your dogs
   may have their share from
   the foe." (68:21–23 NRSV)

Psalm 144

Blessed be the Lord, my rock,
 who trains my hands for war,
  and my fingers for battle;
my rock and my fortress,
 my stronghold and my
  deliverer,
my shield, in whom I take refuge,
 who subdues the peoples
  under me.

O Lord, what are humans beings
        that you regard them,
    or mortals that you think of them?
They are like a breath;
    their days are like a passing
        shadow. (144:1–4 NRSV)

Happy Are Those Who Find Wisdom

Proverbs

Come, let us take our fill of love
until morning;
let us delight ourselves with
love.
For my husband is not at home;
he has gone on a long journey.
He took a bag of money with
him;
he will not come home until full
moon. (Prov. 7:18–20)

A fool takes no pleasure in
understanding,
but only in expressing personal opinion. (Prov. 18:2)

※

❋ Does "sparing the rod" spoil the child?

A nother of the books collected in the Hebrew Writings, Proverbs is often treated as little more than an ancient Hebrew set of Chinese fortune cookies. Like the sayings of Confucius or the pithy advice of Benjamin Franklin in *Poor Richard's Almanac*, more than one thousand traditional sayings and popular adages make up Proverbs. Grouped with the "Wisdom Books" of the Christian Old Testament, the proverbs consist of advice, commands, and admonitions on such themes as correct behavior, purity in mind and worship, avoidance of sin, and above all, the quest for wisdom.

The authors—and there were many spread out over a long period of time—wanted to highlight certain key, timeless virtues: honesty, hard work, trustworthiness, control of one's temper and appetites—sexual and culinary—and maintaining the proper attitude toward wealth and poverty. Some of the sayings are simple observations, but moral values are exalted. There is no ambiguity in Proverbs over the contrast between the righteous and the wicked. Adultery and other sexual wanderings are most frequently condemned, and drunkenness also gets poor marks. In several chapters, a divinely created "Lady Wisdom" speaks, and she is contrasted with the "prostitute," "strange woman," or "Dame Folly" who leads young men astray. While most of the advice is written in classic couplet form, there are also some longer poems, including a final song extolling the virtues of the "ideal wife."

These bits of good advice were traditionally attributed to King Solomon, famed for his great wisdom—although not necessarily for his great moral standards (see page 190). But the book actually consists of several collections of sayings that date from different periods and were composed, or compiled, by a number of anonymous authors, perhaps rabbis or sages who offered moral and religious instruction to young Jewish men. The book is typical of other "wisdom" writings of the Hebrew scriptures and also the ancient Near East, and thirty of the sayings are adapted from the moral instruction of an earlier Egyptian sage, Amenemope.

The Best of Proverbs

My son, if sinners entice you, do not yield. (1:10 JPS)

Hold on to resourcefulness and foresight.
They will give life to your spirit
And grace to your throat.
Then you will go your way safely
And not injure your feet.
When you lie down you will be unafraid;
You will lie down and your sleep will be sweet.
You will not fear sudden terror
Or the disaster that comes upon the wicked,
For the Lord will be your trust;
He will keep your feet from being caught. (3:21–26 JPS)

The path of the just is as the shining light, that shineth more
and more unto the perfect day. (4:18 KJV)

The lips of a forbidden woman drip honey;
Her mouth is smoother than oil:
But in the end she is as bitter as wormwood,
sharp as a two-edged sword. (5:3–4 JPS)

Here is a brief Proverbs version of the familiar fable "The Grass-hopper and the Ant":

Lazybones, go to the ant;
Study its ways and learn.
Without leaders, officers, or rulers,
It lays up its stores during the summer,
Gathers its food at the harvest.
How long will you lie there, lazybones;
when will you wake from your sleep?
A bit more sleep, a bit more slumber,
A bit more hugging yourself in bed,

And poverty will come calling upon you,
And want, like a man with a shield (6:6–11 JPS)

  A sharp warning against the lure of adultery:
For a prostitute's fee is only a loaf of bread,
but the wife of another stalks a man's very life.
Can fire be carried in the bosom
without burning one's clothes?
Or can one walk on hot coals without scorching the feet?
So is he who sleeps with his neighbor's wife. (6:26–29 NRSV)

Hatred stirs up strife,
but love covers up all faults. (10:12 JPS)

Like a gold ring in a pig's snout
is a beautiful woman without good sense. (11:22 NRSV)

He who trusts in his wealth shall fall,
but the righteous shall flourish like foliage. (11:28 JPS)

Those who trouble their households will inherit the wind,
and the fool will be servant to the wise. (11:29 NRSV)

The way of a fool is right in his own eyes,
But the wise man accepts advice. (12:15 JPS)

Hope deferred maketh the heart sick. (13:12 KJV)

The desire accomplished is sweet to the soul. (13:19 KJV)

A soft answer turns away wrath,
but a harsh word stirs up anger. (15:1 NRSV)

Those who are hot tempered stir up strife,
but those who are slow to anger calm contention. (15:18 NRSV)

The human mind plans the way,
but the Lord directs the steps. (16:9 NRSV)

Pride goeth before destruction, and a haughty spirit before a fall. (16:18 KJV)

One who is slow to anger is better than the mighty,
and one whose temper is controlled than one who captures a city. (16:32 NRSV)

He who mocks the poor affronts his Maker,
He who rejoices over another's misfortune will not go unpunished. (17:5 JPS)

A joyful heart makes for good health
Despondency dries up the bones. (17:22 JPS)
     (*Reader's Digest* was right! Laughter *is* the best medicine.)

He that hath knowledge spareth his words: and a man of understanding is of an excellent spirit.
     Even a fool, when he holdeth his peace, is counted wise. (17:27–28 KJV)

A fool's mouth is his destruction. (18:7 KJV)

Before honor is humility. (18:12 KJV)

Whoso findeth a wife findeth a good thing. (18:22 KJV)

He that hath pity upon the poor lendeth unto the Lord. (19:17 KJV)

Bread of deceit is sweet to a man;
but afterwards his mouth shall be filled with gravel. (20:17)

A good name is to be chosen rather than great riches. (22:1 KJV)

Train up a child in the way he should go: and when he is old, he will not depart from it. (22:6 KJV)

Put a knife to thy throat, if thou be a man given to appetite. (23:2 KJV)

Do not wear yourself out to get rich;
be wise enough to desist.
When your eyes light upon it,
it is gone;
for suddenly it takes wings to itself,
flying like an eagle toward heaven. (23:4–5 NRSV)

The drunkard and the glutton shall come to poverty and drowsiness shall clothe a man with rags. (23:21 KJV)

Look not thou upon the wine when it is red, when it giveth his color in the cup, when it moveth itself aright.
    At the last it biteth like a serpent, and stingeth like an adder. (23:31–32 KJV)

If thou faint in the day of adversity, thy strength is small. (24:10 KJV)
("When the going gets tough, the tough get going.")

As a dog returns to his vomit,
So a dullard returns to his folly. (26:11 JPS)

Boast not thyself of tomorrow; for thou knowest not what a day may bring forth.
Let another man praise thee, and not thine own mouth. (27:1–2 KJV)

He who gives to the poor will not be in want,
But he who shuts his eyes will be roundly cursed. (28:27 JPS)

Where there is no vision, the people perish. (29:18 KJV)

Speak out for those who cannot speak,
for the rights of all the destitute.
Speak out, judge righteously,
defend the rights of the poor and needy. (31:8–9 NRSV)

What a rare find is a capable wife!
Her worth is far beyond that of rubies. (31:10 JPS)

And by the way, to those of you who spend a lot of money on dye jobs at the salon, heed a word from Proverbs:

Gray hair is a crown of glory;
it is gained in a righteous life. (16:31)

Does "sparing the rod" spoil the child?

If Proverbs offers some of the best advice on the eternal values of humility, hard work, charity, and wisdom, the book also offers two lines of the worst:

He who spares the rod hates his son,
But he who loves him disciplines him early. (13:24 JPS)

Do not withhold discipline from a child;
If you beat him with a rod he will not die.
Beat him with a rod
And you will save him from the grave. (23:13–14 NRSV)

For centuries, these verses have been used to justify the parent's spanking, the schoolmaster's paddling, the nun's rap on the knuckles with a ruler, and even more severe forms of corporal punishment.

Perhaps the best modern interpretation is that what once was acceptable in a primitive culture is no longer the case. Just as we no longer stone adulterers, society can no longer tolerate the physical punishment of children. Discipline is crucial for every child, but beatings are unacceptable. Just as you wouldn't strike an employee who made a mistake, there is no justifiable reason to hit or otherwise physically abuse a child.

As Rabbi Joseph Telushkin puts it, "Like adults, children need discipline, but the equation of discipline with beating is an example of very bad advice in a good book. In these two verses, morality is turned upside down: People who don't beat their children are made to appear unloving, while those who do beat them (some of whom, one must assume, are sadists) are rewarded by being told that this proves that they are loving parents." (*Biblical Literacy*, p. 344)

There are sure and effective means of teaching lessons, instilling discipline, and even punishing children's misbehavior that do not involve physical violence. In an era of commonplace child abuse, even hinting that the Bible condones such behavior is a grievous mistake.

NOTHING NEW UNDER THE SUN

ECCLESIASTES

Sheer futility, Qoheleth says, everything is futile.
(Eccl. 12:8 NJB)

Of making many books there is no end, and much study is a
weariness of the flesh. (Eccl. 12:12)

uring the 1960s, there may have been no more widely
quoted Bible verses than the words from Ecclesiastes that
provided Pete Seeger with the lyrics for "Turn, Turn, Turn,"
which became a hit single for the Byrds. Americans of a certain
age may also recall that President Kennedy admired these verses
and they were read at his funeral. Ironically, those verses come
from one of the most unusual, and for many, confounding, books
of the Bible.

BIBLICAL VOICES

For everything there is a season, and a time for every matter
under heaven:
a time to be born, and a time to die;
a time to plant, and a time to pluck up what is planted;
a time to kill, and a time to heal;
a time to break down, and a time to build up;
a time to weep, and a time to laugh;
a time to mourn, and a time to dance;
a time to throw away stones, and a time to gather stones
together;
a time to embrace, and a time to refrain from embracing;
a time to seek, and a time to lose;
a time to keep, and a time to throw away;
a time to tear, and a time to sew;
a time to keep silence, and a time to speak;
a time to love, and a time to hate;
a time for war, and a time for peace. (Eccl. 3:1–8)

PLOT SUMMARY: ECCLESIASTES

Anyone who thinks that the Bible is a simplistic book offering
pat answers to challenging questions hasn't read Job or Ecclesiastes. These two books also refute those orthodox and fundamentalist Bible believers who condemn anyone who dares to question
God or the divine plan. While much of the Hebrew scripture depicts an orderly universe in which the faithful can find hope even

in the most desperate moments, Ecclesiastes—like Job—is a searching, skeptical book. Both books not only accept the uncomfortable questions, they honor them. As the editors of the New Jerusalem Bible comment in introducing Ecclesiastes: "The book is valuable for its uncomfortable and questioning faith, and its inclusion in the Bible is a reassurance for all who share this attitude."

The book's first few opening words, "Vanity of vanities! All is vanity" (the Jerusalem Bible uses "futility"), set the author's darkly brooding tone and themes: the futility of chasing after riches and wisdom, and the inevitability of death. At times, the author of Ecclesiastes expresses such hedonistic, cynical ideas that some rabbis sought to suppress the book. Its popularity, its ultimate acceptance of God's will, and the belief that Solomon was its author were apparently enough to secure Ecclesiastes a place in the "Writings," the third section of the Hebrew scriptures. In the Christian Old Testament, Ecclesiastes is part of the "Wisdom" literature that includes the books of Job and Proverbs.

Like Proverbs and the Song of Solomon, the book was traditionally attributed to King Solomon, the idealized "wise man" of Israelite history. But scholars have pointed out that the language, such as the inclusion of certain Persian words in the original text, and the tone of the book make that virtually impossible. Many verses reflect a disillusionment that may have been typical among Jews during the Exile in Babylon. Its composition has been dated as late as 300 BCE, and some historians believe it might be even later than that. Some scholars assert that the book may date from the "Hellenistic" era, the period after Alexander the Great conquered Persia in 332 BCE, a time when the ancient Near East fell under the influence of various Greek philosophers. Literate educated Jews probably would have been familiar with the Greek Big Three: Socrates, Plato, and Aristotle.

BIBLICAL VOICES

I see another evil under the sun, which goes hard with people: suppose someone has received from God riches, property, honors—nothing at all left to wish for; but God does not give them the chance to enjoy them, and some stranger enjoys them. This is futile, and grievous suffering too. Or take someone who has had a hundred children and lived for many years, and having reached old age, has never enjoyed the good things of life and has not even got a tomb; it seems to me a stillborn child is happier. (Eccl. 6:1–3 NJB)

The English title derives from the Greek and Latin versions of a Hebrew word that meant "leader of an assembly or congregation," and the word was loosely translated as "preacher." But the original Hebrew *Qoheleth* may be more accurately translated as "teacher."

Neither history, parable, nor a prophetic book, Ecclesiastes is unique among the Bible books. It might be best to think of it as somebody thinking out loud, a wise but weary old man ruminating to a group of colleagues or students.

Offering a slightly different take on Ecclesiastes in his book *A Poet's Bible*, David Rosenberg sees the author "defrocking" old homilies and clichés. He comments, "No philosophy coheres throughout the poem, much less any theology. . . . The poet, wrapped in the trappings of his stubbornly Hebraic culture, finds a way to embrace a difficult world while seemingly rejecting it. . . . Even today, conventional Bible interpreters, particularly non-Jewish ones, mistakenly assume the book is full of corroding doubt." (p. 169)

More philosophical than religious, the "Teacher's" wanderings all begin from an essential question: "What does one gain by all one's toil?" The author looks for meaning in the typical answers: work, pleasure, riches, but finds none. He even questions the basic issue of right versus wrong, but decides that good is not invariably rewarded and the same end comes for all. All lives end in death, and fate has already been decreed by God. That is a pretty stark departure from other wisdom, contrasting most sharply with Proverbs, which celebrates the modest life of hard work and the continual search for wisdom.

The book's concluding verses read:

> The end of the matter; all has been heard. Fear God, and
> keep his commandments; for that is the whole duty of every-
> one. For God will bring every deed into judgment, including
> every secret thing, whether good or evil. (Eccl. 12:13–14)

This sentiment is so at odds with the rest of the book that
many commentators believe it was added to give this book a more
orthodox and conventionally acceptable message.

THE LOVE MACHINE, ANOTHER GODLESS BOOK

SONG OF SOLOMON

While the king was on his couch,
My nard gave forth its fragrance.
My beloved is to me a bag of myrrh
Lodged between my breasts. (1:12–13 JPS)

※ Black and beautiful?

If the book of Judges was rated "R" for violence, this book is rated "R" for sex. Plain and simple, it is a love poem. But more than that it is an erotic love poem. Check that; it's a *steamily* erotic love poem. Okay, maybe it's not the *Kama Sutra* or *Lady Chatterley's Lover*, but it does get pretty hot.

When memorable Bible verses come to mind, the intriguing line "My nard gave forth its fragrance" doesn't carry quite the same ring as "In the beginning" or "The Lord is my Shepherd." The little ladies who teach Sunday school don't read Song of Solomon aloud very often. It must steam up their bifocals. (By the way, "nard" is an herbal ointment, not some ancient Hebrew euphemism for a part of the female anatomy.)

The Song of Solomon (or Song of Songs, or Canticle of Canticles) is among the most controversial of the Hebrew scriptures. Its place in the canon was still being argued in the first century CE because, like Esther, it never mentions God and doesn't deal with laws, prophecy, or religion. The question is, how did such a sexual poem, richly luscious in its erotic imagery and not overly concerned with marriage, make it into the Bible in the first place?

Placed in the Hebrew "Writings" because of its popularity and the attribution to King Solomon, the Song of Solomon is unique in the Bible. A dialogue between a woman and her male lover— only sometimes called the bride and the groom—expressed in remarkably exotic and erotic language, the poem celebrates the physical love between a man and a woman. The work resembles Egyptian love poetry and Arabic wedding songs that praise the charm and beauty of the bride. There are also parallels with sacred marriage texts concerning the ritual union of the goddess Ishtar and her consort Tammuz, a shepherd-god who was worshiped in the Jerusalem Temple and was specifically mentioned by the prophet Ezekiel.

Some scholars have seen the book as a liturgy for a divine or royal marriage, or at least as derived from such a ritual. While it is impossible to date the Song with certainty, the source of poetry may go back to ancient times before David and Solomon ruled.

The final version was probably composed after the Return from Babylon. Solomon's name is mentioned in several verses and so he was credited with writing the poems. While that is unlikely, the Song probably originated in Solomon's court, filled as it was with hundreds of beautiful, exotic, foreign women.

So what's it doing in the Bible? The traditional interpretation, both in Judaism and Christianity, is that these juicy love poems represent Yahweh's love for Israel. There is some precedent for this notion in the prophetic book of Ezekiel, in which the prophet also offers a sensual expression of God as a lover to a fair maiden (Israel). For Christians, the Song supposedly expresses the love of Christ for his church. Given the sheer eroticism of the poetry, both explanations constitute something of a reach. In presenting the traditional view of the Song as an allegorical model to show the love between God and the Jewish people, Rabbi Joseph Telushkin notes, "The use of such a model suggests the very high regard in which the Bible holds male-female love and sexuality." (*Biblical Literacy*, p. 358)

BIBLICAL VOICES

Oh give me of the kisses of your mouth,
For your love is more delightful than wine. (1:2 JPS)

Your breasts are like two fawns,
Twins of a gazelle,
Browsing among the lilies.
When the day blows gently
And the shadows flee,
I will betake me to the mount of myrrh,
To the hill of frankincense.
Every part of you is fair, my darling,
There is no blemish in you. (4:5–7 JPS)

Awake, O north wind,
Come, O south wind!

Blow upon my garden,
That its perfume may spread,
Let my beloved come to his garden
And enjoy its luscious fruits! (4:16 JPS)

His belly a tablet of ivory,
Adorned with sapphires
His legs are like marble pillars
Set in sockets of fine gold.
He is majestic as Lebanon,
Stately as the cedars
His mouth is delicious
And all of him is delightful,
Such is my beloved. (5:14–16 JPS)

My beloved has gone down to his garden,
To the beds of spices,
To browse in the gardens
And to pick lilies.
I am my beloved's
And my beloved is mine;
He browses among the lilies. (6:1–3 JPS)

How lovely are your feet in sandals,
O daughter of nobles!
Your rounded thighs are like jewels,
The work of a master's hand.
Your navel is like a round goblet—
Let mixed wine not be lacking!—
Your belly like a heap of wheat
Hedged about with lilies.
Your breasts are like two fawns,
Twins of a gazelle
Your neck is like a tower of ivory. (7:2–5 JPS)

Your stately form is like the palm,
Your breasts are like clusters.
I say: Let me climb the palm,
Let me take hold of the branches;
Let your breasts be like clusters of grapes,
Your breath like the fragrance of apples,
And your mouth like choicest wine.
Let it flow to my beloved as new wine
Gliding over the lips of the sleepers. (7:8–10 JPS)

Black and beautiful?

One line in this book has created some translational difficulties.
Here are three versions of a single verse:

- "I am black but comely, O ye daughters of Jerusalem, as the
  tents of Kedar, as the currants of Solomon." (1:5 KJV)
- "I am black and beautiful . . . like the curtains of Solomon."
  (NRSV)
- "I am dark, but comely . . . like the pavilions of Solomon."
  (JPS)

The King James Version says the heroine's skin is black as
"currants," or raisins—which seems a very plausible translation in
light of the sensuous food imagery found elsewhere in the poems.
The other two translations are probably closer to the original Hebrew. "Curtains" and "pavilions" make sense considering the reference to the "tents" of the preceding line.

But was this woman black? Certainly the typical Hollywood
image in which ancient Israelites always looked like fair-skinned,
fair-haired American starlets with veils is way off the mark. The
people of the Bible were Semitic and would have been dark-
skinned. The racial enmity and the equating of "black" with evil

was an unfortunate development in later Europe, devised in part to justify African slavery. To be precise about the Song of Solomon, however, the young woman explains her dark complexion a few lines later. She was required to watch the vineyards and got very tan in the sun. This should not be taken to mean that the Bible is opposed to sufficient sunblock.

Bob Jones, the late fundamentalist Protestant preacher and founder of Bob Jones University, may not have read Song of Solomon. One of his campus rules prohibited interracial dating. But in the Song of Solomon, the Bible offers us a beautiful black or dark woman whose lover has a "belly of ivory," which sounds pretty white. If interracial dating was good enough for Solomon, why not for Bob Jones?

MILESTONES IN BIBLICAL TIMES IV
573 BCE–41 BCE

573 Chaldean King Nebuchadnezzar II captures the port city of Tyre after a thirteen-year siege. He invades Egypt in *568.*

565 Daoism (Taoism) founded by Chinese philosopher Lao Zi (Lao-tse) in Honan province. He sets down principles in *Dao De Ging (Tao Te Ching)*. This liberal philosophy teaches that forms and ceremonies are useless; it advocates a spirit of righteousness but later degenerates into a system of magic.

562 Nebuchadnezzar II dies after a reign of forty-three years. He is succeeded by his son Evil-Merodach (the biblical Marduk), who rules for two years.

559 Cyrus becomes King of Persia. He unites the Medes, Persians, and other tribes and rules for twenty years.

539 Babylon falls to Cyrus of Persia.

538 Cyrus permits the Jews to return to Jerusalem after their forty-nine-year Exile.

530 Cambyses II, son of Cyrus, becomes King of Persia after his father dies in battle near the Caspian Sea.

528 Buddhism has its beginnings in India, where Siddhārtha Gautama, a thirty-five-year-old prince who has renounced luxury, has found enlightenment in the wilderness.

521 A soldier related to Cyrus takes the throne of Persia and reigns as Darius I.

516 Jerusalem's Temple is rebuilt seventy years after its destruction.

495 The Chinese philosopher Kong Fuzi (Confucius) resigns as prime minister and spends the next twelve years as a teacher of morals.

490 The Battle of Marathon marks the beginning of the long wars between the Greeks and Persians continuing until *479 BCE*.

458 Ezra, a Hebrew scribe, goes to Jerusalem to restore the Laws of Moses.

457 Under Pericles, the Golden Age of Athens begins, a twenty-eight-year era in which the city becomes preeminent in architecture and arts while preparing for a conflict with Sparta that will be known as the Peloponnesian Wars.

c. 400 The "Five Books of Moses" receives its definitive form.

399 Greek philosopher Socrates is condemned for flouting conventional ideas and for allegedly corrupting youth. As his students watch, he drinks a potion made from hemlock.

347 Athenian philosopher Plato, a student of Socrates, opens his academy (it will continue for 876 years).

344 Aristotle, a follower of Plato, goes to Macedon to tutor Alexander, the son of Macedon's King Philip.

336 King Philip of Macedon is assassinated and succeeded by his twenty-year-old son, Alexander. Known as Alexander the Great, he carries out his father's plan of fighting the Persians. In *332*, Alexander conquers Egypt and founds the city of Alexandria. By *331*, Alexander conquers the Persians; extends his empire as far as India.

323 Alexander dies in Babylon at age thirty-two. One of his generals, Ptolemy, who is also a student of Aristotle, takes over Egypt.

305 Beginning of rule of Palestine by the Seleucids of Syria.

c. 255 The translation of the Septuagint, the Greek version of Hebrew scriptures, begins in Alexandria.

202 Roman armies conquer Carthage, marking the beginning of Rome's rise to power in the Mediterranean.

167 The Jewish priest Mattathias defies Syria's Antiochus, who has outlawed Judaism. He and his sons will lead a revolt. His third son, Judah, is known as Maccabeus—the Hammerer.

165 Judas Maccabeus retakes Jerusalem from the Syrians.

73 Spartacus, a Thracian slave, leads an army of fugitive slaves against Rome. He is defeated in *71*.

64 Jerusalem falls to the Roman general Pompey. Pompey then conquers the rest of Palestine for Rome.

63 Pompey and Crassus are joined in a triumvirate ruling Rome by Gaius Julius Caesar. Caesar's daughter Julia is married to Pompey, solidifying the triumvirate. Caesar embarks on his conquests of Europe.

49 Caesar leads his troops across the Rubicon River to begin a civil war and defeats Pompey, becoming absolute ruler of Rome in *48*. Caesar follows the defeated Pompey to Egypt, where Pompey is murdered. Caesar remains in Egypt to carry out a war on behalf of Egypt's dethroned Queen Cleopatra.

46 After defeating opposing Roman armies, Caesar returns to Rome with Cleopatra as his mistress and is made dictator of Rome.

44 Julius Caesar is assassinated in the Roman Senate.

43 Roman senator Marc Antony joins with Julius Caesar's great-nephew Octavius and Marcus Lepidus in a second triumvirate.

41 Marc Antony meets Cleopatra, now twenty-eight years old, and follows her to Egypt.

Hebrews 1–Lions 0

Daniel

They brought Daniel, and cast him into the den of lions.
(6:16 KJV)

Many of us may recall a pair of tales of faith featuring a young Jewish boy named Daniel, stories that have been retold recently in William Bennett's bestseller, *The Book of Virtues*. In one of these, three Jewish boys are saved by their faith in God from a deadly furnace. And in the second, Daniel himself escapes unharmed after being thrown into a lion's den. Like most of the simplified childhood versions of Bible tales, these stories are both a lot more complicated. Perhaps you don't recall that when Daniel emerged safely from the lion's den, the men who threw him to the lions were then fed to the lions—along with their wives and children. Rough justice!

While the stories of Daniel and his compatriots are set during the Babylonian Exile of 586 BCE, the book was written much later than that. Daniel is dated with some certainty to 165–164 BCE, making it the last book written to be accepted into the Hebrew canon. That acceptance came around 90 CE, and probably because of this late date, Daniel was placed in the "Writings," or third section of the Hebrew scriptures, instead of with the Prophets. An account of a young man who clings to his faith despite extreme pressure and threats of death, Daniel was written to strengthen and comfort the Jews of Jerusalem who were suffering under the oppressive King Antiochus IV (175–164 BCE), one of the Seleucid kings who ruled the Jews.

The Seleucid Dynasty was named for one of Alexander the Great's five generals, Seleucus I (312–281 BCE). After Alexander's death in 323 BCE, these five generals divvied up the young general's empire. The two most prominent of these were Ptolemy, who established control over Egypt, and Seleucus, who held most of the old Babylonian empire. Like Canaan, Israel, and Judah in centuries past, Judah was now caught between these two old power bases—one in Egypt, the other in Mesopotamia. The Jews of Judah were now governed by a group of aristocrats and priestly families who controlled a senate called the *Sanhedrin* (from a Greek word for "council"), led by the Temple's high priest. This was not an especially proud moment in Jewish history, as the infighting for the position of high priesthood grew intense and conspiracies flourished. It was also a time of conflict and extreme animosity among the Jews because many young men were rejecting their faith and eagerly adopting Greek customs, abandoning circumcision, trading Jewish names for Greek names, and generally viewing themselves as Greeks, rather than Jews. Even two of the competing high priests of this time had the unlikely names Jason and Menelaus. At this time, a group of orthodox, nationalistic Jews called the *hasidim* ("the Pious") emerged to counter the growing "Hellenization" of Judaism, and the author of Daniel may have been one of them.

The turmoil and infighting among the Jews led the Seleucid king Antiochus IV to invade Jerusalem in 169/8 BCE, at which time he sacked and desecrated the Temple, and according to some accounts, slaughtered eighty thousand people. Then Antiochus, or perhaps the high priest Menelaus in the king's name, enforced a series of rules aimed at eradicating Jewish customs. Circumcision, Sabbath observances, the keeping of feasts, and the purity laws were all banned. Claiming that Yahweh, the old Canaanite god Baal, and the Greek god Zeus were all the same, Antiochus dedicated the Jerusalem Temple to Zeus and then assumed divinity for himself, taking the title Epiphanes ("God Manifest" or "Revealed"). Jews were forced to attend ceremonies honoring the "pagan" deity and eat sacrificial meals of pork, which was, of course, "unclean." During this time of extreme religious repression, Daniel's anonymous author told this tale of maintaining the faith in the face of idolatrous, foreign tyranny.

BIBLICAL VOICES

"If our God, the one we serve, is able to save us from the burning fiery furnace and from your power, Your Majesty, he will save us; and even if he does not, then you must know, Your Majesty, that we will not serve your god or worship the statue that you have set up." This infuriated King Nebuchadnezzar; his expression was changed now as he looked at Shadrach, Meshach, and Abed-Nego. He gave orders for the furnace to be made seven times hotter than usual and commanded certain stalwarts from his army to bind Shadrach, Meshach, and Abed-Nego and throw them into the burning fiery furnace. (Dan. 3:17–20 NJB)

Plot Summary: Daniel

Daniel is one of four young Jewish boys taken in the sack of Jerusalem by King Nebuchadnezzar and brought up during the Exile at the royal court in Babylon. The names and dates of the Babylonian and later Persian kings in Daniel are clearly confused, and Daniel should be read not as a work of history but an inspired allegory reflecting events in Judah in the time of Antiochus IV. All four boys have their Hebrew names replaced by Babylonian names. The boys all refuse the unclean food they are offered and amaze the court because they are in better health than those who eat the king's food.

Recalling Joseph in Egypt, who wins favor when he explains Pharaoh's dreams, Daniel is given the gift of dream interpretation by God and he is able to reveal to the king the meaning of several dreams. Like Joseph, Daniel and his friends gain prestige in Babylon. But when the king has a golden idol made and demands that everyone should worship it, three of Daniel's friends (Shadrach, Meshach, and Abed-Nego) refuse the order and are thrown into a blazing furnace. To the king's amazement, the trio survives unharmed with God's protection.

Daniel interprets another of Nebuchadnezzar's dreams as a warning that the king will lose his reason until he recognizes God. His prediction soon comes to pass. Some time later, during a fast given by a later king, Belshazzar, fiery writing mysteriously appears on the wall of the banquet hall. Daniel interprets the writing as a sign that the king will die and his empire will fall to the Persians and Medes. That very night, Belshazzar is assassinated.

Belshazzar's successor, called the Persian king Darius in an obvious confusion, issues a decree that all prayer should be addressed to him, mirroring what Antiochus did. When Daniel refuses to pray to "Darius," he is thrown into a pit of lions—but emerges safely, preserved by God's angel. In amazement, the penitent king throws his court advisers to the lions instead, along with their wives and children. They are all killed by the lions and Daniel is again elevated to a place of power in the court.

The meaning of all of these stories would have been obvious to the author's audience. The tale of Daniel and the other brave boys refusing to defile themselves with unclean food, or bow down to idols, was a clear call to contemporary Jews to resist the Zeus-cult worship decreed by the priest Menelaus and Antiochus IV's pretension to divinity.

In the concluding chapters, Daniel shifts from interpreting the dreams of others to having his own visions. His prophetic dreams contain many references specific to the political intrigues of the day, showing the breakup of the Alexandrian empire and demise of the Seleucids and the Egyptian Ptolemies. Several of the author's specific predictions about the immediate future of these empires were not fulfilled, and he ends the book with words of a final consummation and resurrection of the dead when the faithful Jews would ultimately have victory.

BIBLICAL VOICES

At that time, the great prince, Michael, who stands beside the sons of your people, will appear. It will be a time of trouble, the like of which has never been since the nation came into being. At that time, your people will be rescued, all who are found inscribed in the book. Many of those that sleep in the dust of the earth will awake, some to eternal life, others to reproaches, to everlasting abhorrence. And the knowledgeable will be radiant like the bright expanse of sky, and those who lead the many to righteousness will be like the stars forever and ever. But you, Daniel, keep the words secret, and seal the book until the time of the end. Many will range far and wide and knowledge will increase. (Dan. 12:1–4)

Daniel certainly must have spoken to the people of his day who were confronting the possibility of the extinction of their religion. But his note of hopefulness in such a desperate moment has a timeless quality. Daniel has become the symbol of the oppressed believer, tortured for his faith. His visions of a promised time of "rescue" and "eternal life" have given hope to Jews and Christians ever since.

Between the Books

The Apocrypha or Deuterocanonical Books

❄

Why isn't Hanukkah in the Bible?

With the completion of all the texts considered "divinely inspired" by the Jewish rabbis who established the "canon" of Hebrew scriptures, the Bible comes abruptly back to an old question: "Whose Bible is it?" By the standards of the Hebrew Bible (Tanakh), as well as versions of the Old Testament that follow the order in the King James Version, there is no more to say. But if you're reading a Douay Bible, New Jerusalem Bible, or any of several Roman Catholic Bibles, a few books have been left out. These missing books—or sections of books—often follow the "canonical" books in many Bibles, in a separate section called the Apocrypha.

The Greek word *Apocrypha* refers to a small group of ancient writings whose "divinely inspired" status has long been the subject of debate and controversy. The term means "things hidden away," and there has long been some question whether that meant that these books were somehow heretical and should be hidden away. But in fact, the books of the Apocrypha were never considered secret. In Protestant Bibles, such as the King James or New Revised Standard Version, the books of the Apocrypha are generally placed between the Old and New Testaments. However, in Roman Catholic Bibles these books are interspersed among the other "canonical" books and are referred to as the "Deuterocanonical books," loosely meaning "books added to the canon."

Some of these apocryphal books may have originally been written in Hebrew but were only known to exist in their Greek versions—one of the reasons the rabbis rejected them as part of Hebrew scripture. But they were included in the Septuagint, that Greek translation of the Hebrew Bible that was used by the early Christian church. For the first four centuries of the "Common Era," these writings were accepted as holy by early Christians. The great divide among Christians over these "extra" books began in 382 CE, when Pope Damasus commissioned Jerome, the leading biblical scholar of the time, to make a new translation of the Bible into Latin. In creating what came to be called the "Vulgate," Jerome relied upon Hebrew originals to make his translation. He was convinced that only those books in the Hebrew canon should be regarded as authentic, so he rejected the books found only in Greek, labeling them "apocryphal." But Jerome's views on this question were not accepted by church leaders, and the Christian church retained the apocryphal writings in the Old Testament for the next thousand years or so.

Then, during the Protestant Reformation of the 1500s, the rebellious Protestants sided with Jerome and the rabbis. They pointed to the fact that none of the authors of the New Testament books ever mentioned these apocryphal books, while they frequently referred to the thirty-nine books of the Hebrew canon. By 1530, the Protestant view was that these books lacked divine authority, and Protestants either removed the apocryphal books from their Bibles entirely or placed them in a separate section between the Hebrew scriptures and the New Testament. In response, the Roman Catholic Council of Trent declared in 1546 that the books were divine. These difference weren't simply literary; they involved questions of doctrine that divided the Catholics and Protestants.

The apocryphal books represent several types of writing; there are pieces of outright fiction based loosely on Jewish history, legends and ancient folktales, wisdom books, and historical works that are particularly useful in presenting a picture of Jewish life in Judah in the years leading up to the birth of Jesus.

• Tobit (follows Nehemiah in the Catholic Bible)

Set in Nineveh, the capital of the Assyrians, this book contains some chronological inaccuracies that make it seem fictional. Fragments of the book in Hebrew have been found among the Dead Sea Scrolls. Tobit is a generous, God-fearing Jew who has gone blind. Aided by the disguised archangel Raphael, Tobit's son Tobias catches a magical fish that will restore Tobit's sight and heal a pious young woman, Sarah, who is plagued by a mysterious spirit who has killed seven of her previous suitors. With elements of several ancient folktales, Tobit is essentially a story of righteousness rewarded.

- **Judith (follows Tobit and precedes Esther in the Catholic Bible)**

Like the book of Daniel (see page 311), this story was probably composed during the oppressive rule of Antiochus Epiphanes, perhaps as late as 150 BCE. It tells of brave resistance to a cruel foreigner by a brave Jewish widow, Judith, whose name means "Jewess." It is filled with historical and geographical inaccuracies, which is one reason it was not accepted into the Hebrew canon. The story tells how Nebuchadnezzar—inaccurately described as king of the Assyrians; he was Chaldean—sent his general Holofernes to conquer the rebellious Jews. Taking off her widow's clothes, dressing alluringly, and perfuming herself, Judith goes to Holofernes's camp and offers to help him defeat her people. She gets Holofernes roaring drunk one night, and in his stupor Judith cuts off the general's head with his own sword. Judith returns home, rouses the Jewish people to the attack, and they defeat Nebuchadnezzar's army.

- **Additions to Esther**

The Greek Septuagint includes several passages from the book of Esther (see page 261) for which there is no Hebrew original. In that book, the beautiful young Jewish girl Esther saved her people from a cruel plot by the Persian king's chancellor Haman. In the Hebrew version, God is never mentioned, but these Greek additions contain frequent references to God, and Esther also displays her loathing for the Gentiles and strictly observes the Jewish dietary laws—neither of which are reflected in the Hebrew original.

- **Wisdom of Solomon (follows the Song of Songs in the Catholic Bible)**

Even though it was probably written as late as 50 BCE, and the name of Solomon does not even appear in this book of contemplation, it was attributed to him. The author reflects on his religious faith in contrast to the godless things he witnesses in the world around him, especially among the Egyptians.

• **Sirach (Ecclesiasticus)**

Also called the "Wisdom of Ben Sira," this is a collection of sayings, like Proverbs, that reflect on good behavior, tact, and common sense and celebrate wisdom. The author, Ben Sira, was a scribe and teacher in Jerusalem sometime around 190–180 BCE. Fragments of the original Hebrew text have been found, but the book was translated into Greek by the author's grandson in 132 BCE.

• **Baruch (follows Lamentations in the Catholic Bible)**

The author of this book claims to be a follower of the prophet Jeremiah, who was writing from Babylon with the exiles after 587 BCE. Jeremiah and Baruch were both supposedly taken to Egypt in 582 BCE, and this book was more likely written after the book of Daniel was written around 165 BCE. Like the traditional prophets, Baruch points to the faithlessness and corruption among his people as the reason for the disasters that have taken place. But he believes that the punishment will end, and Jerusalem will be rebuilt.

• **Letter of Jeremiah**

This letter is supposedly written by Jeremiah in Babylon, but Jeremiah went to Egypt after Jerusalem fell. In the letter, "Jeremiah" says the Exile will be long but not permanent and that the exiles should be careful not to pick up any bad foreign habits, such as idolatry.

• **Additions to Daniel**

This book contains three extended passages in Greek that were not part of the surviving Hebrew text of Daniel. "The Prayer of Azariah" is a long hymn of praise as three young Jewish men sit in the furnace into which they have been thrown. "Susanna and the Elders" is a morality tale about a virtuous Jewish woman who is threatened by two men who will accuse Susanna of adultery unless she sleeps with them. Daniel intervenes and saves Susanna's life and the two lecherous old men are put to death. In "Bel and the Dragon (or Serpent)" Daniel scorns a great serpent statue that is offered food daily in the court of King Cyrus. Daniel proves that the statue does not consume the food but, rather, that priests sneak into the temple and eat the food. The king has the priests of the serpent put to death.

- **1, 2, 3 & 4 Maccabees (These are included in the historical writings, following Esther, in the Roman Catholic canon)**

The first three of these books combine to give a historical account of Jewish life under Alexander the Great and his successors in Judah and Syria, the Seleucids, especially the Seleucid king Antiochus IV Epiphanes, the Syrian king who desecrated the Temple. It recounts the rise of a Jewish dynasty called the Hasmoneans, also called Maccabeans, begun by a priest named Mattathias and his five sons.

When Antiochus attacked Jerusalem and later desecrated the Temple, Mattathias and his sons rallied the Jews to resistance. After Mattathias died, his son Judas "Maccabeus" (the "Hammerer") took command and defeated the Seleucids. He retook the Temple, which was purified and reconsecrated. The Jewish festival of Hanukkah celebrates this ritual cleansing of the Temple. But the Hanukkah tradition of a small bottle of oil miraculously burning for eight days is not mentioned in these books.

Judas was killed later and succeeded by one of his brothers, beginning another round of back-and-forth wars between the Syrian Seleucids and the Jewish Maccabeans, or Hasmoneans. The book ends with the rise of John Hyrcanus to leadership of the Hasmonean dynasty in 134 BCE, a period in which the great new world power is emerging from Rome.

- **1 Esdras**

This book retells some of the books of Chronicles, Ezra, and Nehemiah, and includes a parable derived from the Zoroastrian religion of Persia about the "strongest thing in the world," which proves to be Truth.

- **2 Esdras**

With both Jewish and Christian aspects, this book discusses the resurrection of the dead and the coming of the Messiah.

- **Prayer of Manasseh**

In this brief book, the most notorious king of Judah, Manasseh, is depicted offering a prayer of penitence in which he asks for God's forgiveness for all the evil he did as king.

- **Psalm 151**

A psalm said by some to have been composed by David after he defeated Goliath, though other commentators dispute this conclusion.

With the close of Hebrew scriptures, there is a looming presence over the Mediterranean world. It is the dawn of the age of Rome's empire, and everything that happens in the time of Jesus and the early years of Christianity must be viewed against the backdrop of Rome's power. The world into which Jesus was born was a world utterly dominated by the Romans.

Originally a group of villages, Rome developed into a city and slowly gained dominance over all of Italy. In 264 BCE, Rome and the North African city of Carthage confronted each other for control of the Mediterranean in the Punic Wars, a series of battles that lasted until 146 BCE. Founded by the Phoenicians on the north coast of Africa, Carthage was the leading power in the western Mediterranean. Despite the victory of the famed Hannibal, the North African general who marched those elephants across the Alps to surprise Rome with an attack from the north, Rome completed its conquest of Carthage in 146 BCE. Carthage was leveled and Rome controlled the western Mediterranean.

During the next century, Rome also secured complete control over the eastern Mediterranean. By the time of the great general Pompey (106–48 BCE), Judea had been reduced to a client state of the Romans, and Pompey captured Jerusalem in 60 BCE. A chaotic period of civil war followed in Rome but was concluded when Julius Caesar took control of Rome in 49 BCE.

In 44 BCE, Caesar was assassinated and replaced by a ruling triumvirate including Marc Antony and Julius Caesar's great-nephew Octavian. Their partnership also ended in a civil war between the forces of Octavian and Marc Antony, with Octavian emerging victorious after the Battle of Actium in 31 BCE.

Soon after, Octavian proclaimed himself the emperor Augustus. Beginning with Augustus, Rome achieved its world empire with its highly disciplined army, diplomatic skills, and the policy of granting Roman citizenship to all those under its control.

In Judea—the Roman name for Judah—an ambitious soldier named Herod was able to play the Romans against one another before Augustus consolidated his power. Born about 73 BCE, Herod was appointed military governor and became a Roman citizen in 47 BCE. In 41, Herod was made a "tetrarch," or ruler, of one of the five Roman provinces in the area. Herod went to Rome in 40 BCE and Mark Antony made him King of Judea, giving him sole power in the area, secured with the help of a Roman army. But Herod saw which way the wind was blowing and shifted allegiances to Octavian, who defeated Antony. Herod was rewarded when he was confirmed king by the emperor Augustus.

Seen as a cruel puppet of the pagan Romans, Herod was detested for the most part at home. Though he rebuilt the Jerusalem Temple on a scale that surpassed that of Solomon's Temple, Herod was feared and hated, the tyrannical head of a "police state." Herod died at age sixty-nine in the year 4 BCE, and the last years of Herod's rule provide the immediate backdrop for one of the most significant stories in history, a story so familiar to Christians, but a tale riddled with a preponderance of inconsistencies, contradictions, and undocumented events.

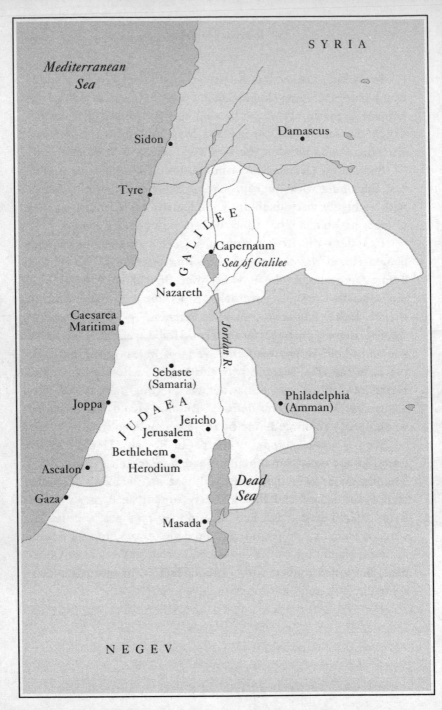

SYRIA

Mediterranean Sea

Sidon

Damascus

Tyre

GALILEE

Capernaum
Sea of Galilee

Nazareth

Caesarea
Maritima

Jordan R.

Sebaste
(Samaria)

Philadelphia
(Amman)

Joppa

JUDAEA

Jericho

Jerusalem

Bethlehem

Ascalon

Herodium

*Dead
Sea*

Gaza

Masada

NEGEV

THE WORLD OF JESUS
This map depicts the general area in which Jesus was born and lived.

part three

THE NEW TESTAMENT

Then Jesus said to the Jews who had believed in him, "If you
continue in my word, you are truly my disciples; and you will
know the truth, and the truth will make you free."
(John 8:31–32)

Jesus Loves me—this I know,
For the Bible tells me so.
—ANNA BARTLETT WARNER
"THE LOVE OF JESUS," 1858

"What if God was one of us?"
—JOAN OSBORNE

❈ What is the New Testament?

❈ Who wrote the New Testament?

❈ Are the four Gospels "gospel" truth?

❈ If there are only four Gospels, then what are the "Gnostic Gospels"?

Thirteen men get off an airplane arriving from Damascus at JFK Airport. Most are unshaven and their clothing smells a little ripe—there is a pungent hint of fish and sheep. Wearing tunics and dusty sandals, they carry no luggage—just walking sticks and sacks holding a spare tunic. Immediately, red lights go off at Customs. A team of inspectors ushers the group into a room to go through procedures. Suspicious Immigration officers stand nearby, guns at the ready. The edgy inspectors assume the obvious: they have a band of Middle East terrorists in hand.

The men are asked routine questions. But their answers are unusual. They have no passports; they say they recognize no governments. They have no money to declare; God takes care of their needs. Their tickets had been paid for by wealthy friends back home. They have come "to teach America the truth," they say. Facing detention, they are quite sophisticated about local ordinances; one of them requests political asylum and an immigration hearing—and he wants that hearing to be in Washington, D.C., in front of the American President!

What would happen if Jesus and his twelve disciples flew into a modern airport? Or Paul and some of the other first Christians walked into a typical American town today? Although accustomed to the fair-haired, blue-eyed image of the "WASP" Jesus, some contemporary Christians might recognize their "Messiah," or the Turkish Jew who founded their church, and welcome them with open arms. But most "believers" would balk at the sight of this motley collection of "foreign," poorly dressed, homeless men. At best, the ragtag group of thirteen would not be invited into the average home. At worst, the FBI would be called to haul them off to custody.

The second part of the Christian Bible, the New Testament, tells the story of these ragged, homeless men (and women!) who changed history.

What is the New Testament?

Unlike the Hebrew scriptures, which span many centuries, the New Testament story covers barely a century and is only about one quarter of the length of the Hebrew scriptures. The New Testament recounts the story of the miraculous birth, works, teachings, execution, and resurrection from the dead of Jesus. For twenty centuries, Christians have professed faith in this Jesus, even though that is not his real name, who was thought to be a Jewish carpenter, although that is only a guess. Besides telling the story of Jesus' life, the New Testament also records the founding and growth of Christianity, first as a sect within traditional Judaism and later as a religion reaching out to the non-Jewish, or Gentile, world. As with the Hebrew scriptures, much of this information was passed along orally until set down by hand in commonly spoken Greek well after Jesus' death and miraculous resurrection.

The central figure in this New Testament drama—one of the most influential people in history—is a good Jewish boy whose name was probably more like Joshua ben Joseph or Yehoshua ben Yosef, the son of a carpenter who, by one account, was a carpenter himself. In the Nikos Kazantzakis novel *The Last Temptation of Christ*, later made into a controversial film by Martin Scorsese, the fictional Jesus the carpenter is provocatively depicted hewing the rough crucifixes on which Jews are executed by Romans.

Like most Jews of his day, Jesus spoke Aramaic, a Syrian language similar to Hebrew that was commonly used at the time, although he surely would have studied the formal Hebrew of the Torah, Prophets, and Writings. Whether he could also speak Greek is anyone's guess. Jesus left no personal writings or other literary remains. There is no physical description of this man. Was he short or tall? Bearded? Was he married? Did he have children? The Bible doesn't tell us. All information about Jesus comes either secondhand, or thirdhand, from his immediate followers, their disciples, or their disciples' disciples.

When several separate and differing biblical accounts are combined, the composite picture shows a Jesus who was miraculously born of a virgin and became a traveling teacher, healer, and wonder-worker who lived most of his life in the vicinity of the Sea of Galilee. Attracting a group of devoted followers who gave up their livelihoods and families to join him, Jesus was eventually viewed as a threat by certain Jewish authorities. They saw to it that he was arrested, tried, and executed by Roman officials on a crucifix, a Roman punishment usually reserved for runaway slaves and rebels. Following his death on the cross, Jesus was reported to appear alive and in the flesh to groups of his followers. To the devout Jews who accepted him, Jesus was the promised Savior who fulfilled the promise expressed in their scriptures of a coming "Messiah" or "anointed one" from the line of David who would deliver the Children of Israel and usher in a new age of peace and God's rule. Though he was later called the "Christ," that is not a name but a title bestowed upon Jesus. *Christos* comes from the Greek, the original language of the New Testament, and originally meant "oil" but was interpreted as "anointed one" or "Messiah."

The twenty-seven books of the New Testament fall into two main sections: the first five books tell about the life of Jesus and the work of his followers in establishing the religion later called Christianity; the next twenty-one books are letters written by some of the leaders of the early Christian church, expanding or interpreting Jesus' teachings and laying out a new set of rules for living and worship very much at odds with their Jewish traditions. The last of the twenty-seven books, Revelation, both letter and "apocalyptic" vision of the Last Days before Judgment Day, is totally different in style and tone from the other books.

Although probably not written first, the four books that are placed at the beginning of the New Testament are called the Gospels. While commonly understood today as the equivalent of "truth," the English word "gospel" is derived from the Anglo-

Saxon *god-spell*—for "good tidings" or "good news." Named for
their presumed authors, the four Gospels are Matthew, Mark, Luke,
and John. Scholars and theologians have traditionally named the
first three the "synoptic Gospels" ("synoptic" is from the Greek for
"viewing together") because they "view" the story of Jesus' life,
death, and teachings in very similar fashion. While the three synoptic Gospels have much in common, they also have some key differences. They relate the same basic account of Jesus' life and death
but disagree on significant details and specifics of chronology and
place. Some of these disagreements are quite startling. For instance,
Matthew, the first of the synoptic Gospels, reports that when Jesus
died, some of the dead of Jerusalem rose and walked—a miraculous
event overlooked by the other Gospels as well as contemporary non-
biblical accounts of first-century Jerusalem. Both Matthew and
Luke provide accounts of Jesus' birth to a virgin, but Mark does not
mention this rather extraordinary event at all.

   John, the fourth Gospel, is very unlike the other three in
biographical details and the author's literary style. A gloriously poetic book, John recounts some of the same events in the life and
death of Jesus as the others, but the book is more figurative and
"spiritual" than the other three. It also contains critical differences,
including variations on so basic a fact as how many times Jesus
visited Jerusalem during his life. Like Mark, John ignores Jesus'
miraculous birth, and John is the only one to report Jesus' first
miracle, in which he changed water into wine at a wedding feast.

   The difficult adjustment for Christians who have grown up
with the merging of the Four Gospels into a historical "biography"
of Jesus is that the word "history" must be used cautiously when
speaking about the Gospels. While they may be divinely inspired,
the Gospels are not works of history or biography. They are not
even personal memoirs. They were written by zealous believers
as a call to faith for their own day, not as documents for some
historical accounting. The authors of the Gospel weren't journalists
"covering" Jesus and eager to capture all the details of his daily

life and report them in a larger historical context. They were devoted followers who wanted to give the world a version of the "Truth" as they had witnessed it.

The four Gospels are followed by the Acts of the Apostles, a brisk narrative recounting how a group of "apostles," Jesus' followers, began to spread the word of Jesus, essentially beginning the Christian church. In the face of deadly persecution by Jewish and Roman authorities, the earliest followers of Jesus were basically an outlaw "cult" until Emperor Constantine converted in 313 CE and Christianity became Rome's dominant religion.

Acts also introduces the New Testament's second most important figure, an educated, pious Jewish tent-maker named Saul, later changed to Paul. Born in what is now Turkey, Saul vigorously persecuted the followers of Jesus. But after a miraculous conversion, his name was changed, and this short, bow-legged, balding Jewish man—the one description of Paul makes him sound a bit like "George Costanza" of *Seinfeld* fame—became the most significant advocate of Christianity in the Roman world. If Jesus "invented" Christianity, Paul "marketed" it to the world. His missionary journeys undertaken to establish and then shore up early communities of believers took Christianity from an offshoot sect of Judaism to a separate, dynamic religion that transformed history. When arrested in Jerusalem for his "heretical" views, Paul demanded a trial in Rome before the emperor, his right as a Roman citizen—the equivalent of that imaginary modern air traveler who wanted a hearing from the U.S. President.

Following the Gospels and Acts, the next twenty-one books fall into the second major New Testament form, a collection of letters, or "epistles," written either to individuals or communities of early Christians. All of them were probably written before the Gospels were composed, and the majority of these letters are attributed to Paul. Two letters are credited to Jesus' first disciple, Peter. Two of the letter-writers, James and Jude, were thought to be Jesus' brothers. Three other letters are credited to the author of the Gospel of John. John was also thought to be the author of Revelation, the New Testament's final book, an apocalyptic vision of God's will for the future, a mysterious prophetic oracle that has fueled speculation and prophecies about the "end of the world" and the "Last Days" since it was written. In particular, its references to the passage of two eras of a thousand years each before Judgment Day arrives has many people wondering if 2000 might be the Big One!

BOOKS OF THE NEW TESTAMENT

The Gospels
    Matthew
    Mark
    Luke
    John
The Acts of the Apostles
Letters or Epistles of Paul
    Romans
    1 Corinthians
    2 Corinthians
    Galatians
    Ephesians
    Philippians
    Colossians
    1 Thessalonians
    2 Thessalonians
    1 Timothy
    2 Timothy
    Titus
    Philemon
General Letters
    Hebrews
    James
    1 Peter
    2 Peter

1 John
2 John
3 John
Jude
Revelation (Apocalypse)

Who wrote the New Testament?

On the face of it, questions about the Christian New Testament should be much easier to answer than similar queries about the Hebrew scriptures, or the Old Testament. Unlike the Hebrew scriptures, whose composition was spread over more than a thousand years, the "books" of the New Testament were probably written within a space of about fifty years, from around 60 to 110 CE. Everything that happened in the New Testament took place in the days of the Roman empire, a fairly well documented bureaucracy, during a "civilized" era when writing was quite sophisticated. A substantial body of "literature"—most of it Greek drama, poetry, essays, philosophy, and law—was available to the educated elite of the Roman world. The Romans were creating their own literature, which lives on in the names of Ovid, Horace, Seneca, Juvenal—a few of the first-century Roman poets and playwrights. Roman historians were recording their own versions of the great empire, and one of them, Tacitus, mentioned the early Christians in his accounts of the period. The Western world's great storehouse of knowledge was in Alexandria, a cosmopolitan Mediterranean seaport in Rome's Egyptian province, where the wisdom of the entire ancient world was supposedly kept on scrolls. That centuries-old knowledge was preserved until 391 CE, when Emperor Theodosius, a Christian convert, ordered all non-Christian works eliminated. The Library at Alexandria, storehouse of the world's knowledge, was burned, the first of many book-burnings "inspired" by Christianity.

Another eyewitness to the events in first-century Jerusalem

was a Jewish rebel-turned-writer named Joseph ben Matthias (c. 37–100 CE). After fighting the Romans during a Jewish revolt, Joseph decided, if you can't lick them, join them. Befriended by some of his Roman enemies, he adopted the Roman name Flavius Josephus and wrote *The History of the Jewish People* and an account of the Jewish uprising that led to the destruction of Jerusalem's Temple by Rome in 70 CE. His colorful and very personalized versions of life and times in Roman Palestine are among the few key documents available for understanding the history of this turbulent period. In one of his books, Josephus makes a brief—and somewhat controversial—mention of Jesus, one of only a few references to Jesus outside the New Testament. One reason for Jesus' absence from traditional "history" is simple. While Jesus and his first followers are so overwhelmingly important today as the founders of Christianity, at that time, they were merely a band of insignificant troublemakers in a far-flung corner of the great empire.

For this and other reasons, despite all the available information, the high degree of civilization in Roman times, and all these learned writers, the authorship of the New Testament books remains clouded in mystery. Just like the unsolved puzzles of Hebrew scripture, there are open questions about the identities of writers, place of writing, and dates of composition for most New Testament books.

Although much shorter than the Hebrew Bible, the New Testament still has its own complex history. Many of the books began in the oral tradition, and because many early Christians expected the "Second Coming" of Christ to happen any day, there seemed to be little need for a written version of the "good news." Eventually, as the first generation of "apostles" who were spreading the "good news" started to die off—either from old age or as the result of persecutions by the Romans—it seemed like a good idea to set these words down. The letters of Paul were the first to be collected, around 90 CE, and sometime after 100 CE there was a collection of the four Gospels. There are no "originals" of these writings. As the early Christian church grew, the Gospels and letters were widely copied to be spread from one Christian community to the next in a day when there was no Kinko's or corner copy shop. Thousands of hand-copied versions of fairly early New Testament documents exist, and they aren't always in agreement. Often composed under pseudonyms, the earliest Christian writings were first written on papyrus or leather scrolls, but around the second century CE the codices (plural for "codex"), or first bound books, began to be used in the early church. Parchment or vellum (calfskin) pages eventually replaced papyrus.

The concept of a "New Testament," an assemblage of holy writings that added to, or even replaced, accepted Hebrew writings, emerged in the second century CE. As with the Hebrew scriptures, there are human fingerprints all over the decision making that led to the compilation of the New Testament. Most biblical researchers presume that other early Christian writings existed, including other letters by Paul, but they were lost or even discarded. Modern scholars also suspect that the New Testament authors had access to a collection of Jesus' sayings, a kind of first-century *Bartlett's Familiar Quotations* or *Quotations from Chairman Jesus* called "Q" (back to alphabet letters for Bible writers!). From the German word *quelle*, for "source," this "Q" document exists only in theory; no such a collection has ever been found.

More controversial is another set of ancient Christian writings that have been found. These include other "gospels" that were written later than the accepted New Testament books. Most of these "other gospels," which later came to be called the "Gnostic Gospels," were rejected by the early church authorities as illegitimate (see page 342). In 180 CE, Irenaeus, a Greek bishop and powerful leader of the early church, wrote that heretics "boast that they possess more gospels than there really are." The early Christian community was not one big happy family. There were deep divisions over very basic questions of what to believe. Groups such as the "Gnostics," a word for a loose collection of early Christians who believed they had access to secret wisdom or knowledge (*gno-*

sis is Greek for "knowledge"), were very much at odds with other Christians over questions of the nature of God, Jesus, and evil. Another group, called the "Montanists," after their leader, Montanus, claimed direct inspiration from the Holy Spirit. The conflict between the church fathers and these "heretics" led to some nasty fights over exactly what constituted "God's Word."

One of the first men to conceive of a "New Testament" as the scriptural foundation for the new church was Marcion of Sinope in Asia Minor (c. 80–155), a renegade Christian leader of the second century. Although not formally called a Gnostic, Marcion was excommunicated for his view that Jesus' teachings were radically different from those of Jewish tradition, and he established his own church in 144. He further distanced himself from the "orthodox" Christians by appointing women as church leaders. Marcion rejected the view of the punishing, wrathful God he found in the Hebrew scriptures. As Elaine Pagels explains in her book *The Gnostic Gospels*, "Marcion was struck by what he saw as the contrast between the creator-God of the Old Testament, who demands justice and punishes every violation of his law, and the Father whom Jesus proclaims—the New Testament God of forgiveness and love. Why, he asked, would a God who is 'almighty'—all-powerful—create a world that includes suffering, pain, disease—even mosquitoes and scorpions? Marcion concluded that these must be two different Gods." (p. 28) Marcion's collection of Scriptures included only an edited version of Luke and ten of Paul's letters, which he also edited in order to remove references to Jewish scriptures. For all of his actions, Marcion was denounced, and largely in response to his "canon" an official "orthodox" Christian canon was produced that emphasized the sacred standing of all four Gospels as well as thirteen letters attributed to Paul.

In 367 CE, Athanasius, a Christian leader in Alexandria, listed all twenty-seven books of the existing New Testament—more than three hundred years after Jesus died. His canon was widely accepted and approved in 382 CE by Christian leaders in Rome, now the center of a legalized and "official" Christianity. When the prominent Christian writer and theologian Augustine (354–430 CE) weighed in and gave his nod to this list, it was accepted by the North African churches. By about 400 CE, most Christian churches recognized the New Testament as it is known today. But there were rebellious splinter groups who thought otherwise, particularly among some of the African and Asian—or Eastern—churches. Some groups accepted only twenty-two books, and the Ethiopian church still recognizes an additional eleven books in its New Testament.

Are the four Gospels "gospel" truth?

Nearly everything known about Jesus comes from the four separate Gospel accounts. Once "canonized," their literal authority and divine stature went unquestioned throughout most of Christian history—just as the Books of Moses were unquestioned by the authorities. Since the nineteenth century, many scholars and researchers have begun to raise questions of Gospel authorship. The precise identity of these writers and when the books were written remain subjects of speculation.

• **Mark**

Although it is placed second in the New Testament order after Matthew, the Gospel of Mark, the shortest of the Gospels, is widely viewed by modern scholars as the oldest of the Gospels. Skipping over Jesus' birth, Mark tells the story of the adult Jesus from the time of his baptism to his Crucifixion and an angel's report of his resurrection. The authors of Matthew and Luke, many scholars believe, relied on Mark's account when they wrote theirs.

But who was Mark? No Mark was listed among the original twelve disciples of Jesus. A person named John Mark is mentioned several times in the New Testament and, according to early Christian tradition, he was a companion of Paul on his missionary travels until they quarreled. Many scholars now believe that the Gospel was written by an unknown early Christian named Mark who drew on a large number of traditions in order to compose his tightly organized narrative. Mark refers to the destruction of Jerusalem by a Roman army in 70 CE, either as an event that may happen soon or as one that has recently happened. Although scholars do not know whether to date the Gospel shortly before or shortly after 70 CE, it must have been written sometime around that significant date.

• Matthew

The author of this book was long presumed to be the Matthew who was one of Jesus' disciples. That Matthew was identified as a tax collector, as unpopular a profession then as it is now. In Mark and Luke, however, the tax collector is also named Levi. The widely accepted modern view is that Matthew was written by a later Jewish-Christian who believed Jesus was the promised Messiah of Hebrew scriptures. There are many references in Matthew to Hebrew prophecies that Jesus fulfills. Matthew opens with an extensive genealogy, tracing Jesus' ancestry back to David—a slight glitch in that the line goes through Joseph, who isn't really Jesus' father, if you accept the Gospel version. Matthew also includes frequent quotations from Hebrew scriptures, meant to convince other Jews of the fulfillment of their prophecies in Jesus. Unique to this Gospel are the Nativity stories of the famous visit of the Magi, inaccurately called the "Three Kings," King Herod's massacre of infant children in Bethlehem, and the "Flight into Egypt," in which Joseph took Mary and Jesus to Egypt to escape Herod's massacre.

Early Christians believed Matthew was written first and placed it first, but modern scholars now consider Mark the earlier book. Relying on literary and chronological clues, they believe the author of Matthew had read Mark, as well as the theoretical collection of Jesus' sayings called "Q." Some scholars believe Matthew was written in Palestine; others favor another early Christian center, such as Antioch in Syria sometime between 70 and 85 CE.

• Luke

The author of Luke, a highly polished narrative that uses the conventions of classical Greek writings, was presumably a well-educated man who spoke and wrote Greek. The same person is credited with writing the book of Acts. Together, Luke and Acts account for nearly one quarter of the New Testament and provide a history of the early Christian faith; Luke tells the story of Jesus, while Acts traces the missionary movement and early growth of Christianity after his death. "Luke's" works were intended to be read together, but when the New Testament was later compiled, the Gospel of John was inserted between the two books of "Luke" to keep the four Gospels together. Mentioned in one of Paul's letters as "the beloved physician," Luke may have been a doctor or a healer who traveled with Paul during his missionary journeys. Several scenes from Jesus' life are unique to Luke, including a genealogy tracing Jesus back to Adam, the story of the birth of John the Baptist, Jesus' trip to the Temple in Jerusalem as a twelve-year-old boy, along with some of the best known of Jesus' teachings in parables, such as the stories of the Good Samaritan and of the Prodigal Son.

Luke's author wanted to give his story of Jesus a sense of historical authenticity, and he included Jesus' age—"about thirty"—when he began preaching as well as specific events—which prove contradictory—for dating Jesus' birth. Luke's message was primarily addressed to the non-Jewish, or Gentile, believers, as the church had aggressively begun to reach out to Gentiles by the time Luke was written. It is now generally agreed that Luke also dates from the decades 70–85 CE and that he may have written from the city of Ephesus (in modern Turkey), a leading center of early Christianity.

• John

The fourth book is the *Magical Mystery Tour* of the Gospels. Complex and profound, it has been attributed to John, one of the disciples closest to Jesus. This Gospel draws a different picture of Jesus' life and teachings, leading scholars to detect an eyewitness-like immediacy in John. Among the more conspicuous and significant differences between John and the "synoptics" (Matthew, Mark, and Luke) are the absence of descriptions of the birth of Jesus, his childhood, the temptation in the wilderness, the transfiguration, the use of parables in teaching, and the agony in the Garden of Gethsemane. John's version of the "Last Supper," in which Jesus eats with his disciples before his arrest and Crucifixion, is presented in an entirely different fashion here than in the other three Gospels. Jesus delivers a long speech to the disciples in John's "Last Supper," and the symbolic breaking of bread and drinking of wine are left out of John. Among the other unique elements of John are the only version of Jesus changing water into wine at Cana and his miraculous raising of Lazarus, a follower, four days after his death and entombment.

For most of two thousand years, Christians accepted that John was written by one of the twelve disciples chosen by Jesus. Since the nineteenth century, the identity of John's author has generated heated controversy. While traditional scholars still believe that John was an apostle and an eyewitness to the events in the book, other biblical historians refute that idea, arguing that a Galilean fisherman could not have written the book's highly polished and poetic Greek. There are a host of possible "Johns," and it is now thought that John was written late in the first century, or by 110 CE.

If there are only four Gospels, then what are the "Gnostic Gospels"?

As if these four Gospels haven't generated enough arguments, somebody had to come up with a few more gospels! In a story combining a little murder mystery with some *Indiana Jones* intrigue, an Egyptian peasant made an extraordinary find of thirteen leather-bound books in 1945. As recounted by Elaine Pagels in her prizewinning *The Gnostic Gospels,* a farmer digging near the town of Nag Hammadi, located on the Nile north of Luxor, uncovered these papyrus books in a buried earthen jar. He took them home, where his mother accidentally burned some of the papyrus as kindling. A few weeks later, this man and his brother killed another local man in a blood feud over the death of their father. Fearing that police investigating the murder would discover the books, the farmer turned his find over to a local priest. Learning of the books, a schoolteacher sent one to Cairo to check its value on the black market for antiquities. The Egyptian government got wind of the books and confiscated ten and a half of the thirteen books and they were placed in a Cairo museum.

But part of another book was smuggled out of Egypt and offered for sale in America. A Dutch historian and linguist heard of the books and purchased the smuggled text. Discovering that parts were missing, he flew to Cairo in 1955, where he was able to see photographic reproductions of the other books. He began to decipher them. The first words he made out were nothing short of revolutionary:

"These are the secret words which the living Jesus spoke, and which the twin, Judas Thomas, wrote down."

The words came from the Gospel According to Thomas. Although other early Christian writings were known to have existed and scraps of a mysterious Gospel According to Thomas had been found previously, the entire text had never been seen. This "new" gospel was the first of fifty-five texts discovered at Nag Hammadi. These were the so-called "Gnostic Gospels," a secret set of early Christian writings. Written in Coptic, a North African dialect used exclusively by an Egyptian Christian sect, they proved to be fifteen-hundred-year-old translations of older Greek writings. Some of the books contained familiar sayings from the New Testament. But other teachings and statements attributed to Jesus were unique and extraordinary, potentially shaking the foundations of Christianity with the questions they raised. In one text, the Gospel of Philip, Jesus is depicted kissing Mary Magdalene, one of his female followers. It is not a brotherly peck on the cheek either:

> ". . . the companion of the [Savior is] Mary Magdalene. [But Christ loved] her more than [all] the disciples, and used to kiss her [often] on her [mouth]." (As cited by Elaine Pagels in *The Gnostic Gospels*, p. xv)

"Gnostics," an early Christian sect whose name comes from the Greek *gnosis*, usually translated as "knowledge," is a term used loosely to identify groups of early Christians who held beliefs very different from conventional Christianity. Just as modern Christianity is split among many contending sects with differing ideas about Jesus, the early church was deeply divided. Gnostics believed, for instance, that Jesus' rising from the dead was spiritual, rather than an actual physical event. They also believed in a spiritual search for inner truth that had more in common with eastern views like Buddhism than with orthodox Christianity. The "Gnostic Gospels" had been denounced as heresy by early Christian leaders who were no longer persecuted victims. *They* had become the authorities. To challenge them was to risk excommunication, arrest, or worse for heresy. About five hundred years after Jesus lived, someone—a monk? there are remains of a monastery near Nag Hammadi—took a set of these banned texts and buried them in the Egyptian desert, either out of self-preservation or for posterity. While the Nag Hammadi discoveries have opened up a great many questions, they also make one thing clear: the earliest Christians did not agree on what we call the New Testament and they may have had more of Jesus' life and words to read and study than the stories and teachings familiar to most contemporary Christians.

This brief look at the evolution of the New Testament provides another reminder that one person's "Word of God" can be another's heresy. And the story doesn't end with the establishment of the New Testament sixteen hundred years ago. A group of devout believers in the God of Abraham, Moses, and Jesus have another holy book, called the Koran, given to their prophet Muhammad, who lived around six hundred years after Jesus lived. Roman Catholics have a catechism to expand on the teachings of the Holy Bible. They also believe the Pope, their earthly leader, sometimes speaks the "infallible" word of God. Another large and growing group of Christians believe in another divine book given to their prophet by an angel. The book could only be read by someone wearing a pair of golden spectacles. That book, deemed holy by the Church of Jesus Christ of Latter-day Saints, is the *Book of Mormon*. So put a Jew, a Muslim, a Roman Catholic, and a Mormon in the same room. All may be sincere, good, devout believers who think they possess the "Truth," or the Word of God. And none can agree on which of them is right.

MILESTONES IN BIBLICAL TIMES V
THE LIFETIME OF JESUS

40 BCE Herod is appointed King of Judea by Marc Antony in Rome and begins a thirty-three-year reign as Herod the Great in *37 BCE*.

31 BCE The Battle of Actium. The Roman general Octavian defeats Marc Antony in this naval battle and becomes ruler of Rome. Marc Antony commits suicide in *30 BCE*.

30 BCE Herod, having denounced Cleopatra and Marc Antony, shifts his allegiance to Octavian.

27 BCE The Roman empire is founded by Octavian, who changes his name to Augustus Caesar and reigns for forty-one years.

20 BCE Herod the Great begins to rebuild Jerusalem's Great Temple in an attempt to restore it to the size and grandeur of Solomon's Temple.

7–4 BCE Possible date of birth of Jesus. The date, place, and circumstances of this event are the subject of considerable speculation.

4 BCE Herod the Great dies; Judea is divided among his three sons.

6 CE The Roman governor of Syria, Quirinius, orders a local census. This is presumably the "worldwide" census mentioned in Luke.

14 CE Emperor Augustus dies; his stepson rules Rome next as Tiberius.

26 CE Pontius Pilate is made governor of Judea; dismissed and recalled to Rome in *36*.

27–28 CE John the Baptist begins preaching; baptism of Jesus.

30–33 CE Possible date of Crucifixion of Jesus. A date as late as *36* is also possible. Tacitus says Jesus was crucified during the reign of Tiberius.

37 CE Tiberius dies; a nephew who is called Caligula rules Rome next.

THE WORLD ACCORDING TO JESUS

MATTHEW, MARK, LUKE, JOHN

I am the bread of life. (John 6:35)

I am the light of the world. (John 8:12)

I am the gate for the sheep. (John 10:7)

I am the good shepherd: the good shepherd lays down his life for the sheep. (John 10:11)

I am the way, and the truth, and the life. (John 14:6)

I am the true vine. (John 15:1)

❋

❋ Was Jesus born on Christmas?

❋ O Little Town of Bethlehem?

❋ Annunciation. Assumption. Immaculate Conception.
Virgin Birth: What's the difference?

❋ Did the word "virgin" mean the same thing two
thousand years ago?

❋ Were there really "Three Kings" and where did
they come from?

❋ Did Matthew's "wise men" meet Luke's
shepherds?

❋ Did Jesus obey his parents?

❋ Why did a young girl want John the Baptist's head
on a platter?

❋ What's the difference between a disciple and an
apostle?

❋ Did Jesus give a Sermon on the Mount?

❋ How does a camel fit through a needle's eye?

❋ Mary Magdalene: naughty or nice?

❋ Did Jesus look down on women?

❋ What's so "Good" about the "Good Samaritan"?

❋ What's so bad about Pharisees?

❋ Why was Jesus so popular?

❋ What is a Transfiguration?

❋ What was the Last Supper?

❋ Who put Jesus on trial?

❋ How does crucifixion kill you?

❋ If you don't believe Jesus was God, what does he have to offer?

Thirty-five years after the death of John F. Kennedy, the American president's life and death continue to fascinate the public and provide an endless source of material for biographers, historians, novelists, conspiracy theorists, and revisionist filmmakers. All make claims about the "real" Kennedy: who he was, what he said, and what he might have been thinking. The flood of conjecture, speculation, and outright fiction continues to pour out despite the fact that there are newspaper accounts, tape recordings, film and television footage, and hundreds—if not thousands—of people still alive who knew John F. Kennedy and worked with him on a daily basis. In spite of all that "evidence," most people still don't know the "truth" about the "real" JFK.

How, then, can anyone possibly get a "true" picture of the "historical" Jesus, a man who left no writings or Oval Office tape recordings? We are not even sure if the people who said they knew him *really* knew him or where they got their stories if they didn't. Nevertheless, since the nineteenth century—and especially in recent years—it has become popular to distinguish between the Jesus of "faith," as presented in the New Testament, and the "historical Jesus." Apart from a scattering of references to Jesus in Roman-era writings, everything we commonly know about the man people called the "Christ," "Messiah," and "Anointed One" comes from the New Testament, on the hearsay evidence of people who had unshakable faith that this man was also the Son of God who died for their sins and then rose from the dead. The Gospels were produced to awaken faith in Jesus as the Messiah and Savior. Just as the Hebrew scriptures contain multiple stories of everything from the Creation to King David and the destruction and rebuilding of Jerusalem's Temple, there are conflicting accounts of Jesus in the New Testament. This section aims to depict the life of Jesus as it is presented in the accounts of the four Gospels, complete with contradictions.

BIBLICAL VOICES

Now the birth of Jesus the Messiah took place in this way. When his mother Mary had been engaged to Joseph, but before they lived together, she was found to be with child from the Holy Spirit. Her husband Joseph, being a righteous man and unwilling to expose her to public disgrace, planned to dismiss her quietly. But just when he had resolved to do this, an angel of the Lord appeared to him and said, "Joseph, son of David, do not be afraid to take Mary as your wife, for the child conceived in her is from the Holy Spirit. She will bear a son, and you are to name him Jesus for he will save his people from their sins." (Matt. 1:18–21)

Was Jesus born on Christmas?

"Chestnuts Roasting on an Open Fire." "On December 5 and 20, Fum, Fum, Fum." "In the Bleak Midwinter."

Throw these and most other wintry Christmas carols out the window. Jesus wasn't born on Christmas. December 25 is basically a date chosen to win over pagan sun worshipers.

Bethlehem? Maybe not. Jesus said he came from Nazareth.

"We Three Kings"? Wrong again. They weren't kings but Persian magicians. And there may not have been three of them.

The elaborate stories and songs woven around Christmas are all part of a complex set of myths and traditions that has little to do with the biblical account of Jesus' birth. The English word "Christmas" literally means "Christ's Mass," the festival of the Christ's birth. The earliest mention of December 25 as the feast day of the "Nativity"—the proper name for the birthday of Jesus—dates to 354 CE. In ancient times, December 25 was the date of the winter solstice, a pagan holiday celebrating the sun god. In Rome, the week preceding the solstice was the Saturnalia, an orgiastic festival that concluded with *gift-giving* and *candle-lighting*. Hmmmmm. Doesn't that sound like a familiar holiday?

Early Roman Christians appropriated the date and then used it to win converts from paganism, a term for the Roman empire's state religion, complete with its set of god and goddesses who had been expropriated from Greek mythology. The word "pagan" was coined by early Christians, loosely meaning "civilian." In other words, anyone who hadn't enlisted in "Jesus' army" was a pagan. Early Christians did not think Jews were "pagan," however, because they still worshiped the same God.

Christians then as now agreed on few things. Following the division of the Roman empire into eastern and western halves in 340 CE, Christianity was also largely split between East and West. Eastern Christians used a calendar in which the solstice fell on January 6, when the birthday of Osiris was still celebrated at Alexandria, Egypt. By about 300 CE, January 6 had become the date of the "Epiphany" (Greek for "manifestation"), a feast closely related to Christmas in the Roman Catholic calendar as the day on which the "wise men" or Magi visited Jesus. In the Eastern Orthodox church, Epiphany is even more popular than Christmas and commemorates the baptism of Jesus in the Jordan River.

Okay, so Jesus wasn't born on Christmas. At least the New Testament tells us what year Jesus was born. Right?

Sorry again. The New Testament actually offers several possible birth years. Pick the one you like. First we have to contend with the "Shifting Calendar" glitch. Since they were in Rome and did as the Romans do, early Christian writers calculated historical dates from the legendary foundation of Rome in 753 BCE. This Roman-based calendar was then replaced by one based on the calculations of a Greek monk who was commissioned to coordinate the festivals of the church. Around 532 CE, the monk, Dionysus Exiguus, dated the birth of Christ to March 25 of the Roman year 754—this translated into the Christian Year 1, starting January 1. This is where "anno Domini," "in the year of the Lord," comes from. But Dionysus Exiguus slipped a bit. Since Matthew dates the birth of Jesus to the days of King Herod, and he died in 4 BCE, the "Year One" fixed by Dionysus Exiguus couldn't have been the Year One.

Like many ancient dating systems, early Christian calendars also referred to the number of years during which a contemporary ruler had been governing. In a modern sense, 1998= the sixth year in the "reign" of Bill Clinton. Luke says John the Baptist, a close relative of Jesus, was born six months before Jesus and started preaching in the fifteenth year of the reign of Emperor Tiberius, which corresponds to between 27 and 29 CE. At that time, Luke says, Jesus was "about thirty years old." Counting back thirty years provides an approximate date for Jesus' birth falling between 4 and 1 BCE. That's a little vague and becomes even vaguer if "about thirty" was Luke's way of saying "thirtysomething." Was Jesus exactly thirty when he started preaching? Thirty-five? Thirty-eight? Or maybe only twenty-five—that's about thirty too. And we're not done yet. This slippery chronology gets even slicker.

Surely Herod's life must offer some clues about Jesus' birth date. The Bible says when Herod was king a big census was taken by the Romans. Somebody must know when that happened. Wrong again. Matthew explicitly connects the birth of Jesus with the government of King Herod. And a reference to King Herod's successor, his son Archelaus, proves that the author meant Herod the Great, not one of his several sons who also took the royal name of Herod. The years during which Herod the Great was king of the Jews are precisely known: Herod was made king of Judea by the Roman Senate in 40 BCE, and he died thirty-six years later, which gives us the exact year 4 BCE. So according to Matthew, Jesus was born sometime before the year 4 BCE.

In Matthew (but no other Gospel), when Herod was told of rumors of the birth of a "messiah" who might threaten his rule, he issued a royal order to kill all the Jewish male infants in Bethlehem. The famed "Slaughter of the Innocents," depicted in great art over the centuries and films like *The Greatest Story Ever Told*, was meant to remind Jews of the Pharaoh who had ordered Jewish babies killed in the time of Moses. When did Herod issue this terrible order? Sorry. Herod did some terrible things in his day and his track record for eliminating opponents was on a par with that of King David, his predecessor as king of the Jews. In 7 BCE, Herod executed two of his sons. Before he died, Herod had a group of religious leaders and their students burned to death for desecrating a Roman symbol that had been placed in the Jerusalem Temple. But there are no records of Herod issuing that gruesome order to slaughter innocent children, and even if there were, the command was to kill the babies under two, implying that Jesus might have been born two years earlier, pushing the date back to 7 or 6 BCE. But outside the Bible there is no historical mention of a massacre of infants that surely would have attracted someone's notice, even though Herod's other brutal acts are well documented. Absence of evidence is not evidence of absence, but there is no way to confirm Matthew's story of this massacre.

What about that worldwide census that the Roman emperor Augustus ordered, as reported in Luke? Like Matthew, the author of Luke agrees that Jesus was born under Herod. In his narrative, however, Luke also connected the birth of Jesus with an enrollment for taxation ordered by Emperor Augustus and carried out under Quirinius, the Roman governor of Syria. Sorry again. According to historical records, no such census of the entire Roman world ever took place at that time. The only enrollment arranged by Quirinius took place in 6 CE, ten years after Herod died. This census, made to gather taxes from Roman citizens, caused a revolt in Judea but did not involve the population of Galilee, where Joseph and Mary lived and where one of Herod the Great's other sons, Herod Antipas, was in charge. Did Luke, writing his Gospel some seventy-five years later, simply get his Herods confused?

So Matthew has Jesus born between 7 and 4 BCE. Luke has him born before 4 BCE, while Herod the Great is alive, and then in 6 CE, ten years after Herod the Great died. These two Gospels disagree by about ten to twelve years. The date is wrong and the year is a mystery. In other words, the birthday of the "Son of God" is a movable feast. If this is divinely inspired, couldn't God get that year right?

BIBLICAL VOICES

In those days a decree went out from Emperor Augustus that all the world should be registered. This was the first registration and was taken while Quirinius was governor of Syria. All went to their own towns to be registered. Joseph also went from the town of Nazareth in Galilee to Judea, to the city of David called Bethlehem, because he was descended from the house and family of David. He went to be registered with Mary, to whom he was engaged and who was expecting a child. While they were there, the time came for her to deliver her child. And she gave birth to her firstborn son and wrapped him in bands of cloth, and laid him in a manger, because there was no place for them in the inn. (Luke 2:1–7)

O Little Town of Bethlehem?

Okay. The day and the year were fudged a bit. But surely we know Jesus was born in Bethlehem? Oh dear. The place of Jesus' birth also raises some problems. If we had only Mark and John to go on, we would assume it was Nazareth because they call Nazareth his hometown, as Jesus himself does. But Luke and Matthew both set the story of Jesus' birth in Bethlehem. Matthew simply states that Mary and Joseph are in this sleepy little town that is six miles (10 k) south of Jerusalem, and a long way from Nazareth, which is north of Jerusalem. In Luke, Joseph and Mary live in Nazareth but travel to Bethlehem for the big imperial census. Even if there had been a worldwide census, Joseph wouldn't need to go to Bethlehem to report to the Roman version of the IRS. Even less likely is a demand that he would have to drag a pregnant woman there.

The exact place of the birth of the revered Jesus within Bethlehem is also unknown. Luke's "manger" may have been a stall with almost no covering, or even a feeding trough in the open; the "inn" was most likely a yard with partial shelter on three sides. Based on current archaeological and other clues, Bethlehem lacked a Holiday Inn two thousand years ago. Another early Christian tradition held that a cave was the birthplace of Jesus; this was according to Origen, a Greek theologian and scholar (c. 185–254) who became an early Christian teacher and said he had been shown the cave. Best remembered for his early attempts to coordinate the Hebrew and Greek versions of the Bible, Origen also castrated himself because Matthew said that some would become "eunuchs for the Kingdom of Heaven." By about 338, the Emperor Constantine built a church over the cave, and it was here that Jerome settled in 386 to translate the Bible from Greek into more commonly used Latin (the "Vulgate").

So why put Jesus in Bethlehem, a small, obscure village? Because to the Jewish people, Bethlehem was not obscure at all. First mentioned in Judges, it took added significance from Ruth, whose heroine went to Bethlehem, married there, and became the ancestor of the future king David. As the birthplace of Israel's greatest king, Bethlehem became an even more significant national landmark. Then the prophet Micah prophesied that a shepherd king, a Messiah to lead Israel, would come from Bethlehem.

There are only two possibilities here. Jesus *was* born in Bethlehem—even though Jesus later says he is from Nazareth and there is no valid historical reason for his parents to be in Bethlehem. Or he wasn't and the writers of Matthew and Luke placed his birth there to conveniently fulfill the well-known prophecy of a Messiah born in Bethlehem out of the House of David. In other words, did the Gospel writers, working about a half century after Jesus died, "cut the foot to fit the shoe"?

BIBLICAL VOICES

In the sixth month the angel Gabriel was sent by God to a town in Galilee called Nazareth, to a virgin engaged to a man whose name was Joseph, of the house of David. The virgin's name was Mary. And he came to her and said, "Greetings, favored one! The Lord is with you." But she was much perplexed by his words and pondered what sort of greeting this might be. The angel said to her, "Do not be afraid, Mary, for you have found favor with God. And now, you will conceive

in your womb and bear a son and you will name him Jesus.
He will be great, and will be called the Son of the Most High,
and the Lord God will give to him the throne of his ancestor
David. He will reign over the house of Jacob forever, and of
his kingdom there will be no end." Mary said to the angel,
"How can this be since I am a virgin?" (Luke 1:26–34)

Annunciation. Assumption. Immaculate Conception. Virgin Birth: What's the difference?

The traditional Christmas story readings familiar to Christians
around the world typically merge the conflicting Matthew and
Luke versions, toss in a handful of Hebrew scriptural prophecies,
and blend it all into a neat, orderly narrative. The problem is that
the "neat" Gospel versions don't agree, as already seen in the
questions raised by the date and place of Jesus' birth.

If these blows to this comfortingly familiar Nativity story are
disquieting, just wait. The plot thickens. In Matthew, the unnamed angel who tells of the birth of Jesus appears to Joseph. He
warns Joseph to take Mary and get out of town because Herod is
up to bad business. Joseph and Mary are not yet married, and her
unexplained pregnancy is a problem. Joseph plans to quietly "dismiss her." But when prompted by the angel, Joseph wakes up,
takes Mary as his wife, and after Jesus is born they leave Bethlehem for Egypt to await the death of Herod (which history tells us
took place in 4 BCE), in the so-called "Flight into Egypt." Without
saying how much time the Holy Family spends in Egypt, an angel
then gives Joseph the "all clear" sign; it is safe for them to leave
Egypt and return to Judah. But instead of returning to Bethlehem,
the Holy Family decides to go to Nazareth, in the district of Galilee. The "Flight into Egypt" of Joseph, Mary, and Jesus is unmentioned in Luke, but Matthew's intentions would have been
clear to Jews. Citing a Hebrew prophecy in Numbers—"I called
my son out of Egypt"—the author of Matthew wanted to show

parallels between Jesus and Moses. Jesus went to Egypt, like Moses, and like Moses and the Israelites, Jesus would be safely brought out of Egypt in a recapitulation of the Exodus.

Unlike that of Matthew, the Gospel of Luke opens with the story of an earlier miraculous birth, that of John the Baptist. Carrying on the biblical tradition of barren women who receive heavenly messengers with surprising maternal news, the angel Gabriel first tells a priest named Zechariah that his aged and previously childless wife, Elizabeth, will bear a son named John. (In Hebrew scriptures, those barren women are Sarah, Rebekah, Rachel, the mother of Samson, and Hannah, the mother of the prophet Samuel.) Like the early Israelite characters Samson and Samuel, this unborn child is also pledged to keep certain vows to God. His job will be to get the people ready for the coming of the Lord.

Six months later, the angel Gabriel goes to Nazareth and appears to Elizabeth's relative Mary, who is engaged to Joseph but not yet pregnant. Gabriel tells this young woman—a "woman" of this time was commonly "espoused" around the age of fourteen—that she will bear a child who will be called "Son of God." Remember, Joseph got the news in Matthew after Mary was already in the "family way." In other words, Mary did not discuss the angelic visitation explaining her mysterious pregnancy with her husband-to-be.

What might you say if your fourteen-year-old daughter sat you down and said that an angel told her that she was going to give birth to the Son of God? But not to worry, Mom and Dad. She'll still be a virgin! The traditional images of the Virgin Mary tend to obscure the fact that the Holy Mother of Jesus was an unwed teenager.

Gabriel's visit to Mary is called the Annunciation, the announcement foretelling the birth of Jesus. (The Feast of the Annunciation is observed by some Christians on March 25, which was also the birth date for Jesus calculated by the Greek monk Dionysus; add nine months and you get December 25!) There is no record of Joseph and Mary discussing their respective angelic visits. Imagine it for a moment, though: Joseph says, "Mary, about that little problem of yours. Well, I had the strangest dream last night."

Surprised, Mary says, "You had a dream? Me too. Six months ago an angel said I would be the Mother of God."

Unlike the other biblical women whose children are predicted by angelic messengers, Mary is told her baby will result from the "Holy Spirit" coming upon her. While all of those older women, from Abraham's wife Sara to Elizabeth, were miraculously foretold of their pregnancies, all conceived by the old-fashioned method. But the presumably teenaged Mary does not conceive as they did; the Holy Spirit comes over her. Mary sets off to visit her miraculously pregnant relative Elizabeth. When Elizabeth sees Mary, Elizabeth's unborn child "leaps in the womb," and the older Elizabeth exclaims, "Blessed are you among women, and blessed is the fruit of your womb."

Mary's response to Elizabeth takes the form of a song that is familiar as the hymn "The Magnificat."

"My soul magnifies the Lord,
      and my spirit rejoices in God my Savior,
for he has looked with favor on the lowliness of his
servant.
      Surely, from now on all generations will call me
blessed." (Luke 1:46–48)

Being the Mother of God is not a matter to be taken lightly, and Mary's position throughout Christian history has been intriguing. After the two biblical birth accounts, very little is said about Mary in the Bible, and even less is said about Joseph, who becomes a missing person in the biblical account after Jesus is twelve years old. Jesus later speaks of his mother in several verses that seem to contradict the commandment to "honor thy mother." On one occasion, his family comes to a house where Jesus is meeting with his followers and asks for him, but Jesus says, "Who are my mother and brothers and sisters?" Continues Mark, "And looking around at those who sat beside him, he said, 'Here are my mother and my brothers and sisters. Whoever does the will of God is my brother, and sister, and mother.' " (Mark 3:31–35) In Luke, Jesus says, "If anyone comes to me and cares about his father or his mother or his wife or his children or his brothers or his sisters or even his own soul, he can't be my student." (Luke 14:26) Jesus' words, which have struck some readers as rather coldhearted, were an unambiguous message that faith in him, which brings a person into his heavenly "family," must be complete and unequivocal.

In spite of the tremendous reverence for Mary and the elaborate mythology that has sprung up around her—thousands of people report "Marian Visions" every year—there are few references to Jesus' mother in the Bible. In John, Mary is said to be at the wedding at Cana and at Jesus' Crucifixion, and she is present with the disciples in Acts after Jesus ascends into heaven. The virginal conception of Jesus isn't mentioned in Mark or John, nor does Paul explore the question of the miraculous birth of Jesus to a woman who hasn't had sexual relations. Paul merely states in a single letter that Jesus was "born of woman." Some biblical historians take this to mean that Mary's virginity wasn't an issue for the earliest Christians, but the authors of the later Gospels were compelled to address the question of how a flesh-and-blood man could also be a divine being, as Jesus was believed to be. Establishing Jesus' divinity was especially important for winning Gentile converts. The notion of gods having sex with humans was commonplace in many pagan traditions, including the famed cavorting gods of Greek myth. But to make it clear that the birth of Jesus wasn't on a par with the Greek myth in which Zeus assumed the form of a swan to mate with Leda, the image of the Holy Spirit as the agent of conception was introduced. Mary conceived Jesus without sexual relations, hence the "Virgin Birth."

Did the word "virgin" mean the same thing two thousand years ago?

Although Matthew and Luke both go to great lengths to make Mary's virginal status clear, the whole question of the Virgin Birth is one more case of mistranslation. Way back in the prophecies of Isaiah, there were many references to a coming Savior. The author of Matthew would have used the Greek translation of the Hebrew prophet Isaiah in which the coming of the Messiah is prophesied. Once Isaiah talked about a son being born to a young woman (see page 225). But the Greek translation for Isaiah's Hebrew "young woman" was a word that can also mean either "virgin" or "young woman." In other words, Isaiah never prophesied a virgin birth, and he wasn't even talking about the Messiah when he prophesied the birth of a child to King Ahaz of Judah. But to fulfill the mistranslated prophecy, the author of Matthew believed that Jesus must be born of a virgin. Since neither John, Mark, or Paul in his writings discuss the Virgin Birth, some theologians have suggested that this aspect of Jesus' birth was a later invention, as with the relocation of the birth to Bethlehem, to fit the Nativity events into a prophetic scheme. Once again, the entire episode of Jesus' birth reminds readers that the Bible is a work of faith, not history or biology.

The "Cult of Mary" that grew over the next few centuries has almost no biblical foundation. But the veneration of Mary quickly grew among early Christians. The title "Mother of God" was used as early as the second century in referring to Mary. But by the fourth century, there were divisive debates among church leaders over the divinity of Jesus and the status of Mary. A monk named Nestorius insisted that Mary was the mother of Jesus, not God. Condemning his teachings, the Council of Ephesus said in 431 that Mary was to be called *Theotokos*, or "Mother of God." Later Christian teaching held that Mary was "ever-virgin," even though there are frequent mentions of Jesus' brothers and sisters in the Gospels. Theologians explained these troublesome siblings away as references to either Jesus' cousins or other near relatives, or children of Joseph by a previous marriage—an interpretation with absolutely no biblical underpinnings. In the birth narrative in Matthew, Joseph is said to have had "no marital relations with her until she had borne a son," certainly leaving open the possibility that Joseph and Mary had "marital relations" afterward.

Later theologians went a step further in a leap that also has no biblical justification: Mary herself was said to have been conceived without "original sin." This belief, the doctrine known as "Immaculate Conception," began early in Christian history and was officially accepted as dogma essential to Roman Catholic beliefs by Pope Pius IX in 1854. "Original sin," a Christian theological idea also not found in the Bible, attributes the universal sinfulness of the human race to the first sin committed by Adam. The prominent Christian writer Augustine, the Bishop of Hippo, didn't coin the term but expanded the notion of "original sin" to mean that the taint of human sin is transmitted from one generation to the next by the act of procreation. The notion of the Immaculate Conception, often confused with the Virgin Birth, was developed in the Middle Ages to explain that Mary not only hadn't had sex in conceiving Jesus but also was free from "original sin."

Mary's popularity grew tremendously during the Middle Ages, particularly during the period of the "Black Death." As the bubonic plague created piles of the dead, many Europeans justifiably thought that the world was coming to an end—the Judgment Day promised in the Bible was upon them. Jesus was more commonly depicted in this time as a supreme, universal judge than as the merciful, forgiving "Lamb of God." As fear of death and the "Last Judgment" grew in response to the plague sweeping across Europe, Mary came to be viewed as the merciful mediator whose intercession would temper the terrible justice of Jesus Christ. The rosary, a devotion originally consisting of 150 "Hail Marys," one for each psalm, came into use at this time.

Roman Catholic and Eastern Orthodox beliefs also grew to include the idea that Mary was bodily taken into heaven and reunited with her soul, in what is called the "Assumption," another concept not founded on any biblical event. The Assumption, based on the sixth-century Feast of the Dormition ("falling asleep"), was formally defined as an article of faith by Pope Pius XII in 1950.

Protestant denominations depart from Roman Catholics on the subject of the Virgin Mary when it comes to both the Immaculate Conception and the Assumption. While the Virgin Birth remains an essential doctrine for most Christians, modern scholars have questioned some of the inconsistencies and issues of translation with respect to Mary and Jesus' birth. Recently, some Christian theologians have begun to cast doubt on the concept of a "Virgin Birth." Like all matters of the Bible, it is ultimately left to individual faith.

BIBLICAL VOICES

After Jesus had been born at Bethlehem in Judaea during the reign of King Herod, suddenly some wise men came to Jerusalem from the east asking, "Where is the infant king of the Jews? We saw his star as it rose and have come to do him homage." When King Herod heard this he was perturbed and so was the whole of Jerusalem. He called together all the chief priests and the scribes of the people, and enquired of them where the Christ was to be born. They told him, "At Bethlehem in Judaea, for this is what the prophet wrote." (Matt. 2:1–5 NJB)

Were there really "Three Kings" and where did they come from?

Leaving out all of Luke's elaborate details about imperial census-taking (which would have happened ten years after Herod died), Matthew's birth account focuses on King Herod, who is told that a new king of the Jews, a "Messiah" (Christ), has been born in

Bethlehem. In a move that would have reminded every Jew of the
Pharaoh's order at the time of the birth of Moses, Herod orders
the slaughter of all the male infants under two years old in Bethlehem. Herod issues this horrifying command after an unspecified
number of "wise men" stop by Jerusalem to ask where the
newborn "king of the Jews" is to be found. They have heard a
prophecy of it and have seen an astrological sign—a star—telling
of it.

So who were these "wise men" who appear only in Matthew?
And were they kings? And were there three of them?

The original Greek calls them *Magi,* the source of the word
magician. The Magi were originally a clan of the Medes, who
formed the priestly class in Persia—modern-day Iran. By the time
of Jesus, the word *magi* had come to refer to professional practi-
tioners of magic or astrology. There is no hint of them being roy-
alty, other than the "fact" that they received an audience with
Herod. Nowhere does Matthew even say that there were only
three of them. The only clue that there are three Magi is the three
gifts they bring the child. There is no reason why three gifts must
mean three people. The fact that Herod orders the death of children under two even suggests that the "wise men" may have arrived in Jerusalem well after Jesus' birth. Although some
translations refer to Jesus as an infant at the time of the Magi's
visit, Jesus is called a "child" in others. The mention of a star
guiding the "wise men" offers a hint that they were astrologers.

Despite the later folktales spun around them, and the establishment of a popular holiday called "Three Kings' Day," the Magi
are anonymous. Their legendary names—Balthasar, Melchior, and
Caspar in western traditions—emerged much later. So did the
myth that one of them was black. That was the product of medieval imagination. The "Three Kings" must have come from the
three known continents, medieval Christians reasoned, so that
meant one of them was African. That meant he must have been
black. This is how legends are born. The Bible does record their
three gifts—gold, frankincense, and myrrh—the latter two aro-

matic herbs obtained from shrubs. Significantly, the Gospels later relate that myrrh was used to anoint Jesus' dead body for burial.

The star the Magi followed has also sent the curious poring over astronomical records. Unlike comets, meteors, or most astronomical events, this was an unusual "star." It moved through the sky until reaching Bethlehem, where it stood still in the sky. An appearance of Halley's comet, often associated with Jesus' birth, occurred in 12 BCE, too early to coordinate with the Nativity, unless the chronology really gets stretched. The Hale-Bopp comet, which attracted so much attention in 1997, was nowhere in sight. In 3 BCE, the planet Jupiter rose in conjunction with Venus, the "morning star," and this might have created a blazing celestial event. Chinese astronomical records, kept very carefully for centuries, also indicate a supernova in 5 BCE, which is a possibility, since Jesus was born before Herod's death in 4 BCE. So starry, starry nights don't help much either in dating Jesus' birth. And the "wise men's" star remains another awkward, misfitting piece of the Nativity puzzle.

BIBLICAL VOICES

> In the countryside close by there were shepherds out in the fields keeping guard over their sheep during the watches of the night. An angel of the Lord stood over them and the glory of the Lord shone round them. They were terrified, but the angel said, "Do not be afraid. Look, I bring you news of great joy, a joy to be shared by the whole people. Today in the town of David a Saviour has been born to you; he is Christ the Lord." (Luke 2:8–11 NJB)

Did Matthew's "wise men" meet Luke's shepherds?

Every Christmas crèche, or manger scene, and every Nativity pageant ever celebrated, has one other key element: shepherds tending their flocks who are told by angels of the birth of Jesus. Matthew neglects this popular Christmas element that Luke includes in his birth story: the shepherds. In Luke, the shepherds go to Bethlehem and pay homage to the child, then leave, saying they plan to tell everyone about this wonderful event. Matthew's wise men and Luke's shepherds never cross paths. Then they all disappear from the Bible. Were they transformed somehow by this miraculous event? Did they join Jesus' followers later?

Symbolically speaking, the announcement to these shepherds was a counterpoint to the homage paid by Matthew's wise men. In New Testament times, shepherds ranked fairly low on the Social Register. Throughout his ministry, Jesus would appeal most directly to the outcast and poorest of Judean society, represented in Luke by the shepherds. It also was a pointed symbolic reminder that Jesus was coming as both shepherd to the flock of Israel and the sacrificial lamb that would be slaughtered to take away the sins of the world.

Did Jesus obey his parents?

According to Luke, Jesus began his ministry when he was about thirty years old. Three of the Gospels omit any mention of Jesus' youth or early adulthood in Nazareth. Only Luke offers a fleeting glimpse of the twelve-year-old Jesus discussing the Law with the sages outside the Jerusalem Temple.

At that time, Nazareth was an insignificant farming village. Mary and Joseph are depicted as faithful Israelites who make the pilgrimage south to Jerusalem each year for Passover. During Passover feasts, Jerusalem was swollen with thousands of pilgrims and Roman soldiers intent on keeping order, as nationalistic, anti-Roman sentiments ran high in these days. In the midst of the crowds, Jesus and his parents are separated and Joseph and Mary assume their son is among the throng of travelers returning to

Nazareth. After the boy is missing for three days, his parents return to Jerusalem and find Jesus sitting among the teachers who congregated outside the Temple to discuss and debate the Scriptures. This twelve-year-old was questioning the rabbis, or teachers, who were astonished at his grasp of the Law. When his parents found Jesus, they were obviously upset and asked why he had treated them that way. His answer confounded them: "Why were you searching for me? Did you not know that I must be in my Father's house?" (Luke 2:49)

Then silence. The next eighteen years or so in Jesus' life are undocumented in the New Testament. Did he follow in Joseph's footsteps and become a carpenter? Did he marry, as was expected of most young Jewish men of the day? Was he a witness to an anti-Roman uprising at that time in nearby Gamala? The Romans razed his neighboring town and crucified the Jewish rebels along the road. There is no record, only speculation.

When next seen, Jesus comes to his relative John, who has become a "baptizer." Descended from a priestly family, John was one of a growing number of Jewish preachers who practiced immersion baptism in the Jordan River. Baptism as a form of ritual purification was not widely practiced among Jews at that time, but the idea of washing off sins with water goes back to Hebrew scriptures. John the Baptist called for repentance and cleansing from sin, symbolized by baptism. While some historians have attempted to fit John into the traditions of the Essenes, the monastic sect who lived at Qumran and apparently made ritual bathing part of their daily life, John seems more to have been a loner, a bit of a wild man who wore clothes made from camel skin and lived on "locusts and honey," preaching the need for repentance and the confession of sins.

John's miraculous birth was foretold by Gabriel in Luke, and he was cast as Jesus' advance man, also in fulfillment of several Hebrew prophecies. The synoptic versions of Jesus' baptism contain slight differences but all three basically agree that at the moment of the baptism the Holy Spirit, in the form of a dove, descended on Jesus' head and a voice from heaven declared, "This is my Son, the Beloved, with whom I am well pleased."

BIBLICAL VOICES

But when Herod's birthday came, the daughter of Herodias danced before the company, and she pleased Herod so much that he promised on oath to grant her whatever she might ask. Prompted by her mother, she said, "Give me the head of John the Baptist here on a platter." (Matt. 14:6–8)

Why did a young girl want John the Baptist's head on a platter?

Sometime after Jesus was baptized, John was arrested on the orders of Herod Antipas, the son of Herod the Great. The Gospels depict John preaching the coming of the Messiah. The Jewish historian Josephus adds to the Gospel record of John the Baptist but his account presents John as a sort of wandering teacher. When John publicly denounced the marriage of Herod Antipas to Herodias, who was his niece and was married to Herod's brother, the angry queen demanded John's arrest. Herod was fascinated by John, but when the daughter of Herodias danced at his birthday party, Herod was swept off his feet and promised the girl anything. The Bible does not identify this young girl as Salomé, although Josephus does. There is also no biblical mention of the famous "Seven Veils" that Salomé sheds as she dances for her stepfather, which figure prominently in Richard Strauss's 1905 opera *Salomé* (adapted from an Oscar Wilde play). Egged on by her mother, the girl asks for, and receives, John's head on a platter. (The operatic Salomé is put to death by her stepfather, but the historical figure actually married Herod's son Philip).

John's severed head raises some more problems of chronology. Traditionally, Jesus was said to have begun his ministry around the time of John's death. But history intrudes once more if the Jewish historian Josephus is to be believed. According to Josephus, John was arrested in 33 or 34. By that time, Jesus was supposedly already dead.

BIBLICAL VOICES

Jesus, full of the Holy Spirit, returned from the Jordan and was led by the Spirit in the wilderness where for forty days he was tempted by the devil. He ate nothing at all during those days, and when they were over, he was famished. The devil said to him, "If you are the Son of God, command this stone to become a loaf of bread." Jesus answered him, "It is written, 'One does not live by bread alone.' " (Luke 4:1–4)

PLOT SUMMARY: THE TEMPTATION OF CHRIST

After his baptism, Jesus heads for the desert wilderness, where he spends forty days, a number of obvious meaning to devout Jews. Moses spent forty days in the wilderness before receiving the Ten Commandments, and then the Children of Israel spent their forty years in the desert. The symbolism would not have been lost on people of Jesus' day. Three of the Gospels report that Jesus was tested during this period. Each Gospel names Jesus' adversary differently. He is the "tester" in certain translations of Matthew, Satan in Mark, and the Devil in Luke. The description in Mark is brief: Jesus was in the desert, was tempted by Satan, and the angels waited on him. Both Matthew and Luke describe a more elaborate, three-part temptation. First, Jesus is urged to turn stones into bread. Citing Deuteronomy, Jesus answers,

> "One does not live by bread alone,
>   but by every word that comes
>   from the mouth of God."

Taken to the top of the Temple, Jesus is told to throw himself down and the angels will save him. He replies from Deuteronomy,

"Do not put the Lord your God to the test." And finally from a high mountain, Jesus is shown all the kingdoms of the world and told he can have it all. Jesus answers again from Deuteronomy, "Worship the Lord your God and serve only him." (That is the order in Matthew; it is slightly different in Luke.) Jesus' references to Deuteronomy, one of the Books of Law, would have reminded people once more of the connection between Jesus and Moses.

BIBLICAL VOICES

As he walked by the Sea of Galilee, he saw two brothers, Simon, who is called Peter, and Andrew his brother, casting a net into the sea—for they were fishermen. And he said to them, "Follow me, and I will make you fishers of men." Immediately they left their nets and followed him. (Matt. 4:18–20)

What's the difference between a disciple and an apostle?

Jesus spent the rest of his life in and around the Sea of Galilee, except for his journey—or annual visits, according to John—to Jerusalem. The Sea of Galilee, or Lake Tiberias, is about twelve and a half miles long and eight miles across at its widest point. The Jordan River enters in the north and flows out due south toward the Dead Sea. Galileans of biblical times were considered country bumpkins or "hicks" to the more cosmopolitan residents of Jerusalem. The common attitude to people of this area was expressed by a future follower of Jesus named Nathaniel in Mark who asks, "Can anything good come out of Nazareth?" when told about Jesus. Thought of as little better than the shepherds of the Nativity on the Judean social scale, a collection of fishermen from Galilee was not exactly the "Dream Team" that would save Israel and defeat the Roman empire.

In Luke, the account varies slightly when the fishermen are

convinced to follow Jesus after he instructs them to cast their nets even though they say they have caught nothing. They catch so many fish their nets nearly break. In Matthew, the four fishermen—Simon, Andrew, James, and John—simply leave their nets and their boats, and follow Jesus. There is still a different version of the call of the first disciples in John, where Andrew is mentioned as a disciple of John the Baptist, who tells his brother Simon about Jesus; there is no mention of "fishing for men" and leaving nets behind. Gradually Jesus singles out twelve followers as his disciples, the number symbolically representative of the twelve tribes of Israel.

THE TWELVE DISCIPLES
(Named in Matthew 10, Mark 3, and Luke 6)

- Simon, whom Jesus nicknames Cephas (Aramaic for "rock") or Peter (from the Greek *petra* for "rock").
- Andrew, Simon's brother, who is later mentioned in John as a follower of John the Baptist.
- James, called the son of Zebedee. (James is a form of the Hebrew "Jacob," a common name among Jews in this period. There are four significant men named James in the New Testament, one of them a second disciple mentioned below.)
- John, the brother of James; Jesus called James and John the "Sons of Thunder." With Peter, they were the closest of the twelve to Jesus.
- Philip is from Bethsaida, the city of Peter and Andrew. In John, Philip tells Nathaniel (next entry) about Jesus, saying Jesus is the one whom Moses and the prophets wrote about.
- Bartholomew, or "son of Tolmai." He is also identified as Nathaniel in John. Tradition holds that Bartholomew went on a missionary journey in Egypt, Persia, India, and Armenia, where he was flayed alive. For that he was named the patron saint of tanners!

- Thomas, who would become known later as the "doubter" because in John he demands physical proof of Jesus' resurrection. A Gnostic "Gospel According to Thomas" is attributed to him, and his name in Aramaic means "twin," leading some scholars to identify him as Jesus' twin brother— a sibling nowhere mentioned in the Bible.
- Matthew, the tax collector, also identified as Levi. He is named the son of Alphaeus in Luke and Mark.
- James is also called the son of Alphaeus, but apparently not the same one as Levi's father. He is also called "the younger" or "the lesser" to distinguish him from James, son of Zebedee, although in some translations he is called "the little," implying he was shorter than James, the "greater."
- Thaddeus; Luke substitutes the name Judas, son of James (the third New Testament James).
- Simon the "Canaanean" or the "zealot."
- Judas Iscariot, the ultimate betrayer. While all the other disciples came from the area around Galilee, "Iscariot" may mean Judas is from Kerioth in Judea.

These twelve were the disciples singled out by Jesus. They were the followers most closely associated with Jesus, but there is frequent mention of many other "disciples," a term used often in the Gospels and Acts. The word "disciples" literally means "learners," or students of Jesus, although it has different connotations in each of the Gospels. The disciples of Jesus were generally those who listened to Jesus, understood him, and even taught what Jesus taught. In Luke, seventy more disciples are appointed by Jesus, in addition to the Twelve. Jesus then sent them out in pairs to precede him to the towns where he planned to go. The number seventy supposedly represented the number of nations in the world as recorded in Genesis. (Other ancient authorities mention seventy-two disciples, reflecting a disparity in translations. The

Hebrew Bible says there are seventy nations; the Greek Bible says there are seventy-two nations.)

In addition to the Twelve and the additional seventy appointed disciples, there was a large and growing "community" of followers who welcomed Jesus and the Twelve when they came to a town.

The words "disciple" and "apostle" are often used interchangeably but mean quite different things. An apostle, from the Greek *apostolos*, for "one who is sent out," generally means a messenger of the gospel. The author of Luke used the word "apostle" specifically for the twelve disciples who had been companions of Jesus, witnesses of the resurrection, and became leaders of the church—excluding Judas, who betrayed Jesus and killed himself. The word is later used in a wider sense to include Paul and other early preachers of the Gospel.

BIBLICAL VOICES

Go on your way. See, I am sending you out like lambs into the midst of wolves. Carry no purse, no bag, no sandals; and greet no one on the road. Whatever house you enter, first say, "Peace to this house!" And if anyone is there who shares in peace, your peace will rest on that person; but if not, it will return to you. Remain in the same house, eating and drinking whatever they provide, for the laborer deserves to be paid. Do not move about from house to house. Whenever you enter a town and its people welcome you, eat what is set before you; cure the sick who are there, and say to them, "The kingdom of God has come near to you." But whenever you enter a town and they do not welcome you, go out into its streets and say, "Even the dust of your town that clings to our feet, we wipe off in protest against you. Yet know this; the kingdom of God has come near." I tell you, on that day, it will be more tolerable for Sodom than for that town. (Luke 10:3–12)

Did Jesus give a Sermon on the Mount?

One of the centerpieces of Jesus' teaching is an extensive talk that Augustine labeled the "Sermon on the Mount." According to Matthew, after calling Simon and Andrew, Jesus got great "word of mouth," as publicists like to put it. He attracted large crowds who followed him to hear his preaching and see him perform healings. One such crowd gathered to listen to him speak as he sat, the typical Jewish position for teaching, on an unidentified mountainside. The "Sermon on the Mount" appears in its entirety in Matthew (more than one hundred verses long) and in a somewhat abbreviated version in Luke. In Luke, this teaching session is similar, though shorter (about thirty verses), and is delivered "on a level place" after Jesus comes down from the mountain where he had been praying.

The differences between the two versions have led scholars to contend that the version in Matthew represents a compilation of many of Jesus' teachings compressed into one long and memorable discourse. In other words, while it faithfully captures the words and teachings of Jesus, the sermon was a "Best of Jesus," edited into a single speech.

In Matthew's version, the sermon opens opens with "The Beatitudes," or "blesseds," a series of promised blessings that emphasize the most vulnerable and empty-handed people who are ready to accept the "Kingdom of Heaven." (There are nine Beatitudes in Matthew; Luke has only four.) Jesus then moves on to a series of "demands" that expand on but don't replace the requirements of the Hebrew Law and Prophets. They include Jesus' version of the "Golden Rule." The "Sermon" includes many of Jesus' most familiar teachings—as well as some of the most enigmatic, difficult, and Utopian—and stands as his great ethical statement.

The Sermon on the Mount
(Matthew 5:1–7:27 NRSV)

When Jesus saw the crowds, he went up the mountain; and after he sat down, his disciples came to him. Then he began to speak, and taught them saying:

Blessed are the poor in spirit, for theirs is the kingdom of heaven.

Blessed are those who mourn, for they will be comforted.

Blessed are the meek, for they will inherit the earth.

Blessed are those who hunger and thirst for righteousness, for they will be filled.

Blessed are the merciful, for they will receive mercy.

Blessed are the pure in heart, for they will see God.

Blessed are the peacemakers, for they will be called children of God.

Blessed are those who are persecuted for righteousness' sake, for theirs is the kingdom of heaven.

Blessed are you when people revile you and persecute you and utter all kinds of evil against you falsely on my account. Rejoice and be glad, for your reward is great in heaven, for in the same way they persecuted the prophets who were before you.

You are the salt of the earth; but if salt has lost its taste, how can its saltiness be restored? It is no longer good for anything, but it is thrown out and trampled under foot.

You are the light of the world. A city built on a hill cannot be hid. No one after lighting a lamp puts it under the bushel basket, but on the lampstand, and it gives light to all in the house. In the same way, let your light shine before others, so that they may see your good works and give glory to your Father in heaven.

Do not think that I have come to abolish the law or the prophets; I have come not to abolish but to fulfill. For truly I tell you, until heaven and earth pass away, not one letter, not one stroke of a letter, will pass from the law until all is accomplished. Therefore, whoever breaks one of the least of these commandments, and teaches others to do the same, will be called least in the kingdom of heaven; but whoever does them and teaches them will be called great in the kingdom of heaven. For I tell you, unless your righteousness exceeds that of the scribes and Pharisees, you will never enter the kingdom of heaven.

You have heard that it was said to those of ancient times, "You shall not murder"; and "whoever murders shall be liable to judgment." But I say to you that if you are angry with a brother or sister, you will be liable to judgment; and if you insult a brother or sister, you will be liable to the council; and if you say, "You fool," you will be liable to the hell of fire. So when you are offering your gift at the altar, if you remember that your brother or sister has something against you, leave your gift there before the altar and go; first be reconciled to your brother or sister, and then come and offer your gift. Come to terms quickly with your accuser while you are on the way to court with him, or your accuser may hand you over to the guard and you will be thrown into prison. Truly I tell you, you will never get out until you have paid the last penny.

You heard that it was said, "You shall not commit adultery." But I say to you that everyone who looks at a woman with lust in his heart has already committed adultery with her in his heart. If your right eye causes you to sin, tear it out and throw it away; it is better for you to lose one of your members than for your whole body to be thrown into hell. And if your right hand causes you to sin, cut it off and throw it away; it is better for you to lose one of your members than for your whole body to go into hell.

It is also said, "Whoever divorces his wife, let him give her a certificate of divorce." But I say to you that anyone who divorces his wife, except on the ground of unchastity, causes her to commit adultery; and whoever marries a divorced woman commits adultery.

Again, you have heard that it was said to those of ancient times, "You shall not swear falsely, but carry out the vows you have made to the Lord." But I say to you, Do not swear at all, either by heaven, for it is the throne of God, or by the earth, for it his footstool, or by Jerusalem, for it is the city of the great King. And do not swear by your head, for you cannot make one hair white or black. Let your word be, "Yes, Yes" or "No, No"; anything more than this comes from the evil one.

You have heard that it was said, "An eye for an eye and a tooth for a tooth." But I say to you, Do not resist an evildoer. But if anyone strikes you on the right cheek, turn the other also; and if anyone wants to sue you and take your coat, give your cloak as well; and if anyone forces you to go one mile, go also the second mile. Give to everyone who begs from you, and do not refuse anyone who wants to borrow from you.

You have heard that it was said, "You shall love your neighbor and hate your enemy." But I say to you, Love your enemies and pray for those who persecute you, so that you may be children of your Father in heaven; for he makes his sun rise on the evil and on the good, he sends the rain on the righteous and the unrighteous. For if you love those who love you, what reward do you have? Do not even the tax collectors do the same? And if you greet only your brothers and sisters, what more are you doing than others? Do not even Gentiles do the same? Be perfect, therefore, as your heavenly Father is perfect.

Beware of practicing your piety before others in order to be seen by them; for then you have no reward from your Father in heaven.

So whenever you give alms, do not sound a trumpet before you, as the hypocrites do in the synagogues and in the streets, so that they may be praised by others. Truly I tell you, they have received their reward. But when you give alms, do not let your left hand know what your right hand is doing, so that your alms may be done in secret; and your Father who sees in secret will reward you.

And whenever you pray, do not be like the hypocrites; for they love to stand and pray in the synagogues and at the street corners, so that they may be seen by others. Truly I tell you, they have received their reward. But whenever you pray, go into your room and shut the door and pray to your Father who sees in secret; and your Father who sees in secret will reward you.

When you are praying, do not heap up empty phrases as the Gentiles do; for they think that they will be heard because of their many words. Do not be like them, for your Father knows what you need before you ask him.

Pray then in this way:

> Our Father in heaven
> hallowed be your name.
> Your kingdom come.
> Your will be done,
>   on earth as it is in heaven.
> Give us this day our daily
>   bread.
> And forgive us our debts,
>   as we have also forgiven
>   our debtors.
> And do not bring us to the time
>   of trial,
>   but rescue us from the
>   evil one.

[See Appendix 3 for other versions of the Lord's Prayer.]

For if you forgive others their trespasses, your heavenly Father will also forgive you; but if you do not forgive others, neither will your Father forgive your trespasses.

And whenever you fast, do not look dismal, like the hypocrites, for they disfigure their faces so as to show others that they are fasting. Truly I tell you, they have received their reward. But when you fast, put oil on your head and wash your face, so that your fasting may be seen not by others but by your Father who is in secret; and your Father who sees in secret will reward you.

Do not store up for yourselves treasures on earth, where moth and rust consume and where the thieves break in and steal; but store up for yourselves treasures in heaven, where neither moth nor rust consumes and where thieves do not break in and steal. For where your treasure is, there your heart will be also.

The eye is the lamp of the body. So, if your eye is healthy, your whole body will be full of light; but if your eye is unhealthy, your whole body will be full of darkness. If then the light in you is darkness, how great is the darkness!

No one can serve two masters; for a slave will either hate the one and love the other, or be devoted to the one and despise the other. You cannot serve God and wealth.

Therefore I tell you, do not worry about your life, what you will eat or what you will drink, or about your body, what you will wear. Is not life more than food, and the body more than clothing? Look at the birds of the air; they neither sow nor reap nor gather into barns, and yet your heavenly Father feeds them. Are you not of more value than they? And can any of you by worrying add a single hour to your span of life? And why do you worry about clothing? Consider the lilies of the field, how they grow; they neither toil nor spin, yet I tell you, even Solomon in all his glory was not clothed like one of these. But if God so clothes the grass of the field, which is alive today and tomorrow is thrown into the oven, will he not much more clothe you—you of little faith? Therefore do not worry, saying, "What will we eat?" or "What will we drink?" "What will we wear?" For it is the Gentiles who strive for all these things; and indeed your heavenly Father knows that you need all these things. But strive first for the kingdom of God and his righteousness, and all these things will be given unto you.

So do not worry about tomorrow, for tomorrow will bring worries of its own. Today's trouble is enough for today.

Do not judge, so that you may not be judged. For with the judgment you make you will be judged, and the measure you give will be the measure you get. Why do you see the speck in your neighbor's eye, but do not notice the log in your own eye? Or how can you say to your neighbor, "Let me take the speck out of your eye," while the log is in your own eye? You hypocrite, first take the log out of your own eye, and then you will see clearly to take the speck out of your neighbor's eye.

Do not give what is holy to dogs; and do not throw your pearls before swine, or they will trample them under foot and turn and maul you.

Ask, and it will be given you; knock, and the door will be opened for you. For everyone who asks receives, and everyone who knocks, the door will be opened. Is there one among you who, if your child asks for bread, will give a stone? Or if the child asks for a fish, will give a snake? If you then, who are evil, know how to give good gifts to your children, how much more will your Father in heaven give good things to those who ask him!

In everything do to others as you would have them do to you; for this is the law and the prophets.

Enter through the narrow gate; for the gate is wide and the road is easy that leads to destruction, and there are many who take it. For the gate is narrow and the road is hard that leads to life, and there are few who find it.

Beware of false prophets, who come to you in sheep's clothing but inwardly are ravenous wolves. You will know them by their fruits. Are grapes gathered from thorns, or figs from thistles? In the same way, every good tree bears good fruit, but the bad tree bears bad fruit. A good tree cannot bear bad fruit, nor can a bad tree bear good fruit. Every tree that does not bear good fruit is cut down and thrown into the fire. Thus you will know them by their fruits.

Not everyone who says to me, "Lord, Lord," will enter the kingdom of heaven, but only the one who does the will of my Father in heaven. On that day many will say to me, "Lord, Lord, did we not prophesy in your name, and cast out demons in your name, and do many deeds of power in your name?" Then I will declare to them, "I never knew you, go away from me, you evil-doers."

Everyone then who hears these words of mine and acts on them will be like a wise man who built his house on a rock. The rain fell, the floods came, and the winds blew and beat on that house, but it did not fall, because it had been founded on rock. And everyone who hears these words of mine and does not act on them will be like a foolish man who built his house on sand. The rain fell, and the floods came, and the winds blew and beat against that house, and it fell—and great was its fall!

Now when Jesus had finished saying these things, the crowds were astounded at his teaching, for he taught them as one having authority, and not as their scribes.

The Sermon on the Mount includes many of Jesus' most familiar words which, in some ways, constituted a new and more ethically rigorous code than even the Mosaic Law prescribed. In the Sermon on the Mount and elsewhere in his teachings, Jesus was laying down a new law that demanded more of believers: legally, ethically, and spiritually. The following section presents a brief selection of some Jesus' most difficult teachings, which make the point, "Piety Is Easy—Christianity Is Hard."

• "Whosoever looketh on a woman to lust after her hath committed adultery with her already in his heart. . . . And if thy right eye offend thee, pluck it out, and cast it from thee: for it is profitable for thee that one of thy members should perish, and not that thy whole body should be cast into hell. And if thy right hand offend thee, cut it off." (Matt. 5:28–30 KJV)

This is the "Jimmy Carter" verse. In a famous interview with *Playboy* magazine when he was running for President in 1976, Carter said he had committed adultery many times, taking this verse as his inspiration.

• "You have heard that it was said, 'An eye for an eye and a tooth for a tooth.' But I say to you, Do not resist an evildoer. But if anyone strikes you on the right cheek, turn the other also; and if anyone wants to sue you and take your coat, give your cloak as well; and if anyone forces you to go one mile, go also the second mile. Give to everyone who begs from you, and do not refuse anyone who wants to borrow from you." (Matt. 5:38–42)

• "Love your enemies, and pray for those who persecute you, so that you may be children of your Father in heaven." (Matt. 5:44–45)

• "Do not judge, so that you may not be judged. For with the judgment you make will you be judged, and the measure you give will be the measure you get." (Matt. 7:1–2)

• "In everything do to others as you would have them do to you; for this is the law and the prophets." (Matt. 7:12)

• "Follow me, and let the dead bury their own dead." (Matt. 8:22)

• "Do not think that I have to come to bring peace to the earth; I have not come to bring peace, but a sword. . . . Whoever loves father or mother more than me is not worthy of me; and whoever loves son or daughter more than me is not worthy of me; and whoever does not take up the cross and follow me is not worthy of me." (Matt 10:34, 37–38)

While the reference to the "sword" may have fired up zealous followers who thought Jesus was actually going to lead a revolt against Rome, this was a metaphorical sword, one that would sever the "old ties." Jesus was telling his disciples that his mission and theirs was not going to be a pleasant one; it demanded unconditional acceptance of his words and complete rejection of their past lives.

• "It is easier for a camel to go through the eye of a needle than for a rich man to enter the kingdom of God." (Matt. 19:24)

How does a camel fit through a needle's eye?

Jesus often said challenging, demanding things. He said confusing things. He even said contradictory things. And sometimes he said puzzling things. This famous verse about the needle's eye is one that many people find puzzling. It was spoken to a wealthy young man who asked Jesus what he needed to do to gain eternal life. The young man assured Jesus that he had kept all the commandments and obeyed all the laws. Jesus told him to sell everything, give away the money, and follow him. The rich young man couldn't do it and left grieving. That's when Jesus told his disciples about the camel and the needle's eye.

A camel, of course, would have been familiar to all the disciples. A needle, perhaps for a tent-maker, was also commonplace. So Jesus was using a hyperbole—an outrageous exaggeration for the idea of something very large being able to get through something small. It made for a curious but understandable image.

There is another simpler view of Jesus' words. The Greek word for "camel" is very similar to the word for "cable," and some early Bible texts used "cable," which can also be translated as "rope." Without changing the essential point, Jesus could have been talking about someone trying to thread a thick piece of rope through a needle hole. Either way—camel or cable—Jesus was saying this wasn't easy.

Where does that leave the rich? Jesus' view of wealth and material goods makes many Christians uncomfortable. He demanded that his disciples give everything away, and they did. Jesus had higher praise for a poor widow who gave to charity her few small coins, all she had, than he did for the wealthy who gave but could afford to give more. Discussing the issue of wealth and the Bible in his bestselling biblical study, *The Good Book,* the Reverend Peter Gomes writes, "Wealth is not what you have; wealth is what you have been given that enables you to give to others."

Luke expresses this sentiment in another memorable verse: "From everyone to whom much has been given, much will be required; and from one to whom much has been entrusted, even more will be expected." (Luke 12:48)

Mary Magdalene: naughty or nice?

The name "Mary," derived from the Greek form of the common Hebrew Miriam, the name of the sister of Moses, makes several New Testament appearances, sometimes creating a bit of confusion over which Mary is which. Jesus' mother Mary makes a few cameos in the Gospels, and she does appear in John at the time of her son's death. Luke tells the story of another Mary, one of two sisters. When Jesus comes to their house, this Mary sits at Jesus' feet and listens to him teach. Her sister Martha performs the usual domestic role of getting the New Testament version of "chips and dip" ready. Martha gets a little miffed because she's working and Mary's sitting. When she lets Jesus know that her sister should be in the kitchen, he cuts Martha short and says that Mary has "chosen the better part" in listening to him speak. Occasionally Jesus' divinity slipped past his humility.

The third significant Mary is usually called Mary Magdalene but is more appropriately named Mary of Magdala, a town near Tiberias (now in Israel). Many people have grown up with the traditional view that she was a prostitute or an adulteress. In the film *The Greatest Story Ever Told*, she is the adulteress whom Jesus saves from stoning. A romantic interest between this Mary and Jesus has also been suggested. For instance, she is the Mary who sings "I Don't Know How to Love Him" in Andrew Lloyd Webber's *Jesus Christ Superstar*. In the film *The Last Temptation of Christ*, she is portrayed provocatively and unambiguously as a prostitute who knows and loves Jesus. The Gnostic Gospels, as mentioned earlier, suggested that Jesus kissed Mary Magdalene passionately, so that gossip must have been making the rounds in early Christianity. Later Christian traditions identified Mary Magdalene as the "sinning woman," presumably a prostitute but possibly an adulteress, described as having anointed Jesus' feet in

Luke 7:37–38. She was also mistakenly linked with the Mary, the sister of Martha, who also anoints Jesus in John 12:3.

If she had a good lawyer, Mary of Magdala could have sued for libel. The images of her as prostitute, adulteress, sinner, or Jesus' girlfriend all reflect either wishful thinking or serious misreadings. Perhaps because Jesus' mother was a "good" Mary, early church leaders wanted to create a "bad" Mary who was saved by Jesus. But the biblical references to Mary of Magdala just don't bear out her wanton image. Luke described Mary of Magdala as one of seven women whom Jesus healed by casting out "demons." She then joined the group of devoted women followers who supported Jesus in his ministry. Her place among the followers was certainly somewhat special, as she is one of the women who goes to Jesus' tomb to tend his body after he died and Jesus appears to Mary specifically after his resurrection.

Did Jesus look down on women?

Though cast in supporting roles in the Gospels, women like Mary of Magdala, Martha, and Mary, the sister of Lazarus, defy the concept, etched into dogma by the church, that women were second-class citizens to Jesus. A woman's place in first-century Jewish society was clearly limited. In the time of Jesus, a woman was "betrothed" or "espoused"—although "bought" might be a better term—at the age of twelve or fourteen. With little more status than a slave, she was meant to have children and maintain the proper dietary laws at home. School was for boys, of course, and women could only enter so far into the temple or synagogues. A woman could not enter a temple during times of "uncleanness," whether her menstrual period or the weeks following the birth of a child. Women had no rights of possession, and though they could sue for divorce, the husband had to grant it.

But women frequently played a central role in Jesus' life and teaching. In one small but rather striking episode told in Mark and Matthew, Jesus ignores a Canaanite woman who asks him to heal her child. Initially he responds by saying that he was sent to tend the "lost sheep of Israel" and rather dismissively and callously tells her, "It is not fair to take the children's food and throw it to the dogs." He means that his message is meant for Jews, not Gentiles; that was a sentiment he expressed in the early Gospels, and there are often disparaging references to Gentiles. But the woman brings Jesus up short when she tells him that even dogs eat the scraps that fall from the table. Realizing that a Gentile can accept his message, Jesus says, "Great is your faith" and he heals her daughter.

There are several other women who play key roles in the Gospels, and Jesus is often depicted talking with women who were outcasts of one kind or another. In a memorable scene recorded in John, he challenges a crowd of people ready to stone an adulteress. "Let him who is without sin cast the first stone," Jesus says, and the crowd sheepishly departs.

Besides the three Marys, Luke also singles out a Joanna and a Susanna who supported and fed Jesus and the disciples. As later biblical evidence from Acts and Paul's letters shows, women in the early church were far from the "mopping, shopping, and dropping" role that Jewish society as a whole, not Jesus, had given them. Although no women were among the twelve disciples, Jesus treated women as equal to men in other respects, including those women who were on the fringes of society. In the Gospels, several women, including Mary Magdalene, were the chief witnesses to Jesus' resurrection. And in the early church, women served as prophets, church leaders, deacons, and missionaries. A reasonable, objective reading of the New Testament—which takes into account the social restrictions placed on women of the first century—goes a long way in refuting the notion of subservience of women in traditional Christianity. But centuries of male-dominated church hierarchy simply placed women in the second class in Christianity.

What's so "Good" about the "Good Samaritan"?

This is how Jesus told the story, exclusive to Luke. A man was going from Jerusalem to Jericho when thieves beat him, robbed him, and left him for dead. A priest, one of the highest religious officials in Judaism, and a Levite, a priest's assistant, both passed by the body on the other side of the road. They either acted out of strict observance of the Jews' purity laws against touching blood, or simple callousness. Then a Samaritan came by, put the injured man on his donkey, tended his wounds, and took him to an inn, where he paid for his care. Jesus, who was being quizzed by several lawyers who wanted to "test" him, asked one lawyer which of these three was the real neighbor. When told "The one who showed him mercy," Jesus said, "Go and do likewise."

What was so special about the story? Samaritans did not have a great reputation among Jews. They were not good neighbors. The Jews and Samaritans had a long and unhappy history. The Samaritans had first come into the land when the Assyrians conquered Israel. An offshoot sect, they followed the Books of Moses but did not treat the rest of the Hebrew scriptures as sacred, and there was bad blood between the groups. To give some sense of how Jewish people then would have viewed a story with a Samaritan as the good guy, a modern equivalent might be called "The Good Palestinian Terrorist."

Jesus' message was simple. Blind obedience to the Law of Moses and strict adherence to religious rules, such as avoiding blood for the sake of "purity," were meaningless motions when unaccompanied by merciful actions toward the needy. In making a Samaritan the hero of his parable, Jesus also underscored his acceptance of the outcasts of Jewish society, an outlook that included the lepers, crazies, sinners, tax collectors, and other "losers" who surrounded him and to whom he actively ministered.

Jesus' use of parables—there are about thirty of them; some appear in all four Gospels, others appear in only one—like that of the Good Samaritan was a characteristic teaching tool. He often used simple stories to make his point. Occasionally these "parables" were not stories but comparisons, riddles, and metaphors, some of them quite complex. Jesus often used these parables not simply to make a point but more importantly to get his followers to think, an activity that later church leaders have not pursued as vigorously.

THE PARABLES OF JESUS

One of Jesus' key teaching methods was speaking in parables, or short stories from everyday life that he used to illustrate a spiritual message. These parables could be a line or two of extended metaphor, such as this description of the kingdom of heaven found in Matthew: "like a merchant in search of fine pearls; on finding one pearl of great value, he went and sold all that he had and bought it." Or they might be more complex stories such as those of the "Prodigal Son" and the "Good Samaritan." While many of Jesus' parables contained very simple moral lessons, others were more Zen-like and obscure. His disciples could sometimes seem very thickheaded about getting the point of them, and Jesus even shook his head once or twice over his slow students. After Jesus told the disciples the parable of the Sower (see below) in Mark, the disciples asked Jesus to explain it to them. "Do you not understand this parable?" Jesus asks them. "Then how will you understand all the parables?"

The parables have a long history of interpretation. In medieval times, they were overlaid with levels of heavy allegorical symbolism, a style of interpretation no longer in vogue. However, that goes to show that people have always brought their own perspective to the parables and to the Bible. There are more than thirty parables in the Gospels, although John does not record any of them. (The Gospel[s] in which each of the following parables can be found is indicated.)

• The Sower: A man sows seeds. Some fall on the path and are eaten by birds; some fall on rocky ground and wither away; others fall in the midst of thorns and are choked; but some fall on good soil and bring forth great crops. The seeds in this parable are the word of God and the soils are the various ways people respond to Jesus' teaching. (Matt., Mark, Luke)

• The Mustard Seed: The kingdom of God is like the mustard seed, the smallest of seeds, but when full grown becomes a great tree. (Matt., Mark, Luke)

• Evil Tenants: A landowner rents out his land to tenants who don't pay and then kill the men sent to collect the rent. The landowner will eventually destroy the tenants. This parable was told to the priests and scribes to illustrate how they were rejecting Jesus. (Matt., Mark, Luke)

• The Divided House: "Every kingdom divided against itself is laid waste, and no city or house divided against itself will stand." (Matt. 12:25, Mark 3:23) Jesus said this after he was accused of casting out demons using the power of the Devil. Jesus was saying that it was impossible to cast out Satan by the power of Satan. In a more practical sense, the verse was paraphrased by Abraham Lincoln ("A house divided against itself cannot stand") in 1858, before the American Civil War, to mean that a divided nation would not last.

• The Fig Tree: When a fig tree blossoms, it is evident what the season is. Jesus tells the disciples that they should look at the signs—meaning himself and his works—that indicated the kingdom of God is also near. (Matt., Mark, Luke)

• Yeast: "The kingdom of heaven is like yeast." God's word is like yeast, which when added to flour allows it to rise into bread. (Matt., Luke)

• The Marriage Feast: The two versions of this parable diverge. In Matthew's version a king gives a wedding feast but all the invited guests beg off for different reasons, so the king sends troops to kill the reluctant guests. (This was a prophetic parable aimed at those who rejected Jesus and referred to the destruction of Jerusalem in 70 CE by the Romans.) Then servants bring in passersby off the streets to fill the wedding hall and when the king sees one of the guests does not have on the proper clothing, he is thrown out and Jesus offers a puzzling moral: "For many are called but few are chosen." Does that mean heaven has a dress code? This has been a tricky one for theologians. The guest was pulled off the streets. Why should he have on the appropriate clothes? Some scholars have suggested that this aspect of the wedding story was a separate parable, which seems like a cop-out. Another interpretation is that even somebody who comes to the feast— "heaven"—needs to come in the right spirit—represented in the parable as a suitable garment. This is an implicit recognition that salvation is not going to be universal. Only those who pay attention to the call will be "chosen."

In Luke, the story is a little more straightforward. The guests who refuse the invitation are those who reject God's summons through Jesus. They too were "called" but rejected the summons and won't be "chosen."

• The Lost Sheep: A shepherd with a hundred sheep will still go and look for the one that is lost. God also wants to bring the lost sheep back to the flock and celebrates when he finds the lost sheep. (Matt., Luke)

• Wise and Foolish Builders: People who hear Jesus and listen are like the wise man who builds his house on rock; the house will withstand the rain and wind. Those who don't listen are like the foolish man who builds his house on sand. That house will not stand. (Matt., Luke)

• The Wise and Foolish Servants: A master leaves his servants alone. One good servant is at work when the master returns. Another gets drunk and beats the other servants. When the master returns unexpectedly, he gives the bad servant a beating. After this parable, Luke comments: "From everyone to whom much has been given, much will be required." (Matt., Luke)

• The Talents: A master gives his slaves varying amounts of money and goes away. On his return, some have invested the "talents" they were given and prospered, while one has simply stored his away for safekeeping. The master is angry at the last for failing to increase the value of what he had been given. (Matt., Luke)

• Wheat and Weeds: When a farmer plants seeds, weeds still sprout up. He lets the weeds grow until harvest time. This is generally viewed as a parable of the Last Judgment, when good and evil will be separated like weeds from the wheat at the harvest. (Matt.)

• Hidden Treasure: The kingdom of heaven is like a hidden treasure. If someone finds it in a field, they should sell everything and go and buy the whole field. (Matt.)

• The Great Net: A net pulls in all kinds of fish, some good, some bad. At the judgment, the angels will separate the righteous from the evil, like good and bad fish in the net. (Matt.)

• The Rich Fool: A wealthy farmer stored up his grain and then relaxed and made merry but died that night. Moral: "So it is with those who store up treasure for themselves but are not rich toward God." (Luke)

• The Secret Seed: The kingdom of God is like a seed that grows overnight and is then harvested. People may not understand how such a thing can happen but should recognize and appreciate the value of this miracle. (Mark)

• The Unforgiving Servant: A servant who owes money is forgiven by his king. But then the same servant tells another servant who owes him money to pay up, and has him thrown into debtor's prison. When the king hears this, he has the first servant punished. The moral: "So my heavenly Father will also do to every one of you, if you do not forgive your brother or sister from your heart." (Matt.)

• The Wise and Foolish Bridesmaids: One group of foolish bridesmaids squanders their chance to greet the groom as he comes for his bride and misses the wedding banquet. Moral: Stay on your toes. You don't know when the kingdom of God is coming. (Matt.)

• The Sheep and the Goats: At the Last Judgment, the "Son of Man" will separate the people as a shepherd separates the sheep from the goats.

• The Lost Coin: A woman who loses a coin searches for it, then celebrates when she finds it. Moral: "There will be more joy in heaven over one sinner who repents than over ninety-nine persons who need no repentance." (Luke)

• The Prodigal Son: A young man takes his inheritance and squanders it so he is forced to take work feeding pigs. He decides to go home and is welcomed by his father. His older brother is annoyed that his father welcomes this unworthy son. The father explains: "Son, you were always with me and all that is mine is yours. But we had to celebrate and rejoice, because this brother of yours was dead and has come to life, he was lost and has been found." A parable of God's loving forgiveness. (Luke)

• The Pharisee and the Tax Collector: A Pharisee goes to pray and thanks God he is not a sinner like other people. A tax collector prays for mercy because he is a sinner. The moral: "All who exalt themselves will be humbled and all who humble themselves will be exalted." (Luke)

What's so bad about Pharisees?

The parable of the "Good Samaritan" contained more than a note of disdain for devout Jews who put the Law above morality. This was a key theme in Jesus' teaching. Obedience to laws without a sense of mercy was empty of spiritual value. Several times, Jesus quoted the prophets who had said, "God desires mercy more than sacrifice."

Jesus reserved a special anger for those he called the "scribes and Pharisees," a group that also might be loosely called "lawyers." Matthew's favorite term for Pharisees is "hypocrites," a term in Greek that was applied to actors, or people who were pretenders. In other words, they were people who said one thing and did another.

In the New Testament, scribes and Pharisees are virtually indistinguishable. Many of Jesus' disputes with the scribes and Pharisees were over points of law and took the form of rabbinical argument, a time-honored tradition in Judaism. Jesus was often depicted as being challenged aggressively by these men on such points as Sabbath observance, divorce, and payment of taxes to Rome. A sect that created the extensive body of Jewish oral teachings that applied Mosaic Laws to contemporary situations, the Pharisees believed in strict adherence to the ritual laws of purity. Jesus condemned some Pharisees for their concern with petty details at the expense of the Law's true purpose as he saw it. In the most hypocritical of these Pharisees, Jesus saw a group of men more interested in the prestige and acclaim of their position than in their spiritual salvation. Still, much of Jesus' own teaching falls in line with that of the Pharisees, and the New Testament view of Pharisees is not one-sided. Jesus is depicted eating in the home of one Pharisee, Simon. One of the greatest of all Jewish rabbis, Hillel, was a Pharisee and he formulated a "negative" version of the Golden Rule: "What is hateful to you do not do to your neighbor. That is the whole Torah. The rest is just commentary." Many historians and scholars have speculated that Jesus might have been a student of Hillel, although there is no biblical evidence to support that theory. But most likely, Jesus would have been familiar with Hillel's teachings, and he may have later rephrased or recast the "Golden Rule" in the familiar form used in the Sermon on the Mount.

The Pharisees were one of several Jewish groups on the Jerusalem scene during the first century, a period in which intense opposition to Roman rule occasionally boiled over into open rebellion. Many Jews of this period believed that the time was ripe for the Messiah's arrival. In the fervor of nationalism, they expected a Savior in the mold of King David, a warrior-king who would lead a military uprising against the Romans, restoring the glory of ancient Israel. A Nazarean carpenter surrounded by fishermen, tax collectors, and lepers, preaching "turn the other cheek," did not fit the bill for the most militant Jews of the day.

Jesus' followers were not the only ones making claims that he was the Messiah. Other nationalistic leaders tried to claim Messiahship in their attempts to gain a following. It is against this turbulent backdrop of contending Jewish groups—some accommodating toward Rome, others looking to rebel—that the last days of Jesus' life must be set. Besides the Pharisees, the other key Jewish groups of this period included:

Sadducees—The "righteous ones" in Hebrew, they were the religiously and politically conservative elite of Jewish society and held a majority of seats in the Jewish council called the Sanhedrin. They also largely controlled Temple matters, and were often at odds with the Pharisees because they adhered to strict written law as opposed to the oral laws devised by the Pharisees.

Herodians—A little-known group that owed allegiance to the Roman-appointed kings descended from Herod.

Zealots—This was not so much a single group, but a catch-all term for a variety of fanatical rebel bands dedicated to the overthrow of the Romans and their Jewish collaborators. The first of them was organized in about 6 CE, and the Zealots included a group of assassins called the Sicarii, named for the short daggers they carried.

Essenes—This somewhat obscure group led a communal, monastic life in the desert near the Dead Sea, removed from Jerusalem because they rejected Temple practices such as sacrifice. Although not all Essenes lived at the Qumran settlement, the group made up the community that presumably produced the Dead Sea Scrolls. The celibate Essenes were avid baptists who looked to a coming war between the forces of "dark and light," asserting that they were "preparing the way of the Lord." Phrases such as these have led some scholars to connect John the Baptist and Jesus to the Essene community. While Jesus may have been influenced by the Essenes, or was reacting to their teachings, he was not one of them. The Essenes excluded women, the handicapped, and the diseased, all of whom Jesus openly welcomed in his ministry. In direct opposition to Jesus' call to love one's enemies, the Essenes also stressed hatred of enemies.

Why was Jesus so popular?

There was no CNN. He didn't have *Oprah* or *Today*. No newspapers, telegraphs, telephones. No Internet. No information superhighway. In fact, no highways at all. Yes, there were Roman roads, but they were paved with rough stones. Camels, donkeys, and horse carts without radial tires were about the best you could expect for getting around. So word moved slowly in first-century Palestine. But somehow, the word of Jesus and his disciples spread. Like the proverbial wildfire. From the obscure village of Nazareth, an out-of-the-way backwater, word of Jesus and his disciples made the rounds of the Galilean countryside. In almost no time, Jesus' fame swept the country and threatened the powerful. "Word of mouth" was all it took. Eventually, the words changed the world.

And what fueled that "word of mouth"? For three years, Jesus and the Twelve have been traveling, teaching, healing—and working wonders. In John, Jesus sets a new standard for wedding guests when he performs his first miracle, turning water into wine at a wedding feast. Others claimed he calmed a storm that came up on the Sea of Galilee and even walked across the water. He had cured cripples, lepers, and the blind. As news of Jesus' miracles as a healer spread his fame around Judea, growing crowds gathered to see and hear him wherever he went. We don't have ratings or polls to gauge his popularity, but he was attracting rock-concert-sized audiences large enough to worry the Jewish authorities.

Contrary to popular notions or misimpressions of the period in Judea, Jesus was not alone in these healing works. Just as other men claimed Messiahship to attract political followers, numerous wonder-workers and healers wandered the Roman empire in that day. Jesus even referred to others who were healing in his name. The Jewish Talmud discusses several wonder-working rabbis of

Jesus' time. But none made the claim that Jesus' followers made: that he had the ability to raise the dead and had done so on three occasions, with witnesses.

When the daughter of a local religious leader was thought to be dead, Jesus spoke to her, saying *"Talitha cum"* in Aramaic, for "Little girl, get up." She rose and Jesus said she wasn't dead, just sleeping, even though others had examined her and said she was dead. In another resurrection, Jesus restored a widow's son to life, and the Jews of his time would have made the connection to similar miracles performed by the Hebrew prophets, Elijah and Elisha. And when Jesus raised Lazarus, who had been dead for four days, he made it clear that he was more than just a wandering wonder-worker. He told Lazarus's sister Martha: "I am the resurrection and the life. Those who believe in me, even though they die, will live and everyone who believes in me will never die." (John 11: 24–26)

Jesus' growing renown was making some Jewish leaders a little uncomfortable. After Jesus raised Lazarus, one Pharisee told another, "You see, you can do nothing. Look, the whole world has gone after him!"

THE MIRACLES OF JESUS

Miracles are as old as, well, Creation.

In the New Testament, as in the Hebrew scriptures, miracles demonstrate God's hand intervening in earthly affairs in extraordinary ways. But New Testament miracles tend to be "personal" miracles, as opposed to miracles affecting the entire nation, such as the Plagues on Egypt or the crossing of the Sea of Reeds and the destruction of the Egyptian army in Exodus.

Apart from his own miraculous birth and resurrection, and the Transfiguration (discussed in the text), Jesus performed more than thirty-five miracles in the Gospels. They fall into three broad categories: Miraculous Feedings; Nature Miracles; and the largest group, Healings, Resurrections, and Exorcisms. This is a list of Jesus' miracles and where they occur in the Gospels:

MIRACLE	MATTHEW	MARK	LUKE	JOHN

• "Four-Gospel" Miracles

MIRACLE	MATTHEW	MARK	LUKE	JOHN
Feeding the five thousand	14:13	6:30	9:10	6:1

Five loaves and two fish feed a crowd of five thousand who had come to see Jesus heal the sick.

• "Three-Gospel" Miracles

MIRACLE	MATTHEW	MARK	LUKE
A leper is cleansed	8:2	1:40	5:12
Peter's feverish mother-in-law is healed	8:14	1:30	4:38
Many possessed people are healed one evening	8:16	1:32	4:40

An interesting footnote to this act of healing is that the demons that Jesus casts out recognize that he is the Messiah and try to address Jesus but Jesus won't listen.

Calming the stormy Sea of Galilee	8:23	4:35	8:22
Demons are cast into a herd of pigs	8:28	5:1	8:26

In this exorcism, Jesus transfers demonic spirits from people into a herd of pigs, "unclean animals," that then drown themselves. Matthew reports that there are two "demoniacs"; in Mark and Luke, there is a single possessed man named "Legion."

A paralytic man is healed	9:2	2:3	5:18
The daughter of Jairus, a religious leader, is raised	9:18	5:35	8:40

This is Jesus' first recorded resurrection.

A woman who had hemorrhages for twelve years is healed	9:20	5:25	8:43

Since blood was considered a sign of impurity, this healing act was especially remarkable to Jews. This woman simply touched the hem of Jesus' garment without his knowledge, but was still healed because she had faith.

continued

MIRACLE	MATTHEW	MARK	LUKE	JOHN
A man's withered hand is healed	12:9	3:1	6:6	

Jesus healed this man's hand on the Sabbath, antagonizing some of the Pharisees. When they confronted him, Jesus asked them, "Is it lawful to do good or to do harm on the sabbath, to save life or destroy it?"

Walking on the water of the Sea of Galilee	14:25	6:48		6:19
An epileptic boy healed	17:14	9:17	9:38	
Blind men healed	20:30	10:46	18:35	

• "Two-Gospel" Miracles

A Roman centurion's slave is healed	8:5		7:1	
A Gentile woman's daughter is healed	15:21	7:24		

When first asked to heal this woman's daughter, Jesus was dismissive because she was a Gentile. But she convinces Jesus that she has faith in him and he responds.

Feeding the four thousand	15:32	8:1		

In this second account of feeding large numbers of people, Jesus takes seven loaves and a few small fish to feed four thousand people.

A fig tree is cursed and withers	21:18	11:12		

This is an odd, somewhat vindictive "miracle" account. When Jesus goes to pick a fig from a tree, he sees that the tree has no fruit. Even though the tree is bare because it is out of season, Jesus curses the tree and it withers. This "tree" miracle has been interpreted as symbolic of the people of Jerusalem who, in rejecting Jesus as the Messiah, "did not bear fruit" and are doomed to "wither" under Roman conquest.

An unclean spirit is cast out		1:23	4:33	

• "One Gospel" Miracles

A demon-possessed mute is healed	9:32			

MIRACLE	MATTHEW	MARK	LUKE	JOHN

When Jesus heals this man, he is accused of casting out demons through the use of demonic powers.

Two blind men are healed	9:27			
The temple tax found in a fish's mouth	17:24			

When challenged to pay the required tax for the temple, Jesus gets a coin from the mouth of a fish caught by Peter.

A deaf mute is healed		7:31		

Jesus heals a deaf mute simply by speaking the Aramaic word Ephphatha *("Be opened").*

A blind paralytic is healed		8:22		
The unexpected catch of fish			5:1	

When Jesus first goes to recruit the disciples who are fishing in the Sea of Galilee, he fills their nets with more fish than the nets can hold.

A widow's son is raised from the dead at Nain			7:11	

The raising of this boy is Jesus' second recorded act of resurrection.

A crippled woman is healed			13:11	
A man with dropsy is cured			14:1	
Ten lepers are cured			17:11	

Of the ten lepers, only one, a Samaritan, shows gratitude.

Restoring a severed ear			22:51	

While the other Gospels report that a man's ear was severed by one of the disciples at the time of Jesus' arrest, only Luke reports that Jesus restored the man's ear.

Turning water into wine at Cana				2:1
A royal official's son is cured				4:46
An infirm man is healed at Bethesda				5:1

continued

MIRACLE	MATTHEW	MARK	LUKE	JOHN
A man born blind is cured				9:1

In this case, Jesus spat onto the ground, made mud from his saliva, and applied it to the man's eyes.

| Raising of Lazarus | | | | 11:43 |

Lazarus, a follower of Jesus, was raised four days after he died; it was thought that the soul departed the body after three days.

| The second catch of fish | | | | 21:1 |

After his resurrection, Jesus appears to some disciples and helps them bring in a great catch of fish after they had caught nothing all night long.

BIBLICAL VOICES

Six days later, Jesus took with him Peter and James and John, and led them up a high mountain apart, by themselves. And he was transfigured before them, and his clothes became dazzling white, such as no one on earth could bleach them. And there appeared to them Elijah with Moses, who were talking with Jesus. Then Peter said to Jesus, "Rabbi, it is good for us to be here; let us make three dwellings, one for you, one for Moses and one for Elijah." He did not know what to say, for they were terrified. Then a cloud overshadowed them, and from the cloud there came a voice, "This is my Son, the Beloved; listen to him!" Suddenly when they looked around, they saw no one with them any more, but only Jesus. (Mark 9:2–8)

What is a Transfiguration?

As Jesus prepared to travel to Jerusalem for the Passover and the climax of his life and ministry, three of the Gospels recount an extraordinary event in which he takes three trusted disciples up a mountain. While the disciples watched, Jesus was mystically miraculously "transfigured," as his physical being was transformed and the figures of Moses and Elijah, the two great prophets of Judaism, stood beside him. The disciples who witnessed this were amazed at this vision and then heard the voice of God speaking directly above them, saying Jesus was God's Beloved Son. It was one of only two times—the other being at Jesus' baptism—in which such a heavenly voice is heard in the Gospels. The accounts all report that Jesus' face shone, recalling the expression on Moses' face when he encountered God on Mount Sinai in Exodus, again cementing the connection between Jesus and Moses for his Jewish followers. The Greek word translated as "transfigure" is *metamorphé*, "to change into another form."

BIBLICAL VOICES

As he came near and saw the city he wept over it, saying, "If you, even you, had only recognized on this day the things that make for peace! But now they are hidden from your eyes. Indeed the days will come upon you, when your enemies will set up ramparts around you and surround you, and hem you in on every side. They will crush you to the ground, you and your children within you, and they will not leave within you one stone upon another; because you did not recognize the time of your visitation from God."

Then he entered the temple and began to drive out those who were selling things there. . . . Every day he was teaching in the temple. The chief priests, the scribes, and the leaders of the people kept looking for a way to kill him; but they did not find anything they could do, for all the people were spellbound by what they heard. (Luke 19:41–48)

PLOT SUMMARY: JESUS, THE FINAL DAYS

Jesus and the disciples go to Jerusalem for the Passover and again the Gospel accounts conflict on numerous points. The first three Gospels treat this as Jesus' first visit to the city, apart from the childhood visit recorded by Luke. But in John, he makes a total of five trips to the city. Jesus sends two disciples ahead to secure a room and bring back a colt for him to ride, again in fulfillment of a Hebrew prophecy. As Jesus enters the city, some of the people cheer him, laying their cloaks and palm branches on the road as he enters the city and calling him the Messiah. This triumphal entry is celebrated by Christians on Palm Sunday. Jesus' growing notoriety, and the notion that more people were coming to view him as the promised Messiah of the Hebrew scriptures, was also creating enemies. While some Jewish leaders saw him as a false prophet, others viewed Jesus as a danger. He might either threaten their own power or provoke a severe and potentially devastating Roman suppression if the Romans detected any hint of rebellion, especially in the crowded Jerusalem of Passover week.

Again conflicting with John, the first three Gospels report that Jesus next went to the Temple. Outraged at the sight of merchants and money changers doing such a brisk business there, he chases them out, furiously overturning their tables and driving the traders out with a whip. These traders sold animals for the ritual sacrifices and exchanged the various coins of pilgrims for locally minted money. Their stalls were placed in the Temple's outer Court of the Gentiles and must have had the chaotic feel of a Middle Eastern bazaar. The actual sacrifice of these animals was performed within the Temple. In another discrepancy, John places this "cleansing of the temple" at the beginning of Jesus' ministry instead of during the last week of his life. This violent assault on the lucrative Temple merchants would have alienated the Temple authorities, who were doing a healthy cash business, and, coming so soon after Jesus' provocative triumphal entry into the city, probably challenged Roman authority, setting in motion the events leading to Jesus' arrest.

BIBLICAL VOICES
Now before the festival of Passover, Jesus knew that his hour had come to depart from this world and go to the Father.

Having loved his own who were in the world, he loved them to the end. The devil had already put it into the heart of Judas son of Simon Iscariot to betray him and during supper Jesus, knowing that the Father had given all things into his hands, and that he had come from God and was going to God, got up from the table, took off his outer robe, and tied a towel around himself. Then he poured water into a basin and began to wash the disciples' feet and to wipe them with the towel that was tied around him. He came to Simon Peter, who said to him, "Lord, are you going to wash my feet?" Jesus answered, "You do not know now what I am doing, but later you will understand." (John 13:1–7)

What was the Last Supper?

In Leonardo da Vinci's masterpiece *The Last Supper*, the disciples are depicted seated at a long, high table on either side of Jesus. What Leonardo didn't know was that Jesus and the disciples would have eaten, as was the custom of the day, while they reclined on couches or mats around a low table. There is some question as to whether Jesus' Last Supper with his disciples was the actual Passover meal. There were apparently no women present, as would have been customary for the Passover meal commemorating the salvation of Israel's firstborn in Egypt before the Exodus. And there is no specific mention of the traditional Passover lamb or customary herbs used in this most sacred of Jewish meals. While the first three Gospels state that it is a Passover meal, John makes it seem that it wasn't. As the men eat, Jesus tells them he will be betrayed by one of them and says he will not eat the Passover meal again until the Kingdom of God comes. In Mark and Matthew, Jesus breaks bread, saying, "Take, eat, this is my body." Then he takes a cup of wine and blesses it, saying, "Drink of it all of you, for this is my blood of the covenant which is poured out for many for the forgiveness of sins." These are words that divided early Christians and still divide Christians over the nature of Jesus' presence in the Eucharist, or communion, commemorating this event. Luke reverses the order of bread and wine and adds a second sharing of wine, and the John account of the Last Supper makes no mention of the bread and wine.

Following the meal, Jesus and the remaining disciples—Judas has slipped away to carry out his betrayal—cross the Kidron Valley to the Mount of Olives and a place called Gethsemane, a name meaning "oil press" or "oil vat." In this garden, Jesus confronts his impending death. Deeply troubled, Jesus asks God to relieve him of the burden he faces. In Mark, Jesus calls on God as *Abba*, an informal Aramaic form of "Father" akin to "Papa" or "Daddy," and asks, "Remove this cup from me; yet, not what I want, but what you want." Although Jesus asks the disciples to stay awake, they fall asleep, underscoring their humanity and Jesus' complete isolation. In the first three Gospels, a band of Temple authorities, led by Judas Iscariot, comes to arrest Jesus. In John, Roman soldiers are on hand to make the arrest. Judas calls Jesus "rabbi" and kisses him to identify Jesus to the arresting officers. Although one of Jesus' followers attempts to fight back and cuts off the ear of the high priest's servant, Jesus counsels nonresistance. In Luke, Jesus even heals the severed ear. Then Jesus is taken off to the palace of the high priest to confront his accusers.

In John, the devil made Judas do it. But the treachery of Judas has provoked some speculation over motives, including the notion that he was an anti-Roman zealot who was disappointed that Jesus had not proved to be the rebel leader Judas expected. In Mark, Judas went to the chief priests to betray Jesus before being offered a bribe, suggesting that he had some other motive besides money. Matthew specifically states Judas asks how much he will be given and he is paid "thirty pieces of silver," in fulfillment of another ancient Hebrew prophecy. Luke reports that he was promised money for his betrayal. The ultimate fate of Judas is a little unclear in the Gospels. In Matthew, Judas repents, returns the money to the priests, and hangs himself. The Matthew account says the priests took the money to buy a "potter's field" in which foreigners would be buried and the place was called the "Field of Blood"—a burial ground purchased with "blood money." But a later biblical account (in Acts) reports that Judas himself used the money to buy the piece of land that was called the "Field of Blood," and died as the result of a fall when "all his bowels gushed out," presumably meaning he suffered some massive accidental injury that disemboweled him.

And how did Jesus feel about Judas? Did he forgive his betrayer? Once again, the four Gospels head in different directions. At his arrest in Matthew, Jesus says to Judas, "Friend, do what you are here to do," which certainly has a tone of forgiveness. But Luke reports that Jesus asks Judas, "Is it with a kiss that you are betraying the Son of Man?"—seemingly a much more damning question. Mark does not report Jesus speaking to Judas or about the fate of Judas. In John, the account is sharply different as Jesus turns himself over to the soldiers without being identified by Judas, depicting Jesus as the master of his own destiny and not a victim of Judas's treachery.

BIBLICAL VOICES

So when Pilate saw that he could do nothing, but rather that a riot was beginning, he took some water and washed his hands before the crowd, saying, "I am innocent of this man's blood; see to it yourselves." Then the people as a whole answered, "His blood is on us and on our children." (Matt. 27: 24–25)

A third time he [Pilate] said to them, "Why, what evil has he done? I have found in him no ground for the sentence of death; I will therefore have him flogged and then release him." But they kept urgently demanding with loud shouts that he should be crucified; and their voices prevailed. (Luke 23:22–23)

Then Pilate took Jesus and had him flogged. And the soldiers wove a crown of thorns and put it on his head, and they dressed him in a purple robe. They kept coming up to him, saying, "Hail, King of the Jews!" and striking him on the face. Pilate went out again and said to them, "Look, I am bringing him out to you to let you know that I find no case against him." So Jesus came out, wearing the crown of thorns and the purple robe. Pilate said to them, "Here is the man!" When the chief priest and the police saw him, they shouted, "Crucify him! Crucify him!" Pilate said to them, "Take him yourselves and crucify him; I find no case against him." The Jews answered him, "We have a law, and according to that law he ought to die because he has claimed to be the Son of God." Now when Pilate heard this, he was more afraid than ever.... From then on, Pilate tried to release him, but the Jews cried out, "If you release this man, you are no friend of the emperor. Everyone who claims to be a king sets himself against the emperor." (Mark 19:1–12)

Who put Jesus on trial?

In the 1960s, archaeologists made a rather startling discovery. The name Pontius Pilate was found inscribed in the city of Caesarea, the seat of Roman rule in Judea. It was the first physical confirmation outside of literature that one of history's most notorious characters existed. Pontius Pilate was governor of the Roman provinces of Judea, Samaria, and Idumaea from 26 to 36 CE and the port city of Caesarea was his base. Most likely as military governor he would have traveled to Jerusalem during Passover week to lead the troop buildup in the city at a time when the city was crowded, anti-Roman sentiment ran high, and insurrection was considered more likely. Pilate seriously offended Jews of the day by bringing Roman shields and flags into Jerusalem. They contained idolatrous images offensive to the Jews. After ten years in Judea, Pilate was eventually dismissed and recalled to Rome after failing to contain a local uprising.

But it was Pilate who had ultimate authority over affairs in Jerusalem when Jesus was arrested, and he held the fate of Jesus or any other criminal in his hands. The question of who tried, convicted, and ultimately executed Jesus is more than a historical "parlor game" or religious "bar argument." In fixing the blame for Jesus' execution on the Jewish people as a whole lies the awful seeds of Christian anti-Semitism, or what Peter Gomes in *The Good Book* terms "Christianity's original sin."

After his arrest at Gethsemane, Jesus was actually tried—or interrogated—twice. The first interrogation took place in the house or palace of Jerusalem's high priest, the highest-ranking Jewish authority of the day. Another Gospel glitch here, though. Two Gospels don't name this high priest. Matthew calls him Caiaphas. But in John, Jesus is said to be taken first before a high priest named Annas, the father-in-law of Caiaphas. Annas had been high priest earlier and then deposed. Annas questions Jesus and then sends him to Caiaphas, the true high priest. In John, there is no account of Jesus being questioned by Caiaphas.

The Jewish council, or Sanhedrin, questioned Jesus on a number of counts. In Mark, false witnesses are brought against him. While they don't agree on Jesus' specific crimes, they chiefly accuse him of plotting to destroy the Temple. When the high priest asks Jesus point-blank if he is the Messiah, Jesus replies, in Matthew and Luke, "You have said so," and in Mark, "I am." That's enough for the high priest, who decides Jesus has committed "blasphemy," a crime punishable under Jewish Law by stoning. But the actual power of life and death still lay in the hands of Rome's representative. So off they all went to Pontius Pilate for a second trial that conformed with traditions of Roman justice.

The men who brought Jesus to Pilate brought along a laundry

list of charges: Jesus is a subversive. He opposes paying taxes to the emperor—which was exactly the opposite of what Jesus had said. He is stirring up resistance to Rome. In all of the Gospels, Pilate is presented as initially reluctant to pass judgment in a case that appears to him to be a local argument among Jews. In Matthew, Pilate's wife even tells her husband that in a dream she has been told that Jesus is innocent. In Luke, Pilate tries to send Jesus to Herod Antipas, the Jewish ruler of Galilee, but Herod sends Jesus back. Many commentators, Jewish and Christian, have detected an overly "apologetic" tone toward Pilate in the Gospels, shifting the "blame" for Jesus' execution to both the Jewish authorities and in a larger sense to the Jewish people. This has been explained by the fact that the Gospel writers, who were confronting Roman persecution, did not want to further alienate the Romans.

This might be a purely academic issue if not for the fact that centuries of Christians preaching that Jews were "Christ killers" underlie the modern history of anti-Semitism. It was not until 1959 that Pope John XXIII removed the phrase "perfidious Jews" from a Roman Catholic prayer said on Good Friday, and before his death he composed a prayer asking forgiveness for the church's anti-Semitism, which he called a "second crucifixion." At a Vatican Conference in 1962, the Catholic church officially exonerated most of Jesus' Jewish contemporaries and all subsequent Jews of the charge of killing God, or deicide. Perhaps you've heard of closing the barn door after the horses have run away? But better late than never.

In spite of the Gospel "spin" on Jesus' death sentence, and Pilate's handwashing, the Roman Pilate was ultimately responsible for Jesus' execution. He may have been reluctant, not so much out of goodness as disinterest in a Jewish matter. What forced his hand was the threat of political pressure from Rome. When Jesus was accused of treachery toward Rome, Pilate could not simply overlook the charge. Doing so would have endangered his own political neck. It is ultimately on this charge of claiming kingship, a direct challenge to the emperor, that Pilate sentenced Jesus to death. Jesus was condemned and executed as a nationalistic freedom-fighter who threatened Rome, not for claiming to be the Messiah. And though the Gospels report that Pilate turns Jesus over to the Jewish crowd, his execution was clearly carried out by Roman soldiers, a fact confirmed by the Roman historian Tacitus (c. 55–117 CE), who wrote in discussing the Christians, "Christ, the originator of their name, had been condemned to death by Pontius Pilate in the reign of Tiberius." This is one of the few references to Jesus' death outside Bible sources.

How does crucifixion kill you?

Many first-century Jews died, just like Jesus, on a cross. Some estimates of the number of Jews crucified in this time for a variety of crimes run as high as one hundred thousand. But not at the hand of other Jews. Crucifixion was not a Jewish form of execution. It was exclusive to the Romans, and it was an extreme penalty, generally reserved for cases of runaway slaves or rebellion against Rome. Whether the Jewish people of Judea knew of it or not, an uprising of slaves against Rome led by the gladiator-slave Spartacus in 71 BCE had resulted in some six thousand crucifixions, the bodies left to decompose as a grim warning. In Jesus' own time, in the nearby town of Gamala, an insurrection by Jews had met with a similar Roman response.

Jesus' Crucifixion, according to historical evidence, was typical of Roman executions on the cross. The condemned man was often scourged, or flogged, to leave him weak and bloodied. He would next have to carry the beam of his own cross through the streets. At the place of execution, his arms were tied to the crossbeam. Sometimes, as in Jesus' case, the hands were also nailed in place. The beam was raised by ropes onto the upright and then nailed in a T shape. The *titulus,* or notice of death, which the victim had worn around his neck, was then set on the cross above the victim's head. The victim's feet were nailed into place. Jesus' death is somewhat unusual in that it came within hours, a fact that surprised Pilate. Some crucifixion victims lingered for days, and they were left for the vultures. Death resulted from hunger, exposure, and loss of blood. Sometimes it was hastened with a blow to the legs, causing the victim's weight to crush the lungs, bringing about suffocation. Other cases show that the victim was lanced to accelerate death, and this was true of Jesus. A Roman soldier pierced Jesus' side and water and blood flowed out.

BIBLICAL VOICES

Father, forgive them; for they do not know what they are doing. (Luke 23:24)

Truly I tell you, today you will be with me in paradise. (Luke 23:43)

Woman, here is your son. . . . Here is your mother. (John 19: 26–27)

My God, my God, why have you forsaken me? (Matt. 27:46; Mark 15:34)

I am thirsty. (John 19:28)

It is finished. (John 19:30)

Father, into your hands I commend my spirit. (Luke 23:46)

This is the order traditionally given to the "last words" ("utterances") of Jesus spoken on the cross.

PLOT SUMMARY: THE RESURRECTION AND ASCENSION

At the moment of Jesus' death, the Gospels report a series of natural phenomena and extraordinary events. Intense darkness overwhelmed the land, a pointed reminder of one of the Plagues upon Egypt. Inside the Temple, the curtain separating the inner Holy of Holies, the place of the divine presence, from the rest of the Temple, was inexplicably torn in two. Matthew alone reports an earthquake, as well as the opening of tombs and the resurrection of "God's saints" who later "enter the holy city and appear to many." The Roman soldiers on duty declare, "This man was God's son," though Luke has a soldier say, "This man was innocent."

After Jesus died, in accordance with Jewish regulations that the dead be buried before sunset, his body was taken away and prepared for burial, either by a group of women in some versions, or two men, Nicodemus and Joseph of Arimathea in John. Jesus' tomb had been purchased by Joseph, a wealthy man from the Judean town Arimathea, who is described as a member of the Jewish council and a secret disciple of Jesus. The tomb, cut from rock in a garden, was sealed with a heavy stone, and a Roman guard was set in Matthew's account, ostensibly to prevent Jesus' followers from making off with the corpse and claiming that he had risen as promised.

Counting the Crucifixion—a Friday, the day before the Sabbath—as Day One, some of the women went to the tomb on Day Three—Sunday—after the Sabbath, to anoint the body, in keeping with burial customs. In Matthew, the women, Mary of Magdala and the "other Mary," go to the tomb to anoint the body of Jesus in keeping with Jewish practice. But an earthquake and an angel have opened the tomb and the guards have fled in terror. The women find the tomb empty and the angel tells them that Jesus is not there. Suddenly the women are greeted by Jesus himself and they are told to instruct the disciples to go to Galilee, where they will see Jesus.

In Mark, the two Marys worry about the stone. But they find it has been rolled away and a white-robed man tells them that Jesus has risen from the dead. They are to go and tell his disciples. Luke's version has "two men" in "dazzling clothes," presumably angels, sitting inside the empty tomb. The women report this to the eleven disciples and Peter runs to see for himself.

John also offers a slightly different account of the first Easter. In this version, Mary Magdalene goes alone, finds the empty tomb, and races back to tell Peter the news. Later, she weeps at the empty tomb and two angels in white ask her why she is crying. Then she meets Jesus face-to-face, initially mistaking him for a gardener. Jesus calls her name and she realizes who he is and what has happened.

During the next few days, Jesus makes a series of appearances to his disciples and followers, individually and in groups, who are seemingly slow-witted about what has happened. Jesus even scolds them in Mark for their unwillingness to believe what has happened. Jesus then blesses the disciples and, in Luke, is "carried up to heaven," is "taken up into heaven" in Mark, and in Acts, is "lifted up, and a cloud took him out of sight."

BIBLICAL VOICES

All authority on heaven and on earth has been given to me. Go therefore and make disciples of all nations, baptizing them in the name of the Father and of the Son and of the Holy Spirit and teaching them to obey everything that I have commanded you. And remember, I am with you always, to the end of the age. (Matt. 28:18–20)

Go into all the world and proclaim the good news to the whole creation. The one who believes and is baptized will be saved; but the one who does not believe will be condemned. And these signs will accompany those who believe: by using my name they will cast out demons; they will speak in new tongues; they will pick up snakes in their hands, and if they drink any deadly thing, it will not hurt them; they will lay their hands on the sick, and they will recover. (Mark 16:15–18)

Thus it is written, that the Messiah is to suffer and to rise from the dead on the third day and that repentance and forgiveness of sins is to be proclaimed in his name to all nations, beginning from Jerusalem. You are witnesses of these things. And see, I am sending upon you what my Father promised; so stay here in the city until you have been clothed in power from on high. (Luke 24:46–49)

If you don't believe Jesus was God, what does he have to offer?

Man or myth? Divine or human? Messiah or great thinker, another Buddha? From its earliest days, Christianity itself was divided over many of these questions. Almost from the start, sects like the Gnostics held views that separated them completely from the orthodox church views. Soon the "church" was a feuding, bickering bunch of thinkers who were all contributing their own take on the life and death of Jesus. Often those opinions had little to do with the biblical accounts. Within modern Christianity there are still boiling arguments over who Jesus was and what he said. For instance, one controversial group of modern Christian theologians has attracted considerable media attention with the so-called "Jesus Seminar," which regards many of the words of Jesus as fiction, creations of the followers who wrote the Gospels. Fifteen hundred—or even five hundred—years ago they might have been expelled from the church, or burned at the stake, as heretics. Now they, and their more traditional opponents, trade arguments and counterarguments in the media and in the bookstores.

At the other extreme end of the spectrum are Christians who believe every single word of the New Testament and that each word is divine truth and should be literally followed. That can cause some trouble. The story has often been told of the old-time fundamentalist who liked to open his Bible at random and do exactly what he read. One day, he flipped around and found, "And Judas hung himself." Turning to another page, he read, "Go and do likewise."

In other words, there is a wide range of Christians in the world today. In America, there are more than two hundred Christian denominations ranging all along the theological spectrum. Some do and some don't accept everything said by and about Jesus as, well, "Gospel."

Since studious, scholarly, sincere Christians can't really agree on what Jesus said and meant, how should the "casual" Christian, or the complete nonbeliever, look at his life and teachings? The question is perhaps even more troubling for Jews, for whom Christianity has not been such a great deal. As Rabbi Joseph Telushkin points out, "Were Jesus to return today, most Jews believe, he undoubtedly would feel more at home in a synagogue than a church. . . . Most statements attributed to Jesus in the New Testament conform to Jewish teachings." (*Jewish Literacy*, p. 128)

However, Rabbi Telushkin also believes that there are three key areas in which Jewish teachings diametrically oppose the teachings of Jesus:

1. Forgiveness of sins. In Matthew, Jesus taught that he had personal authority to forgive sin. ("The Son of Man has authority on earth to forgive sins.") Judaism teaches that God forgives the sins committed against him through atonement on Yom Kippur.

2. Turning the other cheek and loving enemies. While ancient Jewish tradition included the notion of loving neighbors, loving an enemy or persecutor is a different issue. According to Rabbi Telushkin, the Mosaic Law commands a person to offer the wicked man powerful resistance. This is a conundrum for many Christians as well as Jewish believers. How does one turn the other cheek or love the enemy when confronted with the monstrous evil of a Hitler?

3. Jesus as the only way to salvation. In 1980, Bailey Smith, the leader of the Southern Baptist Convention, America's largest Christian denomination, made headlines when he was quoted as saying, "God Almighty does not hear the prayer of a Jew." In 1997, the Southern Baptist Convention again riled people when it announced it was still committed to converting Jews to Christianity. They believe, as do many Christians, that the only way to know God is through acceptance of Jesus as personal Savior. That idea, Rabbi Telushkin points out, denies the teaching of the Hebrew Psalm 145: "God is near to all who call unto him." (*Jewish Literacy*, pp. 128–129)

Telushkin's view is echoed by the Reverend Peter Gomes, who has examined the issue of Christian anti-Semitism, particularly in the writings of Paul. In *The Good Book*, he convincingly repudiates the Bailey Smiths of the world: "Paul's argument is that the cross of Jesus is to Gentiles what the Torah is to Jews, and that both are means of salvation and righteousness. In other words, Jews need not become Christians to obtain the promises—in the Torah they already have the promises as Jews. By the same token, Gentiles need not become Jews and subscribe to the law . . . and because of the cross of Jesus do not need to do so. Paul's argument is for an inclusive God who has provided for both Jews and Gentiles. . . ." (pp. 116–117)

What a lot of Christians still don't get is that Jesus was a Jew. So were his disciples and so was Paul. Jesus' moral and ethical code was tied to strict Jewish Law, and some of his teachings, such as those about divorce, were even more stringent than Jewish Law. His condemnation of some Pharisees as "hypocrites" wasn't a blanket rejection of his own religious background. Jesus often preached that the spiritual life was more important than mere obedience to a careful set of rules and regulations. Jesus said, "It is not what goes into the mouth that defiles a person, but it is what comes out of the mouth that defiles" and "What comes out of the mouth proceeds from the heart." These words have been viewed as a rejection of strict dietary law. Jesus cared more about inner spiritual holiness than outward, symbolic purity. On several occasions, he broke the Sabbath law by healing on the Sabbath. He cited the prophets when he said that God preferred "mercy to sacrifice," meaning that the ideals of justice, charity, forgiveness, and love of neighbor were far more important than going through the motions of obeying laws and then behaving badly

Many people have tried to reduce Jesus to a nutshell, a handful of convenient aphorisms and cute pious slogans—an "Idiot's Guide to Salvation." It's not that simple. Jesus elevated forgiveness. His teachings on mercy and social justice are meant for everyone. In one memorable passage he explained that whenever anyone fed the hungry, clothed the naked, or visited the sick, they were doing the same to Jesus himself. In one of his many comments on the "Kingdom of God," he said that it is within each person, a simple yet profound notion that takes some of the majesty out of all the cathedrals in the world.

But when asked about the greatest commandment, Jesus answered as a devout Jew with the Great Commandment: "You shall love the Lord your God with all your heart, and with all your soul, and with all your mind." Then he added a second: "You shall love your neighbor as yourself. On these two commandments hang all the law and the prophets."

BIBLICAL VOICES

But there are also many other things that Jesus did; if every one of them were written down, I suppose that the world itself could not contain the books that would be written. (John 21:24)

MILESTONES IN BIBLICAL TIMES VI
THE EARLY CHURCH

c. 37 The first Christian martyr, Stephen, a Jewish follower of Jesus, is stoned to death for blasphemy. Among those present is a Pharisee named Saul.

41 After a despotic eleven-year-reign, Caligula is murdered and succeeded by the crippled nephew of Tiberius, who rules Rome as Claudius.

42 Judea's King Herod Agrippa orders the death of the apostle James, son of Zebedee, the first of the original twelve disciples to be martyred.

c. 45 Saul/Paul sets out on his missionary travels.

47 In Antioch, Syria, home of one of the earliest churches, the word "Christian" is coined.

49 Emperor Claudius expels Jewish Christians from Rome.

54 Claudius is murdered at the orders of the empress Agrippina.

Her sixteen-year-old son rules Rome as the emperor Nero.

54/58? Paul's "Letters to the Corinthians" are written.

58 Paul is arrested.

62 Paul is held under house arrest in Rome but then he is allowed to resume his travels.

64 The Great Fire in Rome destroys much of the city. Nero blames the disaster on Christians and begins the first official persecution of the group.

c. 65? The Gospel according to Mark is composed.

68 Emperor Nero commits suicide, ending 128 years of the line that had ruled Rome since Julius Caesar.

69 Roman general Vespasian lays siege to Jerusalem. A coup by Roman generals makes him the next emperor.

70 Jerusalem falls and the Temple, completed six years earlier, is destroyed. All that remains is the wall now famous as the "Wailing [Western] Wall."

73 The Roman siege of Masada near the Dead Sea ends when Romans enter the Jewish fortress and find its Jewish defenders dead in an apparent mass suicide.

79 Mount Vesuvius on the Bay of Naples erupts, killing thousands.

84/85? The Gospels according Matthew and Luke are written.

96 Emperor Domitian is stabbed to death; he is succeeded by Nerva.

98 Nerva dies suddenly and is succeeded by his adopted son, who will rule for nineteen years as the emperor Trajan.

c. 100? The Gospel according to John is written.

• In Revelation, the last book of the Bible, the Christian prophet John writes metaphorically of "Babylon" but is referring to Rome.

Jesus Is Coming—Look Busy

Acts of the Apostles

"Save yourselves from this corrupt generation." (Acts 2:40)

❁

※ How do you tell the world the "good news" if you don't speak their language?

※ What happens when you don't pay your dues to church?

※ Why was Stephen stoned?

※ Was the apostle Paul a chauvinist, woman-hating homophobe?

No Jesus. Judas was dead. The eleven disciples, who had scattered like flies before a flyswatter at their leader's arrest, were probably terrified. They must have been expecting a knock on the door at any minute. Either it would be Jesus coming back or Roman soldiers coming to take them away. Either way, they must have been anxiously thinking, "Now what?"

The beginnings of the Christian church were not like some Mickey Rooney–Judy Garland movie in which the kids say, "Let's put a show." Jesus' earliest followers faced persecution and death, either at the hands of Jewish authorities or the most powerful government on earth. In telling their story, the Acts of the Apostles, a "sequel" by the author of Luke, covers approximately thirty years that roughly correspond with the notorious reigns of the Roman emperors Caligula, Claudius, and Nero. Yet, for those with a taste for the Bible's lurid side, this New Testament saga is fairly tame. At a time when these Romans were inventing the word "decadent," the stories in Acts pale beside the racier details of earlier Bible stories. Sure, there are a few miracles, a prison break, a stoning, a shipwreck, and the death of a couple who don't pay their promised dues to the church. But while Emperor Nero did more than just "fiddle"—he actually played the zither—the first Christians spent much of their time debating kosher food and circumcision. On the other hand, there are a lot of complaints about "fornication" by early church members. But Acts leaves out the seamy details and lacks the wholesale sex and violence that often made the Hebrew scriptures so compelling.

The author of Luke takes up his Acts narrative from the moment Jesus ascends into heaven, and carries it through the establishment of Christian communities throughout the Mediterranean world. Although Acts features a number of early Christian figures, including the first martyr, Stephen, the book is essentially a two-man show. First to be highlighted is Simon Peter (or Cephas), nicknamed "the rock" by Jesus because he would be the foundation on which the church was built. Peter is depicted primarily preaching among his fellow Jews, although he begins to expand his preaching to include Gentiles. Not yet called Christians, the Jewish followers of Jesus called themselves the people of "the Way." Then the spotlight shifts to Saul/Paul, who became the leading advocate of Jesus' message in the Gentile, or non-Jewish, world of the first century.

While modern Christians tend to lump the early Christians together as one big, happy family, working in unison to spread the faith, much of Acts and the rest of the New Testament deal with the tension and rivalries between two factions. The Jewish followers of Jesus initially preferred to remain Jews and retain their laws and traditions. They believed that anyone who wanted to follow Jesus must convert to Judaism first. Opposing them were those, like the zealous Paul, who wanted to take the "good news" to the non-Jewish world, sharply breaking with Jewish Law. The dispute between these factions, the first of many controversies and divisions in early Christianity, led to a council of the apostles in Jerusalem in the year 49 CE, described in Acts. With Peter agreeing that the message should be taken to the Gentile world, this council accepted that Gentiles who wished to follow Jesus did not have to comply with strict Jewish requirements, such as most dietary laws and circumcision. James, mentioned in Acts as the brother of Jesus, now taking a leading position, also accepts the arrangement.

In other words, there's some real Good News, Christians! You can have that burger and shake. And you can rest easy about that awkward little surgical procedure.

Luke and Acts were traditionally thought to have been written by a companion who traveled with Paul. The more popular current view is that the author was not an actual companion of Paul but a later Christian who had access to a "diary" kept by someone who did travel with Paul. Since Paul's presumed execution, sometime in the late sixties, is not mentioned, scholars reasoned that Acts was written before Paul's death. But the book must have been written later than Luke, which is almost certainly later than Mark, believed to have been written around 65 CE. The result is to date Luke's two volumes to sometime between 80 and 100 CE.

BIBLICAL VOICES

When suddenly there came from heaven a sound as of a violent wind which filled the entire house in which they were sitting; and there appeared to them tongues as of fire; these separated and came to rest on the head of each of them. They were filled with the Holy Spirit and began to speak different languages as the Spirit gave them power to express themselves.

Now there were devout men living in Jerusalem from every nation under heaven, and at the sound they all assembled, and each one was bewildered to hear these men speaking in his own language. They were amazed and astonished. "Surely," they said, "all these men speaking are Galileans? How does it happen that each of us hears them in his own native language? Parthians, Medes, and Elamites; people from Mesopotamia, Judaea and Cappadocia, Pontus and Asia, Phrygia and Pamphylia, Egypt and the parts of Libya round Cyrene; residents of Rome—Jews and proselytes alike—Cretans and Arabs, we hear them preaching in our own language about the marvels of God." Everyone was amazed and perplexed; they asked one another what it all meant. Some, however, laughed it off, "They have been drinking too much new wine," they said. (Acts 2:2–12 NJB)

How do you tell the world the "good news" if you don't speak their language?

It was just an average day around the house for the disciples and a few other followers. They were sitting there when, all of a sudden, "tongues of fire" touched each of the followers. They began to speak in other languages. Some people who saw them thought they were drunk. This was the arrival of the Holy Spirit that Jesus had promised. It was a sort of reverse Tower of Babel scene, because the disciples could now go and spread the word everywhere.

To Christians, this was "the birthday of the church" on Pentecost. But many Christians may be surprised to discover that Pentecost is another Christian celebration affixed to a Jewish holiday, once again showing the deep affinity between the two faiths. *Pentecost*, from the Greek word denoting "fiftieth," is used to describe the Hebrew "Feast of Weeks" (*Shavuot*), which takes place fifty days after Passover begins. Originally an agricultural festival marking the end of the wheat harvest, the day later came to commemorate the giving of the Torah to Moses on Mount Sinai. To Christians, it now means the fiftieth day after Easter and the resurrection.

Following this miraculous event, the disciples had become apostles charged with taking the message out to the world. Peter and the others began to preach fearlessly about Jesus as the Messiah. On a single day, after Peter speaks, three thousand converts are reported. Now filled with the Holy Spirit, they begin to heal and work wonders. Peter is able to heal even when his shadow falls on the sick, and he even raises a woman named Tabitha (or Dorcas, in Greek) from the dead.

The Christian tradition of "speaking in tongues," which generally is used to mean uttering an unintelligible, ecstatic speech, rather than speaking in a foreign language, was derived from this first Pentecost. In contemporary Christianity, "Pentecostal" churches are generally a movement of fundamentalist Protestant churches that emphasize being "born again" in the Holy Spirit. Their services typically include "faith healing" through "laying on hands" and "speaking in tongues." Although many conventional, mainstream Christian churches had relinquished these practices over the years, the recent success of the revivalist Pentecostal movement, once dismissed as "holy rollers" and charlatans, has sparked acceptance of the so-called "charismatic" movement within the more traditional, and staid, Christian churches.

What happens when you don't pay your dues to church?

The reports in Acts show how the early church grew as a "communistic" society in which everyone shared. There is a utopian state of harmony depicted in these first days of the Christian community, although they are not yet called "Christians." A young man named Matthias was elected to replace Judas as one of the Twelve, and the group prospered and made collective decisions and enjoyed common ownership of goods, making the early Christians in Jerusalem a practical model for the kibbutz.

This utopian idea didn't always work perfectly. Doing as Jesus had taught and selling one's goods and forking the proceeds over for the common good or relief of the poor was clearly practiced in the early community of followers. A virtuous convert named Barnabas sold a field and gave it all to the apostles. On the other hand there were Ananias and Sapphira. They had agreed to sell their property also, but Ananias, according to Acts, "with his wife's connivance," kept back part of the proceeds from their real estate deal. When Peter asks Ananias how he could do such a thing as lie to the Holy Spirit, Ananias falls down dead. Three hours later, not knowing what happened, Sapphira is asked the same question. When she lies, she drops dead as well. The story ends with a threatening note for all those who haven't paid their church dues: "And a great fear came upon the whole church and on all who heard it." (Acts 5:11 NJB)

It is rather sad to contemplate that the church was growing on goodwill but then fear had to replace the spirit of generosity.

BIBLICAL VOICES

"You stiff-necked people, uncircumcised in heart and ears, you are forever opposing the Holy Spirit, just as your ancestors used to do. Which of the prophets did your ancestors not persecute? They killed those who foretold the coming of the Righteous One, and now you have become his betrayers and murderers. You are the ones that received the law as ordained by angels, and yet you have not kept it."

When they heard these things, they became enraged and ground their teeth at Stephen.... Then they dragged him out of the city and began to stone him; and the witnesses laid their coats at the feet of a young man named Saul. (Acts 7:51–58)

Why was Stephen stoned?

One of the earliest members of the growing followers of Jesus, Stephen was tried by the Sanhedrin, or Jewish council, for blasphemy. In a stinging indictment of the people of Israel who disobeyed God, he had accused them of resisting God and the Holy Spirit. The council believed Stephen spoke against the Temple, saying God, the "Most High," did not live in houses made by human hands. Stephen was taken out to be stoned by a mob. But with his dying words, Stephen forgave his executioners. The death of Stephen sparked a round of persecution of Jesus' followers in Jerusalem and sent many of them fleeing to surrounding cities in Syria, where the early church began to flourish. It was in pursuit of the followers of Jesus, now called "the Way," in cities like Damascus, that a zealous Pharisee named Saul was sent to seek out and arrest more of these "renegade" Jews.

BIBLICAL VOICES

Meanwhile Saul, still breathing threats and murder against the disciples of the Lord, went to the high priest and asked him for letters to the synagogues at Damascus, so that if he found any that belonged to the Way, men or women, he might bring them bound to Jerusalem. Now as he was going along and approaching Damascus, suddenly a light from heaven flashed around him. He fell to the ground and heard a voice saying to him, "Saul, Saul, why do you persecute me?" (Acts 9:1–4)

Barnabas then left for Tarsus to look for Saul and when he found him he brought him to Antioch. And it happened that they stayed together in that church a whole year, instructing a large number of people. It was at Antioch that the disciples were first called "Christians." (Acts 11:25–26 NJB)

Was the apostle Paul a chauvinist, woman-hating homophobe?

For most Christians, Jesus is the centerpiece, the single figure to whom they owe devotion and faith. Even if they are confused by some of the things Jesus said and did, they basically believe in his life, death, and resurrection and his vision of the Kingdom of God.

Somewhat more controversial, especially in recent times, is the figure of Paul. Whether you call him the apostle or Saint Paul, this man with "meeting eyebrows and a rather large nose, bald-headed, bow-legged, strongly built, full of grace" was largely responsible for creating the Christian church. But in setting out many of the rules for Christian worship and life, Paul also stated views that, especially in a modern context, are hard for some Christians to accept. In particular, his views on women, sex, and his fellow Jews have come in for scrutiny.

Paul is introduced in Acts as Saul, named for the ancient Israelite king, who watches the coats of the crowd who stoned Stephen. A Pharisee from Tarsus in Asia Minor, the young Saul went to Jerusalem to learn from the esteemed rabbi Gamaliel, grandson of the legendary rabbi Hillel, the most prominent Pharisaic rabbi of the first century. Given authority by the high priest to arrest followers of the Way in Damascus for blasphemy, Saul experienced a transforming vision that brought about a dramatic change of heart, accompanied by the change in name. He took on the Latinized Paul. Baptized, Paul began to preach the gospel of Jesus, becoming the target of persecution by the Jewish religious authorities himself. In Damascus, he had to be lowered by basket from a window to escape the authorities sent to arrest or even kill him.

Because he had been such a vigorous enemy of the early Christians, Paul was not immediately accepted by the other Christians in Jerusalem. But he was clearly an ardent preacher, and wherever the church leaders sent him to preach he had success. Almost immediately, however, a conflict emerged between Paul and the members of the Way who believed that Gentile converts must obey Jewish Law. At a council in Jerusalem in 49 CE, the apostles and church "elders" agreed that Gentiles need not be circumcised or obey dietary law in order to become Christians. Peter himself had already expanded the mission to Gentiles when he told of a dream in which a sheet filled with "unclean" animals comes down from heaven. A voice told him to kill and eat. The voice tells Peter, "What God has made clean, you must not call profane." Once this issue is settled, with Jesus' brother James weighing in in favor of a compromise that opens the way for Gentiles to be converted, Paul is sent back to Antioch to continue spreading the word.

If only Paul had frequent-flier miles! Over the course of the next decade or so, he made three ambitious missionary journeys, taking advantage of the excellent highway system constructed throughout the Mediterranean world by the Romans. Built so Roman armies could move swiftly and their traders could move efficiently, the Roman roads also contributed to the spread of the Christian message.

Paul's first journey, around 47–48 CE, took him first to Cyprus and then through Anatolia (modern-day Turkey) before returning to Antioch (Syria), then one of the largest cities in the Roman empire. His second journey was even more arduous. Crossing Anatolia again Paul went by sea to Macedonia and Greece, finally reaching Athens. On the third mission, he again went through Anatolia, stopping at Ephesus on the Aegean coast. A major port city, it was also home to a large cult who worshiped the Greek fertility goddess Artemis (called Diana by the Romans). The Temple to Artemis was considered one of the Wonders of the Ancient World. The local metalworkers union did not take kindly to Paul's suggestion that people stop worshiping idols. Paul's preaching started a riot in Ephesus. He escaped and sailed for Greece.

After this third journey, Paul returned to Jerusalem, where he was persecuted by Jewish authorities for trying to persuade people to break Jewish Law. Nearly killed by an angry mob because he had allegedly profaned the Temple, Paul was saved when Roman troops arrived. As a Roman citizen, Paul appealed to the Roman officials, who imprisoned him for two years. In 60 CE, Paul won the right to put his case before the emperor, although the thought of appealing to the ferociously anti-Christian madman Nero seems practically insane. He sailed for Rome, but his ship was caught in a storm and Paul miraculously survived. Bitten by a snake when he arrived on the island of Malta, Paul was again miraculously saved from harm, and after being shipwrecked on the island of Malta, he made it to Italy. Acts ends with Paul under a mild form of house arrest in the imperial capital, preaching the gospel and writing letters to the churches he has established. Acts says nothing further about Paul's appeal or ultimate fate, or that of Peter. Both eventually disappear from the biblical account without specific word of what happens to them. How Peter even got to Rome is a mystery. According to well-established tradition, especially in Peter's case, both apostles were martyred at Rome during Emperor Nero's persecution of Christians after the Great Fire in Rome in 64 CE.

Hated by Roman authorities for their unwillingness to recognize the divinity of the emperor, Christians soon proved to be an appealing target for Nero's depraved appetite for providing spectacles for the citizens of Rome. In *The First Century*, William Klingaman describes the atmosphere in which Paul and his fellow Christians found themselves: "Christians were arrested and tortured until they revealed the names of their brethren; those in turn were crucified, or dressed like wild animals and torn apart by dogs in the arena. But the depths of Nero's cruelty and sadism were revealed only when he impaled scores of Christ's followers on stakes and then burned them alive, as human torches to illuminate the city at night." (p. 301)

Tradition has it that Paul was martyred in 67 CE. Later Christian tales told a story of Peter being executed, requesting to be crucified upside down, since he was unworthy to suffer the precise fate of Jesus.

As the chief proponent of what became the established orthodoxy of the Christian church, first in Roman Catholicism, and after the Protestant Reformation in all of the Protestant churches, Paul has taken a lot of the blame for the traditional sexism of the church. Twice in his letters Paul tells women to keep silent in church. In 1 Corinthians he writes, "Women are to remain quiet in the assemblies." Yet he writes in the same letter, "Man is nothing without woman, and though woman came from man, so does every man come from a woman, and everything comes from God." On a less severe note, he weighs in on whether women should cover their heads in church. It is difficult to reconcile these views with Paul's statement that in Jesus there was "neither male nor female." He seems to want it both ways. But in assessing Paul, there are two important points to recall. First, the early Christian communities and Paul himself were dependent upon the efforts of heroic women who helped keep the church alive by opening their homes as churches, preaching, and providing the material comforts, like "daily bread," that every good apostle needs. The names of Lydia, Phoebe, and Priscilla, for instance, are not as well known as those of Peter and Paul, but they were crucial players in the life of the early church, just as some of the heroines of the Hebrew scripture were in their day. Lydia appears as one of Paul's first converts in Acts who opens her home to Paul, in essence founding an early "church." In Romans, Phoebe is called a "deacon" and is singled out by Paul as "a helper of many, and of myself as well." Prisca, or Priscilla, is also a prominent preacher. Expelled from Rome for her activities there, she forms a church in Ephesus. In fact, in Romans, Priscilla is credited with risking her own neck to save Paul's life.

It is also important to remember the historical setting. Paul was writing in a particular time and place. Readers of the Bible must take into account the role of women in the first century, just as they must look at ancient customs when considering the earlier Hebrew scriptures and their treatment of women. As Peter Gomes wisely puts it: "In the three worlds of which Paul was a citizen, the Jewish, the Greek, and the Roman, women's societal roles were dictated by the subordination principle. His teachings on women, therefore, while reflecting the mores of his time, are no more relevant to an age where those mores no longer apply than, say, first-century standards of dress, of social etiquette, or of dietary rules. Paul is a social and political conservative. . . . So we should understand him, his social teachings, and those who imitate his teachings . . . as writing from within the social assumptions of the age of which they are a part." (*The Good Book*, p. 139)

As for Paul's views on homosexuality, which he condemns in his letter to the Romans, Gomes, himself a homosexual, makes a similar point: "The homosexuality Paul would have known and to which he makes reference in his letters . . . has to do with pederasty and male prostitution, and he particularly condemns those heterosexual men and women who assume homosexual practices. What is patently unknown to Paul is the concept of a homosexual nature, that is . . . something that is beyond choice, that is not necessarily characterized by lust, avarice, idolatry, or exploitation. . . . All Paul knew of homosexuality was the debauched pagan expression of it. He cannot be condemned for that ignorance, but neither should his ignorance be an excuse for our own." (*The Good Book*, p. 158).

BIBLICAL VOICES

"Athenians, I see how extremely religious you are in every way. For as I went through the city and looked carefully at the objects of your worship, I found among them an altar with the inscription, 'To an unknown god.' What therefore you worship as unknown, this I proclaim to you. The God who made the world and everything in it, he who is Lord of heaven and earth, does not live in shrines made by human hands, nor is he served by human hands, as though he needed anything, since he himself gives to all mortals life and breath and all things. From one ancestor he made all the nations to inhabit the whole earth, and he allotted the times of their existence and the boundaries of the places where they would live, so that they would search for God and perhaps grope for him and find him—though indeed he is not far from each one of us." (Acts 17:22–27)

YOU HAVE MAIL!

THE EPISTLES OF PAUL

*If I speak in the tongues of mortals and angels, but do not
have love, I am a noisy gong or a clanging cymbal.
(1 Cor. 13:1)*

The early Christians were forced to improvise, working from "word of mouth," worshiping without benefit of books and established rituals. Remember, when Paul was making his rounds, setting up new communities, there were no Gospels. Before the Gospels were written and circulated later in the first century, letters, also called "epistles," provided the only means to "reach out and touch" other Christians. Although the Greek *epistello*, for "to send to," was traditionally viewed as a more formal letter than a personal message, the terms "epistle" and "letter" are generally interchangeable today. Paul's epistles, or letters to churches and individuals around the Mediterranean world, were the first written documents of the early Christian church. In them, Paul provided guidance on matters of theology, practical advice on local difficulties, and warnings against certain abuses and practices that Paul considered dangerous or sinful. These letters, which constitute nearly one half of the New Testament, cited Hebrew scripture, as well as Jesus, and include some of the most memorable phrases in Christian history, many of which are cited below in excerpts from these letters.

Paul's letters were written as he traveled, and several of them were written from prison. They went out to the early churches, just as Jewish leaders in Jerusalem had earlier sent letters to Jewish communities spread throughout the Mediterranean to instruct or mediate. Probably written on papyrus sheets, which were rolled and tied, the letters would be hand-carried by Paul's personal emissaries, who might read and even supplement the information in the letter. The first collection of these letters is thought to have been made around 100 CE.

Thirteen "epistles" were traditionally credited to Paul, who dictated them to an assistant but then added a personal postscript and his signature. Recent research suggests that some of "Paul's letters" may have been written by later church leaders who used Paul's name to lend authority to their writings. It is also assumed that Paul wrote other letters that have either been lost or discarded. In one of these thirteen letters (Colossians), Paul refers to a letter sent to another church that is missing.

The grouping of Paul's letters in the New Testament is by length, from longest to shortest, rather than in chronological order, or relative importance. They are given the titles of the church or, in a few cases, the person, to whom they were sent. This section offers an overview of Paul's letters, with a selection of noteworthy verses from each.

• **Romans**

In the longest letter, Paul addresses a church that he had not personally founded or visited. The letter was written around 58 CE, probably while Paul was in the Greek city of Corinth, and before the severe persecutions of Christians under Nero begin after 62 CE. Apparently, Paul was planning another journey to bring the Christian message to Spain and was hoping to visit Rome on the way. This letter was to serve as his introduction to the Roman Christians, both for himself and for his teaching. Before leaving for Spain, however, he returned to Jerusalem and was arrested.

Paul says that faith in Jesus leads to salvation, for Jew or Gentile. The new Israel is the successor to the old Israel but is by no means restricted to Israelites. One of the letter's main points is that the Law, meaning strict Jewish Law, is powerless to save. Salvation to all humanity is offered through faith in Christ. Paul also says people must love one another, and love those who act against them.

> For the wages of sin is death; but the free gift of God is eternal life in Jesus Christ our Lord. (Rom. 6:23)

> If God is for us, who is against us? (Rom. 8:31)

> For I am convinced that neither death, nor life, nor angels, nor rulers, nor things present, nor things to come, nor powers, nor height, nor depth, nor anything else in all creation, will be able to separate us from the love of God in Christ Jesus our Lord. (Rom. 8:38–39)

> Let love be genuine; hate what is evil, hold fast to what is good; love one another with mutual affection; outdo one another in showing honor.

Do not lag in zeal, be ardent in spirit, persevere in prayer. (Rom. 12:9–12)

Bless those who persecute you; bless and do not curse them. Rejoice with those who rejoice, weep with those who weep. Live in harmony with one another; do not be haughty, but associate with the lowly; do not claim to be wiser than you are. Do not repay anyone evil for evil, but take thought for what is noble in the sight of all. If it is possible, so far as it depends on you, live peaceably with all. Beloved, never avenge yourselves, but leave room for the wrath of God; for it is written, " 'Vengeance is mine, I will repay,' says the Lord." (Rom. 12:14–19)

• 1 & 2 Corinthians

During Paul's lifetime, the Greek city of Corinth was one of the most important cities in the Roman empire. A commercial bridge between East and West, it attracted merchants, traders, and visitors from all around the Mediterranean area, making it something like the "Times Square" of its day. This gave the Corinthians something of a "reputation." In fact, one of the Greek verbs for "fornication" was *korinthiazomai,* derived from the city's name. In other words, Paul was addressing a church planted in an atmosphere of temptation and immoral sexual practices. Paul says he has heard of one man who is sexually involved with his stepmother. He also singles out for condemnation the "sexually immoral, idolaters, adulterers, the self-indulgent, sodomites, thieves, misers, drunkards, slanderers and swindlers," leaving the impression that Corinth was a very hot town.

There are two letters to the church in this Greek city. The first epistle may have been written as early as 54 CE; the second was probably written a year later. In the first, Paul calls for unity as factions within the Corinthian church are already splintering these Christians among several leaders. Paul also addresses sexual morality, marriage, divorce, the Eucharist, and the importance of love. 1 Corinthians contains some of Paul's most timeless expressions, and when read in context, Paul is far more of an equal rights advocate for women than he is supposed to be.

> The husband should give to his wife her conjugal rights, and likewise the wife to her husband. For the wife does not have authority over her own body, but the husband does; likewise the husband does not have authority over his own body, but the wife does. (Rom. 7:3–4)

> Nevertheless in the Lord woman is not independent of man or man independent of woman. For just as woman came from man, so man comes through woman; but all things come from God. (1 Cor. 11:11–12)

> If I speak in the tongues or mortals and of angels, but do not have love, I am a noisy gong or a clanging cymbal. And if I have prophetic powers, and understand all mysteries and knowledge, and if I have all faith, so as to remove mountains, but do not have love, I am nothing. If I give away all my possessions, and if I hand over my body so that I may boast but do not have love, I gain nothing. (1 Cor. 13:1–3)

> Listen I will tell you a mystery! We will not all die, but we will all be changed, in a moment, in the twinkling of an eye, at the last trumpet. For the trumpet will sound, and the dead will be raised imperishable, and we will be changed. (1 Cor. 15:51–52)

> So we do not lose heart. Even though our outer nature is wasting away, our inner nature is being renewed day by day. For this slight momentary affliction is preparing us for an eternal weight of glory beyond all measure, because we look not at what can be seen but at what cannot be seen; for what can be seen is temporary, but what cannot be seen is eternal. (2 Cor. 4:16–18)

> For God loves a cheerful giver. (2 Cor. 9:7)

• **Galatians**

Written to churches Paul had personally founded in Galatia, a Roman province in what is now Turkey, this letter is believed to be among the earliest written by Paul. Despite extensive research, the exact location of the churches addressed by Paul is unknown.

Paul was apparently writing in response to Jewish-Christian teachers who had arrived in the Galatian churches and were insisting on circumcision as a requirement for Christians. To these Greek converts, the thought of having the tip of their penises shortened was no small matter. Paul told the Galatians to ignore those who say that Christians must follow the Jewish Law and be circumcised. Now that was Good News! Paul insisted that Jewish traditions are not compulsory for Christians, laying out his fundamental idea: faith in the resurrected Jesus is more important than strict adherence to Jewish Law.

> Live by the Spirit, I say, and do not gratify the desires of
> the flesh. For what the flesh desires is opposed to the
> Spirit, and what the Spirit desires is opposed to the flesh;
> for these are opposed to each other, to prevent you from
> doing what you want. (Gal. 5:16–17)

• **Ephesians**

Traditionally attributed to Paul, the letter to the church at Ephesus, where Paul had once gotten into hot water with the Artemis-worshipers who rioted when he preached against idols (see Acts), is now a toss-up of sorts. While Paul might simply have been citing himself, Ephesians paraphrases the earlier—but shorter—letter to the Colossians and is more of a summary of Paul's thoughts than a presentation of new material. There are also questions of style, including an uncharacteristic opening hymn, that seem unlike Paul's more direct voice. Whether it was Paul or not, the author of Ephesians says that believers are neither Jews nor Gentiles: all are Christians and part of God's household. The author calls for mutual respect between owners and slaves, employers and laborers.

> So then, putting away falsehood, let all of us speak the
> truth to our neighbors, for we are members of one another.
> Be angry but do not sin; do not let the sun go down on
> your anger. (Eph. 4:25–26)

• Philippians

The letter is among the so-called "prison letters," thought to have
been written when Paul was imprisoned in Rome from about 60
CE to the time of his death. Addressed to Christians in the ancient
Macedonian city of Philippi, it is personal and affectionate in tone.
He writes that the Philippians have "a place in my heart, since
you have all shared together in the grace that has been mine."

Praising the Philippians for their work in spreading the gospel,
Paul prays that their love for one another continues to increase.
But the question of circumcision is still splitting the ranks, and
Paul also warns them against "evil workers" who insist that it is
necessary.

> Therefore, my beloved, just as you have always obeyed me,
> not only in my presence, but much more now in my absence,
> work out your own salvation in fear and trembling; for it is
> God who is at work in you, enabling you both to will and to
> work for his good pleasure. (Phil. 2:12–13)

> And the peace of God, which surpasses all understanding,
> will guard your hearts and your minds in Christ Jesus.
> (Phil. 4:7)

• Colossians

This letter was addressed to the Christians of the ancient city of
Colossae, another of the churches in Asia Minor (modern Turkey),
near Ephesus. Scholars have also raised doubts about Paul's authorship of this letter. If it is by Paul, it was probably written while
he was in prison, perhaps in Rome. Paul calls upon the members
of the Colossian church to abandon the desires and temptations of
the flesh. Paul's fundamental concern was to alert the Christians
there against an erroneous religious teaching that stressed knowl-

edge (philosophy), rather than faith, advocated a reliance on the worship of angels as the principal means of attaining salvation, and viewed the world as basically evil. He urged instead belief in the crucified and risen Christ.

The letter anticipated the second-century conflict that the church would have with Gnostics, the early Christian sect that departed from accepted Christian teaching. The ideas, or errors, Paul described in this letter were all typical of ideas later embraced by the Gnostics.

> He is the image of the invisible God, the firstborn of all creation; for in him all things in heaven and on earth were created, things visible and invisible, whether thrones or dominions or rulers or powers—all things have been created through and for him. (Col. 1:16–17)

> There is no longer Greek and Jew, circumcised and uncircumcised, barbarian, Scythian, slave and free; but Christ is all and in all! (Col. 3:11)

> Wives, be subject to your husbands, as is fitting in the Lord. Husbands, love your wives and never treat them harshly. Children obey your parents in everything, for this is acceptable duty in the Lord. Fathers, do not provoke your children, or they may lose heart. (Col. 3:18–21)

• 1 & 2 Thessalonians

These letters provoke some controversy because some scholars think the second of them may have actually been written first. Both letters to the church at Thessalonica, the capital of the Roman province of Macedonia (modern Salonica in northern Greece) are believed to be the first of Paul's letters, written about 50 CE. These Christians may have been victims of the earliest Roman persecutions, and Paul congratulates them for their faith in the face of adversity.

Paul was preoccupied with two major practical concerns. The first was sex—Paul specifies keeping away from sexual immorality and says Christians must control their bodies in a holy fashion, not giving way to "selfish lust." And the second issue was hard work. Apparently some people, certain that the second coming of Jesus was due any day, had decided not to bother with work. Paul urges them to refuse food to those who don't work, establishing a precedent later employed by the legendary English adventurer-soldier Captain John Smith, who enacted a similar policy in the British colony of Jamestown, Virginia.

Although some scholars have questioned the attribution of 2 Thessalonians to Paul, it is now generally believed to have been written by him.

> So let us not fall asleep as others do, but let us keep awake
> and be sober; for those who sleep sleep at night, and those
> who are drunk get drunk at night. But since we belong to the
> day, let us be sober and put on the breastplate of faith and
> love, and for a helmet the hope of salvation. (1 Thess. 5:5–9)

• Philemon

This is the only truly "personal" letter of Paul's to survive, the only correspondence to an individual on a private matter. Paul wrote this letter of only twenty-five verses while in prison, where he had met and converted Onesimus ("Useful"), the runaway slave of Philemon, a leader of the church at Colossae. Early Christians kept slaves, like many in the Mediterranean world who could afford to do so. There was nothing unusual or wrong with it in their view. Paul was a "social conservative" who told Christians to obey laws. But there are hints in the New Testament that the attitude toward slavery was changing. Masters were instructed to treat their slaves fairly and give them freedom if the opportunity arose. Even more radical was Paul's teaching that "in Christ" there was no distinction between free and slave.

Paul sent Onesimus home with a letter asking his master Philemon to take Onesimus back. However, he urged Philemon to treat Onesimus not as a slave but as a new brother in Jesus. Paul offers restitution for anything that Onesimus may have stolen when he escaped, and hints that Philemon might free the slave to continue to work for the author in prison.

While Paul did not openly attack slavery, an accepted and legally protected institution, he implied that through conversion to Christianity, Onesimus had become an equal. That Onesimus the slave was "brother" to Philemon, his legal master, would have been a revolutionary idea. It was certainly seen that way in nineteenth-century America when Christian abolitionists cited Paul's letter to refute the ideas of slaveholders that slavery was sanctioned by the Bible.

> Perhaps this is the reason he was separated from you for a while, so that you might have him back forever, no longer as a slave but more than a slave, a beloved brother—especially to me but how much more to you, both in the flesh and in the Lord. (Philemon 15–16)

THE "PASTORAL LETTERS"
1 & 2 TIMOTHY, TITUS

✳

The three "Pastoral Letters" are addressed to disciples and helpers of Paul, and deal with the running of the church and care of the Christian faithful. Both Timothy and Titus were disciples and helpers of Paul. The letters are concerned mainly with organization, the duty of the ministry, doctrine, and Christian behavior. Unlike most of Paul's undoubtedly genuine letters, the authorship of these three is disputed. The letters mention "bishops," a title not used in Paul's lifetime.

The Pastoral Letters are now thought to be the work of a single unknown author of the late first century who pseudonymously ascribed them to Paul. Possibly, he was a disciple of Paul and used some genuine material in his work.

• **1 Timothy**

While Paul had seemed to be of two minds about women in the church, this letter left no doubt about their place. "I permit no woman to teach or to have authority over men," it read. Bishops could marry, but have only one wife. Celibacy on the part of church leaders was practiced from earliest days but was not compelled until medieval times. This letter also makes it clear that the early church was confronting disputes over "false teaching," another indication of the divisions that would fracture the early church into groups such as the Gnostics, who would be branded "heretics":

> The Spirit has explicitly said that during the last times some will desert the faith and pay attention to deceitful spirits and doctrines that come from devils, seduced by the hypocrisy of liars whose consciences are branded as though with a red-hot iron: they forbid marriage and prohibit foods which God created to be accepted with thanksgiving by all who believe and who know the truth. (1 Tim. 4:1–3 NJB)

• **2 Timothy**

In the second of the Pastoral Letters, the author calls upon Timothy to use the strength that comes with the grace of Jesus to bear witness to the gospel. As a teacher of the gospel, he should be prepared to endure suffering, as the author does, for if the faithful hold firm they will reign with Jesus.

• Titus

One of the early Gentile converts who traveled with and assisted Paul, Titus had been one of those at the center of the circumcision debate. In this letter, Paul was ostensibly giving directions on running the new churches on the island of Crete.

> The saying is sure and worthy of full acceptance, that Christ Jesus came into the world to save sinners—of whom I am the foremost. (1 Tim. 1:15)

> For we brought nothing into the world, so that we can take nothing out of it. (1 Tim. 6:7)

> For the love of money is a root of all kinds of evil, and in their eagerness to be rich some have wandered away from the faith and pierced themselves with many pains. (1 Tim. 6:10)

> For God did not give us a spirit of cowardice, but rather a spirit of power and of love and of discipline. (2 Tim 1:7)

> To the pure all things are pure, but to the corrupt and unbelieving nothing is pure. Their very minds and consciences are corrupted. They profess to know God, but they deny him by their actions. (Titus 1:15–16)

> But avoid stupid controversies, genealogies, dissensions, and quarrels about the law, for they are unprofitable and worthless. (Titus 3:9)

MORE MAIL

THE GENERAL EPISTLES

*Be not forgetful to entertain strangers: for thereby some have
entertained angels unawares. (Heb. 13:1–2 KJV)*

*Who is wise and understanding among you? Show by your good
life that your works are done with gentleness born of wisdom.
(James 3:13)*

The letters attributed to Paul are probably the most famous New Testament letters, but there is another group of eight other letters, or "epistles," that includes Hebrews, James, 1 & 2 Peter, 1, 2 & 3 John, and Jude. Most of the "General" or "Universal Letters" are not truly letters but tracts, or even written versions of sermons aimed at early Christian communities. These letters were written either to shore up the nerve of Christians being persecuted or to keep in line those who were starting to wander from the straight and narrow. They reflect real fears in the face of persecution and everyday concerns of the early church. They also treat some of the controversies over teaching that began to split the early Christian world, a community that could be divided by sects and differing opinions, just as modern Christianity is.

• Hebrews

Frequently calling up the names of the "heroes" of the Hebrew scriptures, Hebrews was probably aimed at Jewish converts to Christianity. Few non-Jewish Christians of the early period would have understood the letter's references to Noah, Abraham, Lot, and other familiar Israelite characters. The likelihood is that some of these Jewish converts, faced with the growing persecution of Christians by the Roman empire, may have been wondering if making the switch was such a bright idea. The letter was written to shore up their nerve.

This book has fallen into a kind of literary limbo. It is addressed to no specific church or person and begins without the personal greeting typical of other New Testament letters. The letter's author is unnamed, and for centuries Paul was just assumed to have written it. Augustine, the most influential Christian writer after Paul, accepted that opinion; and when Augustine spoke, people listened. Hebrews was linked with Paul's other letters in early New Testament collections, and some authorities still say it is Paul's work. Other scholars thought it was by another early church leader or an unknown scribe who had recorded Paul's teachings, and the modern scholarly opinion is almost unanimous that Hebrews was not written by Paul.

Since Hebrews makes no specific reference to the Roman destruction of Jerusalem's Temple in 70 CE, many scholars also believe that the letter was written before that date. Others argue for a later date, during the persecution of Christians under Emperor Domitian near the end of the century. They cite this line as a reference to the fallen Jerusalem: "For here we have no lasting city, but we are looking for the city that is to come." (Heb. 13:14)

> Indeed, the word of God is living and active, sharper than any two-edged sword, piercing until it divides soul from spirit, joints from marrow; it is able to judge the thoughts and intentions of the heart. And before him no creature is hidden, but all are naked and laid bare to the eyes of the one to whom we must render an account. (Heb. 4:12–13)

> Now faith is the assurance of things hoped for, the conviction of things not seen. (Heb. 11:1)

• James

Unlike Paul's letters and Hebrews, in which the titles reflect the recipients, this and the other "General Letters" are named for their supposed authors. Which "James" wrote this one is a mystery. The letter was traditionally thought to be written by James, the brother of Jesus, a leader of the Jewish Christians in Jerusalem. There were also two apostles named James and the letter-writer isn't more specific about himself. Possibly because the letter challenges Paul's ideas, a later writer used this "important" name to give his work more authority.

James is addressed to "the twelve tribes in the Dispersion," so it is presumably directed, like Hebrews, to Jewish converts to Christianity. The author addresses a group of Jewish Christians who are told to consider their trials as a privilege, and temptation as an opportunity to do right. They are told to assist the poor especially if they themselves are comfortably off.

Although James was recognized as part of the authorized New

Testament as early as the second century, not everyone accepted it without reservation. The famed German reformer Martin Luther hated the book. Luther (1483–1546) literally ripped it out of copies of the Bible. He felt that parts of it contradicted Paul, and he called it an "epistle of straw."

Luther's objection lay in the book's major theme: the author believes that faith without accompanying "good deeds" is no faith at all. Some of the passages seem to attack Paul's central doctrine of "justification by faith," whereby people are saved by their faith alone, not by "works," by which Paul specifically meant keeping certain religious laws. In other words, is belief in Jesus by itself enough to guarantee salvation? Or must one also be a "good-deed-doer," as the Wizard of Oz put it?

Some modern scholars believe that James and Paul were not arguing over basic doctrine but using similar terms in different ways. James uses "works" to mean acts of charity, performed in the Jewish tradition. To Paul, "works" specifically referred to ritual aspects of Jewish Law, such as circumcision. To Paul, "faith" is a commitment to God, which inevitably produces good works. James was deriding a different kind of "faith," which in his view was merely intellectual belief lacking true commitment. Modern scholars, unlike Martin Luther, acknowledge that Paul and James would both agree that "faith" that does not produce good deeds is false or empty faith.

In refuting that there is a difference between these two Christian leaders, historians also point out the author of James was writing out of concern that some Christians, comfortable with the idea of "faith alone," weren't doing their part in the nitty-gritty work of taking care of the less fortunate. But the letter raises a key question for many people. Can an evil person who gets "faith," repents, and accepts Jesus find salvation? Or can a Nazi claim to be a Christian, as many Nazis did? The answer may lie in James's statement "I by my works will show you my faith." In other words, the true Christian must only do the right thing, not just pay lip service to the Lord.

Be ye doers of the word, and not hearers only. (James 1:22)

What good is it, my brothers and sisters, if you say you have faith but do not have works? Can faith save you? If a brother or sister is naked and lacks daily food, and one of you say to them, "Go in peace; keep warm and eat your fill," and yet you do not supply their bodily needs, what is the good of that? So faith by itself, if it has no works, is dead. But someone will say, "You have faith and I have works." Show me your faith apart from your works, and I by my works will show you my faith. (James 2:14–18)

As the body without the spirit is dead, so faith without works is dead also. (James 2:26)

Who is wise and understanding among you? Show by your good life that your works are done with gentleness born of wisdom. But if you have bitter envy and selfish ambition in your hearts, do not be boastful and false to the truth. Such wisdom does not come down from above, but is earthly, unspiritual, devilish. For where there is envy and selfish ambition, there will also be disorder and wickedness of every kind. But the wisdom from above is first pure, then peaceable, gentle, willing to yield, full of mercy and good fruits, without a trace of partiality or hypocrisy. (James 3:13–17)

• 1 & 2 Peter

In the first of two letters attributed to the apostle Peter, the author offers encouragement to "Exiles of the Dispersion," or Jewish Christians, living in the Roman provinces in the northern part of Asia Minor and facing Roman persecution. Claiming he does not have long for this world, the author denounces false teachers and says that the expectation of Jesus' Second Coming must never be abandoned. The Second Epistle of Peter is addressed "to those who have obtained a faith of equal standing with ours in the righteousness of our God and Savior Jesus Christ," or essentially to all Christians.

Did Peter really write them? Since they are written in excellent Greek, reflect knowledge of Paul's Epistles, and cite the Greek Septuagint, instead of Hebrew scriptures, many scholars doubt that Peter, a Galilean fisherman, could have written them. The place of composition is commonly believed to have been Rome, chiefly because of the phrase, "he who is at Babylon sends you greetings." "Babylon" was a Christian code name for Rome.

> All flesh is like grass, and all its glory like the flower of grass. The grass withers, and the flower falls, but the word of the Lord endures forever. (1 Peter 1:24–25)

> Abstain from the desires of the flesh that wage war against the soul. (1 Peter 2:11)

> Above all, maintain constant love for one another, for love covers a multitude of sins. (1 Peter 4:8)

John's Three Letters

These letters give biblical scholars major headaches. The first of them is highly poetic. The second two read like office memos. A view favored by many commentators is that one and the same author wrote the Gospel of John and all three Epistles and that all of them date from about the turn of the first century CE. A different John wrote Revelation (see next chapter).

• 1 John

The first of three letters opens in a style very reminiscent of the poetic opening of the Gospel of John:

> Something which has existed
> since the beginning,
> which we have heard,
> which we have seen with our own eyes,
> which we have watched

and touched with our own hands,
the Word of life,
this is our theme. (1 John 1:1 NJB)

The author then goes on to denounce those who deny that Jesus appeared in the flesh after the resurrection. The teaching of these "antichrists" may have been an early form of Gnosticism, the religious philosophy that so disrupted the unity of the early churches, and was eventually treated as heresy.

• **2 John**

Trivia fans may want to note: this is the shortest book of the Bible. Consisting of only thirteen verses, the book is by an author who calls himself "the elder." He repeats the warning that believers must not be deceived by those who say that Jesus never returned in the flesh but only in spirit form. It is addressed to the "elect lady and her children," but that is a figure of speech for a church, possibly in Asia Minor.

• **3 John**

Another brief letter, this is addressed to an individual named Gaius, an exemplary member of an unnamed church. The author again calls himself "the elder," and complains that the leader of Gaius's church lacks humility, does not show proper hospitality to guests, and is spreading false accusations.

Beloved, let us love one another, because love is from God; everyone who loves is born of God and knows God. Whoever does not love does not know God for God is love. (1 John 4:7–8)

Many deceivers have gone out into the world, those who do not confess that Jesus Christ has come in the flesh; any such person is the deceiver and the anti-Christ! (2 John 7)

Beloved, do not imitate what is evil but imitate what is good. Whoever does good is from God; whoever does evil has not seen God. (3 John 11)

• **Jude**

Only twenty-five verses long, Jude is written by someone calling himself a "servant of Jesus Christ, and brother of James." For this reason, the letter was attributed to another of Jesus' actual brothers, of which there were said to be four: James, Joseph, Simon, and Judas. The name was shortened to Jude because nobody wanted a letter from somebody named "Judas" in the Bible. This was a tract devoted to combating the "false teachings," again identified with early Gnostics, that had spread throughout the early Christian community.

> But you, beloved, must remember the predictions of the apostles of our Lord Jesus Christ; for they said to you, "In the last time there will be scoffers, indulging in their own ungodly lusts." It is these worldly people, devoid of the Spirit, who are causing divisions. (Jude 17–19)

APOCALYPSE NOW?

REVELATION

Then I saw a new heaven and a new earth: for the first heaven and the first earth had passed away, and the sea was no more. And I saw the holy city, the new Jerusalem, coming down out of heaven from God, prepared as a bride adorned for her husband. (Rev. 21:1–2)

❄

❋ Why is 666 the Number of the Beast?

The author of the New Testament's last book starts off simply enough in the form of a letter to seven churches in Asia Minor. Harshly condemning the sins of the world, he then takes his readers into a nightmarish, kaleidoscopic vision completely removed from the works of Paul or anyone else in the New Testament. Wild images dance across the pages, leaving centuries of befuddled readers and generations of eager "End Is Near" doomsayers in his wake. Strange visions. Earthquakes. Mysterious numerology. Trumpets. Angels. Horses. Blood and Plagues. Death, Doom, and Destruction.

Welcome to the Gospel According to Fellini or Salvador Dalí.

The author calls himself John but he is clearly not the John of the Gospel or the Letters. Nothing in this book's style or message is like those earlier books. The place of composition is presented as Patmos, an Aegean island used as a Roman penal colony, to which the author had been banished for his preaching. There, most likely during the reign of Roman emperor Domitian (81–96 CE), he received an extraordinary prophetic vision of the Second Coming of Jesus and the Last Judgment.

The date of Revelation is crucial to understanding the book's strange symbolism. Like his predecessor Nero, twenty years earlier, Domitian insisted on the divinity of the imperial line and worship of the emperor was required during his reign. Domitian persecuted Christians who refused to worship him, but he apparently did not dream up novel outrages with the perverse gusto that Nero brought to the task. Like his perverse predecessor Caligula, Nero had elevated excessive behavior to an insane art. Convinced of his divinity, he spared no expense. He was transported everywhere in a caravan of one thousand carriages pulled by mules shod in silver. He fancied himself a chariot racer and appeared in the races. He went wild at the betting tables. His sexual excesses were even worse. His incestuous relationship with his mother Agrippina was an open secret, and a "marriage" to a man was performed in public.

Being a follower of Christ in Nero's day was no picnic. Tales of what Rome might have in store for Christians must have still been fresh in the minds of the members of the early church. The Roman historian Tacitus (c. 56–115 CE) wrote one of the few contemporary accounts of the fate of Rome's Christians:

> To dispel the rumor [that he had started the Great Fire] Nero put into the dock instead the group whom the man in the street detested for their vices and nicknamed "Christians," finding highly recondite punishments for them. The name originated with one Christus, executed on the authority of the governor Pontius Pilate during Tiberius' reign. . . . Their execution was accompanied by mockery. They were sewn up in animal skins to be torn to death by hounds, or set on crosses, or prepared for the brand and burned to give light in the darkness when daylight faded. Nero had opened his private gardens for the spectacle, and offered an exhibition in the circus, mixing with the crowd in a charioteer's uniform or riding in a chariot.

When John wrote, Christians heard rumors that Nero, who had committed suicide, was still alive. He was thought to be preparing to return to Rome and retake his throne with a vengeful army. Against this background of persecution and paranoia, John spun out his vision of a coming Judgment Day.

Plot Summary: The Apocalypse

In a dreamlike vision, the author sees a great sacrificial Lamb with seven horns and seven eyes. The Lamb receives a scroll from God and begins to break its seven seals.

The First Four Seals

Four horsemen ride out. The first is on a white horse, an all conquering power; the second is on a red horse, whose rider takes peace from the earth; the third rides a black horse and carries scales, symbolizing the famine that follows war; and finally a pale green horse whose rider's name is Death. The four are given authority over the earth to kill with sword, famine, pestilence, and wild animals.

The Fifth Seal

raises the dead martyrs who are given white robes and told to rest a little longer.

The Sixth Seal

brings a great earthquake and cosmic catastrophes. The sun darkens and the moon turns red; the stars fall from the skies.

The Seventh Seal

there is silence in heaven for half an hour.

Then seven angels blow their trumpets in sequence. The first five blasts bring destruction on the earth; the sixth signals that four angels who had been held ready are released to kill "a third of mankind"; the seventh trumpet blast joins heaven together with what remains of earth. Heavenly voices sing:

"The kingdom of the world has become the kingdom of our Lord and his Messiah, and he will reign forever and ever."

Once again, as with Isaiah, this provides pretty good lyrics for Handel's *Messiah*!

A woman crowned with twelve stars appears. She is in agonized childbirth. A great red dragon awaits the child's birth. But the newborn is taken to heaven, where war breaks out. The angels under the archangel Michael defeat the seven-headed, ten-horned dragon—the Devil and Satan.

Another terrible beast emerges from the sea and is given authority by the other beast. The world worships the beast. Another beast emerges from the earth. The beast has a number: 666.

The day of judgment breaks. Seven angels empty bowls of plague representing God's anger onto the world and over the beast. The cities of the world collapse and vanish. Babylon, the "Great Whore," burns and the world laments her passing. Songs of victory resound in heaven. The new age begins—after which Satan is released for a short time before his ultimate end at Armageddon. This was actually a reference to the city of Megiddo, the scene of several major battles in Israel's early history. Then there is a new heaven and a new earth, and on the earth, a new messianic city of Jerusalem.

Why is 666 the Number of the Beast?

In rock music, books, and films, the number 666 has come to represent Satanism in popular culture. Throughout history, the identity and meaning of the mystical Beast numbered 666 has been applied to such notorious figures as Napoleon and Hitler. In fact, the number has a much simpler and more reasonable explanation. While Satan and the Devil are major players in Revelation, the meaning of 666 was clear to the people of the time. In both Greek and Hebrew, letters doubled as numerals. One simple solution to the 666 puzzle is that the number is produced by adding up the Hebrew equivalent of "Kaisar Neron," or Emperor Nero. Rome, the "Great Whore Babylon" of Revelation, and its butchering evil emperors, were the real villains for the author of Revelation.

BIBLICAL VOICES

I warn everyone who hears the words of the prophecy of this book: if anyone adds to them, God will add to that person the plagues described in this book. If anyone takes away from the words of the book of this prophecy, God will take away that person's share in the tree of life and in the holy city, which are described in this book. (Rev. 22:18–19)

MILESTONES IN BIBLICAL TIMES VII

117 After completing conquests in Mesopotamia, Emperor Trajan dies while returning to Rome. He is succeeded by a kinsman who rules Rome for twenty-one years as the emperor Hadrian.

132 Jerusalem's Jews rise in anger at the construction of a shrine to the Roman god Jupiter on the site of their fallen Temple. The uprising begins a two-year insurrection called the Second Revolt.

135 Roman legions retake Jerusalem and Hadrian orders the site of Jerusalem plowed under.

177 Emperor Marcus Aurelius begins a systematic persecution of Christians in Rome because they oppose emperor-worship and are seen as a threat to Roman order.

c. 200 The bishop of Rome gains his predominant position as Pope.

c. 250 Under the emperor Decius, the wide-scale persecution of Christians increases, producing martyrs who will be revered as saints.

303–311 Emperor Diocletian orders a new round of persecutions of Christians in Rome in an attempt to restore the old religion of Rome.

312 The emperor Constantine becomes absolute ruler of the western Roman empire. Before a battle, Constantine claims to see a vision of a luminous cross bearing the words *In hoc signo vinces* ("In this sign you will conquer").

313 Constantine establishes toleration of Christianity.

325 Constantine summons the Council of Nicaea, in modern Turkey, the first ecumenical council of the church. It supports the doctrine that God and Christ are of the same substance. Christianity becomes the dominant religion of the empire.

326 Constantine moves to the ancient city of Byzantium and renames it Constantinople (modern Istanbul).

367 Athanasius, a church leader in Alexandria, lists the twenty-seven books of the New Testament as they are known today. Church leaders in Rome accept this list in *382*.

391 Emperor Theodosius orders all non-Christian works eliminated and the Library at Alexandria, storehouse of the world's knowledge, is burned.

395 The Roman empire is divided into eastern and western empires, a move that is considered temporary but becomes permanent.

399 North African cleric-philosopher Augustine writes *Confessions*.

Before his death in *430*, Augustine also writes *The City of God* (*426*), which declares that empires like Rome are temporal and the only permanent community is the church. He also states that the purpose of marriage is procreation. His views, more influential than those of anyone besides Paul, dominate church thinking for the next twelve hundred years.

431 The Council of Ephesus. Recognizing Mary as the Mother of God, the Council begins the spread of the cult of the Virgin.

610 In Arabia, the prophet Muhammad secretly begins a new religion, to be called Islam. Three years later, he starts to preach openly and is opposed by Mecca's leaders, who oppose any change in traditional tribal customs. After Mohammed flees from Mecca to Yathrib (Medina)—a flight commemorated as the *Hegira*—a civil war begins. In *628*, Mecca falls to Mohammed's forces and the prophet writes letters to the world's leaders explaining the principles of Islam. He returns to Mecca with the *Quran* (Koran) which means "recitation." It says, "There is no God but Allah and Mohammed is his messenger."

Mohammed dies in *632*, leaving behind an Islamic monotheism that will soon dominate the Near East and North Africa. His youngest daughter also dies that year, leaving two sons—Hasssan and Hussein—who found a dynasty that rules Egypt and North Africa for nearly three centuries.

638 Jerusalem falls to Islamic forces.

AFTERWORD

WHOSE GOD IS IT ANYWAY?

The Lord is a man of war. (Ex. 15:3 KJV)

The Lord is my shepherd. (Psalm 23:1)

"Be perfect, therefore, as your heavenly Father is perfect."
(Matt. 5:48)

The longer I live, the more convincing proofs I see of this
truth, that God governs in the affairs of men. And if a
sparrow cannot fall to the ground without his notice, is it
probable that an empire can rise without his aid?
—BENJAMIN FRANKLIN

I believe in one God and no more, and hope for happiness
beyond this life. I believe in the equality of man; and I believe
that religious duties consist in doing justice, loving mercy, and
endeavoring to make our fellow creatures happy.
—THOMAS PAINE

The foregoing generations beheld God and nature face to face;
we, through their eyes. Why should not we also enjoy an
original relation to the universe?
—RALPH WALDO EMERSON

Religion . . . is the opium of the people.

—KARL MARX

I myself believe that the evidence of God lies primarily in inner personal experiences.

—WILLIAM JAMES

God is dead.

—FRIEDRICH NIETZSCHE

I began this book by asking, "Whose Bible is it anyway?" That question was difficult enough. I end it with another question, a much tougher one: "Whose God is it anyway?"

Or perhaps it would be more appropriate to ask, "*Which* God is it?"

Is it the angry, jealous, temperamental, punishing Yahweh? The war God celebrated by Moses? The God who swept life off the face of the earth in the Flood, killed the firstborn of Egypt, helped conquer the people of Jericho and had them put to the sword, and silently accepted the sacrifice of Jephthah's daughter? The God who took pleasure from the smell of burnt animal flesh?

Or is it the merciful, just, patient, forgiving God? The tender Shepherd of the Twenty-third Psalm? The hunky "lover" of Song of Solomon? The "perfect" Father of Jesus? And could they all possibly be the same God?

It would be very simple—having read all of these stories—to dismiss the Bible and its various images of God as an elaborate set of myths. All of these tales of arks, plagues, battles, burnt-out cities, and miracles might legitimately be viewed as little more than "Just-so stories," as Robin Fox describes them in *The Unauthorized Version*. In Fox's entertaining and provocative book about the Bible, "just-so" stories are tales that men create to explain away rainbows, or the name of a village, or the existence of an unusual pile of stones in a particular place. From the literary, historical, and anthropological perspectives, one could make a convincing case that these biblical tales—steeped in ancient traditions and local folk stories—were all human inventions. The God of Genesis and the rest of the Bible was a brilliant fiction, created by man in his image.

How else to explain the "progression" of God in the Hebrew Bible? The God-Creator who walked in the Garden of Eden. The thunderous mountain God of Exodus. The somewhat removed God who used the prophets as go-betweens. The completely absent God of Esther.

Hand in hand with this view of an "Incredible Shrinking God" stands the rather cynical notion that the rise of both Judaism and Christianity represents another facet of humanity's long Power Play. By adopting the view that human history is essentially about power—getting it and keeping it—the Bible emerges as one more form of power. History usually sees power in terms of muscle, military might, and money. But what hold is greater, what power more terrible, than the one that claims to determine a person's earthly and eternal fate? In this scornful view, "orthodox" religion merely wants to establish the power of the priest over the people and take its place among all the other authoritarian institutions men have devised. God becomes a "Cosmic Carrot-or-Stick." Be good and you will be rewarded—on heaven and earth. Be bad and you will suffer—here and forever.

This dismissive view, quite widely accepted these days, relegates God to mythology—an elaborately fabricated contraption with man-made glitches all over the place. But it is not the only answer to a question that has kept philosophers and theologians pondering for centuries. There are a few distinct alternative responses.

One of them is the answer Job got. This response can be quickly summed up like this: certainly God is still around. But he's awfully busy with all the other things going on in the universe, which you are too puny to understand. So don't even have the audacity to ask! It is short, sweet, and contains its own unrefutable logic. But like the Chinese food of countless jokes, it leaves us hungry for more an hour later.

Then there is the "Big Parent in the Sky" view. In this variation on the paternalistic viewpoint of traditional religion, God is a Cosmic "Ward Cleaver." When we were little, we needed lots of attention, so God was always there for us. This God was a wise, caring, but occasionally imperfect Dad, capable of both unconditional love and a hard swat across the bottom. As time went by, and we humans "grew up," God let us be on our own. This scenario, though naive, is still rather appealing. It means we are no longer bluntly faced with the threat of "Wait until your Father gets home." And it allows humanity the right to make its own decisions and mistakes. People may feel about this sort of God the way many teenagers feel about their parents—"You are really so out of touch."

The "Big Daddy in the Sky" is related to still another view I'll call "Supernatural Selection." In this scheme, God has evolved along with humanity over the centuries in a Darwinian progression. We've both become more sophisticated, less "primitive." As we got "smarter," God no longer found it so necessary to perform flashy parlor tricks with thunder, lightning, and parted seas. This God communicates with us on a more cerebral, or intellectual, level. The American philosopher William James may have had this type of God in mind when he wrote, "I myself believe that the evidence of God lies primarily in inner personal experiences."

A twist on that notion is the suggestion that we humans certainly have changed, but God hasn't. For many years, I wondered why the God of the Bible who spoke to people, performed miracles, and seemed so involved in human affairs had seemingly stopped calling. Had he lost our number? Only recently has it occurred to me that maybe God wasn't the one who stopped paying attention. It was us. Perhaps our "primitive" ancestors, without all the competing noise of modern civilization, were far more able to hear what came to the prophet Elijah as "a still small voice." In *A History of God*, Karen Armstrong suggests that idea when she writes, "One of the reasons why religion seems irrelevant today is that many of us no longer have the sense that we are surrounded by the unseen."

Armstrong's "unseen" offers an alternative—a great, big "On the other hand." If we accept the possibility of the "unseen," it allows us to think that there may actually be something about a set of ideas, morals, and rituals that have survived persecution, ridicule, and doubt for thousands of years. Nietzsche said God was dead. But surprise! God outlasted Egypt, Babylon, Greece, Rome, the Third Reich, and Communism. Each of these "empires" relied upon a distinct belief system. Holding fast to gods of sun or moon, the philosophies of Plato and Socrates, the divinity of the emperor, or the Führer's deranged promises, these earthly empires were founded upon some vision—no matter how perverse—of a perfect world. Needless to say, they all failed.

In other words, if God is dead, "the old boy" looks remarkably well preserved when compared to some of his rivals.

But even that still leaves our question suspended in midair— Which God? Is it the omniscient, omnipresent God of my childhood confirmation classes, the Cosmic Santa Claus who keeps track of who is naughty or nice?

Inevitably, these questions all come down to the "F" word. Faith. The "unseen." You can't buy Faith. You can't sell it, though many have tried. You can't measure, weigh, or dissect it. Do people "believe" because we are spiritual suckers, gullible humans who inevitably fall back on the superstitions of our "primitive" ancestors? Or do we believe because believing is a valid choice?

In a wonderful description of Judaism, Dennis Prager and Joseph Telushkin have written:

> The Jew introduced God into the world, and called all people to live in brotherhood by accepting one moral standard based upon God. Each of these ideals, a universal God, a universal moral law, and universal brotherhood, was revealed for the first time 3,200 years ago, to some ex-slaves in the Sinai desert. Why this particular group of men and women, at that particular time, should have taken upon themselves and upon all their succeeding generations the mission to "perfect the world under the rule of God" is a mystery which perhaps only the religious can hope to solve. (*The Nine Questions People Ask About Judaism*, p. 111)

Jesus was a devout Jew who taught that "the Kingdom of God is within you." The notion, shared by many religions and philosophies, of attaining perfection was one of Jesus' simple—yet seemingly impossible—commandments. In the Sermon on the Mount, he said, "Be perfect, therefore, as your heavenly Father is perfect."

Perfecting the world. Perfecting ourselves. Yeah, right. What ridiculously innocent, utopian ideas!

But for thousands of years, faith has sustained Jews against seemingly impossible odds and difficulties. They have been sustained by the idea that the world is perfectible by revealing the truth about God's moral laws. For two thousand years, faith has sustained individual Christians through persecutions and trials. They have held to faith that miracles can still happen. That death is not an end. That loving one's neighbors is a pretty sound idea. That we have the power—and even the responsibility—to forgive. That we can try to be "perfect as the Father is perfect."

It sure isn't easy. But it beats most of the alternatives.

APPENDIX 1

THE TEN COMMANDMENTS

✳

Then God spoke all these words: I am the Lord your God, who brought you out of the land of Egypt, out of the house of slavery; you shall have no other gods before me.

You shall not make for yourself an idol, whether in the form of anything that is in heaven above, or that is on the earth beneath, or that is in the water under the earth. You shall not bow down to them or worship them; for I the LORD your God am a jealous God, punishing children for the iniquity of parents, to the third and fourth generation of those who reject me, but showing steadfast love to the thousandth generation of those who love me and keep my commandments.

You shall not make wrongful use of the name of the Lord your God, for the Lord will not acquit anyone who misuses his name.

Remember the sabbath day, and keep it holy. Six days you shall labor and do all your work. But the seventh day is a sabbath to the Lord your God; you shall not do any work—you, your son or your daughter, your male or female slave, your livestock, or the alien resident in your towns. For in six days the Lord made heaven and earth, the sea, and all that is in them, but rested the seventh day; therefore the Lord blessed the sabbath day and consecrated it.

Honor your father and your mother, so that your days may be long in the land that the Lord your God is giving you.

You shall not murder.

You shall not commit adultery.

You shall not steal.

You shall not bear false witness against your neighbor.

You shall not covet your neighbor's house; you shall not covet your neighbor's wife, or male or female slave, or ox, or donkey, or anything that belongs to your neighbor.

(Ex. 20:1–17 NRSV)

Appendix 2

The Twenty-third Psalm

❋

These are two versions of the most famous and probably most popular of the Psalms.

King James Version

The Lord is my shepherd; I shall not want.

He maketh me to lie down in green pastures: he leadeth me beside the still waters.

He restoreth my soul: he leadeth me in the paths of righteousness for his name's sake.

Yea, though I walk through the valley of the shadow of death, I will fear no evil: for thou art with me; thy rod and thy staff they comfort me.

Thou preparest a table before me in the presence of mine enemies: thou anointest my head with oil; my cup runneth over.

Surely goodness and mercy shall follow me all the days of my life and I will dwell in the house of the Lord forever.

Jewish Publication Society

The Lord is my shepherd;
    I lack nothing.
He makes me lie down in green pastures;
    He leads me to the water in places of repose
    He renews my life;
    He guides me in right paths
    as befits his name.
Though I walk through a valley of deepest darkness,
    I fear no harm, for You are with me;
    Your rod and Your staff—they comfort me.
You spread a table for me in full view of my enemies;

You anoint my head with oil;
    my drink is abundant.
Only goodness and steadfast love shall pursue me
    all the days of my life,
      and I shall dwell in the house of the Lord
      for many long years.

APPENDIX 3

THE LORD'S PRAYER

✳

The "Lord's Prayer" appears in two versions in the New Testament. The more familiar is the one that appears in the "Sermon on the Mount" in Matthew. The second is a shorter form that appears in Luke.

> After this manner therefore pray ye: Our Father which art in heaven, Hallowed be thy name. Thy kingdom come. Thy will be done in earth, as it is in heaven. Give us this day our daily bread. And forgive us our debts as we forgive our debtors. And lead us not into temptation, but deliver us from evil: for thine is the kingdom, and the power, and the glory, for ever. Amen. (Matt. 6:9–13 KJV; *The Book of Common Prayer* and other versions of the Lord's Prayer use an alternate translation of "trespasses" and "those who trespass against us" instead of "debts and "debtors.")

> Father, hallowed be your name. Your kingdom come. Give us each day our daily bread. And forgive us our sins for we ourselves forgive everyone indebted to us. And do not bring us to the time of trial. (Luke 11:2–4 NRSV)

This most familiar of prayers is learned early by most Christians. Far less familiar are the sharp words Jesus uses in Matthew for the prayer style of many of the pious believers of his time. Before teaching the Lord's Prayer, Jesus said:

> Beware of practicing your piety before others in order to be seen by them; for then you have no reward from your Father in heaven.
> So whenever you give alms, do not sound a trumpet before you, as the hypocrites do in the synagogues and in the streets, so that they may be praised by others. . . . And whenever you pray, do not be like the hypocrites; for they love to stand and pray in the synagogues and at the street corners, so that they may be seen by others. Truly I tell

you, they have received their reward. But whenever you
pray, go into your room and shut the door and pray to your
Father who sees in secret; and your Father who sees in secret will reward you.

Jesus' instruction for proper prayer is especially interesting in
light of the public school prayer debate in modern America. The
notion of making public prayers seems so antithetical to Jesus'
ideas that one can only wonder if the proponents of school prayer
laws, often fundamentalist Christians, have read what Jesus had to
say on this pressing question.

APPENDIX 4

THE PROLOGUE TO JOHN'S GOSPEL

❋

In the beginning was the Word, and the Word was with God, and the Word was God. He was in the beginning with God. All things came into being through him, and without him not one thing came into being. What has come into being in him was life, and the life was the light of all people. The light shines in the darkness, and the darkness did not overcome it.

There was a man sent from God, whose name was John. He came as a witness to testify to the light, so that all might believe through him. He himself was not the light, but he came to testify to the light. The true light, which enlightens everyone, was coming into the world.

He was in the world, and the world came into being through him; yet the world did not know him. He came to what was his own, and his own people did not accept him. But to all who received him, who believed in his name, he gave power to become children of God, who were born, not of blood or of the will of the flesh or of the will of man, but God.

And the Word became flesh and lived among us, and we have seen his glory, the glory as of a father's only son, full of grace and truth. . . . From his fullness we have all received, grace upon grace. The law indeed was given through Moses; grace and truth came through Jesus Christ. No one has ever seen God. It is God the only Son, who is close to the Father's heart, who has made him known. (John 1:1–18)

GLOSSARY

An asterisk (*) indicates words defined elsewhere in the Glossary.

angels: Members of the heavenly court, God's retinue of divine assistants; described as "sons of God," "morning stars," "gods," or the "host of heaven." They are depicted in the *Bible as sent to deliver messages (*angel* is from the Greek for "messenger") and protect God's friends. Although called "angels," *cherubim or *seraphim were not messengers but supernatural creatures with specific roles.

apocalypse: The words "apocalypse" and "apocalyptic" are from a Greek word for "to reveal" or "uncover" and describe a literary genre. There are two truly apocalyptic books: Daniel in the Hebrew Bible and Revelation in the *New Testament; the Book of Ezekiel also contains "apocalyptic" material. Generally speaking, apocalyptic writing contains revelations expressed through visionary experiences, intense symbolic images, and often deals with the "end times" or "final days," when there will be a great cosmic upheaval.

Apocrypha: Writings that are not universally regarded as part of the *"canon," or official list, of either Hebrew or Christian scripture. The word means "things hidden away."

apostle: From the Greek for "send away," used for the envoys of Jesus. Traditionally twelve, but not the same twelve as the *disciples*. Paul is also added to the list of primary apostles, and there are others also considered apostles in a more general sense of the word.

Aramaic: The Semitic language of Aram (what is approximately modern Syria). Closely related to *Hebrew, which it largely displaced by the first century CE. It was almost certainly the language spoken by Jesus and his *disciples.

Ark of the Covenant: A wooden box containing the stone tablets of the Law, carried by the Israelites on their journey through the desert. It disappeared during the sack of Jerusalem in 587 BCE.

Bible: The English word "Bible" is derived from the Old French *bible* which is in turn based on the Latin *biblia* and Greek *biblia* for "books." It is used to refer to the sacred scriptures of the Christian church and also for the canon of Jewish scriptures. The authoritative text in the Jewish community is the *Masoretic text, a collection of thirty-nine books (traditionally twenty-four books, but several have been divided into two parts to produce the larger number), mostly written in Hebrew, and also called the Tanakh. The Hebrew Bible is the equivalent of the *Old Testament in Christian Bibles, although the Roman Catholic tradition embraces a number of other books.

The Christian Bible consists of the Old Testament and the twenty-seven books of the *New Testament, which was composed in Greek by early Christians during the first century and early second century CE.

Canaanites: A collective term for the pre-Israelite inhabitants of *Palestine, roughly equivalent to modern-day Israel and Lebanon.

canon: From the Phoenician word for "reed" and Greek for "rule," these are the books regarded as sacred by the Jews, first established with the *Torah around 200 BCE and eventually closed by 70–90 CE. A number of books and parts of books originally thought to be written in Greek were not included by the Jewish *rabbis who established the *Hebrew canon. Similarly, the *New Testament canon reflects those twenty-seven books accepted by the church leaders as divinely inspired.

cherubim: Not to be confused with cute little winged-baby *angels of Renaissance art. These were great winged creatures similar to the carved stone *karibu*, mythical creatures that guarded Babylonian temples and palaces. They had wings of eagles, human faces, and bodies of a bull or lion. In Solomon's Temple, they formed a frame for the *Ark of the Covenant.

Christ: From Greek *christos*, for "anointed one" or *Messiah.

Diaspora: A collective term for the "dispersion" of Jews living outside the land of Israel beginning with the Babylonian conquest of Jerusalem and the deportation (*Exile) of Jews to Babylon.

disciples: From Latin for "pupil," for the students, traditionally the Twelve, called by Jesus. Judas, a disciple, is replaced in Acts by Matthias as an *apostle.

Easter: The Christian holiday celebrating the resurrection of Jesus, this word does not appear in the Bible. It comes from "Eostre," a Saxon goddess celebrated at the spring equinox.

Evangelist: One who tells the "good news" of the coming of *Christ. In a more restricted sense, it means the four authors of the *Gospels.

Exile: The period of the Captivity of the Jews in Babylon by the Chaldeans.

Gentile: Anyone not Jewish.

Gospel: Literally "good news" from the Anglo-Saxon "god spell."

Hasidim: Originally "the Pious," a group of nationalistic, orthodox Jews in the Seleucid era. Now more commonly, followers of a devout form of Judaism with a strong mystical element.

Hebrew: The language of the Israelites and of most of the original Jewish scriptures or *Old Testament. Displaced as a commonly spoken language by *Aramaic and by Greek. Today it is the official language of the modern state of Israel.

Hellenism: The widespread adoption of Greek language, culture, and customs in the period following the conquests of Alexander the Great— c. 300 BCE until the Roman era.

Masoretic: The text of the Hebrew Bible as preserved by "masorete" scribes and now accepted as the standard for spelling and pronouncing the Hebrew Bible.

Messiah: (Greek *christos*) From the Hebrew for "anointed one." In Jewish and Christian theology, the Messiah is the savior figure who is sent by God to deliver his people from suffering and usher in an age of justice and peace. Christian theology believes that Jesus is the Messiah, who is therefore known as *Christ.

Mishnah: The code of Jewish Law, edited and revised by the early *rabbis. Divided into six major units—agriculture, holy days in the Temple, women and family, damages or political questions, holy things, and purity codes—these rules form the basis of legal discussion and commentaries found in the *Talmud.

Mosaic: No, not the tiles glued into a picture—pertaining to Moses.

New Testament: The second part of the Christian Bible. It bears witness to the covenant (*testament) between God and humanity in the person, ministry, death, and resurrection of Jesus. The New Testament is said by Christians to represent God's final and supreme covenant with the world, supplementing and at the same time superseding the covenant of the Old Testament.

Old Testament: The first part of the Christian Bible, which in Christian belief bears witness to the covenant (*testament) made between God and humanity before the coming of Jesus. The Old Testament is different in some Christian traditions depending on the inclusion of the *Apocrypha.

pagan: Although widely thought today to describe a heathen or nonbeliever, this was an early Christian word, from the Latin word for a "civilian," and used to describe non-Christians other than Jews.

Palestine: The region bounded roughly by the Jordan River (west), the Negeb Desert (South), and the Golan Heights of Syria (north). The name means land of the Philistines and was originally given by the Greeks to the coastal area occupied by the Philistines. "Palestine" is used in this book without modern political connotation.

Pentateuch: The first five books of the *Bible. Also called the *Torah, the Books of Moses, the Book of the Law, the Five Books of Moses, the Book of the Law of Moses.

post-Exilic: Relating to the period of Return to Jerusalem after the Captivity in Babylon.

rabbi: A first-century CE term meaning "master," for a religious teacher. The rabbi served as interpreter of the *Torah and as a judge. In later times, rabbis were thought to have magical powers.

Satan: The Hebrew word is somewhat obscure but many scholars believe it meant "adversary" or "accuser." In the *New Testament, "Devil" and "Satan" are used interchangeably.

Septuagint: The Greek translation of Hebrew scriptures begun by Alexandrian Jews in Egypt around 250 BCE.

seraphim: Flying supernatural creatures who appear beside God in Isaiah. They had three sets of wings; for flying, for shielding their eyes so as not to look at God, and for covering their feet (a euphemism for genitals). Some have described them as fiery dragons or serpents. In later traditions, they are associated with choirs of *angels.

synoptic Gospels: The collective name given to the *Gospels of Matthew, Mark, and Luke, from the Greek for "seen" or "viewed together."

Talmud: (Hebrew for "study" or "learning") The classical rabbinic discussions of the ancient code of Jewish Law. There are two Talmuds; one produced in the land of Israel around 400 CE and the other one in Babylon around 550 CE.

testament: Originally meaning the last will of a person, or an agreement, this word was applied to the Scriptures to describe the agreement, or "covenant," made between God and his people.

Torah: (Hebrew for "Law") The first five books of the *Bible, the *Pentateuch; also the entire body of Jewish Law and teaching.

Yahweh: Occurring 6,828 times in Hebrew scriptures, this was one of the Hebrew names for God (also called the Tetragrammaton, Greek for "four letters"). The name itself was considered too sacred to be uttered, and wherever it appeared in the text, it was read as "Adonai" (Lord). Its source is uncertain, although some scholars trace its roots to the Hebrew verb "to be." In later Christian times, the vowels from "Adonai" were joined to the consonants in YHWH to produce the incorrect translation of "Jehovah."

Zion: An obscure word for the hill of Jerusalem upon which the city of David stands. By extension, Zion can also mean Jerusalem.

BIBLIOGRAPHY

This bibliography includes general references as well as books about very specific areas of Bible study. The emphasis is on recent works that reflect the latest scholarship and archaeological or scientific discoveries, although many older classics are also included. I have also tried to single out those books that are intended for use by the general reader, as opposed to highly scholarly texts. In this bibliography, the original hardcover edition is listed first, followed by the paperback edition whenever available. In addition to these books, there are now many Bible references and resources available in CD-ROM format.

Achtemeier, Paul J., general editor. *The HarperCollins Bible Dictionary*, rev. ed. New York: HarperCollins, 1996. An excellent, illustrated reference aimed at the layperson as well as the scholar.

Alter, Robert. *The World of Biblical Literature*. New York: Basic Books, 1992.

Armstrong, Karen. *A History of God: The 4,000-Year Quest of Judaism, Christianity and Islam*. New York: Knopf, 1993; Ballantine Books, 1994.

Baetzhold, Howard G., and Joseph B. McCullough. *The Bible According to Mark Twain*. New York: Touchstone/Simon & Schuster, 1996. Irreverent writings on biblical matters by America's great humorist.

Barthel, Manfred. Translated and adapted by Mark Howson. *What the Bible Really Says: Casting New Light on the Book of Books.* New York: William Morrow, 1982; Quill, 1983. Bringing recent archaeological finds and newly discovered historical data to bear on traditional interpretations of the Bible.

Bender, David L., and Bruno Leone, editors. *Science and Religion.* St. Paul, Minn.: Greenhaven Press, 1981. A collection of essays on such questions as creation, evolution, and genetic engineering by a group of writers who take both scientific and literal biblical approaches.

Bennett, William J., editor. *The Book of Virtues: A Treasury of Moral Stories.* New York: Simon & Schuster, 1993; Touchstone, 1996. This bestselling collection of familiar morality tales includes a number of Bible stories, which generally retell the familiar, sanitized versions.

Bierlein, J. F. *Parallel Myths.* New York: Ballantine Books, 1994. Examines the common themes, images, and stories found in myths (creation, flood, underworld, heroes) from various times and cultures.

Bloom, Harold, and David Rosenberg. *The Book of J.* New York: Grove Press, 1990. A controversial, bestselling analysis of the Books of Moses that argues that one of the chief authors of the Torah was a woman.

Boorstin, Daniel J. *The Discoverers: A History of Man's Search to Know His World and Himself.* New York: Random House, 1983; Vintage, 1985.

Carter, Jimmy. *Sources of Strength: Meditations on Scripture for a Living Faith.* New York: Times Books, 1997. Fifty-two meditations on the Bible by the thirty-ninth president, who teaches a Bible class in his small-town church in Georgia.

Charlesworth, James H. *Jesus and the Dead Sea Scrolls: The Controversy Resolved.* New York: Doubleday/Anchor, 1992; Anchor, 1995. Addressing recent controversies over the Dead Sea Scrolls, the author presents a balanced, scholarly consensus about the scrolls and their contribution to understanding the Bible, Jesus, and early Christianity.

Clayton, Peter A. *Chronicle of the Pharaohs.* London: Thames & Hudson, 1994.

Cotterell, Arthur. *The Macmillan Illustrated Encyclopedia of Myths and Legends.* New York: Macmillan, 1989.

Ferlo, Roger. *Opening the Bible.* Cambridge, Mass.: Cowley Publications, 1997.

Feyerick, Ada. *Genesis: World of Myths and Patriarchs*. New York: New York University Press, 1996. Photographs and artwork illustrate this excellent survey of the historical background of the Bible's first book.

Fox, Emmet. *The Sermon on the Mount: The Key to Success in Life*. San Francisco: HarperCollins, 1989. A general introduction and spiritual key to the central teachings of Jesus found in the Gospel According to Matthew as interpreted by a prominent twentieth-century English mystic.

———. *The Ten Commandments: The Master Key of Life*. New York: Harper & Row, 1953; HarperCollins, 1993.

Fox, Everett. *The Five Books of Moses: The Schocken Bible: Volume I*. New York: Schocken Books, 1995. A new translation of the first five books of the Bible that attempts to restore the poetic, sometimes primitive, qualities of the ancient Hebrew.

Fox, Robin Lane. *The Unauthorized Version: Truth and Fiction in the Bible*. New York: Knopf, 1992. A historian's investigation by a writer who professes to "believe in the Bible but not in God."

Friedman, David Noel, editor. *The Anchor Bible Dictionary*. (6 volumes) New York: Doubleday/Anchor, 1992. A comprehensive, encyclopedic guide to phrases, names, and concepts. (Also available in CD-ROM format)

Friedman, Richard Elliot. *The Disappearance of God*. San Francisco: Harper San Francisco, 1995. (Published in paperback under the title *The Hidden Face of God*. New York: HarperCollins, 1997.) Combining religion, science, history, and mysticism, the author addresses why God's interaction with humans diminishes as the Bible progresses.

———. *Who Wrote the Bible?* New York: Summit Books, 1987; Perennial, 1989. An excellent overview of the question of the authorship of the Hebrew scriptures, particularly the Torah, or Books of Moses.

Gellman, Marc, and Thomas Hartman. *How Do You Spell God? Answers to Big Questions from Around the World*. New York: Morrow Junior Books, 1995. A rabbi and Roman Catholic monsignor who co-host a radio program answer questions posed by children about such issues as religion and God.

Gomes, Peter J. *The Good Book: Reading the Bible with Mind and Heart*. New York: Morrow, 1996. The Minister to Harvard University discusses the history and the use—and abuse—of the Bible.

Gordon, Cyrus H., and Gary A. Rendsburg. *The Bible and the Ancient Near East*, 4th ed. New York: Norton, 1997. A fascinating overview of the relationship between the Bible and other civilizations of the area; scholarly but written for the lay reader.

Gribetz, Judah. *The Timetables of Jewish History*. New York: Touchstone/ Simon & Schuster, 1993. A chronology of the most important people and events in Jewish history.

Grun, Bernard. *The Timetables of History*, new 3d rev. ed. New York: Touchstone, 1991.

Harris, Roberta L. *The World of the Bible*. New York: Thames & Hudson, 1995. An archaeological, geographic, and historical survey of the biblical lands, profusely illustrated with color photographs.

Helminiak, Daniel A. *What the Bible Really Says About Homosexuality*. San Francisco: Alamo Square Press, 1994. A modern scholarly assessment of the key passages in the Bible that have traditionally been used to condemn homosexuality.

Hill, Jim, and Rand Cheadle. *The Bible Tells Me So: Uses and Abuses of Holy Scripture*. New York: Anchor Books, 1996. A popular overview of how the Bible has been used throughout history by preachers and politicians to support opposing positions on a wide range of controversial issues.

Hinnells, John R. *Who's Who of Religions*. London: Penguin Books, 1996. Originally published in 1991 as *Who's Who of World Religions*, a handy biographical dictionary of leading figures in world religions, ancient and modern.

Jefferson, Thomas. Introduction by F. Forrester Church. *The Jefferson Bible: The Life and Morals of Jesus of Nazareth*. Boston: Beacon Press, 1989. Rejecting established Christianity, America's philosopher-president attempted to distill the moral teachings of Christ as separate from the mystical accounts of his life and resurrection.

Johnson, George. *Fire in the Mind: Science, Faith, and the Search for Order*. New York: Knopf, 1995; New York: Vintage, 1996. A science writer for *The New York Times*, the author explores the intersection of modern physics and faith.

Johnson, Luke Timothy. *The Real Jesus: The Misguided Quest for the Historical Jesus and the Truth of the Traditional Gospels*. New York: HarperCollins, 1996; HarperCollins, 1997. Written in response to a recent outpouring of books about the "historical Jesus," the author argues for the central importance of faith over "historical reconstructions."

Johnson, Paul. *A History of the Jews.* New York: Harper & Row, 1987; Perennial, 1988. A survey of four thousand years of Jewish history.

Kaiser, Walter C., Jr., Peter H. Davids, F. F. Bruce, and Manfred T. Brauch. *Hard Sayings of the Bible.* Downers Grove, Ill.: InterVarsity Press, 1996. A one-volume edition, comprising five separate volumes, that provides scholarly explanation of some of the Bible's most troubling verses, with historical, linguistic, and cultural background provided. Written from a Christian perspective.

Keller, Werner. Translated by William Neil. *The Bible as History,* 2d rev. ed. New York: Morrow, 1981. A useful but now slightly dated overview of the archaeological record of the Near East.

Kirsch, Jonathan. *The Harlot by the Side of the Road: Forbidden Tales of the Bible.* New York: Ballantine Books, 1997. A fascinating assessment of some of the Hebrew stories overlooked or edited out of Sunday school lessons.

Klingaman, William K. *The First Century: Emperors, Gods, and Everyman.* New York: HarperCollins, 1990; HarperPerennial, 1991. An excellent survey for general readers of the hundred years in which Jesus and Paul the apostle lived, the Roman emperors ruled, and China and the rest of Asia were being transformed.

Kugel, James L. *The Bible As It Was.* Cambridge, Mass.: The Belknap Press/Harvard University Press, 1997. A scholarly survey of how the Bible has been interpreted through the ages.

Küng, Hans. *On Being a Christian.* New York: Doubleday, 1976; Image Books, 1984. A monumental study of Christian history and theology.

Kushner, Harold S. *When Bad Things Happen to Good People.* New York: Schocken Books, 1981; Avon Books, 1983. A rabbi's bestselling attempt to explain an age-old question.

Laymon, Charles M., editor. *The Interpreter's One-Volume Commentary on the Bible.* Nashville, Tenn.: Abingdon Press, 1971.

Leeming, David, and Margaret Leeming. *A Dictionary of Creation Myths.* New York: Oxford University Press. An illustrated guide to creation stories from all over the world.

Lehner, Mark *The Complete Pyramids: Solving the Ancient Mysteries.* New York: Thames & Hudson, 1997. A fully illustrated compendium of every major pyramid in ancient Egypt.

Levine, Mark L., and Eugene Rachels, editors. *The Complete Book of Bible Quotations from the New Testament.* New York: Pocket Books, 1996. More than two thousand quotations, arranged by subjects like "Ability," "Jealousy," "Madness," "Wisdom," etc.

———. *The Complete Book of Bible Quotations from the Old Testament.* New York: Pocket Books, 1996. With more than four thousand quotes, a companion to the book above.

Lewis, C. S. *Reflections on the Psalms.* New York: Harvest Books, 1986. The noted British author of spiritual works and science fiction offers a collection of interpretation of selected psalms.

Macrone, Michael. *Brush Up Your Bible.* New York: HarperCollins, 1993; HarperPerennial, 1995. A light but fascinating examination of some of the most familiar verses and common phrases found in the Bible.

Mayotte, Ricky Alan. *The Complete Jesus.* South Royalton, Vt.: Steerforth Press, 1997. A compilation of sayings attributed to Jesus both from the Gospels and other documents that purport to record Jesus' teachings.

Metzger, Bruce M., and Michael D. Coogan, editors. *The Oxford Companion to the Bible.* New York: Oxford University Press, 1993. A rich and detailed reference, combining encyclopedia, dictionary, and atlas of the Bible. Thousands of entries on biblical figures and concepts, along with interpretative essays on the Bible and its impact on history, culture, literature and art, law, politics, etc.

Metzger, Bruce M., and Roland E. Murphy. *The New Oxford Annotated Bible with the Apocryphal/Deuterocanonical Books.* New York: Oxford University Press, 1994. An ecumenical study Bible in the New Revised Standard Version with excellent notes, introductory materials, and many useful articles about Bible history. A fine study Bible.

Michaels, Jonathan A., editor. *Mysteries and Intrigues of the Bible.* Wheaton, Ill.: Tyndale House, 1997.

Miles, Jack. *God: A Biography.* New York: Knopf, 1995; Vintage, 1996. Winner of the 1996 Pulitzer Prize for biography.

Occhiogrosso, Peter. *The Joy of Sects: A Spirited Guide to the World's Religious Traditions*. New York: Doubleday, 1994. An easygoing and very accessible guide to a wide range of faiths and spiritual movements.

Pagels, Elaine. *Adam, Eve, and the Serpent*. New York: Random House, 1988; Vintage Books. The author takes a scholarly yet accessible approach to questions of sin and sex and the Fall of Man.

———. *The Gnostic Gospels*. New York: Random House, 1979; Vintage Books. A prizewinning exploration of recently discovered early texts that challenge and contradict the accepted New Testament Gospels.

———. *The Origin of Satan*. New York: Random House, 1996; Vintage Books. A scholarly accounting of the development of the concept of Satan.

Pelikan, Jaroslav, editor. *Sacred Writings: Volume 1, Judaism: The Tanakh*. New York: The Jewish Publication Society, 1985; The Quality Paperback Book Club, 1992.

Pellegrino, Charles. *Return to Sodom and Gomorrah*. New York: Random House, 1994; Avon, 1995. Solving some of the Bible's ancient mysteries through recent scientific and archaeological discoveries.

Porter, J. R. *The Illustrated Guide to the Bible*. New York: Oxford University Press, 1995. Beautifully illustrated, scholarly yet accessible overview of the Bible's history and contents by an eminent Oxford scholar.

Prager, Dennis, and Joseph Telushkin. *The Nine Questions People Ask About Judaism*. New York: Touchstone, 1986.

———. *Why the Jews?: The Reason for Antisemitism*. New York: Touchstone, 1985.

Pritchard, James B., editor. *The Harper Concise Atlas of the Bible*. New York: HarperCollins, 1991.

Rosenberg, David. *A Poet's Bible: Rediscovering the Voices of the Original Text*. New York: Hyperion, 1991. Modern translations in English verse of familiar books of the Hebrew scriptures.

Sagan, Carl. *The Demon-Haunted World: Science as a Candle in the Dark*. New York: Random House, 1996; Ballantine Books, 1997. While respectful of religion, the famed astronomer makes the case for rationality as he debunks New Age spiritualism, religious fundamentalism, and "faith healing."

Sanders, E. P. *The Historical Figure of Jesus.* London: Allen Lane/Penguin Press, 1993. By one of the leaders of the search for the "historical" Jesus.

Schäfer, Peter. *Judeophobia: Attitudes Towards Jews in the Ancient World.* Cambridge, Mass.: Harvard University Press, 1997. A highly scholarly work that assesses anti-Jewish sentiments in Egyptian, Greek, Roman, and other early cultures.

Shanks, Hershel. *The Mystery and Meaning of the Dead Sea Scrolls.* New York: Random House, 1998. An excellent overview for the layperson of the Qumran scrolls by the founding editor of *Biblical Archaeology Review* and *Bible Review.*

Sproul, Barbara C. *Primal Myths: Creation Myths Around the World.* New York: HarperCollins, 1979.

Strong, James. *Strong's Exhaustive Concordance of the Bible.* Grand Rapids, Mich.: World Publishing, 1986. A revised, updated listing of the words in the Bible cross-referenced by chapter and verse.

Tegarden, William Hollis. *The Bible Nobody Knows.* Princeton, N.J.: Princeton Resource Publications, 1997. A fairly accessible overview of the scholarly strides made in the study of biblical composition.

Telushkin, Joseph. *Biblical Literacy: The Most Important People, Events, and Ideas of the Hebrew Bible.* New York: Morrow, 1997. Excellent overview and commentary about Hebrew scriptures and their place in modern life.

———. *Jewish Literacy: The Most Important Things to Know About the Jewish Religion, Its People, and Its History.* New York: Morrow, 1991.

Throckmorton, Burton H., Jr. *Gospel Parallels: A Comparison of the Synoptic Gospels,* 5th ed. Nashville, Tenn.: Thomas Nelson, 1992. Side-by-side comparison of the synoptic Gospels of Matthew, Mark, and Luke.

Tyldesley, Joyce. *Hatchepsut: The Female Pharaoh.* New York: Viking, 1996. An account of a woman who ruled Egypt in the guise of a man.

VanderKam, James C. *The Dead Sea Scrolls Today.* Grand Rapids, Mich.: William B. Eerdmans, 1994. An overview of the texts found at Qumran by a member of the team translating and editing the unpublished scrolls.

Vermes, Geza. *The Complete Dead Sea Scrolls in English.* New York: Allen Lane/Penguin, 1997. One of the most complete and authoritative accounts of the Dead Sea Scrolls available to date.

Vine, W. E. *Vine's Complete Expository Dictionary of Old and New Testament Words.* Nashville, Tenn.: Thomas Nelson, 1996. English equivalents for the Bible's Hebrew and Greek originals.

Warner, Marina. *Alone of All Her Sex: The Myth and the Cult of the Virgin Mary.* New York: Knopf, 1976; Vintage, 1983. A definitive treatment of the history of the changing role of the mother of Jesus in church history, folk legends, art, and literature.

Weiser, Francis X. *Handbook of Christian Feast and Customs.* New York: Harcourt, Brace & World, 1952.

Wilson, A. N. *Jesus: A Life.* New York: Norton, 1992. Controversial attempt to craft a "biography" of Jesus.

Wilson, Andrew, editor. *World Scripture: A Comparative Anthology of Sacred Texts.* New York: Paragon House, 1991; Paragon House, 1995. A fascinating compilation that brings together selections of writings from the sacred texts from all of the world's principal religions and major offshoots, divided into specific thematic areas.

ACKNOWLEDGMENTS

This book, like many, had its beginnings in my childhood. So I begin by thanking my parents, Evelyn and Richard Davis, for their guidance and love.

Unlike many people, I was lucky to have received my Sunday school lessons from some interesting and challenging teachers. One of them introduced me to the wonder of Giotto's frescoes. Another showed me my first piece of cuneiform. So, from an early age, I had a sense that learning about the Bible meant more than just memorizing psalms and prayers. Similarly, at Concordia College in Bronxville, New York, I had instructors like the Reverend Thomas Sluberski, whose faith did not close them off to the world around us. At Fordham University, I also took classes with Jesuit professors who honored the questioning mind. I consider myself very lucky to have had my education shaped by people like them.

There are many others along the path who have been significant in shaping this book. To Rosemary Altea, who advised me to "write from the heart," I say thank you and "They that wait upon the Lord shall renew their strength; they shall mount up with wings as eagles." (Isaiah 40:31)

I am also grateful to Joni Evans, whose enthusiastic support and friendship I value highly. The staffs of William Morrow and Avon Books have always been loyal friends, and I would like to thank Lou Aronica, Richard Aquan, Michele Corallo, Paul Fedorko, Bradford Foltz, Beccy Goodhart, Mike Greenstein, Rachel Klayman, Lisa Queen, Michelle Shinseki, William Wright, and Will Schwalbe, my former editor, who gave this book such an encouraging start.

My children are a constant source of pleasure, insight, and pride. Thank you, Jenny and Colin, for your wonderful spirits. "I have no greater joy than to hear that my children walk in truth." (3 John 4)

Once upon a time, I worked in a bookstore where a coworker told me I should be writing books, not selling them. I thought she was so smart, I married her. Not many writers get to thank their wife, editor, and publisher all in one breath. I enjoy that remarkable luxury. So thank you, Joann, for everything I need to know but never learned.

INDEX

Numbers in italic indicate maps.